BOUND BY BONDAGE

For more than three decades, the New Netherland Institute (NNI)—an independent nonprofit nongovernmental organization—has cast light on America's Dutch roots. Through its support of the translation and publication of New Netherland's records and its various educational and public programs, NNI promotes historical scholarship on and popular appreciation of the seventeenth-century Dutch mid-Atlantic colony. More information about NNI can be found at newnetherlandinstitute.org.

BOUND BY BONDAGE

SLAVERY AND THE CREATION OF A NORTHERN GENTRY

NICOLE SAFFOLD MASKIELL

CORNELL UNIVERSITY PRESS
Ithaca and London
Published in association with the New Netherland Institute

Copyright © 2022 by Cornell University

All rights reserved. Except for brief quotations in a review, this book, or parts thereof, must not be reproduced in any form without permission in writing from the publisher. For information, address Cornell University Press, Sage House, 512 East State Street, Ithaca, New York 14850. Visit our website at cornellpress.cornell.edu.

First published 2022 by Cornell University Press

Library of Congress Cataloging-in-Publication Data
Names: Maskiell, Nicole Saffold, 1980– author.
Title: Bound by bondage : slavery and the creation of a northern gentry / Nicole Saffold Maskiell.
Description: Ithaca [New York] : Cornell University Press, 2022. | Includes bibliographical references and index.
Identifiers: LCCN 2021051818 (print) | LCCN 2021051819 (ebook) | ISBN 9781501764240 (hardcover) | ISBN 9781501764257 (pdf) | ISBN 9781501764264 (epub)
Subjects: LCSH: Slavery—Northeastern States—History—17th century. | Slavery—Northeastern States—History—18th century. | Slaveholders—Northeastern States—Social conditions—17th century. | Slaveholders—Northeastern States—Social conditions—18th century. | Slave trade—Social aspects—Northeastern States—History—17th century. | Slave trade—Social aspects—Northeastern States—History—18th century. | Slaves—Northeastern States—Social conditions—17th century. | Slaves—Northeastern States—Social conditions—18th century. | Blacks—Northeastern States—Social conditions—17th century. | Blacks—Northeastern States—Social conditions—18th century. | Elite (Social sciences)—Northeastern States—History—17th century. | Elite (Social sciences)—Northeastern States—History—18th century. | Northeastern States—Social conditions—17th century. | Northeastern States—Social conditions—18th century. | Northeastern States—Race relations—History—17th century. | Northeastern States—Race relations—History—18th century.
Classification: LCC E446 .M393 2022 (print) | LCC E446 (ebook) | DDC 306.3/620974—dc23/eng/20211122
LC record available at https://lccn.loc.gov/2021051818
LC ebook record available at https://lccn.loc.gov/2021051819

For Bill and Billy

Contents

Acknowledgments ix

Introduction: Manhunt   1

1. *Neger*: Race, Slavery, and Status in the Dutch Northeast (1640s–60s)   15

2. *Kolonist*: Slaveholding and the Survival of Expansive Anglo-Dutch Elite Networks (1650s–90s)   39

3. *Naam*: Race, Family, and Connection on the Borderlands (1680s–90s)   56

4. Bond: Forging an Anglo-Dutch Slaveholding Northeast (1690s–1710s)   81

5. Family: Kinship, Ambition, and Fear in a Time of Rebellions (1710s–20s)   98

6. Market: Creating Kinship-Based Empires United by Slaveholding (1730s–50s)   123

7. Identity: Navigating Racial Expectations to Escape Slavery (1750s–60s)   140

Conclusion: Gentry   159

Appendices 165
Abbreviations 177
Notes 183
Bibliography 255
Index 285

Acknowledgments

I would first like to thank my family for doing the unseen work that went into making this book a reality. To my husband, Bill, for thousands of hours of editing, hundreds of freezer meals, emotional support and inspiration, thank you feels too small. To my son, Billy, who was a boundless supplier of hugs and laughter, I love you and you can read this book when you are older. My parents have loved and supported me through every twist and turn in my life calling and remain my biggest fans; they are the first people I call after every loss and victory. My brother and sister-in-law have traveled hundreds of miles across California to support my presentations and video conferenced into every speaking engagement since. Endless thanks to my late grandparents, who retold our stories of escape and slavery, mingled with their own experiences as sharecroppers and entrepreneurs in a segregated society, and inspired my interest in the past. My husband's parents—Mom and Dad Maskiell—have offered me the incredible Hudson Valley vista from which to try to imagine a colonial world and have supported and encouraged me for years. Your help and support are so appreciated. I love you all so much.

I feel so fortunate to have found a community of generous people willing to read and critique my writing but also give of themselves to offer so much more. I would like to thank my advisor, Mary Beth Norton, for her tireless support from the very beginning of this endeavor. She helped this idea grow and take shape, advocating for me along the way. I would also like to thank several other scholars who were involved in the earliest versions of this manuscript. Without their help, this book would have never gotten off the ground. Valinda Littlefield, Dan Littlefield, Woody Holton, Andrew Berns, Robert Travers, Duane Corpis, Jeroen Dewulf, Anne Marie Plane, and Chrissy Hosea, thank you for your help and review.

I have been so fortunate to have been a member of several different writers' groups throughout this process to nurture and grow my project. My writers' groups have been an absolute support for me throughout every step of this very long road. Mari Crabtree, Maeve Kane, and Jacqueline Reynoso have been with me ever since our days together in grad school, reading the earliest drafts of my work, offering an incredible amount of scholarly help, and perhaps most importantly, friendship and moral support. Andrea Mosterman, Deborah Hamer, Erin Kramer, and Suze Zijlstra have been my weekly sources of support during these last several years as my manuscript has evolved into its final form, providing equal parts insight, camaraderie, and encouragement. Special thanks also to my OI Atlantic History Writer's Group members for your astute questions and ideas.

Several scholars generously gave of their time to read my manuscript and to offer wonderful insights. Thank you, Susanah Shaw Romney, for spending countless days and nights reading through draft after draft of my manuscript, reading through my various translations, and helping me decode seventeenth-century handwriting. You are an inspiration, and helped center and support me through rocky waters. Marjoleine Kars and Dienke Hondius have provided their expertise and valuable perspectives that have greatly strengthened this book. Thank you each for your time and support! I have been encouraged and inspired by the research and friendship of scholars devoted to uncovering the Dutch past in American life. I would also like to thank my colleague at the University of South Carolina, Saskia Coenen Snyder, who gave me wonderful advice and insights on translating as well as another pair of eyes on these thorny documents. Jaap Jacobs has offered invaluable research, translation, and scholarly help for this project, providing detailed edits and insights drawn from decades studying the Stuyvesants and the Dutch colonial period. Thank you, Jaap, for all of your help!

My editorial team at Cornell University Press has provided a home for this book and I would like to thank Michael McGandy and Karen Laun, whose tireless help, patience, and support have been invaluable. The places that work in my current version are owing to the deep and thoughtful work done by the peer reviewers, which brought this project into clearer focus into my own mind. Their insights, critiques, and suggestions have allowed me to tighten and deepen my project. I owe them an extreme debt of gratitude.

Scholars, including Marisa Fuentes, Karwan Fatah-Black, Jared Hardesty, Wim Klooster, Dennis Maika, Russell Shorto, Ramona LaRoche, Tony Bly, and Katherine Kerrison, have generously read portions of my book, provided very valuable feedback and formal comment, joined me during conferences, and over dinner conversations helped refine my work. Thank you for your help, wisdom, and support.

My students have inspired me every step of the way and I am humbled by their curiosity, intellectualism and kindness. Riley Sutherland, John P. Wilson, and Hannah Bauer have helped extend my research, scrub my writing, and provide three extra sets of eyes during the long process of bringing this story to life.

I owe special thanks to the participants of the various conferences, seminars, and workshops I have been privileged enough to join, each of whom provided valuable feedback and insights that have helped me refine this study. I would like to thank the Carolina Lowcountry and Atlantic World seminar for their comments on portions of an early version of this piece, especially Mari Crabtree, Simon Lewis, and Anne Bennet. Thanks also to Jaap Jacobs and the ministerial and outreach teams of St. Mark's-on-the-Bowery for including me in a series of conversations to examine and explore the impact of slavery on the history of the bowery and the broader world of the Stuyvesants. I would also like to thank the North Carolina Triangle Early American History Seminar (TEAHS), Durham, and the University of South Carolina History Center, Columbia, who gave me the opportunity to showcase and workshop my research at various stages of development.

I extend my deep gratitude and appreciation to the various archivists and librarians who have helped me access materials along the way, at the Stadsarchief in Amsterdam; the National Archives at The Hague; the National Archives in Curaçao; the Clermont State Historic Site in Germantown, New York; the FDR Presidential Library in Hyde Park, New York; and the New York State Archives in Albany, New York. I would also like to give special thanks to the Gilder Lehrman Collection, on deposit at the New York Historical Society in New York, and the Huntington Library in San Marino, California, each of which provided me with fellowship funding to support extended research at their archives.

Many thanks to the circulation and support staff at the Thomas Cooper Library at the University of South Carolina, who supported me through more book requests than I thought possible before beginning this book. I would also like to thank my various public history sources and publishers, including Emily Costello and team at The Conversation for helping me get several of my stories out there. Thanks, to Paul Gunther at the Gracie Mansion Conservancy who, in partnership with the Consulate General of the Netherlands, gave me the opportunity and forum to bring some of these stories to life for the sites' visitors.

Introduction
Manhunt

> A warr.^{t} for Mr Stuyvesants 4 Negroe serv.^{ts} lost. Oct. 6.th Whereas Complaint is made by Mr Peter Stuyvesant, that hee hath lost 4 Negroes (men Servants) These are therefore to desire you to bee ayding and assisting to the bearer or bearers hereof in the apprehending the said Negroes and to cause them to bee brought with safety to New Yorke upon the Manhatans, where they shall receive full satisfaction for their labour and charge, Given under my hand this 6.th day of Oct. 1664 At ffort James in New Yorke. &c.
>
> R. Nicolls
>
> To all Governo.^{rs}, Deputy Governo.^{rs} Magistrates and other office.^{s} whatsoever, in any of his Ma.^{tyes} Colonyes in America, & all others to whom these presents shall come.

Four men escaped bondage together in 1664. The society they fled had counted the enslaved among them since the earliest decades of the seventeenth century. Slave ships docked in the settlements' main harbors and public auctions were held in its towns. Every bordering colony threatened reenslavement, and while local Native groups might offer shelter, they might also recapture those who ran from enslavement. The men were not escaping bondage in the South, but in the newly conquered and rechristened colony of New York. They set off as a group, leveraging collective action to escape and remain out of reach. They had enough political knowledge to choose their timing well. Enslaved people from New York had been traded throughout the region for decades, and there always were colonists willing to clandestinely trade with the enslaved. Like others who had gone before them, these men might have been running toward family and the possibility of connection.[1] Their former enslaver, Petrus Stuyvesant, would use those same human impulses—family, community, and connectedness—to attempt to retain his mastery.[2]

Despite the tumult of the moment, and that he had been recently deposed as leader of the colony, Petrus took time out for a manhunt. It depended on the cooperation of Richard Nicolls, the English governor who had usurped Petrus's position in the colony. Nonetheless, Petrus was issued a warrant for the men, which was posted on October 6, 1664.[3] At first glance, such priorities seem strange. But for all that divided them, colonists like Petrus and Richard were linked in a shared commitment to human bondage. *Bound by Bondage* argues that early Dutch slavery and its successor Anglo-Dutch slave culture were central to the cultural development of the North. What follows is a reconceptualization of the narrative of early Northeastern slavery that centers New Netherland and Dutch regions of settlement as not merely locally important to the development of slaveholding, but regionally crucial to any understanding of the foundations and development of that culture. By integrating familiar sources, such as colonial diaries and narratives, with new English translations of Dutch archival materials, *Bound by Bondage* examines slavery as a central facet of Northeastern cultural development.

Family networks, rather than shifting colonial borders, bound together a slaveholding Northeast.[4] Beginning in the seventeenth century, notions of mastery and conceptions of status entwined enslaved and enslaver across two centuries as a regional slaveholding culture emerged. Slavery was a vital component of familial networks of power during the period of Dutch rule that spread across colonies as these families traded, bought land, and expanded their reach into new territories that ranged from the Chesapeake to New England. Most modern histories assume that slaveholding existed across the Americas but, with the exception of studies that focus on the Native slave trade from the Northeast southward, few have analyzed how early slaveholding societies north of the Chesapeake influenced the spread of slaveholding networks southward. Familial and reputational networks reified connections within and across colonies, and provided avenues along which to conduct trade and grow wealth. Notions of mastery rooted in this shared Anglo-Dutch heritage formed the basis of their ideas of elite identity stretching from the seventeenth century to the final decades of the colonial period.[5] But enslaved people developed their own networks in parallel with the elites who held their bonds. They built, maintained, and utilized alliances across the Northeast. Like the four men escaping Petrus, many set out across a landscape spotted by taverns, farms, and sites of trade alongside waterways, woods, and rival powers. Language proficiency, trade skills, and shared cultural touchpoints would shape a world of connectedness, even as systems of bondage severed ties.

The four men had toiled in a settlement at the edge of a global Dutch empire and were members of an enslaved community that was growing in number. While official figures of those enslaved in New Netherland do not exist, the colony in 1664 has been estimated as having as few as 250 to as high as 500 enslaved people, augmented by 290 people who arrived on the slave ship *Gideon* just before the colony's fall, as well as between 70 and 75 free Black families.[6] The colony was bordered by the Mahican to the North, the Haudenosaunee Confederacy to the Northwest, the several Munsee-speaking groups including the Esopus in the fertile Mahicannituck River valley (that would be subsequently named for Henry Hudson) and the Lenape to the south. If the knowledge and behaviors of these four were similar to other escapees, then they would have followed what were, by the time they ran, well-trod escape routes through New England toward French territory and would have leveraged a knowledge of multiple languages, including European, Bantu, and Native North American tongues. The enslaved community hailed from the various colonies across the Caribbean, Brazil, Spanish South America, and Atlantic Africa. They were four out of the estimated total 700,000 African men, women, and children enslaved in the Americas during the seventeenth century.[7]

Dutch slavery in the Northeast predated the settlement of New Netherland, beginning with the capture and enslavement of two Indigenous boys by Adriaen Block and Hendrick Christiaensen, who were subsequently brought back to the Dutch Republic.[8] European settlers began to take up residence on the island of Manhattan in 1624 and the first recorded slave ship carrying African captives, *Bruynvisch*, arrived just three years later.[9] Slavery grew and evolved with the colony. Enslaved people directly owned by the West India Company (WIC) were put to work in agriculture, construction, maintenance, and defense capacities. Private ownership augmented the ranks of the enslaved. Enslavers traveled throughout the colonies and brought their enslaved people and notions of mastery with them wherever they went. New Netherland–style slavery was exported to settlements along the Delaware River with the Dutch takeover of New Sweden in 1655.[10] Trade with New England led to a common understanding of slavery and mastery that only grew after the English conquered New Netherland in 1664 and renamed it New York. Wealthy merchant families took a particular interest in the plantations and transshipment locations of the Caribbean. Common laws inscribing codes of behavior to govern slavery were introduced throughout the colonies in the late seventeenth and early eighteenth century, regulating the movement, trade, and social lives of the enslaved. Slavery lasted in New York until 1827, fifty years after the thirteen colonies declared their independence and two hundred years after it began, leaving in its wake a wide-ranging web of connections that spread throughout North America.

INTRODUCTION

Earlier generations of historians drew a stark line, representing slavery in the North as much milder than what was practiced in the South. Scholars have since assailed those assumptions, aiming analyses at uncovering the importance of Northern slavery. Beginning in the late nineties and continuing through the first decade of the twenty-first century, historians such as A. J. Williams-Myers, Ira Berlin, Graham Russell Hodges, Thelma Wills Foote, Craig Steven Wilder, Leslie Harris, Jill Lepore, and others began to reexamine the classic split, and led the charge reinterpreting slavery in the North. The last ten years have seen an increase in works focusing on enslaved people and slavery in the North. Historians like Jeroen Dewulf, Wendy Warren, Christy Clark-Pujara, Michael Groth, Jared Ross Hardesty, and Allegra di Bonaventura, just to name a few, have centered the stories of those held in bondage as the focus of their narratives. Others have begun to build on the work of Saidiya Hartman, who challenged archival discourses and questioned the narratives of voyeuristic subjection that distorted the lives and experiences of enslaved people. Marisa Fuentes offered scholars a powerful spatial framework and archival critique in her study centered on enslaved women in colonial Bridgetown, Barbados, and Andrea Mosterman uncovered important new insights about Dutch American slavery using spatial analysis.[11]

Notwithstanding, the debate about enslavement in New Netherland remains framed around assumptions that it was minor, diffuse, and quite peculiar—because enslaved people were allowed certain liberties such as the ability to testify in court, access to baptism, and even freedom itself. Such notions rest on the axiom that the Dutch period was exceptional, and it was only until after the fall of New Netherland to the English that the colony fully entered the broader slaveholding Atlantic.[12] But those theories could not explain what I began finding in the archives: a stalwart and ultimately generational commitment to enslavement in the region among New Netherland's elites that radiated out from the Dutch colony along family lines across the Atlantic world. For a group assumed to be minor players, they were slave trading, expressing developed racist sensibilities, and showing up in some of the most "major" places in the history of slavery at quite pivotal times.

Northeastern slaveholders were united by a dialectical and actual engagement with slavery, which formed a common language and experience.[13] English and Scottish dissidents took refuge in the Dutch Republic, while many among the second generation of such refugees became fluent in Dutch language and culture, frequently departing from the ministerial background of their parents to pursue business careers in the colonies.[14] Anglo and Dutch elites maintained connections in Europe during the heyday of the Dutch Republic.[15] Throughout the founding decades of New Netherland, Dutch elite families held robust Caribbean connections that were also cross-colonial.[16] Such networks expanded into the Chesapeake as well. The Stuyvesant-Bayard families form the first generation of Dutch elites under examination. These families immigrated to New Netherland, laying the foundation for subsequent slaveholding generations in these areas as well as in the Caribbean and southern colonies. The Livingston and Van Horne families intermarried, augmenting the eighteenth-century cohort, whose slaveholding branches in New England, New York, New Jersey, Pennsylvania, and Delaware shaped Northeastern colonial legal, social, and religious history. These families were not the only slaveholders in the colonial Northeast, nor were they the largest. They resided, however, at the center of elite Northeastern culture.[17] Tracing the ways they established and maintained the slaveholding networks they built over nearly two centuries offers insight into how slavery became a vital part of Northern culture.

Across their networks, elites established surveillance and legal regimes to monitor the activities of enslaved people and enforce adherence to their codes of conduct. Legal constructs, enforcement regimes, and channels for disseminating information were built on the back of kinship and trading connections to reinforce notions of mastery and expectations of subservience. We do not know what happened to these four men, but we do know that, in later generations, stories like theirs proliferated in colonial newspapers throughout the Northeast as the wealthy subscribers used their wide reach to mobilize their contacts. Indeed, while many historians will read the lives of the enslaved into runaway slave ads, the attributes and networks of

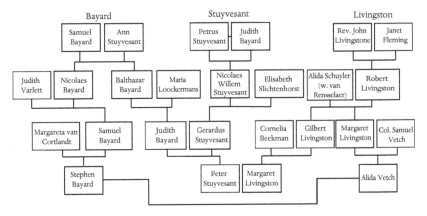

FIGURE 1. Bayard, Stuyvesant, and Livingston family trees showing marriage interconnections.

enslavers are also made legible in their descriptions of "last seen" locales and former sites of captivity.

Mastery was a way of life for Northeastern elites and aspirants. Controlling the lives and actions of enslaved people became a marker of exclusivity and served as a common language to communicate power to others within their network, even among merchants whose business ventures relied most heavily on a mixed white labor regime. Gifting an enslaved worker with an old gentleman's hat or coat turned that person into a sort of walking coat of arms for the family, on display for others in the elite's network. Manning a sloop with a skilled enslaved pilot created a moveable representation of the wealth and power of those who held them in bondage. But enslaved people created alternate meanings out of these trappings and assignments. As other scholars have noted, waterways were sites and avenues of freedom, whether freedom of movement and freedom from observation, or launching points for escape.[18] Clothing could denote either status or a commodity to be traded, and markings, piercings, or hair styles could communicate a sense of belonging or kinship to others who were in positions to provide support. My book seeks to foreground the experiences of such captive peoples and, in so doing, reevaluate the legacies and narratives of Northeastern elites.

Despite the cross-colonial lives of elite slaveholding families, the slave systems that emerged in the middle colonies differed from their counterparts in New England, but each family's slaveholding actions within such societies were as much in keeping with family identities as they were with different colonial environments. When I first became interested in Northern slavery I was captivated by New England, not New Netherland. From passing the first slave law in its Body of Liberties, to the mass enslavement of Indigenous peoples following the Pequot War and King Phillip's War, to the slave ship *Desire*'s early and pivotal role in the entwined Native and African slave trades, New England felt like the epicenter of the story of Northeastern enslavement. New Netherland, by contrast, did not.[19] The Dutch colony has frequently been posited as a unique outpost, interesting but ultimately tangential. Such claims have echoed even more loudly when examining the emergence of enslavement in the colony during the Dutch period. Where New England's seventeenth-century slaveholders are linked to Providence Island, Barbados, and beyond, New Netherland's slaveholders have been positioned as cash-strapped, inconsequential players.[20] At the beginning of this project, I entered the archives with those assumptions firmly in place. But the evidence eroded my preconceptions with one dogged question: Why were New Netherland elites and their family members seemingly appearing all over the slaveholding Atlantic and at key moments of transition?

Because of the emphasis on the relatively *small* numbers of slaves in the Northeast scholars deploy several alternate arguments to display the brutality of the northern variant of American slavery, none more emphasized than the social isolation of the North. The prevalent narrative posits that enslaved people were not able to forge family bonds like their counterparts in the South, a contention that both highlights brutality but also erases the connections that many people have to the past. While writing this book I spoke with many African-descended people with family histories that reached back to the colonial period in the Northeast and learned stories of my own family ties to Elmira. I admittedly became engrossed with finding families, networks, and communities of enslaved people, and along the way discovered violence and separation, but also names passed down from mother to daughter, memories of place and family and community. Such discoveries found me returning to the portrait painted by W.E.B Du Bois, a descendant of New Netherland and the Northeast: of a "rollicking boyhood" and the "hills of New England, where the dark Housatonic winds between Hoosace and Tahkanic to the sea."[21]

In chapter 1, I foreground the narratives of enslaved people within the colony of New Netherland and argue that, despite the ostensibly small population of enslaved people, race and slavery were crucial to shaping social status and hierarchies among key New Netherland elites from the very start of their colonial lives, because the Dutch colony's leadership was deeply embedded in and fully engaged with the wider Atlantic project of enslavement. Centralizing a close reading of personal and administrative correspondence of early elite settlers, this chapter highlights the importance of centering the daily lives and circumstances of enslaved people. Such reconstructed narratives offer wider context for enslavement in the colony, and exposes the emergence of racial sensibilities among white colonists, their direct connections to centers of enslavement in South America and the Caribbean, and the broad influence of their local and ultimately regional power.

Studies have emphasized the interpenetration of seventeenth-century Dutch and Anglo-Dutch networks in the Chesapeake, the Caribbean, South America, and Atlantic Africa, but such approaches, with the exception of a few, have rarely emphasized the importance of family connections. They have also, by in large, downplayed these migrants' actions as slaveholders.

Most highlight the ways in which Dutch transplants were swept along by the prevailing winds of whatever imperium tangentially controlled the colonies within which they found themselves. If slaveholding was a part of the culture, it was one imposed on such émigrés from foreign powers.[22] But I was shocked by how crucial personal and corporate slaveholding was to New Netherlanders' emigration patterns. Indeed, by the middle decades of the seventeenth century, slaveholding remained a key component of regional connections between elites across the Northeast, during a time of imperial enmity. In chapter 2 I argue that it was a central ingredient to the survival of regional Anglo-Dutch elite networks after the fall of New Netherland.

Susanah Shaw Romney's compelling argument about New Netherland specifically, as well as the Dutch Republic and Dutch Empire more broadly, is that it was built by intimate ties.[23] Relationships mattered and understanding them exposes a diverse world of people engaged in sometimes contradictory but ultimately intertwined efforts at connection. For a core group of elite families, such networks of connection endured because of a sustained generational commitment to slaveholding, slave trading, and slave investments. Enslaved human beings were crucial to how some of the region's most influential Dutch-descended families built their wealth, standing, and regional power. Indeed, family prestige and patrician status depended in large degree on claiming hereditary membership in this seventeenth-century slaveholding network, even as mixed labor regimes had always far eclipsed slave labor in the middle colonies and across New England.

Bound by Bondage focuses on the relationships between enslaved people and the forced connections they shared with enslavers to highlight the personal circumstances at the heart of major historical moments during the late seventeenth and early eighteenth centuries. I consciously situate the individual lives and family stories of enslaved Northeasterners within Vincent Brown's "archipelago of insurrection stretching throughout the North Atlantic Americas," and likewise seek to read Northeastern moments not normally analyzed using this framework such as the fallout from the 1690 attack on Schenectady and the pressures surrounding Leisler's Rebellion.[24] What did it mean to run away during such moments? For many Northeastern elite enslavers, it was clearly sedition, with very real political stakes. It also foregrounds the expansiveness of enslaved connections. Such moments have been featured in scholarly works, creating a more nuanced portrait of religious, social, and ethnic tensions in the region, but such events and locales barely register in studies of North American enslavement.[25] But they are crucial to understanding how slaveholding and racial power underwrote the social, cultural, and political ties of regional elites, despite cultural disparities, warfare, and political divisions.

In chapter 3, I examine how the same local and family connections that built dynasties of power among some white colonists were used to criminalize, constrain, mutilate, and marginalize enslaved people, as they struggled to make and maintain connection. Opening with the early business exploits of two men, Tom and Robert, this chapter highlights the wider currents that entwined but ultimately caused their life stories to diverge. Although both men traded within the same wider world and were heavily influenced by connections to Albany's female networks, Tom, a Black man enslaved to Robert Livingston, was ultimately criminalized by such associations, while Robert gained entrance into Albany's Dutch merchant and slaveholding elite through his wife, Alida. Chapter 4 extends that argument by following the business, social, and family connections forged by slavery that bound elites in New York to their counterparts in New England. The seeds planted during the seventeenth century under Dutch rule served to influence and guide the codification of slave laws, culture, and society under the English, as well as grow and expand family slaveholding networks into New England. Although the colony's fall challenged the social power structure, New Netherland's elite class found purchase and social cohesion under English rule by claiming human beings as property. At the same time, other New Yorkers were solidifying both domestic and regional power through racial and gendered claims to the land and enslaved people.[26]

My first experience in an archive was when, as a teenager, I took a road trip down the expanse of the United States. Along the way, I, my parents, and grandparents stopped at small regional archives searching for traces of family in the past. That formative trip also included places outside the archives—visits to physical sites that held vestiges of a traumatic family past that did not show up in vital records. That process has changed dramatically with the onset of digital archives, DNA mapping, and genealogical companies promising to take customers' DNA back a thousand generations, but the impulse for memory and connection with the past remains the same. For historians of Dutch American slavery, such family papers and physical places are vital and are relatively unexplored due to the language barrier, although recent works are changing this trend.[27] Carolyn Steedman wrote of the uncanny ability of archived documents to deflect "outrage." It is in their "folders and bundles" where "the neatest demonstration of how state power has operated" emerges, "through ledgers and lists and indictments, and through what is missing from them."[28] Family power, rather than state (or at times acting in concert) comes through in the neatly bundled and now largely digitized collections used for this work.

Chapter 5 was constructed out of the family papers of the Livingstons, a clan that has inspired multiple works and theories about the emergence of elite society in New York.[29] But the world that jumped off of the weathered pages was one animated by the family stories of many people, including those of enslaved people. The everyday Dutch idioms preserved in the papers connect the eighteenth-century world of enslaved people in the upper Hudson Valley to the seventeenth-century world conjured by elites, like Jeremias van Rennselaer. In recent years, exquisitely conceived work has exposed the interconnected lives of enslaver and enslaved in colonial New England and offered an intimate history of events from Salem to the Boston Massacre.[30] This chapter argues that, despite being a small portion of those who lived on Hudson Valley estates like Manor Livingston, enslaved people's personal and familial struggles impacted regional and local histories. The ambitions and grievances of nonelite white residents of Manor Livingston were likewise bound up with the wider slave culture. I have centralized the stories of those enslaved by the Livingstons to show the human cost of an "expansive slaveholding Northeast," to unpack the personal motives behind a culture of fear that united Northeastern elite enslavers in the wake of Queen Anne's War and the 1712 Slave Revolt, as well as to highlight the political, social, and personal ties of enslaved Early Americans.

Bound by Bondage ends in the mid-eighteenth century. Such a chronology had as much to do with the emergence of developed and expansive Northeastern enslaved networks as it had with the first salvos toward rupture with the colonial past. It is here that New York as the center of a slaveholding Northeastern world feels most familiar, but *Bound by Bondage* examines this as part of an expansive slaveholding past rather than as the first decades of a new era whose slave-trading excess would fuel the later debates on liberty and slavery, as it is most commonly presented. The eighteenth-century world of the final two chapters is constructed from sources well known—and much used—by scholars of slavery: runaway slave advertisements, slave-for-sale notices, slave ship documents, and English-language family papers. Such documents have been used to great effect to uncover a slaveholding Northeastern world that influenced every sector of society, from the docks, to print culture, to academia.[31] Such familiar worlds are deepened when examined against centuries-old networks of surveillance by slaveholding elites with connections to New Netherland's leading families. Chapter 6 argues that elites like the Livingstons expanded their portfolios while including vital and visceral connections to their family's slaveholding

Dutch past. These identities infused their global ambitions for trade and family empire. Northeastern places, and family and regional elites, graced the names of slave ships, and family members' regional footprint in the Chesapeake, South Carolina, and the Caribbean grew alongside increasing Northeastern influence. Chapter 7 highlights the expansive networks of enslaved people that also knit the region together, offering an alternative approach with which to imagine the regions' connections. Although disconnections between enslaved people in the Northeast have long been emphasized, this chapter highlights the networks of connection between diverse enslaved, bonded, and free peoples.

Historians of slavery in the Northeast face a paradox: an archive both prolific and sparse, and every work devoted to the subject, no matter how exhaustive, is, as one scholar has observed, littered with the adverbs "perhaps" or "might."[32] This is in contrast to studies dedicated to the trading ventures, the political machinations, the military campaigns, or the social development of elite European Northeasterners. Those works stand on the certainties of unqualified speech, the identities of familiar actors presented as concretely as if they breathed anew. This is not to say that historians have failed to draw very different portraits based on similar evidence, but rather, that most have never stopped to wonder what all the fragmentary evidence says about the mountain of material drawn on to create the past. It seems logical that enslavers would be suspect when giving an account of the lives of marginalized peoples. But why have scholars not taken the next step and questioned whether or not the gaps in historical knowledge about the enslaved and marginalized call into question the conclusions that can be reached about those "familiar actors" for whom and about whom the archive was intended?

This work seeks to highlight the importance of the choices and daily experiences of early Americans. I have consciously embraced reading evidence against the grain and used a methodology in line with scholars who use critical fabulation in scholarly historical study to excavate the lives of marginalized groups.[33] I believe that such measures are necessary to fully articulate an accounting of the past that does justice to the documents and the lives of historically marginalized people. To support that goal, I am deploying several narrative strategies. First, I am using Dutch words for a number of my chapter titles to symbolically illustrate the survival of the Dutch language in the sources that I use and the outsized influence of Dutch and Dutch-infused culture to the development of the Northern gentry. Second, in most instances where clarity permits, I use first names to refer to both enslaved and enslaver. This is a break from what has become standard historical practice of referring to past actors by their family names. Such a standard has served to buttress systems of oppression and silences. I am consciously choosing to break with this tradition in my use of first names for all historical characters in my book. It must be said, however, that naming itself was an act of colonization and violence directed toward enslaved peoples, but as my narrative will explain, passing down such first names became vital ways for enslaved people to mark their family bonds in the face of separation and sale.

Because of the long colonial history of the word *Iroquois*, I use Haudenosaunee (People of the Longhouse) throughout this work unless directly quoting from the documents. I also use the term *Dutch* to refer to the European families and peoples folded into the Dutch Republic as permanent residents at the time of Dutch rule of New Netherland, but this was a heterogeneous group hailing from Scandinavia, Germany, and French speaking regions of Europe, among other places. The terms *wildt* and *wilden* are most accurately translated as "savage" and "savages." Other scholars have likewise translated the term *neger* as "nigger," although this is less common.[34] These Dutch terms recur many times throughout my text, and I have translated them as Indian and Negro respectively. I made this choice deliberately, to limit the continual violence such terms enact on the minds and hearts of Black and Indigenous people reading my work.

Bound by Bondage reconstructs the names and struggles of those enslaved to offer a multigenerational, and oftentimes migrational, portrait of enslaved families and individuals who loved, lived, negotiated, resisted, and died due to the conscious actions and ambitions of their enslavers. Local geographies stand out in runaway slave advertisements that offer some of the richest archival sources with which to examine the lives of enslaved people and the social experience of slavery.[35] These sources have been mined and counted to uncover a myriad of perspectives—from the development of racial categorization to shifts in literary expectation.[36] Despite the obvious enslaver bias of advertisements, court cases, and letters, such sources offer a way to reinterpret the analytical framework of the colonial Northeast. While elite family histories and archival sources have formed a large amount of the source base for *Bound by Bondage*, recent studies have challenged the archival bias and historical narrative that privileges such elites as actors.[37] What follows emphasizes the ways that Northeastern slave networks affected and were directed by the actions of nonelite actors as well as how the "Northern gentry" was a contested and imagined community that was built on the subjugation of others as much as it was business partnerships and strategic marriages. Such Dutch-descended and Anglo-Dutch enslavers lived lives intertwined with the enslaved.

> **FIFTY DOLLARS Reward.**
>
> RUN-away from the subscriber, three negro fellows, viz. PRIMUS, a very likely fellow, about 22 years of age, speaks very civil and mild; went away the first of October, 1776. SYPHAX, about 34 years old; speaks broken English, very lasey and slow; went away some time in November, 1776. SCIPIO, about 18 years old, went away on Wednesday night the 8th inst. he is a very handy fellow, stoops when he walks, and is apt to stammer when he talks quick.— Whoever takes up said negroes, and brings or sends them to their master, shall have the above reward for the three, or separately for Primus 25 dollars, and for Syphax and Scipio, 12 each.
>
> P. STUYVESANT.
>
> Petersfield, near New-York, Octo. 11, 1777.

FIGURE 2. Runaway slave advertisement in search of Primus, Syphax, and Scipio, posted by Petrus Stuyvesant in *The New-York Gazette*, October 11, 1777. Courtesy, American Antiquarian Society.

More than one hundred years after the flight of the four men, three men would escape the grasp of another Petrus Stuyvesant.[38] Primus, Syphax, and Scipio too would choose a time of tumult and change to make their escape. New York City, which had recently fallen to the British during the American Revolution, offered the possibility of sanctuary, but also peril. They, however, did not run together—a year separates Primus's and Scipio's escapes. That they were advertised together highlights that their enslaver believed them to be connected enough to be found together. Their pursuer was the great-grandson of Director General Petrus Stuyvesant. He was a wealthy slave-holder, owned a Georgian mansion in town, and was the last private owner of the entirety of his family's large Manhattan *bouwerij* (farm). He was a New York merchant working on behalf of an expansive network of slaveholding cousins and would augment his own power through the landed wealth and slaves he had inherited, emerging as the largest New York City slaveholder on the first US Census of 1790. Primus, Syphax, and Scipio had been bequeathed to Petrus in his father Gerardus's will, along with two enslaved women.[39] Like his ancestor had, this Petrus would turn first to racial identifiers, describing the men as "three negro fellows," but the first Petrus worded his notice carefully, denying agency to the men in their flight by eschewing the active verb "run away" for the passive "lost." He had been used to operating within a system of violent vagaries deployed to claim control over enslaved people as needed, while his great-grandson inherited a culture shaped by over a century of human bondage. Unlike the first Petrus's warrant, this notice, ran in a regional newspaper and trained the public's ears toward apprehending the escapees. A would-be slave catcher would have had to linger long enough to be regaled by Primus's "civil and mild" conversation, have heard the "broken English"—perhaps accented by Dutch—that Petrus used to differentiate Syphax, and have caught the "stammer" in his speech to identify Scipio.

The notices that open and close this introduction bookend a period that witnessed the establishment and growth of some of the most powerful dynasties in American history. They represent different end points during the development of what would become an expansive Northeastern slaveholding gentry. The first Petrus existed at the foundation of these networks that were built on the back of kinship, trade, and slave activities. The second Petrus lived at a time when these networks were already established, at the end of the colonial period. This book explores the time between these two points. Beginning in the mid-seventeenth century when New York was still New Netherland and controlled by the Dutch and continuing up to the end of the colonial period, I examine the emergence of an interconnected Northeastern gentry bound by bondage.

CHAPTER 1

Neger

Race, Slavery, and Status in the Dutch
Northeast (1640s–60s)

During the early winter of 1660 in the forested landscape of northern New Netherland, a Black man was compelled to work. He had tied a blanket around his ears to block out the chilly weather as he struggled to ensure that his enslaver's household would have enough wood to make it through the harsh winters that beset the area.[1] With his labor he worked to provide some semblance of the life his Amsterdam-born enslaver Jeremias van Rensselaer had left behind. The work was unrelenting, backbreaking, and commonplace. It was also surveilled.[2] As the man toiled, Petrus Stuyvesant watched him, and wanted his labor for himself. He offered to compensate Jeremias with one of his own slaves or to order another enslaved person from the Caribbean Island of Curaçao.[3] Jeremias agreed to the offer, and the man found his life passed into the hands of another. The following summer, Jeremias sat down to pen a letter to his elder brother, Jan Baptist, detailing the encounter, in which he devoted over half of a manuscript page toward complaining about the enslaved man he referred to, not by name, but by an array of derogatory terms: "the beast" (*het Beest*), a "foul useless beast" (*een onnut vuyl Beest*), "clumsy oaf of a neger" (*een lompe vlegel van een neeger*), and a "dumb beast" (*een domme beeste*). With the last epithet, which he attributed to Petrus, he first wrote and then crossed out "dumb neger" (*een domme negger*).[4] Such crude language rarely opens discussions

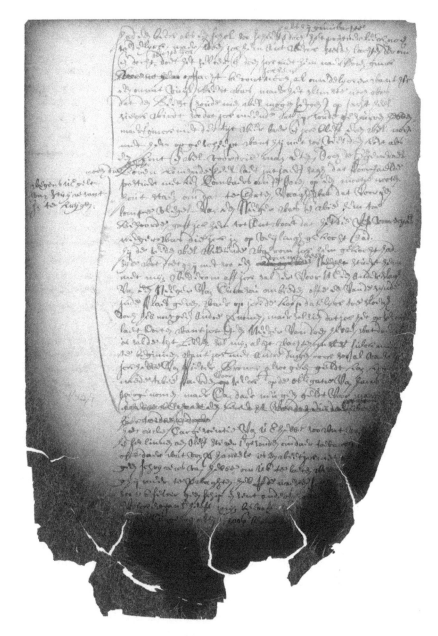

FIGURE 3. Jeremias to Jan Baptist van Rensselaer, June 2, 1661, SC7079 Box 4 Folder 42: Van Rensselaer Manor Papers. From the collections of the New York State Library, Manuscripts and Special Collections, Albany, New York.

of enslavement in New Netherland specifically or in the Northeast more broadly, but it is central to understanding not only the self-perception of enslavers like Jeremias van Rensselaer, but also the cultures of influence they spawned.

Archival sources offer varied reflections of moments lost to time. The unnamed enslaved person described in the letter emerges not as a man at all but a "dumb beast." In writing about an event that had occurred seven months earlier, Jeremias sought not to faithfully capture the exchange, but to conjure for his older brother, Jan Baptist, certain sentiments: disdain, humiliation, and power. A wider gaze captures more than just the perceptions of one man. It exposes the bonds between three men at the furthest outpost of Dutch American settlement. It brings into focus a fourth man sitting in Amsterdam imagining the scene his twenty-eight-year-old younger brother imparted. It interlaces the northern woods with the continental shelf of South America and Amsterdam's opulent canal houses. By the time Jeremias committed his thoughts to writing, a cottage industry of maps marked out the boundaries of the joined colony of New Netherland, which included the southern Caribbean Islands of Aruba, Bonaire, and Curaçao. It was a world connected by waterways and secured by both the expansion and forced depletion of social and kinship ties.

Such an entwining fashioned the colonial experiences of New Netherland transplants. Some European migrants would forge new beginnings, becoming influential in a variety of slaveholding settings in colonial North America. They would build networks of wealth and power that endure to this day. Though steeped in premodern values and mores, these migrants were creating something new. Although the enslaved have been positioned as exotic foreigners on the margins of the heterogeneous tapestry of New Netherland's colonial story, they were far from peripheral. Densely interconnected families built their colonial identities during the period of Dutch rule in no small part through engagement with enslavement. Their efforts consciously constructed networks of slaveholding that would tie the region together far beyond the bounds of New Netherland. Out of such slaveholding experiences, they reconceptualized their environment. They created an interconnected slaveholding network birthed in New Netherland that would ensnare generations of captive people.

Boundaries of Differences

That unnamed laborer's unique existence held value, though the specific contours of his life will never be known. He was perhaps no older than thirty years. Had he been older, it is likely that Jeremias would have mentioned his age in the litany of complaints that he offered about the man. The laborer lived within a wider set of social geographies that knit together enslaved, bonded, and free people in the Dutch colony. The enslaved laborer was not the only person held in bondage by the twenty-eight-year-old Jeremias. An accomplished horse groom named Andries was also claimed by the young man.

In the fall of 1657, Trijntjen (Catherina) Rodenborch sold Andries to Jeremias's older brother Jan Baptist.[5] Who was Andries and where did he come from? The historical record is frustratingly vague. A year before the sale, Trijntjen returned to New Netherland where she had grown up, alongside her husband Lucas (the former vice director of Curaçao), daughter Elizabeth, and an enslaved man, whose name the West India Company (WIC) directors did not bother to record in their letter to Petrus Stuyvesant. The document was not intended as a memorial, but rather to inform Petrus that Lucas had not been paid the "balance of his salary." The WIC instructed Petrus to ensure that Lucas could "balance" his owed wages in New Netherland with "Negroes, horses and whatever else may be of service to him."[6] Eight months later Lucas was dead, and Trijntjen petitioned that some of her late husband's back wages be paid out in specie.[7] Petrus had presumably complied with a portion of the WIC's directive and supplied some of Lucas's back salary in human beings, because by September 1657, Trijntjen placed several enslaved people up for sale.

Rensselaerswijck-based Jan Baptist bought one of these captive people, tasking his brother, Jeremias—who was the family's resident merchant contact in New Amsterdam during the summers—with choosing a person from among the enslaved people that Trijntjen was offering for sale. Jeremias attended the sale with New Amsterdam merchant Oloff Stevensz. van Cortlandt, and they settled on "a tall, quick fellow who can work well." Jeremias promised to send him up to his brother "at the first opportunity."[8] Andries resisted so much during the year following the purchase that Jan Baptist remembered the time as one marked by "trouble and arguments." Nonetheless, Andries's labor was valued—neighbor Jan Labatie offered Jan Baptist 100 guilders a year to hire Andries out.[9] Jan Baptist had not set up that arrangement by the time that he left the colony in the early fall of 1658.[10] Instead, he left Andries on Rensselaerswijck, serving his younger brother Jeremias, who had become the new director, with the understanding that Andries was still his slave.[11] As the months passed and Jan Baptist remained in *patria* that understanding became more fungible, at least to Jeremias. By February of the following year, Jan Baptist decided to sell Andries, and requested that his younger brother affect the sale. By April he had thought better of the decision and requested that Jeremias send Andries to the Dutch Republic: "I need him at Cralo [Crailo] to mind my horse" (*Ick hebbe hem noodtsaeckelijk op Cralo vande [winter] op mij paerdt te passen*).[12] How Andries remained in Rensselaerswijck and the wider community and family context of the episode illuminates the ways in which slavery was made in fits and starts during the first generation of settlement.

Andries spent his days of toil between the patroon's town house in Beverwijck and the lands situated along the flats of the Hudson.[13] The patroonship, the largest in the area, covered a massive amount of acreage, which included islands, rugged mountains, and dense forest. Patroons, according to one version of the "Freedoms and Exemptions," were allotted "twelve black men and women out of the prizes in which Negroes shall be found, for the advancement of New Netherland," although the company did not deliver on this promise.[14] The lion's share of the labor on patroonships like Rensselaerswijck had been planned for tenant farmers. So, how, exactly were the twelve Black men and women, wrested as the booty of privateering raids, going to advance New Netherland? Although the WIC failed to deliver on the initial promise of proposed enslaved laborers, the narratives of two men enslaved to the Van Rensselaers show that their ultimate presence was a catalyst for society building.[15]

The patroonship proposed by the WIC directors, while reflective of land arrangements in the Dutch Republic, would also nod to the new work arrangements that built Dutch colonial aspirations throughout the world.[16] A patroon's identity would be based on racial as much as class difference. This was the edifice on which the entire colonization program would be built. Even if New Netherland would never match the revenue outflow of Recife or become the slave-trading depot for Dutch slavers like Curaçao, it was erected on the assumption of a subordinate class with little hope for advancement.[17] The first patroon, Kiliaen van Rensselaer, intended Rensselaerswijck to contribute to the larger Dutch Atlantic economy that was fueled by slavery, exporting its grain harvests to Brazil, which would be deployed to feed the company slaves.[18] Rensselaerswijck relied on a tenant, bonded, and enslaved labor force and exported goods to Native societies and throughout the Atlantic world. As Kiliaen explained, "As to the farm of *Bijleveldt*, I see that your honor has it worked by one farm hand and one negro, which may well be done and it still yield profit." He sought to expand such a mixed work scheme for the farm belonging to Coenraed Notelman, the *fiscael* of the WIC at New Amsterdam.[19] After Kiliaen's death, his eldest son Johannes inherited the title of patroon of Rensselaerswijck, though, like his father, he never left Holland.[20] Instead, his half-brother Jan Baptist traveled to New Netherland to manage the patroonship until 1655 when he returned to Amsterdam, leaving the directorship to his younger brother Jeremias.[21]

Rensselaerswijck became the only financially viable patroonship. Although technically in the hands of distant patroons such as Kiliaen and Johannes van Rensselaer, it would be governed by directors who spent a considerable amount of time in the Hudson Valley, such as Jan Baptist and Jeremias, men who would construct a colonial environment, created in part by enslaved labor. They would build their dynasties through strategic marriages executed in Dutch Reformed churches while sitting on courts that slowly eroded and invalidated the social and community ties between the enslaved. They would pass down dowries and legacies that honored the connections made at baptisms through carefully chosen witnesses. The relationships and community built by enslaved and freed people using the same avenues were systematically closed, as over time baptism, witnessing, and marriage became institutions reserved for the freeborn and not the enslaved.[22]

Andries was pulled between chaos and tumult. Jeremias complained that Jan Baptist had left the patroon's house in such an awful condition that it needed considerable repairs.[23] Jeremias's town house, gallingly zoned within the boundaries of Beverwijck after a violent and contentious dispute between the patroonship and the colony, was newly completed and decorated with flourishes of his family's wealth, but crowded, serving as the meeting place for colony business and housing an enslaved and a servant staff.[24] In contrast, the van Rensselaer home on the Keizersgracht was opulently appointed, decorated with goods purchased as a result of the family's precious gem business as well as dividends from the Dutch East India Company.[25] The family manor named Crailo, located on feudal lands held in Het Gooi, would have been the closest approximation of life in Rensselaerswijck, and is where Jan Baptist planned to place Andries to tend his horses, but the flat expanse of the Dutch countryside would have contrasted sharply with the rolling foothills that marked the northern river valley.[26]

Andries would have already seen the *grachten*, or canals, of Amsterdam by the time of Jan Baptist's letter, if he was the unnamed man who arrived in New Netherland with his former enslaver, Trijntjen Rodenborch. Jeremias compared Andries's "worth" to the price of other enslaved people who had lived thirteen to fourteen years in the Caribbean, and two "here among the Dutch," implying Andries had such Caribbean experience in addition to his service in New Netherland.[27] As Andrea Mosterman argued, his skill with horses could point to Andries's origins in Senegambia. Colonial enslavers in the Caribbean and Spanish South America highly prized Senegambian captive people for their cattle and husbandry skills.[28]

Andries's skill attending horses offered him some leverage. Andries's position as a groom is certainly what spared him from being sold in February 1659 as Jan Baptist had initially planned. Jeremias noted that during the winter, Andries had "taken care of the horses alone and has done it so well that during my time the horses have never looked so fine."[29] Alone in the brutal winters of the Hudson River Valley, Andries took care of his enslaver's horses. He might well have understood that Jan Baptist had a mind to sell him and used his skills to remain in the community by impressing his indispensability to Jeremias, a young man who engaged in winter sports and boisterously raced sleighs with his comrades.[30] Andries would have known the danger of sale that Jan Baptist's departure posed to him if he had witnessed other enslaved people sold away. When Jan Baptist reversed his previous decision to sell Andries and instead requested that Jeremias "do not forget to send the Negro," it was to tend his new "roan piebald horse, a 3-year-old Spanish mare, being full of worms."[31] Andries could have had experience leveraging his skilled labor as a groom while living in the Caribbean. Aruba, Bonaire, and to a lesser extent, Curaçao supplied horses to New Netherland, and at least some enslaved people used their knowledge of horses to escape.[32]

In any case, using his skill as a groom to avoid the life disruption of sale was a gamble because it was this skill that led Jan Baptist to desire him in Holland. Amsterdam merchant families were heavily invested in the slave trade and enslaved people were held captive in the Northern European city, as well as others throughout the republic.[33] Such a relocation could have afforded Andries opportunities to connect to the Black community in Amsterdam, living in Rembrandt's neighborhood near the Jewish section that Mark Ponte highlights inspired the painter's artistic renderings of urban life.[34] However, Jeremias was loath to let his brother's enslaved man go, so he stalled. He never sold Andries outside the family following Jan Baptist's February letter, and after sending a letter in May praising Andries's skill attending his horses, he pointedly ignored his brother's request to send Andries to Holland.[35] By August, Jeremias wrote to Jan Baptist that "friends here have advised me against [sending Andries to Holland], saying that it would be nothing but foolishness to try to have him serve you in a free country (*vrijlandt*), as he would be too proud to do that."[36] For Jeremias, Rensselaerswyck specifically and New Netherland in general was no free land; even in Rensselaerswijck whose enslaved population was overshadowed by New Amsterdam's in terms of numbers, Jeremias imagined that Andries's actions and even sentiments were controlled by a communally and socially enforced bondage. Jan Baptist knew better; enslavement was a reality everywhere: both in the Dutch Republic and in its broader empire.

Andries continued to resist. Jeremias complained of the difficulty "to get him to do anything for anybody if I have not expressly ordered him to do so."[37] Andries clearly had options: he lived at the crossroads of several different settlements and cultures and was a part of the working community of Beverwijck. Andries lived and worked alongside laborers of different social statuses. A maid worked in the patroon's house and two Dutch servants lived in the house during the same period as well. A tailor would board in the house on occasion. Later, another two enslaved people—one Native—would also live and work there. Two enslaved people named Mookinga (which appears to be a Dutch transliterated version of the Angolan name, Muxima) and Manuel had been sold at auction in New Amsterdam and sent up to the fort to labor.[38] Though he tried to present his retention of Andries as a favor to Jan Baptist by highlighting Andries's behavior, Jeremias ultimately admitted, "To tell the truth, I could not spare him very well." He offered to pay his brother "de somma 50 heele bevers" or the equivalent of fifty whole beavers (roughly 400 guilders).[39]

Jeremias was uninterested in sending Andries on what he believed would be a one-way trip to Holland, but was keener to trade enslaved people with powerful New Netherland colonists. The young Jeremias was surrounded by friends who did not hesitate to offer their opinion of proper mastery. Such slaveholding friends could have included the Van Cortlandts who resided in Manhattan and the Schuylers who lived in Beverwijck. As Janny Venema notes, other friends also included fur traders Volckert Jansz Douw, Jan Thomasz, Pieter Hartgers, and town surgeon Abraham Staets.[40] Jeremias's friendships maintained his family's prestige as one of the four controlling trading families in the colony.[41] Indeed, he noted that he had purchased the laborer mentioned at the beginning of this chapter on the suggestion of Petrus Stuyvesant for his brother's account in order to settle debts.[42] Such ties illuminate the social importance these colonists placed on shoring up local relationships through ties of bonded reciprocities.[43] Jeremias would rather hold onto the labor and life of a captive Andries, following New Netherland-based friends' advice, than send him across the ocean to toil for his brother. Such penchant for following local friends rather than the desires of his distant blood relations, would lead to Jeremias courting and ultimately marrying Maria van Cortlandt without asking his mother Anna's permission.[44] Perceptions that equated the Dutch Republic and other Western European lands with freedom—despite the sharply contrasting realities of those enslaved within European societies—would persist as imagined boundaries of empire. Jeremias's slaveholding actions should be read as part of a continuum of constructing difference at work throughout the Dutch overseas empire, but it was also profoundly local. The language that Jeremias used to describe these two enslaved people—one "a dumb beast" and the other "too proud"—would come to define not just the intrinsic and labor-based value they each provided, but also their relational worth for establishing status and prestige within expansive American dynastic families.

A *Bouwerij* in Lower Manhattan

When the laborer formerly enslaved by Jeremias left southward down the Hudson toward New Amsterdam, he was headed toward an uncertain future.[45] His story highlights how much silence remains in the recounting of history, shadowing not only his name, identity, and past, but also the motives and ministrations of his captors. Yet such fragments also contain the power to disrupt. Various firsts have opened the story of enslavement: the arrival of the first slave ships or the stories of the first African-descended residents. His journey away from Rensselaerswijck and toward New Amsterdam presents alternate focal points for the narrative of early American enslavement. The Stuyvesant family's properties would ultimately include holdings in Wiltwijck (present-day Kingston) and Bergen County (in New Jersey).[46] But their domestic lives were mostly spent on their properties in Manhattan—the house in town that the English would rechristen Whitehall and their *bouwerij* (bowery). The bouwerij was a place of enslavement as well as a place for creating networks between free Blacks. It served as both a physical and social place for connection and disconnection, and became the locus from which an expansive network of slaveholding connections was formed, yet it was immortalized in the written record as a "place of relaxation and pleasure."[47] The man's sale, and those like it, connected the lives of enslavers to each other and to the far-flung reaches of the Atlantic world, but the veneer applied to this network of oppression was one of peace and calm—an intentional dissonance that, like Jeremias's descriptions of both Andries and the unnamed laborer, fed into the self-perceptions of enslavers and the cultures they influenced. By following the lives of the Stuyvesant family; their transatlantic migration as well as the social elements of their American lives revolving around church, household, and neighborhood, I highlight the process of becoming enslavers.

In the 1660s, the bouwerij was a compact village of its own, situated on the shores of lower Manhattan. A number of New Amsterdam's enslaved workers lived nearby. Composed of a farmhouse and barn chapel surrounded by gardens where foodstuffs were grown, the bouwerij's landscape would have differed from that in the northernmost reaches of the colony.[48] By then the wooded landscape that had covered Manhattan had been cut back and cleared for the island's southernmost settlement. Such labor was completed in part by numerous Black workers. An enslaved man named Balthazar, who had been held captive in the Spanish Caribbean, seized by French pirates, before being sold in New Amsterdam, toiled for Petrus.[49] Enslaved and free people worked the bouwerij's fields of wheat and garden plots. Others owned by the WIC toiled on the chain gang, to relime the fort and construct the palisade.[50] An Angolan woman, named Mayken, enslaved to the WIC who had been among the first group of Black people to arrive in New Netherland, worked as a domestic in one of the Stuyvesants' Manhattan houses. She labored alongside her friends Lucretia and Susanna.[51] The bouwerij sported a chapel—one of the last construction projects for the bouwerij carpenter Frederick Philipse, before he secured a contract to trade tobacco and enslaved people in Virginia.[52] In good weather, the services there would be led by twenty-three-year-old Henricus Selijns, who remarked to his superiors back home of the mixed community that he found, one which included forty Black people from the "negro coast" (modern-day Congo and Angola).[53]

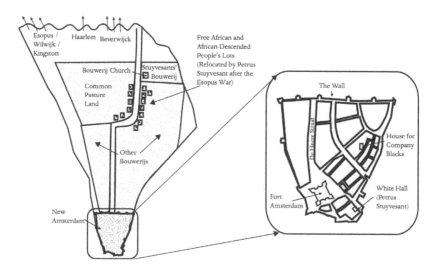

FIGURE 4. Map of New Amsterdam, the bouwerijs, and the southern portion of Manhattan Island. Based on the Castello Plan of 1660. From The New York Public Library.

Petrus Stuyvesant's domestic world in 1660 included his wife Judith and two sons, Balthazar who was thirteen and Nicolaes Willem who was twelve.[54] From the beginning of their colonial American lives, the Stuyvesant family's experience was entwined with enslavement. By the winter of 1660, the family had become so comfortable with enslavement that the lives of men, women, and children became currency that underwrote their personal and professional relationships. But their lives in New Netherland, surrounded and supported by bondage, was little more than a decade old. Before then, only Petrus had been exposed to the Atlantic slave market. He had begun his American career sometime before 1635 as a commissary or supercargo on the Fernando de Noronha island chain off the northeastern coast of Brazil. By 1639, he had been posted on the island of Curaçao, starting as a commissary but working his way up to director in 1642.[55] Petrus's tenure was marked by raids against the Spanish and, as director, he had considerable access to and control of the people enslaved by the WIC who endured a brutal existence on the island. The enslaved were given just enough rations to survive, despite being set to work on the salt pans. They were subjected to whippings and sale. They frequently ran away in protest. In a resolution dated May 19, 1643, drawn up at Fort Amsterdam on Curaçao, by Petrus Stuyvesant, Brian Newton, and Lucas Rodenborch, the group found it "necessary for the maximum security of the island, as long as the Negroes remain working there, to keep 3 to 4 horsemen there together with 8 to 10 soldiers, in order to provide a guard for the countryside both against surprise (Spanish) attack and the escape of Negroes."[56] On May 26 the following year they whipped and sold a group of four enslaved "Negroes and Mulattoes" caught attempting to escape the harsh island regime by building "a raft near the east point." Judging the groups' escape seditious, they counted the punishment mercy, noting "we did not sentence them to death, which they well deserved, but found it most profitable for the Company, after whipping them severely, to send them off to St. Cruz or other Caribbean islands to be traded for provisions."[57] The dramatic difference in perspective between enslavers viewing the vulnerability of their political positions, which partially depended on the "allegiance" of peoples highly motivated toward insurgency, and those of freedom seekers was stark. This sentence reflects the intersection between the fear of high treason and the desire for continual profit from the sale in human beings, which motivated the group's flight.

Later in 1644, Petrus's leg was crushed by a cannonball during a siege against St. Martin. He returned to the Dutch Republic to recuperate where he met and married Judith Bayard. Around a year after their wedding, the pair departed from the island of Texel on the *Prinses Amelia*, bound for New Netherland and Petrus's new role as the director general of the joint colonies of New Netherland and Curaçao "and the islands thereof" (*en d' Eylanden van dien*, which included Aruba and Bonaire).[58] Seven months pregnant, Judith received her introduction to enslavement on the island of Curaçao during the spring of 1647, when the *Prinses Amelia* docked there for a month before continuing on to New Amsterdam.[59] Petrus's half-sister Margrietje, full sister Anna, and Anna's four children—Balthazar, Petrus, Nicolaes, and Catharina—would emigrate seven years later, following the death of Anna's husband Samuel Bayard, who was also Judith's brother. Petrus had business on the island—he was tasked with briefing island management of the details of the transition to his new administration.[60]

Even from the ship they would have witnessed the work routines of the enslaved enforced by institutionalized torture and heard the cadence of different languages. Some captives were brought by the Spanish in the sixteenth century from Sierra Leone and Senegambia. Others could have been traded from Caribbean islands like St. Christopher, from Spanish South America, or from Dutch Brazil. In the early years of the trade, such captives were the plunder of Dutch privateers who attacked Portuguese slave ships in Africa and then shipped the enslaved people to the Americas, but by the time that the Stuyvesants arrived in Curaçao the Dutch were firmly entrenched for direct trade from the Gold Coast to Pernambuco. Those arrivals who hailed from West Central Africa—an area that encompassed the Kongo basin and in the south, Angola—would have spoken a variety of Bantu languages. Those who hailed from the Kongo would have had exposure to Roman Catholicism and a number of captives would have been baptized Catholics before arriving in the Americas. A debate as to the numbers of this trade persists, but for the period of the Dutch slave trade, nearly 500,000 African captives were transported to Dutch America, with more than 200,000 arriving during the seventeenth century. The Dutch represented nearly 12 percent of the slave trade during the seventeenth century but were eclipsed during the eighteenth century by the meteoric numbers attained by the British. Numbers from the direct trade after 1651 indicate that most of Curaçao's enslaved population hailed from West Central Africa and the Bight of Benin. The Bight of Biafra and the Gold Coast made up another large share of the imported Dutch captive population during the period, with much less coming from Senegambia and Sierra Leone.[61]

Lucas Rodenborch, the island director who had worked closely with Petrus, lived on the island with Trijntjen. The Rodenborchs' household was served by people enslaved to the family and those owned by the Dutch West

India Company.⁶² Judith would have observed the expectations of deference from captive people that enslavers such as the Rodenborchs had come to expect. Though she had no doubt encountered Dutch maidservants in the United Provinces and understood those customs of decorum, and lived in a society where Black servants in various states of unfreedom were present (across Europe during the early modern period), she would have seen new patterns of behavior imposed by torture.⁶³ She also would have encountered another side to Petrus, the only one of them who would have been accustomed to a world dominated by enslavement. In the years to come, he would help implement the WIC's vision for a more expansive slave footprint in the North American colony.⁶⁴ Judith was getting a crash course in how to function as an enslaver.

By the time the family arrived, Curaçao had a legal framework for slavery, which included punishments for running away and admonitions against sex with African and Native women that emphasized the contact as "unchristian-like intercourse." Such laws could have been a reaction to sexual abuse, a reflection of a racially rooted unease, or a disgust with sex outside of Christian marriage but likely were an acknowledgement of the key role nonwhite female agriculturalists served on an arid island where famine was constant. As Linda Rupert has noted, the early legal code included strict protections for enslaved gardens, a potential nod to the dire need for such enslaved women's agricultural prowess.⁶⁵

The same year that the Stuyvesants stopped in Curaçao on their way to New Netherland, Englishman Richard Ligon arrived on the island of Barbados, at the very beginning of the sugar boom. Sugar was still worked in part by European servants, but it was quickly being racialized. Ligon's *A True and Exact History of the Island of Barbados* would describe the beginnings of sugar on the island as well as circulate for a seventeenth-century Northern European market an image of Atlantic slavery and African cultures.⁶⁶ Likewise, the families that would depart the southern Caribbean island for the northern colony of New Amsterdam would inscribe a narrative of their lives that would be intertwined with the struggles and hardships of the enslaved. Such stories would circulate in accounts of captivities, in the margins of financial records, within the pages of baptismal records, and perhaps more prevalently, in the laws and cases that stood as an enduring monument to their attempts to control. But before the emergence of a slave society in the Chesapeake, before slavery followed the condition of the mother, before slave patrols tracked down runaways and enslavers published their hue and cry, a group of family members and their friends learned what it meant to be colonists in the teeming cauldron of the Caribbean. Thus initiated, they would have left the island of Curaçao armed with a set of expectations for their lives in colonial North America, one that foregrounded slavery.

New Netherland contained a small community of enslaved people by the time of the Stuyvesants' arrival in 1647 and, unlike in Curaçao, the institution was not codified into the legal structure of the colony. The first official shipment of Africans arrived in New Amsterdam in 1627, when the *Bruynvisch* landed.[67] Additional captives would come on further ships before Petrus and his family set foot on Manhattan, but as scholars have rightly pointed out this first generation of New Netherland's enslaved people did not face the legal and social restrictions of later generations.[68] How much of this is owning to the uniqueness of New Netherland's culture is debatable. Access to landowning, the courts, and even church membership existed in the Chesapeake during the same time and was not restricted until the 1660s and later, although Virginia's 1639 law did prevent arming "Negroes," in contrast to what was practiced in New Netherland. There is no evidence to suggest that Black New Netherlanders owned white indentured servants as was the case in the Chesapeake, nor did any free Black landowner in Manhattan rival the social status of Anthony Johnson.[69] New Netherland colonists with sufficient financial resources were permitted personal ownership of enslaved people, and their ability to buy and sell these individuals was safeguarded. In a 1642 resolution of the Amsterdam chamber of the WIC, the company directors explicitly state that former director Wouter van Twiller "may dispose at his pleasure of his cattle, movables, Negroes and all that belongs to him" on his former company farm.[70] The use of Black people enslaved by the company for construction and defense was also well established in the colony. Slavery's growth was encouraged by company leadership in Amsterdam, although they could not always be the sole channel for delivery of enslaved labor.[71] In 1646, two years after eleven formerly enslaved individuals successfully argued for freedom for themselves and their spouses (a freedom that would exclude their children), the WIC issued instructions to the new director general and the Council of New Netherland that, "for the promotion of agriculture there, it is deemed proper to permit, at the request of the Patroons, colonists and other farmers, the conveyance thither of as many Negroes as they are willing to purchase at a fair price."[72]

After Petrus had settled in, he began his tenure as the only director general of a newly joined colony. He entered the position with a picture in his mind of how the space he inhabited should be arranged, one that was shaped by his experience in a slaveholding colonial environment. Petrus began his colonial career in Dutch Brazil in 1635, serving partly under the direction of the governor general, Count Johan Maurits van Nassau-Siegen. Johan Maurits was heavily invested in the slave trade, as Carolina Monteiro and Erik Odegard argue, carving out an extensive slave-trading network and personal ownership of over thirty individuals in addition to the control of another fifty people enslaved to the company by the time that Stuyvesant assumed his post as director of Curaçao in 1642.[73] Under Petrus's predecessor Willem Kieft's term, in 1646, the slave ship *Tamandare* docked in New Amsterdam, dooming some of its compliment of enslaved men women and children to toil in New Netherland, while Willem sold most for export. Petrus inherited Willem's company responsibilities, which included an expanded desire for enslavement in the northern Dutch colony and, a year after his installation, Petrus received word from his superiors that they felt "more negroes could be advantageously employed and sold" in New Netherland than "the ship *Tamandare* has brought." At the very beginning of his term, Petrus would have had to keep the WIC's 1647 guidance in mind, which pronounced the company's own proslavery stance at the beginning of his tenure: "We shall take care, that [in the future] a greater number of negroes be taken there."[74] In 1648, the WIC made explicit their commitment to encouraging the importation of Angolans who were intended to "be employed in farming."[75] For his own part, Petrus asked for a salary increase as well as "the transfer of a *bouwerije*, stocked with two horses, six cows and two negro boys."[76]

Shortly after the Stuyvesants began their new lives on Manhattan, a free Black family gathered for the baptism of their son Sebastiaen, an effort to secure their social and religious standing.[77] The little boy's father, Jan van Angola was joined with his chosen witnesses Emanuel Congoij and Marie van Angola. The geographic origins embedded within their surnames suggest that Jan, Marie, and Emanuel could speak to one another in several languages, Kimbundu, Kikongo, Portuguese, a creole form of Portuguese similar to what would become Papiamento, and Dutch. Like the multicultural settlers that populated New Netherland, they were creating their own American community out of networks of family, land, language, and religion. It was, as Susanah Shaw Romney, Jeroen Dewulf, and Graham Russell Hodges have argued, an Atlantic African community that would have been recognizable throughout the Americas, but with creole as well as identifiably Dutch elements. There are several enslaved men named Jan in the records during these years, including Jan de Neger who was enslaved in Rensselaerswijck and had, in 1646, performed one of the area's first executions.[78] Rensselaerswijck's *domine* Johannes Megapolensis requested freedom for Jan

Francisco, the younger, due to his service to the colony, causing Van Laer to speculate that this was the same Jan who had served as executioner.[79]

Jan sought to incorporate his son as a member of the free African community, claiming Christian liberty through baptism, and physical freedom by naming him Sebastiaen, after Bastiaen, the leader of the free Black community. Bastiaen, who was known as the "captain of the Negroes," could have been a sailor, a WIC employee who had been granted freedom by the company in 1640.[80] Sebastiaen's baptism was one of the five within the African and African-descended community that evoked his name "based on Bastiaen's exceptional connections."[81] They exemplified Ira Berlin's "Atlantic creole" who thrived during the "charter generation," of Black settlement.[82] A West Central African man, Paulo de Angola, had been granted "a certain parcel of land on the east side of the Klock of the Fresh water" in 1645.[83] Paulo and a group of ten other people enslaved to the West India Company had been granted their freedom and those of their wives in return for an annual tax of their harvest.[84] Their children, however, remained enslaved to the company. Enslaved and free parents would struggle to protect their children from the abuses of slavery, frequently appearing at the baptismal font or in New Netherland's courts in pursuit of such aims. Their aspirations to build a thriving free community were zealous, like many other inhabitants of the diverse colony, but their racial otherness and the competing aims of family building by white settlers made such strivings a daily struggle. While they lived in community with one another, they also had relationships with white neighbors, many of whom had business, religious, and personal connections with the Black community.

Judith Stuyvesant's life had been drastically transformed in her new colonial home. She had lived most of her life a single woman in the Dutch Republic and, within a year and a half of marriage to Petrus Stuyvesant, that life was gone forever. In its place were new duties as a new mother, and as the wife of the director general, stationed at a small but expanding outpost of the Dutch empire manned by a mixed workforce that included enslaved people.[85] While the society she left did have a population of enslaved people who served in Dutch centers like Amsterdam and Delft, the immediate diversity both in background and circumstance of the denizens of New Amsterdam would have made for a glaring change. Three months after arriving, on August 11, 1647, a very pregnant Judith stood alongside commissary Hendrick van Dijck, Van Dijck's wife Lydia, and two others to witness the baptism of twins Jan and Aelje. Two weeks later another child, Jan, the mixed-race child of captain Jan de Vries, was baptized in the Reformed Church in New Amsterdam.[86]

Another seven weeks later, Judith's first child, Balthazar Lazarus—named for both her and Petrus's minister fathers—was baptized in new Amsterdam.[87] His witnesses were chosen from the leaders of the colony and included the Huguenot physician Jean de la Montagne, whose tobacco plantation, named Vredendael, had been recently destroyed by warfare, and Cornelis van Tienhoven. As secretary, Cornelis formalized the sale of enslaved people to New Netherland's denizens shortly before the Stuyvesants' arrival and helped place an unfree African child whose parents had successfully wrested freedom from their captors.[88] Alongside them stood Anneken Bogardus, whose husband, Everardus, had facilitated the baptism of many of the community of enslaved and free Black people that populated New Amsterdam.[89] These elite neighbors stood and promised to raise Balthazar in the knowledge of the Reformed faith, and their example would school him on the earthly engine of empire. He and his brother Nicolaes Willem, baptized a year later, grew up on the bouwerij surrounded by a community of free and enslaved Native, African, and African-descended men, women, and children.[90]

Such enslaved laborers would have served Judith and her young family, cleaning the house and preparing the food that had come to represent the taste of the republic in its far reaches of empire. In later generations, the enslaved population's grasp and syncretic transformation of Dutch culture became a defining aspect of life in colonies with old Dutch populations.[91] Judith's American life would be spent in close living proximity with the enslaved in and around the bouwerij, as well as a group enslaved by the West India Company who lived in a house on the Slijksteeg in New Amsterdam and fifteen free Black households who lived and farmed along the wagon road in parcels of land granted them by Petrus in 1659. Henricus Selijns, the Brooklyn minister who visited the bouwerij on Sunday evenings, would have preached to a multiracial congregation that incorporated flocks as far as New Amsterdam. Ægidius Luyck, a schoolmaster and future minister, had been hired as rector of New Amsterdam's Latin School. As he was married to a relative of Judith, he doubtless visited the bouwerij regularly.[92] The Stuyvesants were surrounded by a host of relatives and friends who lived nearby. Many of them would marry and create networks of slavery that would crisscross the Americas. A Northeastern slaveholding culture that would last for two centuries was born out of communities in lower Manhattan.

Dishonorable Work

Unlike the discoverable lives of the Stuyvesant family, the laborer who opened this chapter and sailed down to New Amsterdam in 1661 was drawn in the barest of terms. He suffered from some unnamed chronic ailment or injury, and he had been employed at strenuous work. The scars of such a life sunk so deeply that they would be still visible in the bones of enslaved people excavated centuries later.[93] By calling the enslaved man a "dumb beast," Jeremias (and presumably Petrus as well) evoked an animality and carnality that underlay nascent notions of racial difference. Jeremias could have deployed the adjective *dumb* to mean that the man could not speak or had trouble speaking, evidencing a certain unease toward disability that was infused by racial disdain. Jeremias's earlier description of the man began by noting he had a "mouth that looked like a flounder ^when he grinned" (*een beck als een schol soo scheen ^als hy gruickacten*) suggest the man had a facial paralysis consistent with a stroke or cerebral palsy. It could also have been a racialized disparagement of the man's lips, just as other Dutch travelers read monstrosity in African women's breasts.[94] Jeremias's choice of the work *beck*, which evokes an animal's beak rather than a human mouth, linked his assessment to popular travel literature describing African people as beasts. Jeremias also described the man as clumsy and noted disparagingly that he tried to break the piece of wood by standing on it as opposed to swinging an axe. He complained that the man could do less work than a child despite looking fit and eating as much as three men (*hy niet soo veel doen [cost] als een kint & wel voor drie man eten*), and freely expressed that he regretted the man had not died when he had earlier fallen ill (*ick bleft even wel noch met hem op gescheept*).[95] His words are laced not only with racial antipathy but with clear disgust for the man's physicality. Despite Jeremias's criticisms, Petrus clearly intended a future of labor for the man, one that would be both backbreaking and dishonorable. He could have even been sent to war. Several months earlier, Petrus had requested that the slaves the Amsterdam directors had ordered sent to New Netherland should be "stout and strong fellows" (*heel cloecke ende starcke negros*) who were "fit to work on this fortress and other works; also, if able, in the war against the native neighbors, either to pursue them, or else to carry the baggage for the soldiers."[96] Notions of race were intimately tied to conceptions of capabilities and honor, and this racially coded world shaped relationships between Petrus, the Esopus and other regional Indian nations, Africans, Creoles, and New Amsterdam's other white settlers.

Hogs, cows, horses, and goats infested the island of Manhattan in the 1640s leaving destruction in their wake. Petrus lamented the deplorable condition of the fort, crumbling and overrun with the settlers' uncontrolled animals. He saw an island in need of cleaning and construction, if any hope of proper defense or social order could be achieved. He set enslaved

Africans and white company servants to the arduous repair of the fort, but after toiling for two summers their work was ruined by settlers' animals left to run free.[97] Petrus was incensed by the destruction, and assigned the company-appointed fiscael, Hendrick van Dijck the task of prosecuting colonists who failed to keep their animals in check. Hendrick was offended, not by the animals, or the destruction, but by the implication that the assignment he'd been given by his superior was one more properly suited for a "negro." Or so he claimed, in the testimony he gave to the States General in 1652, against Petrus. He recounted that he was ordered to "look to the fort's hogs" and keep them "from the fort."[98] Hendrick complained that Petrus employed him "mostly as his boy; ordering me to look to the hogs and keep these from the fort, which a negro could have easily done."[99] In phrasing his complaint this way, Hendrick deliberately tried to cast Petrus in a bad light and ignored that his duty was not to herd hogs himself, but to prosecute colonists who flouted the colony stipulation to keep their animals controlled. By this time, Hendrick and Petrus had an acrimonious relationship and Hendrick's account of past events was no doubt soured by their bad blood. Hendrick chose to express his anger at his debasement in terms that both referenced the omnipresence of enslaved labor in the colony and connected to the concept of honor in the minds of authorities in the Dutch Republic.

Both men had lived in the Dutch American colonies, at different poles of empire, and both understood the socially infused decorum of race and enslavement. This was not Hendrick's first time in New Netherland. He served as an ensign during the series of battles that would come to be known as Kieft's War and, in 1642, was tasked with helping to lead an attack on a Wappinger town located on the mainland, northeast of the island of Manhattan, near the present-day town of Pound Ridge, New York. The raid occurred at night, and the colonial forces shot and killed 180 people and then set fire to the town, marking one of the most brutal episodes of the war with the deaths of over 700 men, women, and children.[100] After such bloody actions, Hendrick ultimately returned to the Dutch Republic where the WIC appointed him *fiscael*, and sent him back to America along with Petrus.[101]

Petrus's actions toward Hendrick disturbed the fiscael because of their social and racial implications. In his testimony Hendrick complained that during the group's sojourn on Curaçao before continuing onto New Netherland, Petrus confined him to the ship for "some three weeks," while allowing "all the other officers, nay, even the soldiers" to leave "immediately on their arrival," because Petrus did not recognize his authority to act as fiscael on the island of Curaçao.[102] If so, then confined to the ship, Hendrick's thoughts could have been drawn to the slave ships that coasted off of Atlantic African shores. Such vessels were filled with men, women, and children, some of whom had been branded with the mark of the Dutch West India Company, before arrival in the Americas.[103] Although Curaçao would not transform into a major transit depot for the slave trade until a number of years later, by 1647 the enslaved would already be omnipresent on the island, visible even from within the holds of the ship—they would have toiled at every servile occupation and were closely watched. The contrasts between white and Black work must have been in Hendrick's mind constantly.

Colonization afforded European newcomers latitude in reinvention. While new modes of labor, such as the large-scale mechanized sugar works became racialized from the start, other tasks that had been worked by Europeans on the continent, such as tending hogs, building fortifications, and serving as executioner, underwent a more gradual process of racialization.[104] It was this process that came to define the ways that elite colonists across North America came to construct themselves against racial slavery. Three years after his complaint against Petrus, Hendrick was called on to argue a case for his son-in-law, Nicolaes de Meyer, that hinged on understandings of difference. Hendrick maintained that another colonist named Gabriel de Haes had no evidence to support a suit of assault against Nicolaes because the witness statement was "a declaration only of a negro, or a young Indian, which in law is invalid."[105] However, Hendrick was arguing based on perceived cultural practice, not legal precedent. In this case, the court ignored the legal argument and decided that, as the accusation pertained to a criminal matter, it should be prosecuted by the New Amsterdam *schout*.

Creating a group of people who were forever enslaved and who carried that condition as a hereditary curse was a process that was neither completed until well after the English takeover, nor was it a straightforward linear development. It was a reactive process, borne out of social fears as well as hopes for what European settlers would make from the new environment. Every space that opened for an individual act of resistance both shaped and reaffirmed the images that the elite held of themselves. By the middle decades of the seventeenth century, the families that settled in New Netherland did not come wholly ignorant of cultural expectations between themselves and those they held in perpetual captivity. Stock notions of slaves and enslavement promulgated by biblical texts and popular exegesis, the fear of being enslaved that inhabited popular rhetoric in the wake of Dutch independence, and the Black Legend all had several centuries to imprint an outline of slavery in the minds of those who departed for New Netherland's shores.[106] They did not merely use those expectations unquestioningly but instead transformed the expectations that they held for the enslaved in the wake of changing personal and social conditions.

Work and dishonor were closely linked, but in the presence of race-based slavery, they were transformed. This was not a phenomenon unique to the Dutch outpost in North America—a process of racialization was at work across the Americas—but its North American variant can be traced as firmly to the banks of the Hudson as to the Chesapeake Bay. On February 3, 1639, Gijsbert Cornelissen Beyerlandt was accused by the colony's fiscael, Ulrich Lupoldt, of being a "trouble maker" who had wounded some soldiers at Fort Amsterdam. Who exactly was involved in the altercation or what it was about, remains unclear. It was so violent that the wounded soldier required the services of a surgeon and resulted in Gijsbert's banishment from the colony. Before he was set to depart, he was "condemned to work with the Negroes for the Company until such time as the first sloop shall sail for the South River and to serve the Company there and furthermore to pay the wounded soldier fl. 15, the surgeon a fee of fl. 10 for his services and the fiscael a fine of fl. 10."[107] The sentence of being forced to work with those who filled lowly positions was not a new one. In Amsterdam, high-status convicts or debtors were forced to fill humiliating positions as punishment for crimes against the state that did not merit a traitors' death.[108] It was a symbolic act that attacked the status of the prisoner, yet in this case, there was an undeniable racial caste. Gijsbert's experience was clearly intended to travel with him. Back in the Dutch Republic, he would carry as his final memory of the colony of New Netherland, his experience of being condemned to work alongside the enslaved at the most repulsive and back breaking labor that the colonial authorities could conjure.

Being made to work like enslaved people was humiliating to European colonists and surfaces often in the records when parties perceived their honor was at stake. In 1652, Brant van Slichtenhorst was the director of the patroonship of Rensselaerswijck, fulfilling an administrative role that would have been similar to Petrus's, albeit on a smaller scale. The director controlled the resources of Rensselaerswijck and, to a certain extent, the actions of his tenants, which put him at odds with WIC employees when it came to the harvesting of firewood. Petrus and his council received complaints, and they were not amused with the "impertinent, unbearable and unchristian-like tyranny of the present commander or, as he styles himself, director of the colony of Rensselaerswijck." Forbidding WIC employees from cutting firewood in the public woods and prohibiting the inhabitants of the patroonship from bringing firewood for the fort, "both the officials and servants of the Company are compelled to carry the firewood, which they have begged from him, on their shoulders as bondservants [*dienstbaerheyt*] . . . to the disregard, indeed, contempt of the honorable Company, its officials and good servants."[109] In his 1647 Dutch-English dictionary Henry Hexham defined dienstbaerheyt as bondage or servitude, and thus I have used the term bondservant to more closely capture this meaning.[110] Nearly a decade earlier dienstbaeren had already begun to be used interchangeably with *slaven* on the Dutch coastal forts in Guinea.[111] The "disregard" and "contempt" associated with the work would have only been deepened by such association.

Petrus's social and physical worlds were increasingly bound up in the promotion of agriculture and remained tied to local politics with regional import. While Petrus was headed down the Delaware River in a successful bid to capture the colony of New Sweden, fighting broke out in and around New Amsterdam. Provoked by Dutch aggression, several hundred members of various Indigenous groups launched a series of attacks on several New Netherland towns. After the fighting ceased, almost thirty farms and a large amount of grain was burned, five hundred to six hundred head of cattle were lost, fifty colonists were killed, and another hundred taken hostage.[112] Scholars have deepened our understanding of this moment: Jean Soderlund argued that the fighting was the result of political alliances that originated with Lenape groups allied with the Swedish on the Delaware, and Andrew Lipman posed the action as highlighting the importance of Native maritime power.[113] When the directors in Amsterdam wrote to Petrus in 1656, outraged over reports of Hendrick van Dijck's role in precipitating the battle, they were reacting to a report that all of the fighting had been avoidable and began only after Hendrick killed a Native woman who took some peaches from his yard.[114] Such fights over the products of and rights to the land were not perfunctory and the racial and gendered import of the action remains crucial to understanding the ways that colonists and colonial administrators conceived of the world they sought to claim.

While it is unclear what punishment, if any, Hendrick received, it is clear that some of Petrus's subsequent actions were also inspired by defense of his own personal interests through the physical control of the free and enslaved community of New Netherland. In the years following this incident, he manumitted several other enslaved people and granted them land, albeit land that abutted his bouwerij. "In the years 16[59 and] 1660, I ordered and commanded the Negroes listed below to take down their isolated dwellings for their own improved security [and] to establish and erect the same along the common highway near the honorable general's farm."[115] But this was not purely for their "own improved security." In a letter to provincial secretary Cornelis van Ruyven in 1660 warning him to be ready for attack after a successful battle against the Esopus, Petrus closed with an admonition to "let the free and the Company's negroes keep good watch on my *bouwerij*."[116] The use of free and enslaved Black people for defense extended beyond the director general's bouwerij. Black and Indigenous people were used as messengers, for logistic support, and as soldiers. Jeremias van Rensselaer was traveling through the Maquas' (Mohawk) country in early June 1660 when an enslaved man arrived with an urgent message. Vice Director Jean de la Montagne entrusted him with "a note saying that in the Esopus there had been trouble between the Dutch and the Indians and that on both sides people had been killed."[117]

Under Petrus's tenure, in the aftermath of the Second Esopus War, the sentence of working with the Negroes was given to Indigenous combatants, a racially coded punishment rooted in dishonor. In a letter sent during the summer of 1660, Petrus Stuyvesant sentenced several of the young Esopus leaders who had spearheaded the attack to Curaçao "to work with negroes."[118] Such action was not taken in a vacuum. By the mid-decades of the seventeenth century, a burgeoning Indian slave trade from the Northeast and Southeast to the Caribbean, South America, Bermuda, Europe, Atlantic Africa, and beyond promised a permanent exile that hung like a conjured threat. While the economic commitment to slavery in New Netherland increased in the final decades of Dutch rule, the social construction of a racial system based on identifiable difference had already begun to infuse the culture of the northern Dutch colony before the tenure of Petrus Stuyvesant.[119] While certain forms of work had always been associated with dishonor, the impact of Atlantic slavery constructed a culture of expectation that racially coded modes of work. Thus transformed, slavish work held vital significance to the ways that white colonists imagined their social fortunes within the Dutch colony.

In the spring of 1664, after enduring the journey from Rensselaerswijck to New Amsterdam, Jeremias van Rensselaer was not in a jovial mood. His rancor would have been lessened somewhat if the New Amsterdam delegation had not objected to him, as the representative of the oldest court in the colony, presiding over the New Netherland colonial assembly. The meeting was convened by Petrus Stuyvesant to discuss the state of the colony. In April 1664, Rensselaerswijck, New Amsterdam, and other towns and patroonships met to discuss improving New Netherland's defense, but by September, the entire colony would be lost without a fight to the English. Yet, for Jeremias, all that lay in the future. While in New Amsterdam, he also protested to the West India Company for handing out parcels of land in an area claimed by Rensselaerswijck. Piqued by the attitude of the West India Company, Jeremias wrote to Jan Baptist. In the letter, he described the company's negative reception of his protestations, writing they had treated him "als oft het mÿn neeger geseijt had" ("as if my Negro had said it").[120] His choice of imagery vividly illuminates how the slavery he encountered in the Dutch American colony informed his own self-perception and how Jeremias processed all that he conceived as improper in the boundary dispute between Rensselaerswijck and the West India Company. Communities of acquisitive settlers exploited and reified preexisting racialized conditions to build their family fortunes. Drawing from their everyday experiences, such families created networks of power that traded on distinctions in value attributed to racially coded activities and individuals. Nevertheless, the traumas of a racially coded system of bondage persisted within the Dutch colony even though no formal slave code was issued.

CHAPTER 2

Kolonist

Slaveholding and the Survival of Expansive Anglo-Dutch Elite Networks (1650s–90s)

On a spring day in 1664, a mother and her child were sold at public auction in New Amsterdam. Their names were not recorded—they exist in the record only as "female negro with a child" (*een negerin met een kint*)—but they remain connected to one another as family.[1] Yet their family ties survive the ravages of time alongside the price a slaver placed on them, and the other three enslaved people sold as property in the northern Dutch colony. This was a violent moment, one of debasement, voyeurism, and profound loss. These human beings were destined to bondage, brokered by the Varlet family, a fate that forcibly entwined their lives to the Dutch leadership of the colony. Eight years earlier, when in the autumn of 1656, Anna Stuyvesant stood before the minister in the Dutch Reformed Church at the base of Manhattan Island, her environment and circumstances contrasted sharply with the first time she was wed.[2] She had lived with her first husband, Samuel, in Alphen aan den Rijn where he taught French.[3] When he died, he had not left her penniless, but his death created a considerable social and financial void.[4] Her father, a Reformed minister, was dead, and her brother Petrus and sister-in-law Judith had relocated to New Netherland.[5] It was a tumultuous time, and Anna had four children to care for. In Alphen aan den Rijn, she had lived a middling life and was familiar with the community. Several men, including local merchants, ministers, or

FIGURE 5. Mr. and Mrs. Samuel Bayard, ca. 1644, oil on wood, 34 1/2 x 48 in. (87.6 x 121.9 cm) 1915.7. Luce Center. Courtesy of the New York Historical Society.

public servants, could have served as potential spouses.[6] As a wife of one of these men, she would have been expected to be an able *huysvrouw*, keeping a keen eye on the maidservants—who Dutch literature and painting cast as a necessary albeit potentially devious element in the household, and performing some market tasks.[7]

But she left the Dutch Republic in 1654 alongside her four children accompanied by her half-sister Margrietje, when, despite official enticement, other Dutch citizens were loath to emigrate.[8] The two women sailed toward family. Anna would carve out an existence for herself and her children that would differ significantly from the one that she left behind in the United Provinces. Her new husband, Nicolaes Varlet, traded tobacco and enslaved people from New Netherland to the Chesapeake and Curaçao, continuing the business connections forged by his father, Caspar, who had held such connections to Brazil.[9] His sisters had married tobacco planters and relocated to the Chesapeake, where they, too, traded tobacco and human beings along with their husbands and maintained trade and slave ties to New Netherland.[10] Margrietje was married a year before Anna in New Amsterdam, to Jacobus Backer, who would build his own trading presence in part through enslavement.[11] Elite slaveholding family networks connected Albany to Maryland and Curaçao to Boston. What caused some white colonial families to thrive

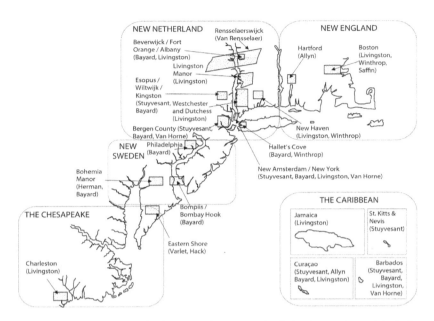

FIGURE 6. Map of New Netherland, New Sweden, New England, the Chesapeake, and the Caribbean. Based on "Pas caarte van Nieu Nederlandt uytgegeven door Arnold Colom" of 1656. Map reproduction courtesy of the Norman B. Leventhal Map and Education Center at the Boston Public Library.

while others were suffocated by the transitions of swiftly changing colonial environments? For a core group of elite interconnected families, a vital component in their strategy for survival was slavery.

Expanding Communities

Northern elite slaveholding families were geographically expansive, bursting through administrative boundaries in pursuit of economic opportunity built on ever-growing familial networks and the labor of the unfree. Anna and Nicolaes Varlet made their home in New Amsterdam, while a contingent of their close family, friends, and business associates migrated to the Chesapeake. They arrived as experienced slaveholders. Nicolaes's sister, Anna Varlet, married Dr. Joris Hack—her first cousin—and relocated to the Chesapeake, settling with her family to Accomack County on the eastern shore of Virginia in 1651 alongside a number of Dutch émigrés and, in 1658, purchasing lands in Cecil County, Maryland, near brother-in-law Augustine Herman, who had also relocated from New Amsterdam.[12] The Varlet Hacks were slaveholders with considerable property, including a nine-hundred-acre plantation located on Pungoteague Creek, a four-hundred-acre plantation on Matchotank Creek, and one hundred acres located on local islands.[13] Anna owned land in her own right and controlled the ships that traded in tobacco, slaves, and other goods as the family's Chesapeake contact.[14] She formed a key node in the broader familial network and ever-expanding community.

The transactions that underpinned these networks benefited the elites, but they could be exceedingly cruel to the enslaved. During the summer of 1655 in New Amsterdam, a man named Nicolaes Boot purchased a dying enslaved woman at public auction.[15] Nicolaes was a well-connected merchant who traded in tobacco, and other goods, and trafficked in human beings along the Eastern shore.[16] His ventures were backed by the wealthy New Amsterdam investor, Jacob Moesman. The connections and story of the captive woman he acquired remain lost to history, except for her final moments. She fell to the ground and uttered a painful plea of *"Ariba"* [*sic*] ("come on" or "up") as she actively struggled to move. Despite the evidence of her unsteady gait, her fixed and dilated eyes, and foaming mouth, the carpenter of the slave ship *Wittepaert* assured Nicolaes that she was not in pain, but merely "drunk."[17] She tried again, this time gesturing to her constricting chest and saying: "More, More" (her cry, transliterated into Dutch for the written record, was probably some conjugation of the Spanish verb *morir*—either *mori*, which means "I died," *muero*, which means "I am dying," or *moriré*, which means "I will die"); they were her last known words. Nicolaes continued home with the woman, although she had to be "carried in a wagon," the rest of the way to his house. The woman suffered for five more hours before the surgeon "found her very low," and she died "within half an hour in their hands," a casualty in the pursuit of trade.[18]

On September 6, Meyndert Lourisen, skipper of the *Wittepaert*, sued Nicolaes Boot for the purchase "at public auction [of] a negress, according [to] the conditions, for the sum of fl. 230," who "died on the following day," a result for which the "deft. refuses to pay."[19] For Nicolaes and Meyndert, this was a transaction, nothing more, and accounts had to be settled. The callous dismissal of her final moments was offered as evidence of fraud in the court, rather than an appeal to human empathy. Meyndert had no doubt scanned the tortured faces of hundreds of captive people. He was moved by profits, not pity. Whatever succor might have been afforded her in her last moments was denied by the reading of her actions as drunkenness, a charge (while leveled against many New Netherland settlers) commonly attributed to Indigenous peoples and the enslaved. Meyndert would soon die himself, a casualty of the hostilities that broke out on Manhattan stemming from an act of violence directed against a Native woman.[20] While the case captured the final agonizing moment of an enslaved woman, it was far from the last foray into the slave business for her purchaser and former enslaver, Nicolaes Boot. Nicolaes did not remain in New Netherland. He relocated to Virginia in the early 1660s after divorcing his first wife, and by 1667, his merchant ties secured for him an advantageous marriage to the now-widowed Anna Varlet Hack.[21] The two were able to get a solid start in their new home after receiving headrights on the Black people that they brought along with them, enslaved people most likely from New Netherland.[22]

These wide-ranging family networks provided much-needed support when addressing challenges from outside the colony. In 1663 English privateers seized the Dutch yacht named *Wapen van Amsterdam* (or the *Amsterdam Coat of Arms*) during its crossing to America, and its complement of eighty-five enslaved people, who had been loaded in Guinea, landed in Virginia on September 10. Nicolaes Varlet, then commissary of the Dutch West India Company, went with "Councillor Johan de Decker" to "reclaim them."[23] Nicolaes's knowledge of the Virginia slave market, borne of decades of family trade, and inroads with the local merchants would have been invaluable. His father, Caspar, had been heavily invested in the Virginia tobacco trade market alongside his uncle Daniel, although the two men remained based in Utrecht and then Amsterdam.[24] They had invested in the *Rensselaerswijck* (1636) and the *Wapen van Leeuwarden* (1639), which had traded New Netherland goods for Chesapeake tobacco.[25]

Nicolaes was not venturing into unknown terrain, but rather into an environment of family contacts: specifically, that of his female kin. The society that Nicolaes encountered on the eastern shore of Virginia in 1663 was changing rapidly amid social transformations that would ultimately create a racially determined slave society.[26] While the influence of local cases and events on the development of race-based slavery has been explored, the impact of Northeastern transplants remains understudied.[27] The regional influence of enslavement flowed along family lines and in both directions, although Northeast to Southeast is rarely emphasized outside of studies of Native slavery. Such emigration was vital to the strengthening of Atlantic merchant ties during the first generation of the Stuyvesant-Bayard network. While regional forces were undoubtedly crucial to establishing the type of slaveholding activities that each branch of the family undertook, the commitment to the project of family expansion was pursued hand in hand with slaveholding.

By the time that Nicolaes was sent down to Virginia with his grievance over the seizure of the *Wapen van Amsterdam*, his sister, brothers-in-law, and their children were in the midst of a naturalization process, cementing the

CHAPTER 2

family's position in the southern English colony.[28] Just seven days after the *Wapen's* arrival, the Maryland Assembly ordered "an Acte of Naturalizacon be prepared for Augustine Herman, and his Children and his brother in Lawe George Hack and his wife and Children."[29] Even though Joris had previously denied his Dutch heritage during the Anglo-Dutch wars, publicly substituting a German one instead to keep his trade unmolested by seizure, the Varlets still relied on family connections to keep the trade conduit of tobacco and enslaved human beings open between the Chesapeake and New Netherland.[30] Anna, not Joris, was that contact. The West India Company directors relied on the strength of the Varlet family network in the bid to reclaim the lost slave ship and the eighty-four captives on board, although they were ultimately unable to accomplish this.[31]

Family transplants were not the only ones to benefit from their association with the budding slaving dynasty. In 1660 the former carpenter on the Stuyvesants' bouwerij, Frederick Philipse, got his start in a regional trade corridor connecting New Amsterdam to the Chesapeake, pioneered by the Bayard/Varlet family and other Northeastern émigrés such as Augustine Herman. On September 20, 1660, the company passed a resolution to allow Frederick, identified as "late [the director's] carpenter," to charter the company's sloop to make a trading voyage to Virginia.[32] His connection with Petrus and the director's vast network had offered him a way into a lucrative trade corridor in a society where the racial underpinnings of slavery were calcifying. That same year the Virginia assembly's laws already assumed lifelong enslavement for runaway "negroes." Elizabeth Key's successful freedom suit decided in 1656, would be met five years later with *partus sequitur ventrum*, or the pseudo-Roman notion that slavery followed the condition of the mother, an overturning of centuries of English precedent.[33] Two years later, in 1662, Willem Beeckman, whose family had arrived in the colony alongside the Stuyvesants on the *Prinses Amelia* and who was stationed as the vice director of Fort Altena on the Delaware River, asked Petrus to send him "a Company Negro; I require one to perform various services."[34] Such enslaved people had built the trade opportunities and even helped to construct the geography of forts and walls that surrounded elites such as Petrus, and others hoping to emulate his model.

Other community members built on the network laid down by the elite families and their associates. Enlarging the contingent from New Amsterdam to the Chesapeake was aspiring minister Michiel Zyperius and his wife Anna, who used the move as another moment to escape the bad reputation that had followed him across the world. Michiel had first been posted to Curaçao where he married Anna and was censured for baptizing enslaved people.[35]

They sailed up to New Amsterdam on the *Spera Mundi*—a ship that carried enslaved children, several of whom were earmarked for Petrus—where their tenure was likewise brief.[36] In 1661, just months after the still unordained Michiel commenced his duties as reader (*voorlezer*) in the village of Nieuw-Haarlem on Manhattan, the classis sent a scathing letter to Domine Samuel Drisius who served as minister in New Amsterdam to a linguistically and ethnically diverse congregation. In it they warned that they received "a bad report" and that they had "been reliably informed that the same Michiel Siperius has from his young years onward been a bad person who in school at Alkmaar he was publicly chastised before all the scholars." This public censure occurred due to "many wicked acts, such as obtaining goods from shops in the name of the rector, and taking them to a pawn shop."[37] His lackluster performance in Nieuw-Haarlem could not survive the additional rebuke, and Michiel departed New Netherland for Virginia.

His reputation lingered. On August 5, 1664, Samuel Drisius noted Michiel's departure in a letter to the Classis of Amsterdam, writing, "Ziperius left for Virginia long ago. Through drinking, cheating and forging other people's writing, he behaved himself most scandalously here, so that he was forbidden not only to preach, but also to keep school."[38] This created a shortfall in ministerial labor, which required that his Nieuw-Haarlem congregation attend services given by Henricus Selijns on Petrus Stuyvesant's bouwerij. Drisius himself, fluent in English and Dutch, would be part of a delegation sent to Virginia.[39] For his part, despite his disgraceful exit, Michiel and his wife Anna were not banished, but followed a well-trod route of emigration from New Netherland to the Chesapeake forged by the Varlets and the Hermanns. By the mid-1660s, they settled on the North River Precinct (present-day Kingston Parish in Matthews County), whose location was just across the Chesapeake Bay from a prolific tobacco and slave district that was the headright established in Accomack County by Anna Varlet Hack Boot, Petrus Stuyvesant's cousin by marriage.[40] Michiel ultimately became an Anglican, was finally ordained, and by the 1680s, became rector of the North River Precinct. The broad geographic reach of elite slaveholding networks led to an expansive community of individuals whose shared cultural ties followed them across colonial lines.

Crossing Colonial Lines

Men, women, and children also served as alternative currency that offered liquidity across contested borders. On May 31, 1664, the New Netherland Council passed a resolution agreeing that in exchange for "a quantity of pork and beef equal to 6000 lbs., the beef at 4 and the pork at 5 stivers the pound" that the West India Company would pay Captain Thomas Willet "in Negroes at such a price as may be agreed on" or "in case of not agreeing, in beaver or goods, beaver price."[41] While the resolution was timed in anticipation of the arrival of the *Gideon*, the business deal had been four years in the making. On October 28, 1659, Petrus requested more "negroes," complained about Jewish trade competition for enslaved people, and discussed his association with Thomas Willet of New Plymouth as well as John Allyn of Connecticut. Thomas offered surety for the colony that year with the promise of payment in "negroes," "beavers," or other "goods."[42] After four years of nonpayment—not an exceptionally long time for a frontier colony in want of hard specie—Petrus backed up his promise made on behalf of the council, by securing a loan from two wealthy slave-owning contacts, Johannes de la Montagne and Jeremias van Rensselaer, who assured that Thomas would be "reimbursed satisfactorily either in good Negroes or other goods."[43] Payment "in negroes" was a matter of course across the Dutch Atlantic and had become a way of life in New Netherland, as the example of Lucas Rodenborch and Jeremias van Rensselaer, demonstrated. But Thomas's acceptance of the payment illuminates the regional penetration of the practice: Captain Thomas Willet was a New Englander.[44]

In 1636, Thomas Willet wed Mary, daughter of John Browne, and relocated to Wannamoiset (near Barrington, Rhode Island).[45] Before immigrating to the Narragansett Bay, he had spent time in Holland as a Puritan refugee and gained fluency with Dutch language and culture, a familiarity that he would transform into a brisk trade with New Netherland and then revisit again when, nearly thirty years later, he became the first English mayor of New York.[46] Although he arrived in Plymouth, Massachusetts, in 1630, he would go on to ply intracolonial trade and slave ties. His cross-colonial slave experience would not be a singular occurrence, but rather presage centuries of commercial slave ties. By the middle decades of the eighteenth century, Rhode Island and New York would emerge as prolific Northern ports, and although Newport would dwarf New York City in numbers of transatlantic slave ship departures, New York would eclipse Rhode Island in slave population and transatlantic voyages that returned to the colony.[47]

Thomas began trade with the Dutch colony during Willem Kieft's tenure, though his qualifications came highly recommended to Petrus Stuyvesant by New Plymouth's governor, William Bradford.[48] New England traded with its Dutch neighbor, and ships laden with salt from Bonaire would arrive in Boston and in turn be loaded with provisions destined in part to feed enslaved workers on the Dutch Caribbean island.[49] Despite the persistent request for more enslaved workers to support the citizens of New Netherland, the WIC directors earmarked such captive cargoes for English markets in the Chesapeake, and Petrus used them to square accounts like Thomas's in New England. Petrus's connections with Thomas, John, Jeremias, and Johannes evidence a long-term investment in an expansive slave network that would survive the fall of the colony.[50]

By the middle of the seventeenth century, the Stuyvesants had an Atlantic household, with their eldest son Balthazar following in his father's footsteps and seeking to advance his career on the island of Curaçao.[51] That same year, a group of enslaved people, including children, who had lived, served, and worshipped on lower Manhattan found themselves thrust onto the Caribbean slave market.[52] The Stuyvesants had used Caribbean marketplaces to purchase several enslaved children before, but the group with children whose fates made it into the family correspondence were unusual: they had been sold by mistake.[53] Although Vice Director Matthias Beck wrote to Petrus Stuyvesant his message was clearly meant for Judith: "Among other things, I have noticed in your honor's welcomed letter the great mistake that has been committed here in the trading of your honor's slaves; especially the small children, since they had been presented for baptism with good intentions by Mrs. Stuyvesant, your honor's beloved."[54]

Judith's "good intentions" to baptize the enslaved children were made during a heightened decade of activity when her name appeared in the baptismal records as witness nine times.[55] During their baptismal service, she would have most likely heard the familiar words of Genesis 17:7 intoned: "I will establish my covenant between me and thee, and thy seed after thee, in their generations, for an everlasting covenant."[56] The covenant that she witnessed for these children was everlasting, a heritage to be passed down to successive generations. Baptism, the minister (likely Henricus Selijns) would have reminded, was intended in place of circumcision, and as recipients, "infants are to be baptized as heirs of the kingdom of God, and of his covenant. And parents are in duty bound, further to instruct their children herein, when they shall arrive to years of discretion."[57] The daughter of the Reformed minister Lazare Bayard, and mother to two sons, Judith would have been familiar with the parental responsibility to raise such baptized children in the faith.

Standing before the *predikant*, Judith Stuyvesant was performing an officially unsanctioned act, one that would leave no trace in the Reformed Church Baptismal record: all notations of slave baptisms ceased between 1652 and 1665.[58] Henricus Selijns had assured his superiors in 1664 that he stopped the practice of slave baptism because enslaved parents only wanted freedom for their children and had little interest in deep and abiding faith.[59] But, perhaps it was Judith's presence that encouraged the exception. The maintenance of the Reformed faith was keenly important to the Bayards: due to Judith's father Lazare's position as a minister to a small Walloon congregation in Breda, the family had been forced to leave the city after it fell to Spain in 1625. They resided in Amsterdam as religious refugees before Breda was restored to the United Provinces, and they returned in 1637.[60] As the wife of the director general, she was well-positioned to fulfill the promises she had made to these children before God. Yet her promises came to ashes. Although her family's Reformed identity had persevered even when forced from their birthplace, Judith's role as the children's spiritual guide was stymied under the force of slavery.

Judith, herself, was not merely a bystander in the children's ultimate end as her family was heavily dependent on the slave market in the Caribbean. The Stuyvesants were not shocked by the children's presence in Curaçao—implying that they could have been the agents of the relocation that would have severed any ties the enslaved people held in New Netherland—but instead, they were upset about their sale. Petrus had already sent an enslaved couple, Lucia and Joseph, down to the island to tend cattle "at pasture there" along with "Paulo and Diego or Jacob."[61] Curaçao was certainly squeezed for enslaved people. Enslaved people were sometimes borrowed from private enslavers on the island to fulfill transshipping contracts. In one notable instance, the colony's vice director, Matthias Beck, gathered sixty-two individuals from various parties around the island to fill three Spanish ships, which had arrived to pick up enslaved people from the not-yet-arrived transatlantic slave ship *Eyckenboom*.[62] Arguably, such an enslaved group, sent down to Curaçao by Petrus to work primarily on company landholdings could have been caught up in such a scenario. It was not the first, nor the last of such clandestine sales.

Children were churned by the Curaçao market, some destined for Petrus and his wider network of friends and kin. Matthias Beck facilitated such transactions. Petrus could have met Matthias in 1655 while the latter was in Barbados after being exiled from Brazil following the Dutch colony's fall to the Portuguese, although it is possible that they met during the 1630s while they were both stationed in Brazil.[63] It was Petrus's only known trip to the English island, but it would mark an overture for the family's cross-colonial designs in the Caribbean, one that mirrored Petrus's earlier efforts in New England. Matthias had owned a sugar mill with two hundred enslaved people in Brazil and was interested only in enslaved captives who could be worked the hardest; any others, he argued in a letter to the West India Company's Amsterdam leadership, were not worth the provision of feeding.[64] In 1659, Matthias reported that "two boys and a girl" had been set aside from *Coninck Salomon* a slave ship from Guinea. Another two children pulled from a compliment of three hundred captives—people who could have been the children's parents, siblings, or other relatives—were selected "for the commissary Van Brugh" and "two young Negros" purchased by the commissary Laurens van Ruyvan "for the account of his brother." Matthias also sent Petrus, "a young female Negro for Mr. Augustinus Heermans," in Maryland.[65]

The Stuyvesants and Becks were tied by marriage to one another, bonds that linked them to the Chesapeake contingent. Judith and Petrus entrusted the well-being of their eldest son to Matthias's care, trusting that he would be able to see to it that Balthazar was set up properly on Curaçao.[66] A month before Petrus sent Judith's complaint along to Matthias, the West India Company organized a slave auction held in New Amsterdam. Among the purchasers were the wealthiest settlers in the colony. Petrus's own brother-in-law Nicolaes Varlet bought five new enslaved arrivals, including the enslaved woman and her child (*een negerin met een kint*) who opened this chapter at public auction for 360 guilders.[67] In total he spent 1,035 guilders for five human beings. Another brother-in-law, Jacobus Backer, bought three enslaved people, one man and two women spending 1,175 guilders. Such purchases were part of a wider market for enslaved people. Captive Indigenous people had been traded from the Northeast and the Chesapeake to Curaçao and other islands since the 1640s, a policy enacted for New Netherland under Willem Kieft and continued by Petrus's regime.[68] Slavery ultimately trumped salvation, and material family ties overshadowed spiritual bonds.

Blood and Enslavement

Despite Petrus's expansive trading ties, 1664 closed with the English invasion of New Netherland. As ships approached, the colony's council descended into chaos. Amid the melee, a group of Black people who held a provisional freedom from the WIC secured their full freedom for themselves and their children.[69] In a later certificate, drawn up during the English period to prove the freedom of these Black families, their deference is dramatically emphasized—they were described as falling to their knees and praying. That this episode does not appear in the request itself but rather as proof of the veracity of their manumission highlights that they were not hoping for heavenly deliverance, but an earthly assurance of freedom.[70] Their status was already an anomaly but their successful negotiation of freedom at the fall of the Dutch colony, reads almost mythically. It was as Susanah Shaw Romney noted, "The penultimate act" of the Dutch colony, affected by a ragtag council on Petrus's personal bouwerij.[71] Their success would ensure the continued existence of one of the oldest free Black communities in North America. The Dutch colonial experiment with slavery would be situated by later generations of scholars as a much milder regime, the calm before the storm of English rule, with its burning pyres of Black men.[72] Yet the elite families that formed the core of the Northern slaveholding regime remained, and their networks established under Dutch rule proved resilient and flourished under the English.

Of course, the Dutch era had its own public burning, a year before Petrus's tenure.[73] Despite the English takeover, Petrus retained his standing among the community of former Dutch colonists and his identity as a slaveholder. Several colonists living on his bouwerij testified that the day before the arrival of the English, Petrus "had as much grain as possible threshed by his own Negroes and servants and brought into the fort every day, whilst the frigates remained at the Narrows. This we are ready, at all times, to confirm by oath."[74] Such measures were in addition to the call from council leaders for all residents to work alongside the enslaved to prepare the city against invasion.[75] If the memory of the punishment of laboring with the enslaved lingered in the minds of New Amsterdam's populace, social revulsion in addition to the overwhelming numbers of the English invasion fleet, might explain the colonists muted response. Notwithstanding his actions on behalf of the Black people who he emancipated during the fall, Petrus remained a committed slaveholder. On October 6, 1664, the newly installed English governor Richard Nicolls issued a Hue and Cry on behalf of a deposed Petrus Stuyvesant, demonstrating that despite grappling with the fall and impending official censure, the former Dutch leader still prioritized tracking down people he claimed as property. His personal resources had been severely limited by the loss of the colony but, nevertheless, he promised to give any slave catcher, "full satisfaction for their labour and charge."[76] The final transactions that Petrus made as governor and his first act as a private citizen were dark reflections of one another.

After being relieved of his command, Petrus had time to contemplate his excuse for the colony's fall. His initial testimony included the want of provisions occasioned by the burden of the joined colony of New Netherland

and Curaçao. The second added to his first explanation, the strain that the slave ship *Gideon* had placed on the colony: "That about 14 or 16 days before the arrival of the frigates . . . came, in the ship Gideon, between 3 and 400 half-starved Negroes and Negresses who alone, exclusive of the garrison, required one hundred skeples of wheat per week."[77] The specifics within Petrus's testimony should not be taken at face value, as he was incentivized to embellish by the particularities of the Dutch Republic's legal system.[78] Despite the dire picture he drew for the Amsterdam leadership, Petrus had a third of the *Gideon*'s captive people sent to Fort Altena, a city colony on the Delaware.[79] Some of them had survived the middle passage from Guinea or Angola, where nearly half of the captives had been weakened by an outbreak of typhus and remained on Curaçao's seasoning camps.[80] Others were people in their mid-thirties, already "seasoned" on the island of Curaçao, and judged old by colonists eager to purchase the lives of others.[81] Upon arrival at Fort Altena, they were taken into Willem Beeckman's custody. They would ultimately be seized by the invading English, the fate that befell most of the people formerly owned by the West India Company.[82]

Petrus was allowed to leave and returned to the renamed colony of New York.[83] A pear tree sapling planted on the bouwerij would in later generations come to symbolize the Stuyvesant family's rootedness to lower Manhattan.[84] Among their neighbors were a diverse group of fellow colonists that included Africans who had lobbied for their freedom on the eve of English conquest.[85] A generation of community members would celebrate their nuptials on the bouwerij, and its mixed character would stand out to later travel writers. Although much had changed, much remained the same. Following the transition, the Stuyvesant family was still intimately tied to the slave trade and seasoning camps of the Caribbean, and they still owned human beings.

The wide-ranging geographies of elite networks provided security and constancy even at times of upheaval. Petrus's eldest son Balthazar's short vagabond life was steered by Caribbean trade markets and his connections to New York. He traded between Curaçao and New York after the fall of the Dutch colony to the English.[86] Balthazar first settled on Curaçao. Matthias Beck, the man tasked with setting up Balthazar on the island, had already put a sugar mill on St. Joris, a former company garden that in later years would also be used for "seasoning" new African arrivals.[87] Balthazar continued to communicate to his family in New York via his cousin Nicolaes Bayard.[88] The two maintained their family relationship and social prominence; they also remained large landowners in New York, Kingston (Esopus), and New Jersey.[89]

Other elite Dutch colonials maintained their ties to the Caribbean and expanded their slave-trading connections after the English takeover. Cornelis Steenwijck directed a portion of his vast fortune toward slave trading. In 1667, he co-owned the *Leonora*—a four-hundred-ton frigate sporting thirty-six mounted guns—bound for Ardra on the Bight of Benin.[90] Captained by Jacob Dircksz Wilree and Dirck Jansz Klinckert, the *Leonora* left the Bight of Benin with 338 enslaved captives but arrived in its first American port of call—Fort Amsterdam, Curaçao (modern-day Willemstad)—with 291.[91] Those who had survived the journey together could have found themselves herded onto St. Joris, Matthias Beck's land and seasoning camp, while others continued onward to Martinique. Two years later, in 1669, Cornelis co-owned the slave ship *Vergulde Posthoorn*, along with three other investors, one of whom was Amsterdam-based Jan Baptist van Rensselaer.[92] The vessel arrived first in Elmina on April 21, 1668, continuing on to Ardra, where it loaded up with 548 enslaved human beings. It arrived in Fort Amsterdam, Curaçao, with 471 enslaved captives, weakened by an ordeal that had only just begun. Like the enslaved from the *Leonora*, the group would have been seasoned on the island of Curaçao before the lion's share—387 people—departed for sale in Martinique and St. Kitts.[93]

Balthazar Stuyvesant also had slave trade connections with Steenwijck. In 1668, he coinvested alongside his cousin Nicolaes Bayard and Cornelis Steenwijck in the *Leonora and Leeuwinne*, a Dutch *pinas* (pinnace) built for speed and easy maneuverability in the harbor. The ship departed Ardra in the Bight of Benin on November 10, 1668, with 147 captives bound for Willemstad, Curaçao, though only 126 people lived to disembark.[94] By the time of the cousins' investment, Curaçao was firmly entrenched as the Dutch transshipment center for enslaved captives, but it was only one island in a burgeoning landscape of Caribbean profits. Curaçao was made a designated transshipment location for Spain's newly restored *Asiento de Negros* by 1662, when a contract was made for two thousand enslaved people to be delivered to the island. 1668 brought a new contract for an additional four thousand enslaved people.[95] In 1672, Balthazar moved to the Danish Island of St. Thomas, which had, until 1666, been a Dutch colony before its loss to Denmark, and was in the process of transforming into a sugar plantation colony and slave depot for the Danish West India and Guinea Company.[96] He moved again, this time to St. Eustatius, a Dutch island that had become a regional center for the clandestine slave trade and was where his two daughters were born.[97]

Cousins Nicolaes Bayard and Balthazar Stuyvesant shared a common engagement with slavery that would have been foreign to Nicolaes's father

Samuel, after whom Nicolaes chose to name his firstborn son, and the Calvinist grandfathers for whom Balthazar was named. Balthazar Stuyvesant was Samuel's godfather.[98] His final move, to Nevis, occurred during the heyday of the island's seventeenth-century traffic in human beings. In 1673, it became the Leeward base of trade for the Royal African Company, and five years later, Nevis's Black population would soar after a shift to large-scale sugar works.[99]

Balthazar's family connections were intertwined with slave networks and persisted after his death. Nicolaes Bayard took Balthazar's two surviving children, daughters Judith and Catherine, into his household. He married his stepfather's sister, Judith Varlet, becoming ever more enmeshed in the slavery kinship networks originally forged by his mother, Anna, in her second marriage.[100] His landholdings included a large portion of the north side of Wall Street, land that had formerly been set aside by the West India Company as "Negro lots," where he rented to members of the free Black community.[101] And he remained a slaveholder. His 1703 household inventory included three enslaved people: two men and one little girl, who, if they were not sold by the time of his death, likely ended up owned by his son Samuel.[102]

Links to a broader regional slavery increased over time. Petrus Bayard, Anna's eldest son and Petrus Stuyvesant's namesake and nephew, ventured away from New York, drawn by the religious pietism of the Labadists, to Cecil County, Maryland.[103] There, on August 11, 1684, with Peter Sluyter, Jasper Danckaerts, John Moll, and Arnoldus de la Grange, he signed the deed for 3,750 acres bounded by the Bohemia River that would come to be known as the Labadie tract.[104] The group's members hailed from Friesland, New York, and Delaware.[105] The world was in constant flux around them, as a wholescale demographic shift was underway, one that would end with the emergence of the Chesapeake as the central slave region.

But that slave-centered destiny was not preordained, but rather the result of individual choices and compromises. The Labadists embraced antislavery in Europe and debated as to the prudence of American settlement citing the vices of tobacco and slavery.[106] When in 1680, the Labadist party led by Jasper Danckaerts and Peter Sluyter scouted the site that they would eventually settle in Maryland, their language was disdainful of the tobacco cultivation and servitude that they encountered. Jasper compared the food's coarseness to the dogged treatment endured by the denizens of Maryland, but though his meditation dwelled on the wretched condition of the servants, he offered little but passing concern for those enslaved.[107] The Labadists quickly lost any antislavery scruples with the establishment of two settlement ventures—in Maryland and in Suriname, the first-named Bohemia Manor and the second

Providence Plantations. According to one polemicist, Peter cruelly treated those enslaved at Bohemia Manor.[108] In the end, economic promise trumped religious conviction.

Those without such landed slave ties struggled during the English takeover. The lives of colonists and traders were often subject to the whims of the lords who decided colonial boundaries. Bohemia Manor existed in Lord Baltimore's Maryland after the fall of New Netherland and was supplied by New York traders who sailed around New Jersey and up the Delaware River, continuing the relationship between the regions that was established during the period of Dutch rule when they were New Amsterdam and the Colony on the South River. William Penn changed that when he convinced his friend, the Duke of York, to grant him the west bank of the river as part of his Pennsylvania colony. Traders without landed connection to the area would need to work with Philadelphia merchants to bring goods to the Delaware Valley, unless they sailed much further south to the mouth of Chesapeake Bay and back up around the peninsula. Jacob Leisler did not have these landed connections, while the Bayard family did, and so their fortunes began to diverge.[109]

Religious zeal could threaten family unity, but slaveholding ambitions overcame those challenges, in part because discourses of difference had deep roots in Judeo-Christian ideologies. Although Peter Bayard traveled with the Labadists to Maryland, and copurchased land that came to be known as the Labadie tract, he did not remain in Maryland. He had initially abandoned his wife Blandina to become a Labadist, but by the final decade of the seventeenth century, he returned to New York, renounced his vow of chastity and a country life in favor of a house in the city. Peter also participated in the regional slave culture that bound his scattered family in one purpose, like his former coreligionists in Maryland had done. In 1693, his wife inherited from her mother, Sara Roelofs's estate a "negro boy, Hans."[110] At the time of the 1703 city census, Peter's household inventory listed an enslaved woman.[111] Thirty enslaved individuals were held by his extended family who were nearby neighbors.[112] The Bayards did renew their physical presence in Bohemia Manor. Peter's son Samuel permanently settled on the tract in Cecil County with his brother-in-law Hendrick Sluyter.[113] The Maryland and Pennsylvania branches of the Bayard family would remain deeply enmeshed within the political, merchant, and slaveholding elite of the region.[114] Slave-owning overcame religious and geographical divisions to bind this family together.

Several interconnected trader families expanded their own social footprints beyond the boundaries of New Netherland during the final decades of Dutch rule by capitalizing on slaveholding connections. These colonists created migratory networks of power that followed the Delaware River into Maryland, the tobacco trading routes onto the eastern shore of the Chesapeake, and into New England. Wide-ranging networks of power and colonization forged through the trading of commodities, which came to increasingly include human beings, were indelibly shaped by gender, race, and community. Such colonial links were not forged solely along patriarchal lines but were dependent on female networks of family and friendship. Enslaved people offered liquidity to their transactions and meaning to their constructed social identities. From English émigré Thomas Willet to Caribbean transplant Balthazar Stuyvesant, Curaçao's burgeoning transshipment economy in captive human beings continued to be a part of such elite business portfolios. Controlling a considerable number of enslaved people was a key element of the colonial identities of the Stuyvesants, their cousins, and wider networks, even as they also allowed the existence and landed status of a free Black community of New Netherland.

Chapter 3

Naam

Race, Family, and Connection on the Borderlands (1680s–90s)

Tom and Robert were both local entrepreneurs. They traded in the same supply of materials and tapped the same community of people. They traveled the streets of Albany and understood the politics and danger of the tensions between their position and New France. Both men's origins lay a continent away, and both stood condemned by the Albany court. Yet for all their similarities, the two men were separated by one glaring difference: Tom was enslaved by Robert. Family name (*achternaam*) separates the ways enslaved and enslaver are remembered, segregating them in many analyses. Such names obscure not only race but the relevance of gendered relationships in creating social circumstances. But centralizing the *similarities* between diverse colonials uncovers how racial difference emerged out of specific local and regional circumstances to become a crucial determinant to understandings of legitimate or illegitimate trade, mastery, and networks of belonging.

On March 30, 1682, Robert Livingston was "condemned to pay the costs of the proceedings" related to the prosecution of his enslaved man named Tom, whom he had brought before the court due to the man's alleged "theft" of several items.[1] Tom and an associate named Jack were charged with trading linens, beaver skins, clothing, and various household items to two local families, primarily on Sundays during church services, in exchange for tobacco, rum, and unmolested moments of camaraderie.[2] The everyday lives and trading activities of Albany's enslaved residents, lay embedded in court and vital records, documents that criminalize their actions and monetize their lives. Such records must be read thoughtfully, and as Marisa Fuentes contends, used in a way that, "purposely subverts the overdetermining power of colonial discourses."[3] Approached carefully, such remnants can offer insight into the enslaved community of late seventeenth century Albany and the upper Hudson Valley.

Tom was enslaved by Robert Livingston and lived on Prince Street in the patroon's house with Robert's wife Alida Schuyler and their two young children. Jack, his trading partner, lived in town near the stockade's North gate and was enslaved to the fur trader Tjerk Harmense Visscher, his wife Femmetje Jans, and their children. Tom testified that he traded with another captive man named Symon, offering him one of the shirts allegedly taken from Robert Livingston. Symon was enslaved to Jacob Staets, the town surgeon who lived nearby. A man named Jan, enslaved by Alida's father Philip Pietersz Schuyler, would have come into frequent contact with Tom as the Schuyler family home in Albany was nearby the Livingstons. He also likely spent time on the Schuyler property in the Flatts. He was stabbed to death by an Indigenous man a month after Tom's case concluded. A mother named Mary toiled for Willem Teller and Maria Verlet, another local merchant and landowning family, embedded within the broader Stuyvesant/Bayard/Varlet network. She would face the humiliation of court censure when they sided with the white colonist whom she accused of fathering one of her children. She was far from alone, as the sexually coerced lives of two other local enslaved women—Mary and Pey—would make their way into the court record. Another man, whose name never appears in the court record, except in relation to his enslaver Jacob Casparsz, lived in Albany next to the Norman's Kill. Two months after Tom's case, in July 1682, he would murder two of his enslaver's children and his enslaver's father-in-law, Hans Dreeper, before being found dead in the woods. The manhunt for him began on Pieter Schuyler's order, and his body was hung up to terrorize the community. A man named Barent Emanuelse, who was born in New Amsterdam before the first fall of the colony, toiled for the local minister, *domine* Gideon Schaets, who had likewise settled in the area when it was under Dutch control. Tom strategically timed his trading ventures to occur on Sundays when the domine ministered to his flock, a time when clandestine trades could be executed with less surveillance.[4]

The record of Tom's life begins and ends with Albany's criminal court documents; in contrast, Robert's life story was preserved in archives across the world, but most prominently within the massive Livingston Family

Papers, housed at various New York State archives. Robert's own clandestine actions, while equally stretching the finer points of the law, have been situated as part of his wealth-building strategy. Tom's actions were quickly censured and severely punished. Robert Livingston was born in December 1654, in Ancrum, Scotland, a few months after the conclusion of the First Anglo-Dutch War. During his childhood, northern European powers struggled over control of slave ports and increased the numbers of enslaved people brought into their American colonies. Such battles underwrote the wealth of the age and the stability of the Dutch Republic that offered his family shelter, when his minister father John Livingstone was exiled from Scotland. Robert was nine years old. Laws ensuring the heritability and violent control required to enslave would be enacted across the Atlantic World. As a teenager Robert learned to keep proper merchant accounts in Amsterdam, studying his trade within a society in which merchant families were the ultimate power brokers.[5] Families, like the Amsterdam-based Van Rensselaers, were helmed not only by men but by moneyed trade savvy women.

His own family connections offered him an entrée to Boston, in 1673. In New England, he quickly became embedded within the fur trade and regional economy as part of John Pynchon's Springfield operation. John Pynchon who had visions of wresting the fur trade from Albany, also held connections to the Caribbean economies and was an enslaver. By the autumn of 1674, Robert relocated to New York after the second and final fall of the colony to the English and was living in the city when former Dutch director Lord Anthony Colve transferred power of attorney to Nicolaes Bayard onboard the warship *Suriname*, so named for the South American slave colony where the Dutch had staked a claim as part of the terms that ended the Second Anglo-Dutch War.[6] Robert moved to Albany, where his bilingual background embedded him within the primarily Dutch trading environment, and he became secretary to the director of Rensselaerswyck, Nicolaes van Rensselaer.[7] The family operation in the Northern settlement had included bonded and enslaved labor as part of their diverse portfolio for at least three decades. Within a year, his employer would die, and Robert marry his widow, the locally connected and merchant-minded Alida Schuyler.[8]

Robert was able to rely on societal privilege that drew on the power of Dutch names and connections that his wife Alida brought to their relationship, ties which elevated him in society and insulated him from much of the judgment that would befall those with more limited networks. Alida was born in Beverwijck in 1656, to the fur trader Philip Pietersz Schuyler and Margaretha van Slichtenhorst.[9] While the male connections through her first husband Nicolaes van Rensselaer's family and her father's Schuyler family were valuable, Alida's trading network vitally leveraged a traditionally Dutch approach to ownership and the market economy wherein women enjoyed inheritance rights and could operate with autonomy.[10] Her female family members and friends extended her reach throughout the colony, acting as factors and lenders, both in her name and (with the transition to English rule) her husband's name. Her unmarried aunt, Hillegont, would function in later years as Robert's factor in the newly renamed town of Kingston, several miles south of Rensselaerswyck on the western shore of the Hudson River.[11] Alida's mother was also a factor in business with her sisters, and her grandmother Aeltje had a reputation for tracking down people in her debt.[12] Robert was a happy beneficiary.

Conversely, the bane of Tom's existence were those same female networks leveraged against him. At the dawn of colonial New York, slavery fueled the integration of immigrant newcomers into interconnected webs of trade and slavery forged during Dutch rule, whose connections cemented the Northeast into a coherent culture of enslavement. The political instabilities of perpetual warfare created opportunities for the enslaved to expand and exploit their own networks, even as it made them the targets of tightening legal strictures and borderland violence. Members of the Stuyvesant-Bayard family network constructed a legal edifice of slavery in New York that emerged out of an earlier era of intercolonial rivalries. Engagement in the slave economy as an investor, merchant, and enslaver was a vital part of Robert Livingston's ascent from an immigrant debtor to a well-connected merchant. The same commodities that enlivened Robert and Alida's ventures fueled the supplies of enslaved entrepreneurs whose mobility, customers, and markets were systematically closed off by their white merchant counterparts.

Race and "Legitimate Trade"

Northeastern elites sought to control their world by establishing legal and normative constructs that would reinforce their claims to economic and social dominance, though such hegemony was never absolute. They used the courts to safeguard those claims, ensuring that those who might challenge them would be stopped in a public and exemplary manner. Three years before Tom was brought before the court, on August 29, 1679, Barent Emanuelse was condemned to "receive 30 lashes on his bare back" and "to be branded on his right cheek as an example to other rogues."[13] A courtroom full of enslavers, who sold men, women, and children at auction, and financed slaving voyages as far-flung as the Caribbean and the Gold Coast of Africa, had condemned Barent as a "rogue" and a thief.[14] By 1679, elite men across the colony had spent nearly three decades of sitting on and adjudicating cases that linked the enslaved with criminality. They strengthened their networks of wealth and security through the purchase, auction, and prosecution of enslaved individuals. Conversely, enslaved people such as Barent lived lives marked by insecurity and surveillance.[15] Their enslavers utilized the bonds of family to build dynasties supported by layers of unfree labor and buttressed by systems of law and practice.

People held in bondage were frequently forced into states of extralegality. Barent was no stranger to Albany's court system. He had been charged with theft two other times. Barent stood in the courtroom, stripped of a right to a jury by his peers—indeed his only peer, the enslaved man Claes Croes, had been sentenced to "receive at the hands of the public executioner 20 lashes on his bare back."[16] Whipping alone was deemed too lenient a punishment for Barent, he needed to be made an example of for others. He was sentenced to be whipped and then branded on the face.

The man who claimed his body as property protested the verdict. His enslaver, the Dutch Reformed minister, Gideon Schaets, requested that Barent be "branded on the back instead of on the cheek," which the court was "pleased" to honor.[17] Unlike Barent, Gideon was facing not a room full of angry enslavers, but congregants. A month earlier, he had married the court secretary, twenty-two-year-old Robert Livingston, to Alida Schuyler.[18] Alida's father, Philip Pietersz, an elite Indian trader and another member of Gideon's congregation, served as the trial foreman. Robert's star had recently risen in Albany; just one year earlier, he had been a pariah, shunned by at least one New York woman that he pursued as being too grasping.[19] The marriage had not allowed him to thoroughly shake that identity, and marrying his recently deceased employer's much younger wife, might have been more scandalous had not Nicolaes van Rensselaer's co-minister, Gideon Schaets, officiated at their nuptials.[20] If Barent's sentenced facial brand had been carried out, the mark would have threatened the minister's investment, lessening Barent's value on the slave market by advertising to prospective buyers that he was trouble. Gideon's public reputation was granted clemency while Barent's body was condemned to abuse. On Saturday, August 30, Barent Emanuelse was stripped from the waist up, tied to the public whipping post, and forced to endure the lash, thirty times. Afterward, his shredded back was seared with a brand.[21] Barent's torture was meant to terrorize enslaved people like Tom and disincentivize any activities that might be branded subversive. Regardless, it did not stop the engine of commerce: a month later Barent was in court again, this time charged with "stealing" several items with another enslaved man and giving them to a woman named Marietje

Damen, who was a wealthy trader that lived in Schenectady, to be made into silver breeches buttons.[22]

Manipulating the inequalities in the legal system, and understanding the power of local female networks, was du rigor for some aspiring entrepreneurs hoping to gain entrée into the higher (and mostly Dutch-descended) echelons of Albany society. Robert Livingston trained his attention toward making himself indispensable in Albany society by becoming a local merchant and holding public office. As secretary of the colony, he witnessed loans, backed up by human beings, including "a Negro boy named Wynamus, about nine years old, together with another Negro named Bock, about twenty-one years old," presented as surety for Jacob Jansen Gardiner's debt to Andries Teller.[23] The same debtor, put up the nine-year-old again several months later to settle with brickmaker Pieter Meesz Vrooman a transaction that Robert facilitated as secretary. Upon marriage to Alida Schuyler in 1679, Robert moved into the patroon's house, a short relocation from his lodgings next door but an extremely symbolic leap forward in fortune. Robert was quick to begin leveraging his new wife's network. Alida's brother-in-law, Jacobus van Cortlandt, who was already deeply involved in the Barbados market and had slave dealings with the Van Rensselaers, offered him an introduction to the New York merchants who controlled the docks.[24] Along the journey down to New York City from Albany, Robert Livingston would have encountered enslaved men who were piloting the boats or loading and unloading the cargo from ships that had arrived from Barbados.[25] Jacobus was positioning his brother-in-law Robert to reap a portion of a booming New York shipping trade that had received unprecedented growth due to the passage of a 1678 law that gave New York merchants exclusive rights to shipping.[26]

Legal constructs provided a robust latticework on which upwardly mobile newcomers could build and grow their social and economic networks. Robert had been contacted by English merchant James Graham who proposed that he diversify his supply markets by including the Barbadian market as the source of some of his supplies, inquiring "if any Barbados goods be proper, viz., Rhum, Maleasses, Sugar," and continuing "I having a great Quantity of that trade."[27] This was a contact that he made several months before his marriage.[28] Trade, fueled by the massive proceeds due to sugar and slavery on Barbados, had made the island a sound investment. The same currents that increased the numbers of slave ships filled with enslaved people that pulled into New York also carried Robert's early profits. Although Robert gained status through his marriage, his networking and shipping accounts had already begun to bear fruit, allowing him to pay back several of his debts before he wed.²⁹ Indeed in the same letter where he encouraged Robert to enter the Barbados trade, Graham sought to leverage Robert's local connections, for advice as to his own nephew's merchant prospects: "I should be willing to board him in your parts hoping he may better learn the Dutch Tongue."³⁰

Although some of his supplies streamed in from the Caribbean, Robert remained a local vendor—focusing his time on shoring up his status in the Albany community. He kept the accounts of others in the community, including one for provisioning captive white Virginia prisoners held by the Oneida.³¹ If Tom entered his household as part of Alida's dowry, then his working world would have, like Andries before him, included both Albany and Rensselaerswyck. Alida appeared in court on December 31, 1678, seven months before her marriage to Robert but while he was acting as official secretary, to secure her estate.³² While the inheritance of specific enslaved people during the seventeenth century remains opaque, due to the Dutch practice of passing down the entire estate unbroken, enslaved people were a form of moveable property that conveyed status to white women and were owned by them outright.³³ Tom's extensive connections to the broader white community in Albany indicates that he had lived there for some time, and could have even been born in the community or brought there from New York, like Barent.

Tom's language ability is unmentioned in the court record but can be implied from context. He would have needed to be conversant in Dutch—a linguistic dexterity that would have been a feature of living in a mixed culture household such as the Livingstons. The case was recorded in English, though the testimony may have been given in Dutch. Robert and Alida spoke Dutch at home, though Robert traded frequently in English. When questioned about the whereabouts of some stolen handkerchiefs, Tom answered that he took them to "Pautje's" using the Dutch familiar diminutive to refer to Paulus Martense.³⁴ Tom, like Robert Livingston, networked locally, choosing Jack, identified as "the Negro of Tierk Harmense" as his partner. The other Albanians named in connection to this suit were Claes Janse Stavast, who owned land between the highway and the river, "Symon, the Negro of Jochim Staets," who appeared in the 1697 list of Albany householders as Jacob Staets, and Jack's enslaver Dirck Harmense.³⁵ These overlapping networks of enslaver and enslaved knitted the community together.

Just as Robert was building his business based on networks that had been laid down under Dutch rule, so too Tom benefited from a century's-old network. The Black community of Albany dated from the first decades of Dutch settlement.³⁶ Tom dwelt and toiled in the patroon's house, though not the same house as Andries had nearly two decades earlier, as that one had been completely destroyed by an ice flow in 1666.[37] Jack and Tom were two of the most common names given to men in English-speaking enslaved communities throughout the Atlantic World, and may have come into the Albany community through neighboring New England or from the Caribbean. Although some historians point to the prevalence of such shortened forms as evidence that white enslavers were demeaning African-descended people through diminutive names, the argument that they were anglicized forms of African names is a persuasive possibility. If this is the case, then Jack's name could have been derived from the Akan day name Quaco for Wednesday; whose shortened form was Quack. Tom (or perhaps Tam as he was likely known in the primarily Dutch-speaking Albany), could have been a transliterated form of the Yoruban Taiwo, which translates as the "first born of twins."[38]

Tom and Jack kept up a brisk, albeit clandestine local trade. The items they were accused of stealing were the same supplies that Robert and Alida were using to augment their trade networks in Albany, including beavers, rum, tobacco, and linens. Tom clearly accompanied Robert Livingston on his business trips down to New York City. Among his traded inventory were listed "four fine shirts" that Jack testified belonged to Robert Livingston, but Tom elaborated that "he had brought them from New York."[39] Tom's testimony highlighted the illicit nature of the transactions indicating that he traded with Claes Jansz Stavast's wife Aefje "when her husband was in church" and to Paulus Martense' wife Catherina "when he went to fetch milk."[40] Claes Jansz and Paulus Martensz both owned property in Albany and were active in the land market that Robert Livingston sought to corner, with Paulus engaging in several local land transactions.[41] Tom took beavers, empty bottles, and linen items that he obtained from the Livingston household and, using the wives as points of contact, he in exchange received tobacco and rum.[42] Tom and Jack's clandestine business was in alcohol, and the main points of contact identified during the court testimony were local married Dutch women, and an enslaved man named Symon, who was identified as "the Negro of Jochim Staets."[43] While Robert and Alida might not reach these particular buyers, Tom and Jack managed a parallel trading network in the same goods.

Tom's ability to develop a trading business was at least in part an artifact of laws and practices that had not yet fully limited enslaved people's movement, though those laws were rapidly tightening, as Andrea Mosterman has shown.[44] Tom's freedom of movement allowed him to ply his own business. Although he likely lived in a secluded corner of the Livingstons' house in Albany, he held relationships and familiarity with a cross section of Albany's

CHAPTER 3

population.[45] On Sundays, he would walk from place to place, laden with the wares that he would trade for spirits. Such mobility was not unprecedented among enslaved people generally or in the case of the Livingstons in particular.[46] Yet the legal situation for enslaved people was tightening, and entrepreneurs like Tom, as well as others, found their freedom severely curtailed. As an enslaved man serving in the house of Robert Livingston, who at least sometimes traveled with Robert down to New York City, Tom would have been issued a pass and might have been able to produce one if encountered by the authorities.[47] Though the absence of this pass could have ultimately been his undoing. A year before Tom's trial, a law was passed in New York City in 1681 (and was copied by New Jersey the next year) that prevented free inhabitants from purchasing items directly from enslaved vendors, explicitly stipulating that such people "frequently steal from their masters and others what they expose to sale at distance from their habitations."[48] The next year black codes stipulated penalties against "Negroes and Indians slaves, their frequent meetings and gathering themselves together in great numbers of the Lords Days and at other unseasonable times using and exercising severall rude and unlawful sports and pastimes to the dishonour of God."[49] This tightening legal regime served to affirm the rights of white traders, while making the actions (and even the pastimes) of enslaved people increasingly illegal.

Tom had carried on his business right under the noses of the Livingstons, though it is unlikely that either Alida or Robert were wholly ignorant of the two men's activities. While the enslaved men received censure, the female colonists were acquitted, free to continue the clearly popular practice facilitated by enslaved traders of other neighbors. Neither the enslaved nor trading environment of the Livingstons' household were a province manned only by Robert. Alida was the primary household manager when Robert was away, and he ensured she had full legal control of the estate when he would go on long trips, a position mirrored by other women in the colony during the years of Dutch rule.[50] Alida could have offered introductions to the social and trading worlds of Albany's female population. Alida's marriage to Robert upset many in the Van Rensselaer family, since her status as Nicolaes's widow effectively transferred control of Rensselaerswyck to Robert when she wed, and her personal network provided great leverage and access through members of her Schuyler and Van Slichtenhorst families, which were among the most well-connected in the colony. Tom could have even provided Alida with some remuneration for allowing the business.[51] Such funds certainly would have allowed Tom to live more independently and lessened the amount that the Livingstons had to pay for his maintenance.

Tom's trade business was deeply connected to the broader local economy that fueled the tensions between the English colonies and New France. His trading of Robert Livingston's beavers joined him to the brisk beaver trade emanating from within the Haudenosaunee Confederacy.[52] His linen supply was but a small part of a much larger market for English linens that were in demand among the Haudenosaunee, a preference that gave the English both a trade and negotiating advantage over Quebec, one that the French governor Louis de Buade, Comte de Frontenac argued the English used to their military advantage.[53] During the 1680s, Robert Livingston's actions as commissioner for Indian affairs were purely unofficial.[54] Nevertheless, his activities offered him an in-depth understanding of both the economic and political situation. He had provided his house in Albany as a refuge for the families of English-allied Haudenosaunee fighters during a flare-up of tensions between the English and French allied groups in the 1680s.[55] Tom could have heard the details of the situation from countless conversations engaged in before him, or on numerous trips to New York, since Robert was frequently in New York on business, and would have understood the broader value of the items that he traded for his supply of spirits. According to Jack's testimony, Tom denied stealing "four fine shirts" from Robert Livingston but, instead, claimed to have "brought them from New York," demonstrating command of a long supply chain stretching the length of the Hudson.[56] The harshness of the sentence carried out against him hints at the influence of the broader political situation, as the court condemned him to the more severe penalty of "39 lashes on his bare back" for his punishment and "an example to others."[57] Elites occasionally overlooked the clandestine trade of an enslaved person, but not when it had implications for the intercolonial balance of power.

Tom's business was a satellite of Robert's own trading in spirits.[58] Robert's diversified supply portfolio included merchant contacts with the Mahicans, the Haudenosaunee, New England, Amsterdam, and London, in addition to the Caribbean.[59] His marriage contacts had offered him inroads into the beaver market by way of his brother-in-law Brandt Schuyler, a relationship that Alida actively facilitated. These relationships transformed him from a debtor into a creditor.[60] Robert's Massachusetts connections, cultivated before making inroads in Albany's elite, were deeply embedded in New England's slaveholding and slave-trading culture. During the 1670s, Robert's main creditor was Springfield merchant, John Pynchon, a relationship he kept up until 1680. Robert's early trade appears modeled after John's, whose trade in rum and supplies along the Connecticut River made him prosperous and who also held African slaves in Massachusetts and in Antigua.[61] The slave connections between the two colonial regions and the rest of the Atlantic World were not always legal. Cases of smuggling and theft of enslaved people on the borderlands did not cease after the fall of New Netherland but continued to be tried in regional courts.[62]

Tom was not the only vendor that Robert called to account, just merely the one with the most exposure to the full brunt of the law and the least protection under it. Cases involving enslaved participants were not the only reason that Robert frequented the court; in addition to his position as court secretary, his newfound status as a creditor made him very litigious. Between 1676 and 1685 Robert Livingston was the plaintiff in twenty-eight cases brought before the Albany courts. While some cases dealt with collecting back excise taxes, most were brought against his neighbors in relation to accounts owed or reimbursement for defective merchandise. By contrast, Robert was sued only seven times during that same period and served as a lawyer for other people's cases ten times.[63] In fact, one year earlier, Robert Livingston had sued a tavern keeper for trying to make a bit more money by evading the excise taxes.[64] Despite his exuberant use of the courts, Robert's own trade connections were not strictly legal.[65] Robert's canniness would make him a powerful (if not always respected) member of Albany's community, the same characteristics that caused Tom and Jack to be branded malefactors.

The details of the case Robert brought against Tom uncover a broader interconnected world of gender, race, and trade in Albany. Though she was never named in the suit, Alida Livingston's presence is crucial to understanding the broader implications of the case, as well as to social relationships within the northern settlement. Among the myriad stolen items were everyday objects and included nine marked children's shirts—likely with a recognizable family monogram—and a child's night cap. At the time of the case, Alida's son, Johannes was two years old and her daughter, Margaret was an infant.[66] As one of the wealthier members of the community, visibly stationed in the patroon's house, Alida's sartorial choices for her children were more than personal, they communicated status. Tom's everyday duties brought him close enough to the children's living space to take these items to trade. According to Tom's testimony, Catharina van Kleeck and Aefje Gerrits clearly valued the items as well. These neighbors took the time to painstakingly remove the identifying marks on the children's shirts with a needle, in exchange for rum, some of which Tom, and his partner Jack enjoyed at Catharina's house.[67]

Such local transactions made up the fabric of everyday life in Albany. Understanding the primacy of women's domestic economy within Albany uncovers the central role that women held within networks that encompassed enslaved people.⁶⁸ Alida herself was embroiled in a row with Maria van Rensselaer, her former sister-in-law, over the land she had inherited from her first husband Nicolaes van Rensselaer, and though the two women expressed their involvement in the affair in correspondence sent to their male relatives, Maria trained her frustrations specifically against the Schuyler family, terming them a "bitter family" (*Bittere geslacht*) a jab aimed directly at Alida.⁶⁹ Both sides of Alida's family wielded local power. Alida's father Philip Pietersz Schuyler had, eight years earlier, purchased the Flatts from Arent van Curler, land that her mother Margaretha would control in the years following his death.⁷⁰ Her uncle, Gerrit, owned a considerable amount of land at Claverack, part of the lower manor of Rensselaerswyck, holdings which he would pass down and would largely fall under the control of his daughters.⁷¹ Thus, Alida's closest family represented a considerable amount of the landed wealth in Albany. They were, likewise, enslavers.

Claverack's connection to female slaveholding networks emerged prominently in a paternity case brought by a Black woman named Mary in 1679, who accused a local baker of fathering all three of her children. The court proceedings revealed that Mary had been questioned as to the identity of the father by the court-sworn midwife, during transition—the final and most painful part of active labor—in the presence of her enslaver, Trijntie Wessels Staets.⁷² Trijntie Wessels was married to Abraham Staets, and they lived on land in Claverack. The court's use of female officials and high-status women in childbirth was not unique; what was distinctive about this case was what it revealed about the racial implications to gendered life in Albany.⁷³ Such testimony given during the most painful part of labor was considered very persuasive, due to its connection to the life-threatening nature of the moment and the belief that the pains of childbirth were effective tools of veracity. Yet the man contested Mary's testimony and was acquitted of the paternity charge, by highlighting that she was a heathen woman.⁷⁴ Such an implication conjured the racial debate, which centered on the widely circulated view among Northern European travel writers that Black women felt childbirth pangs differently from white women because Black people sprung from a different origin than whites, who were under Eve's curse. Such beliefs were among the myriad circulating theories of racial difference, some of which were tangentially justified by conjuring biblical precedent.⁷⁵

The Dutch women implicated in the case against Tom would likewise lean on gendered and racial supports to exonerate themselves of wrongdoing. They were in real danger. As Erin Kramer has demonstrated, women's tapping activities were viewed with unease, because of the "semi-private" domestic setting and mixed gender an ethnic composition of such gatherings, and threat to social order. Cases involving women charged with violations of the liquor laws would often result in stiff penalties imposed on such women.[76] Catharina and Aefje took shelter under English legal norms which stripped married women of a separate legal identity apart from their husband. Documented in the court record not by name but as "the wife" of their respective husbands, Catharina van Kleeck and Aefje Gerrits swore under oath that they had not carried on trade with Tom and Jack. The court believed this testimony and added defamation to the charges of theft leveled against the two enslaved men, solidifying the notion that nonwhite trade could not be legitimate.[77]

Mastery and Borderlands

During a time of perpetual struggle and war against Indigenous groups and other Europeans along the borderlands, the leaders of the English colonies used legal codification of free and slave categories as a way to assert ideas of mastery over both people and territory throughout the colonies. By the closing decades of the seventeenth century, some elite Dutch families managed the transition to English rule in part by wholeheartedly adopting a more stringent slave system. In October 1682, New York aldermen Frederick Philipse and Willem Beeckman gathered in court together along with a number of their elite colleagues. They convicted three Black men—Robert Seary, Mingoe, and Cane—of the crime of "Breaking Prison" and "Stealing A Boate" to "Runn Away with out of the Mould or Harbour of this Citty," and sentenced them "to be Tyed to A Carts Arse and to Receive tenn Lashes or Strips on the Bare back att Each Corner Round the City And to be Branded in the forehead with the Letter R."[78] The men, if the testimony of sheriff John Collier can be believed, had run away from Virginia and Maryland, perhaps following routes of freedom that piggybacked the slaveholding networks elites used to connect their Atlantic ventures.[79] Legal action provided colonial leaders with a way to reassert their mastery of these men and secure their position of dominance over their networks.

If they had actually taken the boat—Robert Seary protested his innocence—they had confidence on (and likely *in*) the water.[80] Mingo's name offers some insight into their shared past. If he received his name in the Caribbean, a combination of African day name traditions and a shortening of the Iberian word for Sunday, Domingo, then Mingo and his compatriots could have gained their familiarity with seafaring in the Caribbean as part of a crew or as pearl divers.[81] Alternatively, if Robert, Mingo, and Cane worked the docks in the Chesapeake, then they could have carried their skills with them across the Atlantic, a treasured retention of their old lives or a secret inheritance passed down from the experiences of others.[82] Nevertheless, the elite men ensured that their punishment was public and would be seen by the entire enslaved and free populous of the city. Additionally, their status as "runaway" would be branded not just on their flesh but on their *faces*. Such disfigurement was meant to cause horror and alienation for the rest of their lives.

Keen to control the movement of the enslaved, during that same session, the council of elites introduced "An Order Concerning Negroes and Indian Slaves," intended to stop meetings and gatherings of enslaved peoples on Sundays and at "Other Unseasonable times using and Exercising Severall Rude and Unlawfull Sports and Pastetimes to the Dishonour of God."[83] The law has been read as a correction of the "freedom of movement allowed slaves under the Dutch," and if so, it was a change made by men who had lived decades of their lives under the Dutch system, rather than a group of newly appointed English transplants.[84] The act also came with a penalty to settlers who hoped to trade with the enslaved lacking their enslaver's approval: they would be fined five pounds. To be a freeman was not enough to govern and engage the trade and pastimes of the enslaved—the council ensured that only moneyed slaveholders would be able to control commerce and recreation.

Elites pursued control of the slave trade along legal, commercial, and familial avenues. Aldermen Willem Beeckman and Frederick Philipse, who were shoring up their power through business deals and strategic marriages, made slaveholding a key part of their business growth strategy. By 1682, Willem was the deputy mayor of New York and the newly minted lieutenant of the militia. Just seven months after the passage of the slave act, he managed a shipment of "thirty-eight negro slaves" who had voyaged from Angola to their first port of disembarkation, Nevis, ultimately bound for London but were waylaid in New York.[85] His family had long been intertwined with the slaveholding elite, arriving in the colony on board the *Prinses Amelia* with the Stuyvesants. His sister Maria, although dead by the time of the law's passage, had been married to Nicolaes Stuyvesant, Petrus Stuyvesant's youngest son.[86] Frederick Philipse, who had immigrated to the colony from Friesland as an employee of the West India Company, was keen to increase the output of his mill investment in Westchester.[87] Three years after the law's passage, Frederick invested in the slave ship *Charles*, which brought forty enslaved people from the Kongo to New York. These people formed the core of the workforce at Philipsburg Manor, which would go on to be one of the most extensive slave manors in the region.[88] The interaction of personal networks, legal protections, and commercial ambition formed the basis of elites' power.

CHAPTER 3

Maximizing power necessitated minimizing challenges to that power, so elites attempted to circumscribe the actions of nonelites. In 1683, a law was brought before the Common Council of New York and Cornelis Steenwijck, the merchant slaveholder and slave trade investor who was then mayor of New York City, that curtailed the movement of enslaved Black and Indigenous people. The text of the law included the injunction "that noe Negro or Indian Slaves, Above the Number of four, doe Assemble or meet together on the Lords Day or att Any Other tyme att any Place, from their Masters Service within [the City]."[89] A peace treaty with the Haudenosaunee had just been signed in Albany during the previous fall, during which Alida Schuyler's grandfather, Gerrit, served as interpreter.[90] This ostensibly brought an end to a series of skirmishes throughout Virginia and the Chesapeake, but Steenwijck's desire to control the assembly of the colony's enslaved population, whether "Negro or Indian," likely stemmed from his personal experience as a slaveholder. A year later, New York's General Assembly passed "A Bill Concerning Masters, Servants, Slaves Labourers and Apprentices."[91] The law set up the legal boundaries of slavery: prohibiting "no servant or slave either Male or Female" to "Give Sell or Truck any Comodity Whatsover during ye Time of their service," "any person whatsoever" from extending "credit or trust" to "any servant or slave for Clothes Drinke or any other Comodity," and setting up the legal justification for pursuing runaways.[92] This legal edifice—in theory if never fully in practice—protected elites from any challenges to their dominance.

Notions of mastery were entwined with claims to dominance over the land. Concern about the transition to English rule weighed heavily on the landed elites of the former colony of New Netherland. Indigenous land grants were crucial to laying claim, and a reaffirmation of old grants and new ones that showed knowledge and ignorance of usage rights among the Mahican, Wappinger, other upper Hudson Valley Indigenous peoples and Haudenosaunee proliferated. The nearly one million acres of Rensselaerswyck had been under the Van Rensselaer family's control since Kiliaen was confirmed as the patroon in 1630, and the new English governor Thomas Dongan reaffirmed the family's patent in 1685, though he would request a portion be sectioned out for the independent town of Albany the following year.[93] Robert and Alida Livingston, meanwhile, sought to carve out a similar landholding, acquiring through a series of purchases and land grants more than 160,000 acres just south of Alida's former home between 1683 and 1686. In 1687, one of the manor's first lessees would be Mattheus Abrahamse, whose term included "a strong Negro of 14–15 years."[94] As landholdings grew at the end of the century, so did the commitment to slave ownership.

Mastery over others was, as Danny Noorlander contents, a symbiosis between commerce and theology. The slave regime of New York was under review by Governor Thomas Dongan at the behest of the newly crowned King James II. In a 1686 report to the king, Thomas wrote that the inhabitants of New York "take no care of the conversion of their Slaves."[95] This was, in part, because of the previous belief held over from the Dutch period that baptism could lay the foundation for freedom; it had been an organizing principle for the networking of the free Black community, although that changed with the increasing demands of commercial empire.[96] The former Duke of York, King James II, saw no contradiction in enslaving Christians within his former duchy, nor threat to his commercial stake. A major shareholder in the Royal Africa Company, he directed Governor Edmund Andros in April 1688 "to find out the best means to facilitate and encourage the conversion of Negros and Indians to the Christian religion," "pass a law for the restraining of inhuman severity" used in punishing enslaved people, and asking that "the wilfull killing of Indians and Negros be punished with death."[97]

At the same time that James issued this guidance through governmental channels, a few Quakers in Germantown, Pennsylvania, began to agitate for the rights of enslaved people within their community of faith. Francis Daniel Pastorius authored a protest alongside three others, declaring "the reasons why we are against the traffik of men-body" and asking their leadership to discuss the case of slavery at their next quarterly meeting.[98] This marked the first time that an organized protest against slavery by whites was conducted in North America, and contrasted with the restrictive *Code Noir* (Black Laws) that were drafted in 1685 to govern the institution and practice of slavery in the French colonies and was circulating throughout that empire. The year 1688 would also mark the end of King James II's reign, as the "Glorious Revolution" forced him into exile in December of that year.

James II's successor demonstrated a more robust commitment to the institution of slavery from the moment of his installation. An anonymously published broadside entitled *A True and Exact Relation of the Prince of Orange: His Publick Entrance into Exeter* featured William of Orange's arrival in England along with "200 Blacks brought from the Plantations of the *Neitherlands* in *Americe.*" Such men were the second group described as accompanying the new monarch during his entrance into Exeter, just after *"English* Gentlemen Richly Mounted on *Flanders* Steeds." The Black grooms were described as clad in "Imbroyder, lined with white Fur, and plumes of white Feathers, to attend the Horse." They enjoyed pride of place over "200 *Finlanders* or *Laplanders* in Bear Skins taken from the Wild Beasts they had Slain," and even a banner with the inscription "GOD *and the* PROTESTANT RELIGION."[99]

CHAPTER 3

When news of the takeover reached the colonies, the townspeople of Boston erupted into revolt, capturing Governor Andros and other members of his government in early 1689. In New York, the lieutenant governor of the Dominion of New England, Sir Francis Nicholson, faced his own rebellion, as the local militia, led by Jacob Leisler, removed him from power.

Northeastern elites were not a single, unified block, but rather a collection of individuals with competing aims and varying levels of integrations into the network. Jacob Leisler was part of a broad community of elites within New York and the wider colonial region. A German immigrant who arrived as a soldier during the last years of New Netherland, Jacob elevated himself within the colonial society through extensive fur and other trading activities, and by 1676, only Cornelis Steenwijck had amassed greater wealth within the New York City limits, based on taxable records.[100] He achieved prominence and became captain of the militia, but made enemies of those who held the most elite stations during the rule of King James, a list that included the Van Rensselaers, Bayards, and Livingstons. Jacob, a staunch Calvinist, took issue with the preaching of Reverend Nicolaes van Rensselaer, who had been appointed by the future King James in 1676.[101]

Jacob Leisler made efforts to establish his own elite network through intercolonial trade, though this put him at odds with other networks. By the time of the rebellion, Jacob had added enslaved people to the list of his trades. He was co-owner of a vessel that delivered five enslaved people from New York to Maryland in 1677 as part of a series of trades that he executed with New York's former South River colony.[102] Marylanders may have been inspired in part by Jacob's 1689 actions when they rebelled against the Lord Baltimore later that year. Leisler's Rebellion itself had been infused with the language of mastery and slavery. The Anti-Leislerians, of which Robert Livingston was a prominent member, had been termed the "whites" and the pro-Leislerians, the "blacks." Such terms had their roots in European political discourse, but by this time had come to also denote racial distinction, as Jeroen Dewulf explores, one that could not have been lost on the population of elite enslavers, some of whom had recently hailed from the slave society of Barbados.[103] Tension and dissention between old and new elites permeated Leisler's Rebellion, propagated along network connections and exploited racial stereotypes.

The unrest caused by the Glorious Revolution created an opportunity for the French and their Indigenous allies to destabilize England's hold on its colonial possessions. On the cold and snow-covered morning of Sunday, February 9, 1690, the town of Schenectady was attacked by a joint expeditionary force of French and Indigenous forces from Canada under the command of Sieur Le Moyne de Sainte Helene and Lieutenant Daillebout de Mantet. By the end of the day, most of the houses were burned to the ground, many of the livestock were slaughtered, sixty inhabitants lay dead, and an additional twenty-seven people were captured, while only two raiders lost their lives during the assault.[104] The assault heavily impacted Black people, who represented more than 20 percent of all victims, despite making up only 8 percent of the population of Albany county in 1687.[105] Among those killed were thirteen enslaved or free Black people, while another five were among the captured. As the violence that would come to be known as King William's War continued throughout 1690, attacks spread into the heart of Maine country, a central route for self-emancipated escapees from New York and New England headed toward Canada. Following Schenectady, a March attack destroyed a settlement in Salmon Falls, and in May, attacks engulfed Casco. The traumatized refugees from these sites would stream into New England towns such as Salem village, making up a significant portion of witchcraft accusers. Others would become tenants on Robert Livingston's manor, which bordered Albany.[106] This would create a new baseline from which further growth and contests for mastery and control would be waged throughout the remainder of the decade.

Running Away during Rebellion

The political economic and social worlds of powerful white colonials were shaped by notions of mastery and networks of influence. But enslaved people held their own networks, even though they emerge in the written record as anonymous or devoid of family name. Scholars have approached the era of Leislerian Rebellion from various perspectives yet none have done so from the point of view of the enslaved. The borderland violence that erupted served as a crucial moment of resistance and change for the enslaved and was understood in racially inflected ways by enslavers. One man took advantage of this moment to make a dramatic change. His act endures in the archival record as a few lines in a letter written in the spring of 1692 between Hartford-based John Allyn and Robert Livingston: "I received Mrs. Schuyler's [Alida Livingston] Letter & have made the best inquiry I can for her Negroe but find him not. I can hear nothing of him there was one last year as soon as I heard of him I did take him to be a run away & sent a warrant to the constable to secure him but before the constable had y warrant he was runn from there & so I could not come at him."[107] Once the hunted man stepped away from the Connecticut house that he determined to be his last place of captivity, to turn back would have meant severe reprisals. He was a fugitive now, a runaway. His first name would be lost to history, replaced forever by "runaway," the title meant to criminalize his status but one that also challenged Alida's claim on his body.[108] It was a decision that would survive for centuries in the correspondence of those who pursued him, a lasting epitaph to the feat. He started his journey away from his captors, the Livingstons, sometime during the eight months between August 1690 and March 1691, when the family had been forced away from Albany into exile in Connecticut. His position in the household was not recorded, but that he had been Alida Schuyler's enslaved man, offers clues to his origins. This suggests that he toiled on their house in Prince Street, or Rensselaerswyck and entered the Livingston household as part of Alida's marriage dowry. If that were so, he could have left family in the Hudson Valley, people whose connections he utilized to aid his escape. He certainly either knew or acquired a broad enough knowledge of the countryside that he had managed to evade capture for one year. His networks, like those of many who escaped slavery, provided him with support and cover as he pursued his flight.

Networks of enslaved people came into conflict with networks of elite enslavers at the moment of evasion and escape. A successful escape required an understanding of the obstacles that stood in the path to freedom, as well as more than a little luck. The white inhabitants of the colony, who were connected by friendship or family ties to his enslaver, constituted the severest obstacle. In March of 1690, Robert had been forced into exile by Jacob Leisler's authorities, who were determined to arrest him for his vocal opposition to Jacob's government and refusal to allow his officials into the city of Albany. After a few months of separation, while Alida, her children, and those she enslaved remained in a deserted Albany bracing for attack from without and enduring a virtual house arrest under Jacob's supporters from within, Robert returned to the city under the protection of his friend, Fitz-John Winthrop.[109] Fitz-John was the grandson of Massachusetts first governor, John Winthrop, who had maintained a mutual relationship with Petrus Stuyvesant, and who had enslaved and traded Pequot captives to Barbados for the first "parcel of negros" brought into Massachusetts aboard the slave ship *Desire*.[110] Fitz-John had been recently appointed by a regional committee to defend vulnerable settlements against joint French and Indian attack, after the destruction of Schenectady. Thus, able to leave unmolested by Jacob's supporters, the Livingston family sheltered in Fairfield, Connecticut.[111] Their correspondence, nevertheless, reflects the vast networks they held across the colony—from New London to Hartford. John Allyn, their main contact in Hartford, had made his money as a mariner, even stopping in Curaçao to receive enslaved people on credit from Matthias Beck. He cultivated ties with Petrus Stuyvesant, as one of his New England contacts. After the fall of New Netherland, John maintained his relations with the Dutch population of New York.[112] Those networks would have created a formidable challenge to the escaped man.

Elite networks represented challenging obstacles that escapees must navigate, turning to their own social resources as a sort of compass or guide. Upon arriving in Hartford, the self-emancipated man would first have had to get past John Allyn, whose house was situated along the banks of the Connecticut River and was the point of disembarking for ferries that sailed the waterway.[113] He was directly involved with the river traffic and was compensated "4d ye horse & 2d ye man" for each fare that crossed the river.[114] It is clear that John knew Alida as well, in that he referred to her following the Dutch convention using her maiden name as "Mrs. Schuyler," even though Alida herself signed her personal correspondence "Alida Livingston."[115]

The Livingstons and Allyns also shared another cultural similarity: they were slaveholders. The son of Matthew Allyn, one of Hartford's founders, John grew up in a community that included slaves. His father, Matthew, bought the estate of William Holmes of New Plymouth in 1638, including "all the lands, houses, servants, goods, and chattels of the Town of Windsor."[116] William's "servants" could have included some Pequot war captives.[117] Acting as secretary of the colony in 1650, John Allyn estimated that Connecticut's enslaved population consisted of thirty captive people who had been purchased from Barbados.[118] He was also a slaveholder in his own right. John was Petrus Stuyvesant's contact in Connecticut and a mariner who captained the "ketch named *Rebecca*" to Curaçao in the spring of 1661. While on the island, he purchased on credit from Matthias Beck "twenty horses and five Negroes."[119]

John Allyn was deeply embedded in New England's slaveholding networks. He was related to John Pynchon through marriage, as his wife Ann was John Pynchon's niece.[120] Had Alida's enslaved man tried to smuggle his way across the river, he would have had to devise a way to not only evade John Allyn but also the passengers that took the ferry willing to give up information about a suspicious-looking runaway. That may have been how John received the report in 1691 that a Black man fitting the description of Alida's escaped man was in Hartford. Regardless of who he actually was, the man was able to elude John's grasp and escape. The man successfully navigated the landscape of elite networks in his bid for escape.

The self-emancipated man exercised new connections that he had made in Connecticut to successfully run away, taking advantage of the brief instability of the Livingstons' situation. Any escape was a risk, as slave catchers and a network of slaveholders stood between each potential escapee and their chosen destination.[121] But had fortune favored the formerly enslaved man long enough to spirit him past the reach of the Livingstons, he would have had to then contend with an active war zone. Jacob Leisler's seizure of New York's government, which had caused Robert to flee or be thrown in jail, coincided with the outbreak of King William's War.[122] When the French and their Mohawk, Algonquian, and Onondaga allies attacked the village of Schenectady, killing more than one hundred people, including eleven enslaved people, Robert protested Jacob's sluggish reaction taking his grievances in person to Connecticut and Boston, and in writing, across the ocean to England.[123] This event would have featured in conversations throughout the region.[124] The man who determined to run away from the Livingstons could have had family members among the fallen or had others who were carried into captivity. Some, such as the enslaved laborers of slain Schenectady minister Peter Tessemaaker, also used the moment to escape.[125]

When Alida Livingston's escaped man was brought to Connecticut with the family, he would have entered a colony containing some free African-descended people. By the late 1680s, Hartford and the surrounding area had a small but growing free Black community. One man, named Tony, owned ten acres of land in and around Norwich. In 1689 Tony was bequeathed his freedom from John Olmsted in Norwich as well as "3 acres in the little plain, 3 acres in the Great plain and 4 acres at Wequetequock." Philip and Ruth Moore owned farmland and woodland in Hockanum, near Hartford, and lived there along with their children, Philip and Susannah, son-in-law Cato Sessions, who was indentured to the Reverend Timothy Woodbridge, and their grandchildren. Sampson lived in Farmington, just six miles from Hartford. Mareah was newly freed from her service to Alexander Pygan and living in New London. Alida's escaped man could have sought shelter among Connecticut's free Black community. Such sheltering was enough to occasion New York's 1692 law which fined free Black people for entertaining enslaved people.[126] He might well have been offered shelter by white inhabitants of the region, a reality that as Graham Russell Hodges noted, was reflected in the runaway notices that warned against people harboring escapees.[127]

The connections between the Livingstons and Fitz-John Winthrop's family would have occasioned interactions between their enslaved people.[128] For the duration of the time that the entire Livingston family was in Connecticut, Fitz-John himself was in Quebec trying (but ultimately not succeeding) to win an offensive against New France. His daughter, Mary, remained in New London, but she would have not been alone.[129] A household that included indentured servants and enslaved people toiled for the Winthrops and would have come into frequent contact with the domestic slaves that arrived with the Livingstons, on their visits to their friends' household.[130] Robert Livingston's father, the Reverend John Livingstone, had been friends with the elder Winthrop, and those ties were the basis on which Robert started up a new friendship with Fitz-John.[131] The enslaved people who were forced to follow would create their own networks.

Likewise, the enslaved communities within Connecticut held links to those of New York. When Hartford was part of New Netherland, enslaved denizens of New Amsterdam could find themselves traded across the colony.[132] Yet these enslaved communities remained, and despite the capriciousness of sale and bequest, as well as the smaller sizes of Black and mixed-race families, enslaved people made connections with one another, relationships that they maintained, if only in memory, despite separation.[133] When Alida's enslaved man arrived in Connecticut, he could have been reunited with family or have been following the family connections of other members of enslaved household laborers. In 1690 the entire enslaved population of African descent in Connecticut totaled about two hundred people, a number that more than doubled in ten years.[134] Demand from elites like Robert would fuel the importation of enslaved people into the region. The man's flight coincided with a time when Robert Livingston was directly investing in the slave trade: in 1690 he invested in the slave ship *Margriet* (also the name of his nine-year-old-eldest daughter) with his brother-in-law Jacobus van Cortlandt.[135] Such newly arrived enslaved people would have been brought into the community by seasoned enslaved people like the escaped man, a pattern that occurred elsewhere in the Atlantic world.

Enslaved messengers and pilots gained familiarity with travel—even routes across contested territory—knowledge they could use for their own purposes. The Livingstons rarely traveled the countryside without a Black groom or sloop pilot. Tom traveled with Robert to New York, as evidenced by the trial testimony.[136] Later in the decade, in 1698, Alida referenced "ons Hendricken," an enslaved man who, according to Alida, had duties ferrying goods on the river so she placed him on the boat to New York. But he was not fully in charge of piloting the yacht, as she expressed annoyance that among the group of other men that Robert had sent up to assist the job not one of them had expertise piloting, because Hendricken "could not do it" (*de neger kon niet doen*). She fumed, "It is a wonder that there was not one man with them who understands the river" (*het is wonder dat er zijn niet een man bij had die de ravier verstaet [verstaat]*).[137] By March 1700, Alida sent Robert a letter giving an account of her experiences managing local vendors and moving inventory up and down the Hudson. She made sure to specify that

CHAPTER 3

when she visited Robert in New York she would not be alone, writing that in two weeks she and "the negroes" (*de neghers*) would bring "shirts and other clothing" (*hemde [hemden] en andre kledings*) to ensure that Robert and her son John represented the family with the proper accouterments.[138] If the man formerly enslaved to Alida transported her throughout the region, he would have continued to perform that duty while in Connecticut. He could have known Jan, a man enslaved by Alida's father, who was stabbed "in the belly, under the short ribs" during a scuffle with two Indian men who had insulted Philip Schuyler and harmed his horse.[139] If his circle were wide enough, he would also have known the two Native men who labored for the Livingstons, such as "Jan de wilt," or "Jan the Indian," and a man Alida referred to only as "de oude wilt," or the "old Indian."[140] Jan was a husband and father, a local Mahican, who traded in Albany and appears in merchant Evert Wendell's account book, alongside his son Waskaemp. Presumably, the other man was also a local Mahican man as well. Mahican people held hunting and fishing rights to the manor as part of the agreement they made with Robert in 1683. Jan's family relationships appear in the account book in relation to his wife, and although unnamed, her presence is crucial: his son Waskaemp is referenced as "the son of Jan's wife" and Evert notes sister in the same manner.[141] Such responsibilities and diverse workforce, linked by their own kin relationships would have quickly offered the formerly enslaved man a working map of the area.[142]

The community of enslaved people that populated Connecticut and New York's settlements would have held numerous commonalities. They would have spoken similar languages, as the populations of the area had been formed from captive Black people hailing from Caribbean locales such as Curaçao and Barbados, two islands that had been connected in the slave trade and gained population from West Central Africa and increasing numbers of people from the Gold Coast.[143] Slave depots in the Caribbean were never so walled off as the navigation acts should have made them, and the enslaved community of the Northeast reflected the colonists' local business deals that skirted the letter of the law.[144] The community would have had similar holiday celebrations.[145] The multiethnic population included individuals conversant in Indigenous languages and geographies, a knowledge that would have aided any person seeking to survive their flight.[146] They would have also been constrained by a Black Code that was passed in 1690.[147] These commonalities would have served to unify the broader enslaved population of these cities.

In his flight, the man joined his struggle with other bonded people who set off away from their enslavers, a daunting task that could just as likely end in failure. Robert's correspondence with John Allyn intended to track down Alida's escaped formerly enslaved man was not the only cross-colonial runaway search conducted that year between the Livingstons and their Connecticut contacts. In September 1692 Hartford-based William Pitkin sent a letter including thanks for all of Robert's efforts in trying to track down his runaway servant named Edward Blake.[148] The interconnection of Blake and the unnamed Black self-emancipated man's stories shows the intercolonial reach and prevalence of bonded unfree labor as highlighted by Jared Ross Hardesty, to building hierarchical networks of influence in the early modern world. For all that can be reconstructed about those who set away from bondage, most can never be known. The man's name, his personal history, where he hoped to go, and all he hoped to accomplish are lost to time. Yet, the effort to repopulate the canvas of what can be known about such narratives, highlights an early Northeast connected by hidden networks and escape routes of captive peoples.

News of Jacob Leisler's arrest sent the Livingstons back to New York, without one son and one enslaved man. They left their eldest son, John with Fitz-John to be educated in Connecticut. In the years that followed, their houses in Albany and Manor Livingston became Alida's base of operations. There she managed a household with a diverse workforce, one that was served by a large contingent of enslaved domestics.

"Slavery and popery" was a pro-Leislerian faction touchstone, though arguments about the former predated the events of the 1690s. Jacob had lost a protracted fight with Nicolaes's brother, Balthazar, over the lower Manhattan estate of his father-in-law, Govert Loockermans, one that included some enslaved people. When Maria Sr., Govert's widow, drafted her will, she made provisions for the eventual emancipation of two enslaved boys, Francis and Manual. She cut her stepdaughter Maria Loockermans out of her will, an omission that led to a fifteen-year court battle between Jacob Leisler and Balthazar Bayard.[149] In 1702, his followers got their revenge by pronouncing his rival Nicolaes Bayard, Petrus Stuyvesant's great-nephew, as part of a more massive conspiracy to establish "popery and slavery" in the colony.[150] Although the phrase is used as part of stock constellations of appellations against tyranny, it would have held a more immediate local resonance for their intended audience. Nicolaes had inherited a considerable amount of land from the estate of his elite ancestors, which included the north side of Wall Street, which had formerly been designated for Black residents. He and his wife, Anne, were also slaveholders. While not decrying the real practice of enslavement, such words could easily be read as condemnations of

Nicolaes's disordered mastery.[151] Popery and slavery were inexorably linked with the enslaved population of New York.

To elites, slaveholding was a crucial avenue toward building their networks of power and mastery. When Robert returned to New York, he quickly set about conferring with his business associates about his trading empire, none more important than Stephanus van Cortlandt. On November 15, 1691, Stephanus updated Robert on the trade dealing that he had in Albany, which included the exchange of "small beer" and other supplies with his nephew Kiliaen van Rensselaer, for which the later purchased the life of an enslaved boy to square accounts.[152] Robert's relationship with Stephanus van Cortlandt had temporarily soured relations between Stephanus and his sister Maria, who amid the fight had nothing but disdainful words for her brother.[153] The fight was distant enough for Stephanus and Kiliaen that they were trading supplies and the life of one enslaved boy. Stephanus's letter also included the debts owed to him by local community members, including a widow, who owed him money for an enslaved man that she had purchased from him.[154]

The time of revolution, rebellion, and warfare during the late 1680s and early 1690s provided an opportunity for enslavers to at once reinforce and benefit from their elite networks within and across colonial boundaries. Utilizing pathways and connections established during the period of divided rule that began with the separate Dutch, Swedish, and English colonies, northern elites could expand their locus of control over the land and the lives of enslaved people beyond their own personal and immediate environment. These networks provided trading opportunities, aided in the capture of runaways, and served as a bulwark or shelter in the event of physical or political attacks, uniting disparate colonies and locales more effectively than Andros's Dominion of New England ever could. These elite networks, built on the names, honor, and reputations of the wealthiest and most well-connected families of the region, established cross-colonial bonds that provided the basis for future, continued growth.

CHAPTER 4

Bond

Forging an Anglo-Dutch Slaveholding Northeast (1690s–1710s)

When traveling from New England to Albany for treaty negotiations with the Five Nations in August 1694, Reverend Benjamin Wadsworth of Cambridge described the route as a "hidious, howling wilderness."[1] He was not alone. Along with him for the journey was a coterie of New England elites, including Colonel John Pynchon of Springfield, John Allyn of Hartford, and Judge Samuel Sewall of Boston. The group "met a negro coming from Albany" who they determined was "very suspicious" so they immediately detained and "pinion'd" the man.[2] The accosted traveler, who maintained he was a former soldier from the fort at Albany, was able to break free of the bonds and escape. Benjamin admitted that "tho we saw him no more, yet we thought of him." Upon arriving at Albany, they encountered a bevy of regional elites amassed for the diplomatic conference including Governor Benjamin Fletcher, his close ally Nicolaes Bayard, as well as Albanian Peter Schuyler and colony secretary Robert Livingston. Benjamin Wadsworth continued to gather information on the Black man, and ultimately "understood yt this negro had been a souldier there and had run away from thence." Despite hailing from very different colonies, the group displayed a unity of purpose in policing the actions of a "suspicious" Black man and a dogged desire to establish his status as a runaway.

The men continued their journey to the "very stately farm of Mr. Levistone's." The Livingstons had not yet built their manor house, and the property had only a few tenants, but Benjamin Wadsworth described being "Baited, and refreshed horse and man."[3] Passive constructions erased the identities of the people who served the elite group, but the Livingstons' typical manor laborer was a debtor or unfree. Nonetheless, the Livingstons used enslaved people to project power in a way that land, commodities, and investments could not, because they were a form of movable property that could be *moved*. Enslaved people were traded to forge alliances and tighter cultural touchstones that were legible across colonies and even oceans, and also to demonstrate dominion. Legal frameworks enacted by interconnected kin centralized control through the surveillance and criminalization of the enslaved. The bonds that knit together a diverse yet interconnected Northeastern slaveholding elite during the final decades of the seventeenth century would tighten around the enslaved like a vice, and be used to naturalize legal, social, and racial notions of mastery that were deeply gendered.

Pirates and Businessmen

Northeastern elites used enslaved people as a kind of currency that underwrote their power and connections, and knit their diffuse network together across a wide area. When three enslaved children—two boys and one girl—disembarked from the *San Antonio* in the summer of 1699 bound for Gardiner's Island, a privately held island situated just on the east end of Long Island Sound, they had little idea of what the future might hold.[4] Their journey thus far would have been eventful; they were not only captives on Captain William Kidd's sloop, but they were also earmarked as William's personal plunder.[5] The haul included buried treasure intended to buy William's way out of a piracy charge, a charge that would ultimately lead to his formal conviction as a pirate and his execution in 1701.[6] The children were handed over to John Gardiner, the proprietor of the island, a man who resided in a large manor house and whose family wealth descended from his grandfather Lion's purchase of the island sixty years earlier after the Pequot War.[7] In the end, their fates were not only entwined with William Kidd's and John Gardiner's but also bound together with those of Robert Livingston and his Boston-based business partner Duncan Campbell.

Robert had put up a bail of ten thousand pounds for William, a man that he had had business dealings with in the past, and in exchange William promised one of the enslaved children along with "a forty pound bag of gold" that he had kept secretly hidden until he could determine the severity of his social predicament.[8] Duncan, likewise, received one of the captive children plus other gifts in exchange for helping William secure a pardon. Enslaved children were the currency on which William hung his prospects. Their lives were co-opted to weave an intricate tapestry of obligation connecting Robert, William, and John.[9] These ledgerless transactions implied a distinct hint of complicity in piracy, at least to some government officials, and although John, Robert, and Duncan were deeply involved with privateering activities, they managed to escape the moniker of pirate that was attached to William by denying that they knew that the payment was ill-gotten.

Robert Livingston had spent the better part of three decades networking among the colonial elite of Albany, New York, Massachusetts, and the Caribbean, creating a bulwark of families and associates linked by marriage and by slaveholding ties. In 1692, Robert bought a house from William Kidd, a fellow Scotsman and longtime friend. The property was on New York's Dock Street, a center for business and slavery.[10] Enslaved workers manned the marina, building and maintaining ships, some of which would be engaged in trading people who, like them, were captured into the vice of slavery.[11] In 1693, Robert, charged with smuggling, faced a grand jury of which William was the court foreman. Robert was acquitted of that charge likely owing to his networking ability.[12] Robert's friendship with William netted him a long-term real estate foothold where he could profit from proximity to slavery. Ten years after Robert's purchase of William's Dock Street property, 25 percent of the Dock Street Ward, which was bounded by the East River, Burgher's Path, Broad Street, and Prince Street, were listed as enslaved.[13] Robert maintained trading links to Curaçao—New York's former southern Caribbean region and slave depot—for four decades, a relationship that his son Philip continued. Stephanus van Cortlandt, Robert Livingston's business partner, enslaver, and trader, as well as the former brother-in-law of Robert's wife Alida, maintained connections in St. Christopher, Nevis, and Curaçao that had been forged during Dutch rule.[14]

But the tension evident during several diplomatic meetings with the Onondaga recorded by Robert evidences that the use of racial slavery in regional patois dating back to the Dutch era had wide-ranging consequences. During peace negotiations between the French allied nations and New York on February 3, 1699, the influential Onondaga Sachem and diplomat Teganissorens relayed the experiences of a community member named Cohensiowanne who encountered the French diplomat Maricour (known as "Stow Stow" due to his adoption by the Onondaga), while traveling to Canada to visit family. Stow Stow reportedly told Cohensiowanne that when Robert's brother-in-law, Captain Johannes Schuyler, was last in Canada, he had greatly disrespected the Five Nations. He called them "disobedient" and, when asked "why the Sachims of the 5 Nations did not come to Canada,"

Johannes purportedly replied "here is the 5 Nations, and pointed to a negroe he had with him." The New York delegation took immediate umbrage to such a characterization, and reconvened three days later "upon the request of Capt. Johanns Schuyler" to publicly insist that they were "scandalous and malitious faleshoods."[15] In January 1699, New York governor Richard Coote, the first Earl Bellomont, received correspondence from the Lords of Trade eager to know the results of the talks with the Onondagas in order to retain "them in their subjection to the Crown of England" as well as to declare William Kidd a pirate, a decision which imperiled Richard's own position as one of William's original investors.[16]

When Robert Livingston and William Kidd met in Boston, they pledged their continued fealty through the exchange of hard money and enslaved children, a currency that had bound the region since the mid-seventeenth century. By the turn of the eighteenth century, Boston still had only a small enslaved population, especially when compared to the bustling slave port of New York.[17] Nevertheless, the elite maintained a commitment to slavery and slaveholding that they had forged throughout the seventeenth century. Robert's American migration had begun in New England, under the direction of Springfield-based John Pynchon and in concert with his nephew, Elizur Holyoke. He had served as John's factor at a time when the Springfield merchant became ever more invested in both Caribbean and local slavery.[18] John's model of such regional slave diversification also became the model that Robert followed.

By the time that Robert was embroiled in the William Kidd affair, slavery had infused the cultural fabric of Massachusetts's elites. Massachusetts minister, Cotton Mather hotly defended his father's threatened position as president of Harvard College by directly referencing the slavery that had come to shape how he too encountered the world. The object of his rage, Judge Samuel Sewall, recorded the scene and the charges the incensed Cotton made against him, in the margins of his diary: "Mr. Cotton Mather came to Mr. Wilkins's shop, and there talked very sharply against me as if I had used his father worse than a Neger; spake so loud that people in the street might hear him. Then went and told Sam, That one pleaded much for Negros, and he had used his father worse than a Negro."[19]

Just as Jeremias van Rensselaer's contempt for the enslaved spilled out as superscripts and strikethroughs, Samuel's annoyance bleeds off of the main page and into the margins allowing modern readers to encounter the sights and sounds of the day. Cotton Mather stormed into the shop of Richard Wilkins who was the Boston bookseller to whom Samuel Sewall's twenty-three-year-old eldest son and namesake Sam was apprenticed, shouting so loudly that his voice carried into the street.[20] The incensed Cotton did not bring his argument to the elder Sewall but rather "went and told Sam": a move, no doubt intended to shame Samuel Sr. in front of his son's master. Wilkins had sold Samuel's published work in the past, but the jurist had decided to circulate his antislavery tract, *The Selling of Joseph*, privately, perhaps worried that the subject matter might cost him the bookseller's continued favor. The elder Samuel transcribed the scene as Cotton screaming the Dutch pronunciation of "neger" in public. It was only indoors, after he confronted Samuel's son, that Cotton reverted to using the English "Negro."

This slaveholding culture would be translated and disseminated to a wider public through the proliferation of the newspaper. John Campbell, a fellow Scottish émigré, was appointed Boston's deputy postmaster general in 1693 after the post had been taken over by royal administration. His brother, Duncan Campbell, who was embroiled alongside Robert Livingston in the William Kidd affair, was Robert's close friend and business associate. In 1704, John would go on to found the *Boston News-Letter*, the first newspaper established in the colonies.[21] In it, advertisements assessing the value of Black men women and children would appear alongside those that tracked their flights away from slavery across the expanse of the Northeast. If, as one historian has argued, "slavery and the newspaper grew up together in Massachusetts," it was a relationship forged on the back of friendships and contacts across the Northeast between colonists like Robert, Duncan, and John.[22]

Both Robert and Alida had instilled the values of profit and mastery into their children, a shared culture that entwined the business lives of his two eldest children, John and Margaret. By April 1701, a then married John, and his brother-in-law Samuel Vetch, Margaret's husband, partnered with Boston merchant John Saffin in the trading ship *Mary* (likely named for John Livingston's new bride, Mary Winthrop), which traded illegally in Quebec.[23] John Saffin was heavily invested in the Chesapeake as well as in the Atlantic slave trade; markets exploited a generation earlier as an interpenetration of Dutch and English ventures.[24] A month before the *Mary* set sail, Adam, a man enslaved to John Saffin, sued for his freedom. John had promised to free Adam on New Year's Day 1699 after he had worked on his farm in western Massachusetts, but had reneged on the deal. The case was heard several times, first before Samuel Sewall, then subsequently in a court where John Saffin assumed the roles of judge and jury in addition to defendant. Samuel Sewall protested the biased court and intimated it was stacked by John.[25] Enraged at Adam's audacity, and the support of justice Samuel Sewall for

86 CHAPTER 4

Adam's cause, John published his *A Brief and Candid Answer to a late Printed Sheet Entitled the Selling of Joseph* in 1701.[26] In it, he answered Samuel's *The Selling of Joseph* with the same anger that impelled Cotton Mather to scream into a Boston Street that Samuel had treated his father, Increase, "worse than a Neger." An acclaimed poet, John communicated his hatred in verse:

> Cowardly and cruel are those *Blacks* Innate,
> Prone to Revenge, Imp of inveterate hate.
> He that exasperates them, soon espies
> Mischief and Murder in their very eyes.
> Libidinous, Deceitful, False and Rude,
> The Spume Issue of Ingratitutde.
> The Premises consider'd, all may tell,
> How near good *Joseph* they are Parallel.[27]

The court found in Adam's favor. As John Saffin's hold on Adam crumbled, his joint investment in the *Mary* tanked. The *Mary* was discovered, and her hold of illegally traded goods was seized. John Livingston bore the brunt of the failure and was plunged into crippling debt.[28] In the ensuing years, his attempts to rebound from his imprudent investments would tear an enslaved Connecticut family asunder. Ten years after the loss of the *Mary*, John Livingston represented New London enslaver Samuel Beebe's claim to a mixed-race woman named Joan and her children against the counterclaim of her free Black husband, John Jackson. Victorious, John Livingston was awarded ownership over the Jacksons.[29]

The Livingston family's far-flung connections and business deals were tied together through slavery. Enslaved children served as currency across regional boundaries and the family's dual identities—Dutch and Scottish—were shaped by enslavement. Robert's transatlantic family correspondence at the turn of the eighteenth century shows how the language of slavery infused the family's transatlantic communications. In December 1699, after only narrowly having escaped implication in the William Kidd affair, Robert received a letter from his business associate John Borland in Boston. In it, John solicited funding for Caledonia, an attempted Scottish colony established on the Isthmus of Panama.[30] John Borland was a fellow Scottish refugee whom Robert had met in Amsterdam two decades earlier.[31] The Scotland-based Livingston family supported the scheme, which was vigorously opposed by the English who did not support Scottish competition so near Jamaica.[32] Robert's nephews, James and Andrew, immigrated to the colony, only to be captured by the Spanish authorities. On January 4, 1700, James Livingston wrote his younger brother from Edinburgh detailing the two Livingstons' desperate fortunes: there was no word from John (James's son), though Andrew had written that summer "from the prison of Carthagina" describing himself as being "worse treated then their slaves."[33] This description disturbed James, who relayed the following to Robert: "[Andrew's letter] gives me just cause to judge that if my son John be on life he is in the same condition amongst thos people that [are] worse then savages our collonie in Darien [Panama] their deserting has been [a] matter of great Greift in this Countrie."[34]

James feared that if his son John was alive, he was being treated—like his cousin Andrew described—as worse than "their slaves" by Europeans who had descended to a state described as "worse than savages." Such language shows that the Edinburgh-based James imagined a colonial world defined by bondage and savagery. While the dire condition of the Darien refugees inspired such florid language from the Scotland-based Livingstons, it reflected the tenor of their American cousins' correspondence. Also, these Scottish Livingstons were not insulated from slavery, as the enslaved were brought to Edinburgh to labor under bondage that was not officially recognized by British law.[35] If James had been an avid reader of the *Edinburgh Gazette* or any number of the active newspapers out of London that reprinted their news and advertisements in Scotland, he would have found runaway slave notices that advertised the abuses slaves endured as identifying marks to aid in capture.[36] The distant, though none the less desperate, father employed the language of savagery to demean the characters of the Spanish officials, imagining them as "worse than savages" imagery that had been deployed a century before by Nicholas De Meyer and Jeremias van Rennselaer in conceptualizing their own difficulties. Slavery and the savagery of bondage framed the way that the Livingston family made sense of Andrew and John's experiences.

Margaret's husband Samuel Vetch had survived the Darien misadventure to create a truly Northeastern network. In 1704, the town of Deerfield in Massachusetts was attacked; Samuel Vetch networked with Massachusetts governor Joseph Dudley, volunteering to travel with the French governor Pierre de Rigaud de Vaudreuil and Dudley's son Paul to quell regional tensions, and enticing him with the prospect of profits. Although the governor signed off on the scheme, many in the Puritan guard were not as solicitous. By ingratiating himself with Dudley, Samuel had made an enemy of the Mathers who still smarted over Dudley's decision to place John Leverett in charge of Harvard College. Therefore, when he arrived back in Boston, Samuel was thrown in jail. Although he managed to secure release, he was tried for illegally trading in Canada. Samuel fled to London, where he appealed his case and won by promising to defeat the French-occupied territory and bring it under the control of Queen Anne in a circulated paper entitled "Canada Survey'd."[37] He would organize and helm an invasion force, augmented by Indigenous fighters to enact this plan.[38] Samuel would continue to expand his network of power across the region to achieve his dream of English territorial expansion, relying on the regional Anglo-Dutch connections of his in-laws, while destructively laying claim to the lives of enslaved human beings.

Old and New Networks

Rather than being an imposed English legal innovation, slavery was reconceived by a core group of elites with roots to the Dutch period through their own shifting notions of mastery. Although the cohort had figured as collaborators or anglicizers, their connections forged during the Dutch period remained crucially important throughout the seventeenth and well into the eighteenth century. Tightening slave laws during the English period emerged as much out of the will of these enslavers as from their English overlords. On April 9, 1700, when his wife Margaretta van Cortlandt was just one month away from giving birth, Samuel Bayard attended the meeting of the common council in New York City. He served as an assistant to the aldermen, who included Jacobus van Cortlandt, his father-in-law; the merchant Brandt Schuyler; and David Provoost, the mayor who had been a longtime business associate of the Bayards. As part of the regular business of the council, the group passed a law meant to constrain the lives of their enslaved people.[39] Meeting time brought enslaved people of all walks of life together to mingle not just among themselves but to enlarge their networks. Court records indicate that during the "time of divine service," the enslaved had expanded trade with colonials, both women and men, engaged in leisure activities, and strengthened social ties. The surveillance and criminality placed on such activities had been a top priority of colonial elites even as they strengthened their networks through legal and extralegal means. By limiting the group number to less than three, the colonial councilors were forbidding not just potential conspiracy but the meeting of families.

The councilors, whose roots dated back to the Dutch period, and their families, were the heirs of a militaristic ethos and planned empire-building that fueled Dutch Atlantic pursuits before the early 1670s.[40] Their larger overseas empire had fallen, and its metropolitan directors turned to a smaller model of conquest, but the families who had ventured out during the heyday of Dutch rise still held onto grand visions of empire.[41] Indeed, many of the colonists were lured away from the burgeoning economy of the Dutch metropole only by the dream of building their personal empires abroad.⁴² Thus, a subsequent generation in the later decades of the seventeenth century enacted strict control over dependent populations: with none more draconian than those passed against the enslaved. The enslaved represented a group against whom experiments of control could be trialed throughout generations, with the contingency of mastery serving to uncover avenues of protest the system allowed. With each challenge, the elite adapted to erect a series of legal and economic levers that ensured the survival of their system of control. Holding fast to the power and importance of ever-expanding kin groupings, elites such as the Stuyvesants, Bayards, the Van Cortlandts, and the multiethnic Livingstons systematically sought to strip the dispossessed of access to family and social networks.

Thus, by the time that Samuel began his tenure on the council, his uncles Balthazar Bayard and Nicolaes Varlet along with fellow Dutch elites who had been brought up in New Netherland, set up the legal apparatus of slavery in the new colony named for the Duke of York. If indeed those who assembled sought to harden the murky lines of legal slavery that had existed under Dutch rule, such strictures were not a forced adaptation to English authority but were conceived and enacted by a group that was overwhelmingly made up of members of the Dutch elite. Such legal strategies were also focused on the further dispossession of Native peoples and free Black people at the turn of the eighteenth century. The Bayard-Varlets focused on building up family landholdings in New Jersey and New York City. Atlantic slavery was a vital component of that effort. Nicolaes had been granted the "Patent of Hobocken" by Petrus Stuyvesant in 1663.⁴³ Eight years later, he and Balthazar were given a grant of land in Bergen County, where Balthazar served as *schepen* in 1663 and 1664, and as a representative to the General Assembly of New Jersey in 1668.⁴⁴ Balthazar, removing to New York to take up primary residence in the city alongside his brothers and sister, served as schepen in 1673 during the brief recapture of the colony by the Dutch and as alderman in 1691.⁴⁵ In 1686, during Balthazar's term as a council assessor, an ordinance was passed that "noe Negroe or Slave be Suffered to worke the bridge as a Porter about any goods either Exported or imported from or into this Citty," one that specifically singled out race as a criterion.⁴⁶

By the close of the seventeenth century, Samuel's father, Nicolaes Bayard, was busy buying up land on the bowery, including lands that had been formerly owned by free Black families.⁴⁷ The Bayards lived in neighborhoods surrounded by other elite slaveholders as well as the individuals and families that they enslaved. The laws they worked to pass against the enslaved were motivated by a history of insurgency. A generation earlier those enslaved to the Bayard family had posed a direct threat, one that arguably lingered in the minds of the Bayard brothers as they sought to pass laws to contain the enslaved population. In 1669 an enslaved man named Emanuel was suspected of having attempted to burn his master and slave trader Nicolaes Varlet's home to the ground. On March 15, 1669/70, Emanuel was brought before the "Justice and Magistrates of Bergen," which included Nicolaes Varlet as well as his new brother-in-law, Nicolaes Bayard.[48] Such attempts to curtail domestic insurrections were passed down along lines of kin over years of increasing influence, economic gain, and legal precedent.

For lineal slaveholders like the Bayards the political was frighteningly personal. On April 25, 1691, Balthazar Bayard, alongside fellow aldermen Willem Beeckman (who had arrived in the colony aboard the *Prinses Amelia* with the Stuyvesants), Brandt Schuyler, Willem Merrett, Johannes Kipp, and the other members of the council "ORDERED that no Inhabitant of this City Shall Sell to any Indians any Rumme or other Strong Liquors under the Quantity of fifteen Gallons" and that no settler "harbor Entertaine or Countenance any Negro or Indian Slave in thier house or otherwise or Sell or Deliver to he any Wine, Rumm or other Strong Liquor without leave from thier Master."[49] Legal restrictions were personal, targeting an enslaved population that was, to a large extent, in the hands of such elites. On April 29 they met again to pass more regulations to control the lives of Black people:

> ORDERED that Every Male Negro in the Citty with Wheele barrows and Spades perfume one dayes Worke about Said lotts as they Shall bee ordered by Mr. Schuyler and Mr. Clarke On fayler of any Negroes Working as afore the Mr. of Said Negroe so neglecting to worke Shall forfeite one Shilling & Six pence to the Use of the Citty.[50]

Unlike the earlier laws, this order demanded action, rather than prohibited it, but the effect was similar—by constraining the amount of free time that was available, the number of activities that free and enslaved Black people could engage in decreased. Lineal slaveholders trained such laws at their own enslaved population. By the turn of the eighteenth century, the Bayards lived in Dock Ward and East Ward and owned twelve enslaved people in the city between all siblings with the family name. When in-laws and cousins are taken into account that number increases, including such slaveholders as the Van Cortlandts (14) and the Stuyvesants (11), and encompassing the Out, West, Dock and East Wards. The legal restrictions created by these slaveholding families targeted an enslaved population that was already largely in their families' control. These laws, therefore, should be seen not as separate constructs, but as extensions of household mastery.

The intimacies of that history of legal action against the enslaved population perpetrated by such elites is apparent in the language of the law passed by the New Jersey council "Regulating Negro, Indian and Mallatto Slaves."[51] It called for castration for an enslaved man suspected of sexual violence against a white woman, a clause that was rejected by Lord Dartmouth and Whitehall as "one that inflicts inhumane penalties on Negroes &c not fit to be Confirmed by Your Majesty." Ultimately, "the said Act be repealed."[52] Despite the repeal, the elites who conceived of the law were keen on maintaining their power and conceived of that power in terms of lineage and race. At its core, the law revealed the discomfort that interracial sex would pose to the passing on of power. New Jersey's castration statute showed that there was a considerable amount of unease about a free population of African and African-descended people. Such unease about the growth of free Black groups was not peculiar, as such communities consistently challenged the racial boundaries erected within colonial societies.[53] What was unique was that Dutch-descended elites, such as the Bayards, who had previously seen a benefit in contributing to older free Black communities, were committed to closing the possibilities of such future communities with violent force.

By the turn of the eighteenth century, the colony of New York passed some of the strictest slave laws in the region while elite families solidified their grip on colonial power. Unlike the Livingston-Schuyler alliance, the Bayard family was not a newly created dynasty but a generation old, and even though members such as Nicholas Bayard had sought to adopt anglicized identities to retain their power, they remained ethnically Dutch. Like other families in the region, the Bayards continued to expand power that was both local and Atlantic. Although they had enjoyed power during Dutch rule, they had to weather the transition to English, a feat that was not without difficulty. They had done not only that but had built a network of connections that provided others with the ability to expand their fortunes—which were made in concert with the growing regional slave market. For example, Adolph Philipse's fortunes as a slave trader and landowner did not merely emerge from the grist of shrewd business dealings but an earlier grafting into the orbit of elite family networks: his father had begun as a carpenter on Stuyvesant's bowery.[54] Slave trading from Madagascar to New York was likewise booming in the city at the turn of the century due to the shortages caused by King William's War, and the same conditions that created the circumstances encountered by a group of enslaved children traded between

92   CHAPTER 4

Robert Livingston, William Kidd, and John Gardner as collateral fueled the profits of elite slave networks.[55]

Neighborhoods

Control over enslaved people was central to the masculine identity that was emerging as a key component of elite family identities. When Elizabeth Stuyvesant recalled her embattled marriage to English captain George Sydenham, she characterized her existence bluntly: "I lived in hell" (*leefd ick in hell*). She testified that in 1704 George forged her name, forcing her to rent out the bouwerij to Christopher Rousby for a nine-year period agreeing to an annual rent of £102.2. The agreement included the forced labor of two men named John and Samson alongside "10 milch cows, 8 working horses, 10 young cattle, 170 sheep, 1 sow & her pigs, 16 geese & other cows, 2 waggons, 1 plow, 1 harrow, 1 wood sleigh"[56] The horror that John, Samson, and the other enslaved people endured at George's hands survives in Elisabeth's testimony. In 1703, the Sydenhams were listed as having ten enslaved people, four men, two women, two little boys, and two little girls.[57] Elisabeth recounted that George would torture them to exert his control: he "tied the negroes up and whipped them for nothing" (*bondt de negers op en geselt ze voor niemendal*). The verb *geselen* which translates into English not only as to whip, but to flog or even to horsewhip, conveys the violence of his assaults. George sadistically used their pain to demonstrate his dominion over his household and such abuse would have been etched into the memories of the four men, two women, two little boys and two little girls held captive in that household. Additionally, George withheld food from Elisabeth's children by her first husband, and Petrus Stuyvesant's youngest son, Nicolaes Willem, requiring her to hide rations "in the cellar under the tub" because George "locked the cupboard that contained the food, yes not so much as a drink of beer for myself or for the children." Elisabeth testified that he "threatened to cut the tongue from my throat if I said anything against him; his wife was his own as long as he did not beat her to death."[58]

George's abuse was targeted against those he deemed dependents in specifically gendered ways that reflected not only his personal designs at mastery but also a regional shift in notions of power. George sought to exert control over land—specifically properties that tied Elisabeth to New Netherland's ruling Dutch elite—as well as wrested Native land and enslaved people. While historians have long pointed to shifting legal realities to explain the cultural and gendered shift from the Dutch to the English period, the story of the lives of individuals bound together in abuse on the bouwerij illuminates the importance of racial mastery to that region's gendered transitions. In Nicolaes Willem Stuyvesant's 1698 will he passed "all estate, both real and personal, lying in the Bowery in New York," to his wife Elisabeth, and for his "eldest son Petrus, one Negro boy over and above his third" part of the estate that Nicolaes Willem expected Petrus would divide with his two other siblings.[59] With the gesture of a pen, Nicolaes Willem ensured that both land and slavery would become a crucial part of the Stuyvesant legacy into the eighteenth century. But widowhood presented Elisabeth the challenges of running the massive bouwerij by herself as well as raising three young children. Just two months after Nicolaes Willem's will was proved, on November 4, 1698, Elisabeth applied for a marriage license with an English officer named George Sydenham and, sometime thereafter the couple, Elisabeth's children by Nicolaes Willem, and their enslaved people resided together on the Stuyvesant family properties in Manhattan at the bouwerij.[60] It was a decision that she would live to regret.

Elisabeth had been born in Albany and grew up in the Van Slichtenhorst home. She was the daughter of Albany trader Gerrit van Slichtenhorst whose father had been the director of Rensselaerswyck and, in addition to Nicolaes Willem's bequest, she had inherited "60 morgen" of land "lying at" Claverack, the lower manor of Rensselaerswyck, land that had been purchased from the Mohawk leader Red Hawk and other members of the Haudenosaunee Confederacy (*van de wilden gekocht; rodthasvik [Rode Havik] de wilt en andere meer*).[61] She had grown up in a household with enslaved people and her father had sold enslaved people on several occasions.[62] By the time that she wed Nicolaes Willem in 1681, she was living in her family's house along the Hudson in Esopus, which, during the Dutch period, had been a site of warfare, death, and ultimately dispossession for the Munsee. In less than two decades, these Dutch families claimed the land by planting a burgeoning farming community with a growing enslaved population.[63] Nicolaes Willem's older brother Balthazar had also owned a bowery in Esopus, and when the two wed the record noted that they held ceremonies in the Hudson Valley and Manhattan. Nonetheless, Elisabeth left that life behind for a new one on the bouwerij.

Nicolaes Willem, by then a widower, had been previously married to Maria Beeckman, whose father had conspired with Petrus to keep a large portion of the enslaved captives of the *Den Gideon* at Fort Altena. The bouwerij's landscape of orchards, meadows, and marshes would have connected it to the world of Nicolaes Willem's childhood, and its retinue of villagers included enslaved people.[64] Their marriage had symbolically mended the rift that had opened between Petrus and her grandfather Brandt over the relationship between Rensselaerswyck and New Netherland, but her father's will included the clause that "the land left to his daughter, Elizabeth, wife of Nicholas William Stuyvesant, is not to be estranged or alienated by her husband or anyone else without her free will," showing that full reconciliation required the surety of law.[65] The will itself was witnessed on the bowery. The clause gave Elisabeth considerable control over her own land, which was itself contested due to differing notions of land-rights between the Mohawk and the Dutch. So, during the tumult of King William's War, Elisabeth sought to protect not only her own but her sisters' claims. In testimony given years later during her trial against George, she detailed that she bought three more parcels after her sister Bata was forced to flee, another sister Alyda's holdings were burned twice, and yet another sister Hillegont was in financial straits. With the aid of her first cousin's husband, Robert Livingston, and without Nicolaes Willem's knowledge she purchased her sisters' lands, giving Elisabeth an additional 120 acres at Claverack. She explained she had Robert acting in his capacity as secretary forge the transaction in Nicolaes Willem's name (*en had Robber[t] Lifvenston [Livingston] wie de secretaris was in Stuyvesants naam het schrijf*) but without his knowledge (*sonder't weten van Stuyvesant*).[66] She ultimately confessed her secret purchase to Nicolaes Willem on his deathbed. He confirmed his intention that Elisabeth should retain control of Claverack in his will, writing "all that tract or parcel of land lying situate and being up Hudson River commonly called or known by the name of Clavarack . . . which land I have always held and enjoyed in right of my said wife and it is but just and lawful that unto her and her heirs forever I should return it."[67] Upon Elisabeth's death their three children, Petrus, Gerardus, and Anna stood to inherit an equal part of the family lands.

Elisabeth's life with Nicolaes Willem on the bouwerij had been a multiracial one. A year after their marriage, two free Black neighbors, Pieter van Kampen and a woman recorded only as the widow of Lovijs Angola (*wed[e]. van Lovijs Angola*) were married on the bouwerij.[68] In 1689, another neighbor, Manuel Pieters, wed Maijken d'Angola, on the bouwerij.[69] In 1691 Pieter Lucaszen and Marijken Jans, a free Black couple were married on the bouwerij.[70] The community of free Black people had survived the English transition but were steadily being eroded by a suite of ever more stringent laws passed by councils filled with members whose own families also dated back to the Dutch period. These same white neighbors were the ones who in 1671 made "diverse complaints" that two free Black residents "Domingo and Manuel Angola" did "from time to time" entertain "sundry of the servants and negroes belonging to the Burghers and inhabitants of the City to the great damage of the owners."[71] At the fall of the colony, Petrus held both direct and indirect sway over the greatest number of enslaved people in the region. By the turn of the eighteenth century, his wider family network still owned twenty-three enslaved people, or 3 percent of the total population. The Out Ward, where the Stuyvesant bouwerij stood, counted seventy-two enslaved people, with ten living on the bouwerij, the third largest number of enslaved people held privately in the city.[72]

Elisabeth's broader family connections and new marriage to Captain George Sydenham quickly unraveled. In 1702, Elisabeth and George sued her sister Hillegont for gifts that they had exchanged throughout the years, as well as a continued shadow over the land title that Hillegont had sold to Elisabeth under Nicolaes Willem's forged name.[73] The rancor had actually gone so far that on the eve of Nicolaes Willem's death, Hillegont was briefly jailed.[74] A few years following Elisabeth's marriage to George Sydenham, another suit by the Beeckmans (Nicolaes Willem's first wife's family) against Nicolaes Willem's estate also commenced.[75] Throughout the varied litigious affairs, Elisabeth had a dreadful secret, she was being physically and emotionally abused by George. It would take ten years for Elisabeth to make her abuse claims public.

George Sydenham had his sights trained on Claverack. He and his friend Paroculus Parmyter compelled Elisabeth during a fit of delirium induced by a difficult pregnancy to sign the title of her lands over to him. When she still refused to ascent, George adopted ever more violent tactics that targeted enslaved people and the Manhattan holdings Elizabeth had brought into her marriage. He ultimately had her imprisoned in jail after she attempted to retake the bouwerij. After being in the "Comon Goale of this City about Eight months," Elisabeth was assumed in one family history to have taken refuge with her adult widowed daughter, Anna Stuyvesant Pritchard, in New Jersey.[76] The enslaved people had no such outlet. Even after the proceedings the abusive George retained their lives and labor. Due to English marriage laws, he also held title to the lands in Claverack, though the bouwerij passed to Gerardus Stuyvesant, Elizabeth's remaining living son by Nicolaes Willem. In November 1713, George sent his enslaved man from Claverack to Robert Livingston's mill "with corn to grind." He expected that Robert would send the man back with various goods, including "pease," "gunpowder," and "pidgeon." George included a veiled threat to his erstwhile cousin by marriage, compelling him to "comply with this . . . otherwise" he would "go to Albany" and take his business with him.[77] What fate befell the ten enslaved people on the bouwerij remains unknown. Gender and masculinity were becoming more entwined with mastery in the early eighteenth century, with the rights afforded white women as propertied land and slaveholders during the previous Dutch era increasingly under attack.[78] While Robert Livingston engaged his female family members as crucial members of an expansive trading network, and even helped Elisabeth secure her property rights during Nicolaes's convalescence, George sought to consolidate power to himself and his male supporters, using brutality against both family members and enslaved people as enforcement.

By the turn of the eighteenth century, an expansive Northeast navigable by ties of enslavement had come into existence. Networks forged between kin-traders were central to the creation of an elite culture that such slaveholders navigated with ease. Enslaved men, women, and children served as the surety on loans and even clandestine transfers of power, just as they were passed along with rental properties and as inheritances. Northeastern elites shared a cultural expectation for racial surveillance and deployed a shared language of dishonor that linked blackness with degradation in personal and political negotiations. These expanding networks were not the result of the fall of Dutch rule, but rather were a continuance of older networks. The maintenance of Dutch ties and the active prevalence of Dutch legislators steered the legal trajectory of New York City during the last decades of the seventeenth century, in contrast to the prevalent notion that such laws were English transplants that arrived with the final downfall of Dutch rule. Elites made it their business to erect a favorable legal environment that created a foundation for expansion in local enslavement as well. They would call on their social, religious, and economic connections to nourish and expand their power, which was in every place they settled tied to slavery.

But, in the final decades of the seventeenth century, the ethnic characters of such family groupings changed. The networks became more Anglo-Dutch than Dutch in identity, and their approach to the control of the enslaved reflected this shift. Shifting gendered notions fed into the emergence of racial strictures and codes that had not existed at midcentury. Nevertheless, one crucial strategy for dominance facilitated the melding (if at times uneasily) of the English and Dutch imperial projects: the importance of family networks. Even as the Dutch lost official power at the end of the seventeenth century and did not dominate the slave market in the numbers that the English did, they did offer critical inroads into markets that were controlled by family networks. Marriage was the way into such networks and served to expand the influence of the subsequently blended family networks toward the creation of a coherent slave system. Although such families worked to shore up their power, they were not the only engine of empires. During the eighteenth century, emigration continued to offer a diverse ethnic population and a community of free workers whose desires drove the direction of policy and whose lives surrounded and intersected those of the elite. Slave policy, networks, and slaveholding became a way to create connections within families and across ethnic, political, religious, and social borders.

CHAPTER 5

Family

Kinship, Ambition, and Fear in a Time of Rebellions (1710s–20s)

Sometime during the second half of 1713, a little girl named Isabel was sent away from her family in the Hudson Valley to Boston. Her mother Diana worked in the Livingstons' manor house, and her father, Ben, traversed the Hudson on the Livingstons' bark, lumbered, and operated the gristmill with other enslaved men, in addition to serving as the Livingstons' personal attendant.[1] She had at least two other sisters named Eva and Gritta, and one half-brother named Caesar who was mixed race.[2] Her forced relocation destroyed her family and set a series of events in motion that devastated the enslaved community on Livingston Manor. One year earlier, in 1712, Margaret Livingston Vetch—Robert and Alida's eldest daughter—moved with her husband Samuel Vetch, daughter Alida, and son to a property located on the corner of Tremont and Winter Street in Boston, overlooking Boston Common and the public granary.[3] In the same year, Benjamin Wadsworth's *The Well-Ordered Family* was published.[4] Very little of the Vetches' household would meet Benjamin's standards for order to *"dwell together* as constantly, as their necessary affairs will permit."[5] They frequently lived in Albany, New York City, spent some time in Nova Scotia, where Samuel was governor, and finally Boston. Samuel Vetch was chronically financially overextended, constantly away chasing investments, military schemes, and shady business deals throughout the Atlantic world. But their destructive claim on a young girl's life fit neatly within Benjamin's expectations for household management (he only urged enslavers to allow *"Food, Raiment, Sleep"* and "careful rendance in case of Sickness"), as it did the worldview of those within his wider network of elite slaveholders. Nonetheless Margaret's domestic expectations swept Isabel in its wake, shattering the young girl's home life.[6]

Enslaved people and their families also shaped the social, cultural, and political development of the Northeast during the early decades of the eighteenth century. When reconstructed as part of an integrated history, their personal circumstances are as potent as the generalized tableau marshaled by many scholars to describe the tightening vice of enslavement across the Northeast during the early decades of the eighteenth century. Isabel's family connections emerge across various documents of the Livingston correspondence, through a kinship web anchored by her mother Diana. Other Black kin networks and families likewise emerge connected to Black women enslaved on the Manor, though some, as in the case of Isabel include male kin relationships. Diana and Ben worked on the manor; Diana's daughter, Isabel, as well as several other children, were bequeathed to various Livingston family members. And in 1728, Diana's grandson, Daniel, was bequeathed to Philip Livingston, as was a miller named Joe and his son Hannibal, Jak Piet, Piet blak, and a woman named Saar.[7] Some of them would live and die on the

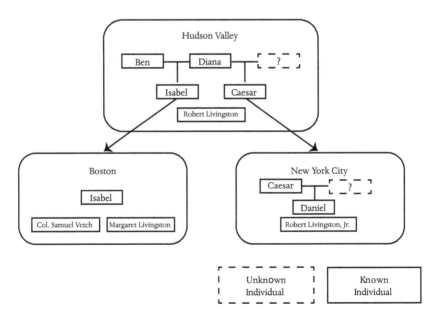

FIGURE 7. Chart showing an enslaved family separated by the Livingstons.

CHAPTER 5

manor, while others would be sent to New England or as far as Madeira. Their lives and severed connections made possible the Livingstons' slaveholding web built on networks of kin.

Domestic Troubles

By the first decade of the eighteenth century, the Livingston estate fifty miles south of Albany had become the family's locus of trade and daily life. The manor was a community filled with varied people from across the world, including local families displaced by the violence on the northern borderland, white indentured servants, Indigenous neighbors, and a contingent of enslaved Black and Native people. The manor was not primarily a slave operation. But it was shaped and defined by slavery nonetheless. It was one of the four manorial estates in the region that included Rensselaerswyck, Philipsburg Manor, and Cortlandt Manor. Such enterprises produced myriad products, including grain and corn destined for the slave markets in the Caribbean, and were a center for Black life in the Hudson Valley.[8] Before Isabel's departure tore a family and community asunder, the clash between the domestic struggles of the enslaved and the will of their enslavers fed a network of fear that bound elites together. Scholars have begun to examine the central place of borderland conflict in shaping colonial events like the Salem Witchcraft crisis.[9] What has not been fully understood is the wider regional context of the 1712 New York Slave revolt. By centralizing the actions of enslaved people in the upper Hudson Valley during the borderland conflicts of the early eighteenth century, the brutal reaction to 1712 emerges as one part of a regional white culture of fear stoked by the domestic narratives and political actions of bonded people.

Diana's archived story, like those of countless enslaved women across the Atlantic world, is jarringly brief, disjointed, and filled with violence. She neither speaks with her own voice, nor writes in her own hand. Her name never comes up in the hundreds of pages of Livingston personal correspondence. She remains, like Saidiya Hartman's Venus, frozen in death, on a document meant to be unsealed upon the death of her enslaver. To approach the fragments that bear Diana's name is as Hartman warns "to enter a mortuary."[10] What follows, consciously wrestles with the constructs used to conjure narratives of the past. Tropes of home, family, resistance, and mastery all emerge from archival remnants, to create a framework within which the past becomes somewhat more accessible. They are familiar tools used to conjure the worlds of northern elites, to understand the political, social, and cultural context of bygone eras. Few temporal signposts place Diana or her children in time, making one line in the 1721 version of Robert's will distinctive: "I do give and bequeath to my son Robert and his heirs and assigns a molatto Boy called Cesar about 17 or 18 years of age son of Diana."[11] Robert's numerous wills preserved Diana's motherhood as a commodity, one borne quite bluntly of rape and coercion. Bondage, not nativity mark the scant evidence of Diana's daughters—Isabel, Gritta, and Eva—who were parceled out to Alida's daughters, Margaret and Joanna. Robert carefully mapped her and other captive people's location "at the manor" to conjure the expanse of Livingston holdings and construct an ideal of home.

On October 18, 1710, Robert closed his letter to Alida noting that an enslaved man named Tam had been to visit his family (*zijn volk*), but returned "home" (*thuijs* [*thuis*]) to the manor.[12] Tam, who clearly had familial ties to the wider community, could have been the same man that he sued for theft and was ordered whipped in 1683, or perhaps he was his son who visited his parents still enslaved in Albany. Both Tam's journey and Robert's possessive claim to notions of home and family, were legible across the slaveholding Atlantic world.

Ben's fatherhood and relationship to Isabel emerges, not on a baptismal ledger but within the court record of an attempted murder case, where his lament that his daughter was sent out of the colony to serve within the household of Robert's eldest daughter Margaret, was coerced out of another man enslaved on the manor.[13] The Livingstons commanded a large enough workforce to put several girls through the intensive training required to be a lady's maid. Indeed, Isabel's two sisters may have been vetted in this way, and there was at least one other enslaved family named in Robert Livingston's 1721 will, who would have had girls eligible for such training. In the decades of childhood, such service could have kept Diana's daughters close for a time.

Discounting a brief time in New York City at the beginning of their marriage, Samuel's frequent absences kept Margaret in in the Hudson Valley, surrounded by family, where she occasionally conducted trade.[14] In 1708, while Samuel was away in England, news reports of the gruesome deaths of the Hallett family on Long Island led to fear of a wider conspiracy. They had been slain by an enslaved couple—an Indian man named Sam and a Black woman—who hacked all five of them to death with a hatchet. In response, the enslaved people were put to gruesome deaths: the woman was burned alive, while the man was forced to straddle a "sharp iron" in a gibbet until he died of blood loss and exposure.[15] Other enslaved people, branded as confederates were subsequently tried and executed. The regional tensions of war and dispossession coupled with the violence of domestic slavery filled the hearts of Northeastern enslavers with a common terror.

Such stories also reflected the seventeenth-century family and slaveholding roots that bound New England and New Netherland. The Halletts descended from Anne Winthrop, John Winthrop's niece who, in the seventeenth century, had been banished to New Netherland due to a marriage her community deemed bigamist. She and her new family had ultimately settled at the *Hellegat* (Hell Hole, also commonly referred to as Hell Gate)—a tidal area of the river between Manhattan and Long Island—after being granted refuge in New Netherland by Petrus Stuyvesant. They had enjoyed financial success, which translated into a household with a number of enslaved people.[16] The slain Halletts were distant cousins to the Livingstons (through John Livingston's marriage to Mary Winthrop) and would have lived a life familiar to Margaret. The murder itself was over domestic concerns—the enslaved couple was not allowed to go to abroad during Sunday services, an attempt to prevent them from intermingling with others. They attacked the family while they were sleeping, during the hours of the night when enslaved domestics were compelled to remain in a state of watchfulness lest their enslavers need them in the night. Neither the pregnant woman nor her children were spared. The dramatic story of the Halletts' deaths percolated into Boston's *News-Letter* through networks of New Yorkers such as paper editor Benjamin Coleman's friends, the Livingstons, and would no doubt have influenced how Margaret approached her own enslaved household staff. An enslaved maid that the Vetches had purchased from the New York merchant Thomas Wenham on Robert Sr.'s account in 1707 toiled for Margaret.[17] Perhaps latent fears of domestic rebellion stirred up by sensational news stories, influenced Margaret's desire to request a young enslaved lady's maid from the manor, someone she knew, whose parents were known and had grown up around Margaret.

By 1709 she moved with her family to Boston. In 1710, Margaret gave birth to a little boy whom she nicknamed Billy, and whom Samuel presented for baptism at the Brattle Street Church.[18] Despite Margaret's new arrival, her father Robert did not explicitly leave her family enslaved laborers in a will he drew up in 1710.[19] He did bequeath Isabel's sisters, Eva and Gritta, to her younger sister Joanna, who had yet to wed, ensuring that, at least for the short term, Isabel's family would remain intact. Isabel and Caesar were unnamed in the 1710 will. Thus, they remained with Ben and Diana, with the portion of the estate that passed to Margaret's mother, the elder, Alida. These concessions, which kept their family together, may have been won because of Diana or Ben's negotiations, considering their access to the Livingston family. But that world was tenuous, continually threatened by marriage and family as much as by border warfare, disease, and internal rebellion.

In 1710 the population of the manor dramatically increased when thousands of refugees from the German Palatine were settled on adjacent lands purchased by New York Governor William Hunter.[20] The massive resettlement ratcheted up regional tension with the Mohawk, who saw the population explosion as a very real threat that would further erode their holdings.[21] Robert, who had hoped to profit from the massive resettlement, instead became financially overextended. He passed the fallout to Alida and, ultimately, enslaved workers when, on July 21, 1711, he instructed Alida to stop baking bread for the Palatines because they were underwater on their settlement investment due to a shortage of labor. The shortage was caused because of the loss of Palatine labor due to conscription for Queen Anne's War, with Robert noting "300 Palatines must go to Canada" (*Moet 300 Palatijns naar Canada*). The Livingston operation baked bread to supply the troops in Boston and Albany. Robert's baking instructions were meant for the hands of three enslaved bakers: "Henrick and Thomas and Dego." Robert insisted that they continue to bake "hard bread" (*hart broot* [*hard brood*]).[22] Robert had been given a victualing contract by the crown to provision the new arrivals with beer and bread, a task that fell to Henrick, Thomas and Dego, and it was they who would have to face an increasingly disgruntled population when Robert pulled back promised supplies in a bid to save money.[23]

Such news was not taken lightly by the Palatine tenants who violently protested the reduction in their rations.[24] Adding to the tension on the manor, Robert viewed their labor in tandem with those he enslaved when he instructed Alida on September 21, 1711, to "let the negroes or Palatines be employed in" winterizing the manor's mill pump, emphasizing that "it is very important"[25] Alida responded to Robert: "Our negroes have no time" (*onse neggers hebben geen tijt*) to winterize the mill pump, because they had to harvest corn and wheat "and cut wood for the brewery" (*hackt het hondt* [*hout*] *voor de brouwerij*).[26] The Palatines were tasked with sapping the trees on Livingstons' property to provide pitch and timber for the crown. Unhappy with being settled on the less fertile Livingston lands, instead of the promised Schoharie tract that had formerly been claimed by Nicholas Bayard, but remained firmly within the control of the Mohawk, the Palatines were frequently at odds with the Livingstons, a simmering resentment that would break out into a tense armed standoff.[27]

Additionally, Alida wrote that she received a report from an Indigenous man that "8 Indians" were "shot to death" in local skirmishes during Queen Anne's War. By then, the Livingstons had an inflow of news from Native informants for at least two decades, as in 1692 when Alida mentioned "our Indians" (*onse wilde*) bringing war news. Such phrasing bandied in private correspondence reflected the possessive and bondage-evoking way that elites like the Livingstons began to refer to their Mohawk and Onondaga allies, although some Indigenous people living among the Livingstons were enslaved.[28] At the turn of the first decade of the eighteenth century, the manor and its environs had suddenly become a small society of its own. The transformation caused enough chaos to allow for an opening of escape for two enslaved people on Livingston Manor, who networked with a local Native contact—perhaps one of the myriad of people listed as dropping by the manor in the Livingstons correspondence—and escaped to French territory.

During the late fall of 1711, several people enslaved by the Livingston family ran away from the Hudson Valley toward Montreal.[29] Their escape would have been particularly perilous: they were setting out during Queen Anne's War, and if caught, they would be killed. An act passed by the New York Council six years earlier had proscribed death to self-emancipated people found more than "forty Miles above the Citty of Albany or above a Certain place called Sarachtoge" in order to ensure that "no Intelligence be Carryed from the said City and County to the French at Cannada."[30] Thus, when they set off away from New York, they understood that it would be either liberty or death. They were also facing the dense network of contacts at the Livingstons' disposal. Robert Livingston held family and business contacts that ranged from the Caribbean to New France, but the war limited the ability of those contacts to apprehend runaways using their usual means. By the time that a member of the Livingston family managed to locate them, they had reached their destination in New France and understood the power that they held as a result. Philip, the second oldest son who was managing the family's trade connections in Montreal, communicated as much to his mother, Alida, in a letter dated October 23, 1713, saying that he "could not convince our Negroes there to go home, they said they would rather stay there, & as long as they say that there is no likelihood of getting them from there except having the Indians steal them which will cost a great deal the Indians are quite afraid of the French."[31] Although Philip entertained the possibility of kidnapping as an option for forcing back into slavery the newly self-emancipated people he referred to possessively as "our Negroes," his first strategy was to convince them to go "home."

Philip Livingston, in his letter, written in Dutch, employs the verb *bewilligen*, which can be rendered as to convince or to persuade.[32] This was not the only choice at his disposal. He might have used the word *consenteerden* (to consent), which appears four times in 1581 in the Dutch Act of Abjuration

(*Plakkaat van Verlatinghe*), whose structure and appeal to the consent of the Dutch people under the rule of the Spanish king, later inspired the writers of the American Declaration of Independence (one of which would be Philip's own great-nephew Robert R. Livingston).[33] Philip's choice of "bewilligen" rather than "consenteerden" reflects the power that he still felt over the lives of the self-emancipated people. But no matter what meaning of the verb Philip conjured, the two newly minted denizens of New France held most of the cards. They had left Manor Livingston armed with a savvy knowledge of the Native-French alliances and political landscape. An abortive invasion of Quebec helmed by Samuel Vetch, a month before their escape, left the Livingstons allies and all of the bordering northern colonies on high alert of impending attack.[34] The self-emancipated people confederated with a "River Indian" to enact their escape, likely a local Mahican. Upon arriving in Canada, one sought asylum with the governor of Montreal, Claude de Ramezay. The escapees from Livingston Manor traded information for sanctuary. Robert was informed they "told ye french yt there was 8 more negroes from whence they Run upon wch ye french had sent" thirteen Indians to this "Place in Particular to take ye negroes." Robert was desperate enough to forget the threat of insurrection he had faced from the Palatines the year before and arm a troop of "20 Palantines" to "keep guard" on the manor for "5 or 6 Days" expecting imminent attack. But the liberation party was sent to Albany instead.[35] The enslaved people had escaped, not just for themselves, but so that more people might be liberated.

If in his private communication to his mother, Philip admitted that persuading the enslaved would be easier (or at least more economical) than brute force, his father made public steps to ensure that the choices for other enslaved people so inclined would be severely limited. Robert sent his letter noting the political maneuvering of his formerly enslaved people just four days before the outbreak of a series of fires in New York City set by enslaved people keen to revenge themselves on their white captors. One and a half years later, Robert Sr., in his capacity as the representative from Livingston Manor to the state council, passed an act that would "revive" and "continue" the earlier law that deemed running to New France a capital offense, despite an end to the hostilities between England and France.[36] Across the Northeast, slaveholders like the Livingstons shared a constant fear of rebellion and anxiety over the growing numbers of enslaved people that they bound to lifelong heritable service, a terror that was legible and popularized by print culture. It would ignite with the New York Revolt of 1712 and the public and draconian response to that event, but continue to smolder for years later. From Long Island to Manor Livingston, the first few decades of the eighteenth century brimmed with social and political unrest that was amplified by the anxieties caused by the daily insurgencies of slavery played out against the backdrop Queen Anne's War.

Insurrections

Networks of fear bound the region's slaveholding elites and fractured enslaved families. Sometime in the intervening tumultuous years, Robert Sr. sent Isabel to Boston. What could have caused such a devastating decision? The choice to send Isabel, a punishing blow to Ben, Diana, and their family, might have been a reaction to the 1712 New York Slave Revolt and a public power play to establish dominance over his slave population. In April 1712, a mixed group of enslaved New Yorkers from the Gold Coast and others whose Indigenous identities had been flattened under the term "Spanish Indian," enacted a secret rebellion by setting fire to a dwelling in the East Ward. When white men came to put out the flames, the enslaved attacked, killing nine and wounding seven. Of the thirty-nine enslaved people accused of participating in the 1712 slave revolt, twenty-five received the death sentence. Three of those were burned to death, with one man tormented over a slow fire for "eight to ten hours until dead and consumed to ashes," while another man named Robin was gibbeted until he succumbed to starvation and the elements. The rest were hanged. Nevertheless, sixteen men were pardoned by Governor Hunter, and others were let go on the promise of testifying against others.[37] Scholars have offered in-depth readings of the revolt's wider relevance, uncovering the importance of Gold Coast identities, Obeah, the racialization of enslaved "Spanish Indians," and the regional legal fallout of the events that unfolded during the spring of 1712.[38] But the domestic circumstances of slave owners and those they held in bondage can uncover how the event both united and destroyed families, and remained alive in the lingering fear of domestic unrest and regional borderland violence.

According to the Livingstons' correspondence, Philip narrowly escaped the violence. By April 1712, Samuel Vetch and Margaret Livingston entertained John Borland, a family business associate at their home in Boston, who brought news of the slave revolt. John relayed his meeting to Philip, writing that Samuel and Margaret "are all aware & much concerned for ye sadd acct of such a villainous Murther by ye Negroes & Indiens att York as are many of our people are yet [to] hear it I am Glad your Self & my [&] yr acquaintance escaped."[39] Slave revolt information first spread regionally within elite slaveholding networks before being disseminated in the newspapers they controlled.

News of Philip's narrow escape of the April 6 slave revolt traveled in just one week to Margaret and Samuel's household in Boston. From there, the heightened fear and suspicion caused by the event radiated to "many of our people" in Boston, which certainly would have included the Colemans, the Livingstons' contacts at the *News-Letter*. Two weeks later, the harrowing details appeared on page two of the *News-Letter* along with a description of the investigation and punishments. The article noted "about 70 Negro's in Custody," most of whom "knew of the Late Conspiracy to Murder the Christians." Six committed suicide, three were executed brutally—"one burnt, a second broke upon the wheel, and a third hung up alive"—and "nine more of the Murdering Negroe's are to be Executed tomorrow."[40] Such fear would have reverberated in Boston's slaveholding households who looked out and saw increasing numbers of enslaved African arrivals within the city.[41] In an atmosphere like that, what might Isabel have faced upon arriving in the Vetch household? A month later, when George Vane, a military engineer, sent an official appeal to London, he described Samuel's style of governing Nova Scotia as treating the inhabitants "more like slaves than anything else."[42] Robert Sr. was instrumental in passing the 1712 "act for preventing suppressing and punishing the conspiracy and insurrection of Negroes and other slaves," which allowed enslavers latitude in slave punishment just short of death.[43] Regional tensions influenced the style of mastery adopted by elites in both their domestic and public lives.

Insurgencies arose out of the domestic violence attached to enslavers family dramas, and the external pressures of epidemic disease. The choice to send Isabel to Boston might have also been solely borne out of need. In September 1712, Margaret became pregnant with her third child, but the nine months of her pregnancy were tumultuous. Sometime during 1712, Margaret's elder brother John began a relationship with a local Boston woman named Elizabeth Knight while his wife Mary was dying of breast cancer, an action that sent shock waves throughout Margaret's family.[44] Margaret's sister Joanna moved to Connecticut to care for Mary, who had just returned to New London after having undergone several surgeries in New York to fight her breast cancer—including the earliest recorded mastectomy in colonial America.[45] Joanna evidently traveled with one of her ladies maids—Eva or Gritta—Isabel's sisters, a blow that Diana would have felt keenly. In July 1713, Joanna complained that Boston was too expensive and she was "forst to sence Clod my neger gurel from top to Botham [forced to since clothe my neger girl from top to bottom]."[46] While she was in New London, Joanna would have also been served by the Jacksons, an enslaved family that toiled for the Winthrops. A then-pregnant Joan Jackson likely completed the dirtiest tasks, such as changing Mary's bandages or soiled linens. Mary's death in January 1713 did not send Joanna home, which would have reunited one of Isabel's sisters with their mother Diana, but rather on to Boston to help her sister Margaret whose baby was due during the summer of 1713.[47] Upon arrival, though, Joanna fell ill, her sickness coinciding with a measles epidemic that tore through New England, killing a considerable number of people. Against the background of this outbreak, Joanna reminded her mother of her promise to send a "negro maide" to attend Margaret's little Alida.[48] The request would have put Isabel directly in harm's way, as the measles epidemic disproportionately ravaged the enslaved population.[49] On August 2, Margaret's child named Mary was baptized in Brattle Street Church. Her death shortly thereafter could have been a result of measles, as both Alida and Billy came down with the illness.[50]

Joanna's request would have traveled along the New England postal route to Albany, likely passing through enslaved hands on its way to Manor Livingston. Perhaps Ben himself delivered the parchment, which held the future of his family in a hastily scrawled sentence.[51] Just two years earlier, on October 26, 1711, Alida wrote: "I could not get our Negro Ben to Tachkanick he is so scared and I am also very scared when the night comes but I hope God will keep and protect us" (*Ick kon ^onse negger ben niet naar tachkannick kryghen soo bangh is hij en ick ben ook heel bangh als de nacht aan komt doch ick hoop Godt zal ons bewaren en beschermen*).[52] Despite Ben's fear, his ability to refuse Alida's request also emerges from the interchange. He lived his life in daily proximity to the Livingston family and enjoyed some direct influence on them. But Joanna's request would change Ben and Diana's lives forever.

A culture of public violence against enslaved Black and Native people arose out of elite attempts to reconcile and control the small fractious diverse societies of laborers that worked in Northeastern households and lived on manorial estates. The Livingstons were inundated with the fear of violence. Tenant protests, war, and 1712's slave uprising had placed them on particular alert. So, when in the winter of 1714, Tom, a man enslaved on Manor Livingston, stood accused of attempting to kill his enslaver, Johannes Dijkeman, a tenant living on Robert Livingston's vast estate, Robert feared a deeper conspiracy. The constable brought Tom to be interrogated by Robert who did not question the captured man about the reasons he had attacked Johannes. Instead, he wondered "whether his Negro Ben or any other of his Negro's were Privy to this barbarous murder."[53] With that, the focus of the court fell on the domestic unrest within the Livingstons' household.

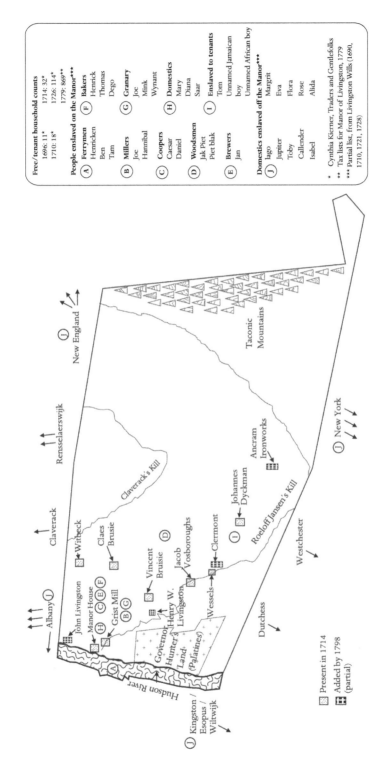

FIGURE 8. Map of Livingston Manor. Based on the John Beatty Map of 1714 and the John Wyman Map of 1798. From The New York Public Library.

CHAPTER 5

Robert feared a secret slave conspiracy stretching from the manor house to the tenant's residences, a fear that was influenced by Diana and Ben's personal loss, the events of 1712, the political instabilities with Indigenous groups in the area, and slaveholding among white nonelite tenants on Manor Livingston. The enslaved population on the manor was a mix of people from the Caribbean, the Gold Coast, enslaved Native peoples from various regions and others who likely descended from older regional populations. The previous spring, several tenants on the manor purchased enslaved people from the Livingstons. Robert scoured New York City's slave market, searching for people to send up the Hudson, but complained to Alida on April 21, 1714, that he could not fill the requests of his tenants Jeremie and Japick: "No negroes procurable who are worth a penny; perhaps they will come through."[54] Seven days later, he revised his assessment: "They are such beautiful negroes (*schoune* [*schoon*] *negers*) as I have ever seen & do not sell them for less than 50£, please, for they are worth it. One, the oldest, speaks good English, has been a sheep herder, was born in Jamaika; the other was born in his land, knows nothing but negro."[55] A month later the lives of the two enslaved people, whose names Robert did not note because they would be overwritten by whatever suited the fancy of their new enslavers, were in the hands of two of Manor Livingston's tenants, with another human being on order for a third. Alida wrote Robert: "Jeremie got the negro boy who knows English for 50£ he shall pay us when you come and the other was too small [for] Japick. Roelef has the small one for 50£ to be paid in winter so that for Japick you should send up a big one like Jeremie's."[56] By the winter three new captive people would, like Tom, toil for manor tenants.

Although he owned Tom, Johannes Dijkeman could not claim membership among the elite enslaved gathered to decide the fate of his enslaved man. He was a refugee, a tenant attempting to rebuild his life after escaping the Schenectady massacre three decades earlier. The census of 1714 indicated that Tom was the only enslaved person living in his household, a group that included Johannes Jr., one other man, and two women.[57] He was likely the only labor that Johannes could afford after rent and the supplies necessary to farm and lumber his plot located on Robert Livingston's estate.[58] Tom also probably lived with Johannes next to the falls of the Roeloff Jansen's Kill [present-day Roeliff Jansen Kill]. Johannes might have saved money by taking on an indentured servant or paying for temporary labor, but he opted instead to buy an enslaved man, a decision that likely also represented his social aspirations.

Johannes descended from a family who had immigrated to the colony from Amsterdam during the seventeenth century, while it was under Dutch control.[59] His father had been an official of the Dutch West India Company posted as the constable in Beverwijck before he had lost his position after suffering what was most likely a stroke.[60] After his father's death, Johannes's family was listed at Beverwijck's poor house and Johannes was indentured to his older half-brother Cornelius.[61] By 1688 he was married and had moved to Schenectady, starting out his life on a small plot of land given to him by his father-in-law, Cornelis Cornelissen Viele, who owned the local tavern.[62]

With old Dutch roots in the area, land, and a well-connected new family, Johannes Jr. was poised to begin his life with a solid start. With his relocation to Schenectady, he found himself in a new, primarily Dutch settlement. Its location placed it along central trade routes into Iroquoia. Several of its most extensive landowners had households with enslaved people and, though Johannes's was not among them, he would have come into daily contact with the enslaved.[63] That life was destroyed in the winter of 1690 when a group of French allied with Indigenous groups came down from Quebec, launching a coordinated attack that had been planned for Albany. At nightfall, as heavy snow was falling, the group did not follow their plan but, instead, shortly before midnight attacked Schenectady. Johannes benefited from the fact that his small plot of land lay slightly outside of town.[64] He and his wife Jannetje were part of a group of residents that escaped Schenectady with their lives, although the majority of Jannetje's family were killed during the attack. Among the sixty dead were eleven enslaved people.[65] Of those who survived, twenty-seven former denizens of Schenectady were taken captive, including five enslaved people. The story circulated throughout the English Atlantic world: from New England to Barbados alongside tales of slave conspiracies emanating from the British Caribbean.[66]

Johannes and Jannetje escaped with only the clothes on their back in the dead of winter. In the days that followed, the former young landowner appeared on a list of rations given to the refugees.[67] The haggard escapees had fled to Albany, over twenty miles away in snow that was described as knee-deep. It was perhaps in Albany that Johannes met Robert Livingston. Little detail of Johannes's life after the massacre remains, except that he was given a farm to tend at the border of Robert Livingston's property, but he was no longer an owner, he was a tenant. In 1715 he was also listed as being a captain in the militia.[68] As such, he would have had a crucial role to play as protection detail for Robert's property and would have been deployed for border defense against guerrilla fighters that made periodic sweeps of the area.[69]

Johannes Dijkeman was one of Robert's longest-term tenants with a prominent place in controlling the community of the manor. After the successful escape of some of the manor's enslaved population, and the 1712 slave revolt, Robert was out to set an example. Was there a slave revolt brewing on Manor Livingston? Perhaps. There was a plot on manor Livingston—at least in Robert's mind—and it hewed too close to the details of what had occurred in the city. Like the 1712 rebellion, this imagined action was sealed with a blood oath. This one did not follow the African brotherhood rights, but rather was the oath between father and daughter, a bond that mattered to Robert, and one that he fundamentally understood. Some of Manor Livingston's enslaved population—from the new people that Robert and Alida had procured for their tenants to the veterans of the Livingstons' slave ships—doubtless held African ethnic identities in common with the rebels in New York City. The popular named used to describe one such people "Coromantee" was as Walter Rucker demonstrates, not only the name of a Fante settlement but also of the trading Fort Kromantine on the Gold Coast that had been erected by the Dutch, and then taken by the English, much like New York. When the Dutch took it back again, Rucker notes, they renamed it "Fort New Amsterdam," evoking the connection directly.[70] Hudson Valley enslavers and slave ship owners like Robert enjoyed the profits of trade in human beings from the Gold Coast and the Caribbean, inroads such networked elites had followed since the Dutch era. In Robert's case, embedding himself in his wife's Dutch network had offered him entrée into the world of mastery and rule he so assiduously cultivated in Albany and on the Manor. The violence on the Manor had, like 1712, been trained against a nonelite slaveowner, and it would not have taken much of a mental leap for Robert to wonder if upon escalation the true targets would emerge as himself and his family. Robert need not think too hard to remember the confederates he formerly enslaved, who had made their own alliances with Indigenous peoples, to successfully seize freedom. Their ultimate designs had been for mass escape of several of Albany's captive people.

After interrogation, which included torture if it followed the patterns of other such ordeals throughout the Atlantic world, Tom gave up intimate details that reflected his relationship with or at least knowledge of Ben's domestic troubles. He maintained that neither "Ben nor any other of Mr. Livingston's Negro's knew nothing of his design of killing his Masters or any other Person but that he had done it alone and that Ben had never said anything but that he was sorry his Master had sent his Daughter to Mr. Vetch."[71] His testimony reveals the tension that simmered on Manor Livingston: the pain of an enslaved father, grieving the loss of a daughter who had been sent away, the fact that elites like Robert understood that breaking the familial ties of captive human beings could come with deadly consequences. It also reveals how little we can know of the events that unfolded in the final days of January. Forced to confess before his aggrieved enslaver and a room packed with white members of the community, Tom faced a prejudiced court but resolutely refrained from naming any coconspirators. Perhaps Tom's actions saved Ben's life and those of the other members of the enslaved community living on Livingston Manor. But Robert's punishment was severe. Tom was burned at the stake. The execution would have been a public affair intended to terrorize the manor's enslaved population, witnessed by men, women and children. Robert had an executioner brought up from Kingston for the occasion. Ben was never mentioned again in the Livingstons' correspondence, after Tom's trial and execution.[72]

After the opaque reference to Isabel's fate in Tom's testimony, she was last directly referenced in Robert Livingston's 1721 will. He wrote: "I do give and bequeathe to my Daughter Margaret wife of Coll Samuel Vetch & Their heirs and assigns a negro girl called Isabel Daughter of Diana."[73] By the time of this official recording, Isabel had lived away from her family for nearly a decade. In Boston, Isabel would have labored for little Alida: waking her in the morning, and attending her at the toilette, at social functions, and when her dress needed mending. She would have been required to maintain a neat appearance that advertised the Livingstons' status and would have been versed in the vagaries of decorum.[74] She was there as a servant and as a lesson, intended to teach young Alida the ways of slaveholding and how to properly be a Livingston. She would have accompanied the Vetches to Boston's Brattle Street Church and encountered an entirely different community of free and enslaved Black people, some of whom were baptized members of the congregation.[75]

Several clues within the historical record hint at more of Isabel's travail after the last explicit mention of her name in 1721. In 1717, Margaret decided to relocate to England and join Samuel, after enduring a prolonged separation following his departure in 1714 for London to get back his appointment as governor. She sold off most of her Boston assets to finance the trip and, although she brought Billy along, she left Alida behind with her family in New York. Samuel Vetch was mired in debt, and Robert continually hounded him for repayment of the funds he and Alida used to support their granddaughter. One ready way many northern colonials used to gain access to quick cash was the sale of human beings. Robert had planned to leave Isabel to Margaret as an inheritance and might well have sold her to square accounts. Joanna (nicknamed Naetye) informed her mother about the progress of just such a sale of an enslaved woman to the merchant James Bradish whose family had resident ties to Long Island and did business with Robert Livingston.[76] On June 7, 1722, the younger Alida (nicknamed Veets) was placed in charge of the woman's sale but was hampered by the enslaved woman's efforts: "Bradis said that the negro woman said she was always ill and he asked Veets about that. And she sent for the negro woman and he said he wanted to buy her; and she set a price for her, but the negro woman said she did not want to be sold and said what illness she had."[77] Was the woman Isabel? One detail in Samuel Vetch's account supports such a reading. Two months later, on August 1, Robert Livingston noted that he charged Samuel Vetch for: "1 negro girl of 5 years of age called Dina," who was given to Alida Vetch.[78] The little girl wore Isabel's mother's name and her age means she was born in 1717, while Isabel toiled for the Vetches in Boston, and at a time of financial stress. Isabel's fecundity may have marked her as salable, as it did so many other Northeastern enslaved women. If so, then Isabel fought hard against being sold away from the little girl that bore her lost mother's name. But, ultimately, like her mother, she was forced to suffer the violence of a child's loss to serve the Livingstons' needs.

In Robert's final will, Isabel's family was parceled out among several different households of Livingstons: her sister Grita (or Margarit) ended up with Gilbert; her half-brother Caesar, now a father of a boy named Daniel, was passed to Philip. Isabel, along with her mother, Diana, and sister, Eva, were unmentioned. Instead, Robert willed to Margaret "a negro man calld Toby and a negro Boy calld Calender, and also ye Time of a Palatin girl calld Anna Cogh w^h I have by Indinsure till she attain to nineteen years of age."[79] Born in the Hudson Valley, Isabel's archived story ends in Boston, willed to serve people who were familiar but who had effectively destroyed her family.

Defiance

Such tragedies made Manor Livingston a cauldron of turmoil. The tightening vise of enslavement during the eighteenth century reflected a culture of mixed-descent elite families in New York who celebrated their Dutchness by maintaining trading connections from the Dutch era, using the Dutch language and marrying within the group. These were not changes, then, that were at odds with traditions developed in the Dutch era, but rather were extensions of them. While Robert was away creating policy, which would shape the life, death, and surveillance of enslaved people, Alida, her sons, and the manor overseers were the ones who were engaged with daily managing manor Livingston's enslaved, indentured, and tenant population. Their names appear most frequently on the cover pages and throughout the family correspondence, joined by those of the major tenants who owed debts to the Livingstons and who served as overseers and workers. Such people have formed the bedrock of inquiries into the everyday working of Manor Livingston and the interethnic and class realities of the large estate. But another

FAMILY

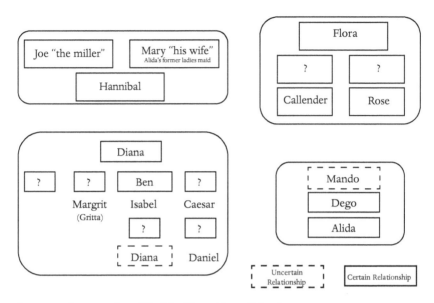

FIGURE 9. Reconstruction of Black families on Manor Livingston.

group of names also emerges from the family correspondence and wills: enslaved men, women, and children whose production was essential to the output of Manor Livingston and whose resistance served as a constant tension.[80] Some even held Livingston family first names or shortened forms. Flora toiled in the household, and her children Rose and Callender were listed as gifts in Robert's 1721 will. A valet named Dego and his daughter Alida toiled for the Livingstons, as did Joe (alternately spelled Syoo or Sjo or Jos), who worked as the miller, and Jupiter, Minck, Trebie, and Wynant.

On May 3, 1717, Alida gave Robert a report that presented an environment full of stress and disorder. Alida recounted the fears their Native ally and neighbor Katerickseet and his brother expressed of reprisals due to an Indigenous man that Alida and Robert's youngest son Gilbert held in bondage (*de wilt dat ghysbert has*) and would not sell back. A Native man had already come to Manor Livingston and girdled two trees, making deep circular trunk cuts that would kill them, and sending a powerful threat to the enslavers. Alida also complained about the state of "Minck's packages" and that Trebie's barrels were "too small," apparent sabotage that forced Alida to purchase bigger barrels from an outside vender, and delay the shipment.[81] These enslaved laborers from different stages of the production process worked together to resist by attacking the Livingstons' business. Enraged, Robert replied: "Joe, Mink, and Wynant are godless gits on earth" (*Jos mink & wynant zynd godtloos guyts op aarde*). According to Robert, the enslaved men had gone beyond slowing down work by purposely packing the flour in packages that were too small, but they had also included "coarse bran" with the corn so that the Livingstons would need to incur an additional expense to have it rebolted (resifted). Although Robert assessed their result as due to "merely slackness" (*alleen slattigheijt*), his choice to describe the three as "godless gits" (*godtloos guyts*) evidence that he certainly understood the purposeful intention of their actions. As for the flour, despite Alida's attempts to countermand the sabotage, they were still "2 barrels short."[82] While the enslaved turned to sabotage and work slowdowns to express themselves, Robert, like Jeremias before him, turned to early modern portrayals of the enslaved as lesser beings, characterizing them as "ungodly gits," childish tricksters who were firmly outside the church, and thus below Christians.

Such dehumanizing treatment marked the Livingstons' dealings with another enslaved couple. Joe "the miller" recurred in the Livingstons' correspondence beyond the mention of his actions in sabotaging the flour and corn. Documented family events do not frame the narrative of his life as they do the lives of his elite enslavers, although he was the only enslaved person listed as having a wife in Robert's many wills. His wife was Alida's lady's maid, Mary, and they had a son named Hannibal. Instead of being constructed out of the family events of marriage, birth, and everyday life, his life emerges as a list of problems posed to the Livingstons. On November 5, 1720, Alida included a report of Joe's illness to Robert.[83] Two years later his ill health was in her correspondence to Robert again, and on June 13, 1722, Alida reported that he was "so out of order" (*soo niet order*) for nearly a week. She explained that a tenant named Leendert Konijn carried Joe out of the forest "purely mad" (*puur dol*). She detailed her remedy, saying that she treated by administering a "vomit drink" (*spugen drank*) bloodletting and purging him.[84] With Joe sidelined, Alida put Wynant to the task of milling. Alida's practice of herbal medicine was a vital part of her daily routine, and the vomit drink may have been a famous Winthrop recipe called rubilia (salt peter mixed with antimony) that she received from her friendship with Fitz-John.[85] She frequently used such cures to self-treat illnesses, as for example, earlier in the letter she expressed her aversion for pills, opting instead to treat her swollen feet with sour buttermilk.[86] Mary, Joe's wife, would have been tasked with attending Alida's increasingly numerous ailments, for it was Mary who lived in closest proximity to Alida. Mary spoke fluent Dutch and could sew. Her first duty would have not been to Hannibal or Joe, but rather to Alida, and Mary would have had to weather an increasing degree of hostility from her enslaver.

Mary, whose job it was to always be near Alida, would not have been far when the herbal remedy was applied to Joe, a cure that was just as likely also a punishment. Alida did not describe Joe as sick but instead observed that he was "out of order" for "6 days," a condition that—despite his previous record of illness—she interpreted as "trouble" (*trobbel*). Such wording betrayed that Alida believed Joe might be feigning his illness and Robert's response, "I am sorry to hear that Joe has become so cunning (*so slim*)," supports that Alida was acting with a good measure of punishment when administering the "vomit drink."[87] This treatment would have racked Joe's whole body as unrelentingly as a flogging, and the bloodletting and purging would have drained his strength.[88] Such torture could have indeed made him come "to his sense somewhat" in Alida's mind. After ten days, she had clearly decided that Joe was sick and not resisting, when she closed her letter, "Sjo is reasonably healthy."[89] Bloodletting, purging and administering emetics to a "cunning" and "ungodly git" in the presence of his wife, was most likely a tailored response to perceived resistance.

Defiance could take many forms and some enslaved people augmented work slowdowns and disobedience by exploiting the physical revulsion that some elites felt toward the enslaved. While Joe labored in the saw and grist mills, an enslaved man named Tam ferried the bolted corn, flour, timber, and other goods for the Livingstons.[90] Tam utilized his physicality to directly resist not only Alida's management but the social identity of the family that she so assiduously cultivated. In the same letter where she described Joe's illness, Alida wrote that "Tam does not do anything and does not want to do anything and is fat and slick (*vet en gladt*). He wants to keep his letter himself, he said, or he will do evil. I am afraid he will do something evil—set something on fire." Alida looked externally for support, turning to a "High Dutch woman" on the manor who "has had him for 4 days, and she did not get it sorted. She says additionally that he might be willfully doing it in order to get away. Have him sold or sent away."[91] Tam was not the only member of the enslaved community at Manor Livingston to offer resistance, a fact that Alida alluded to when she said that she was having "trouble enough here with our people" (*hier trobbel genoeg met ons volck*), but his was the only anecdote that she chose to include in her correspondence with Robert. She used the word "*gladt*," which has been translated as greasy by other scholars, but also carries the dual meaning that he was slick, or sly, someone who could not be trusted. It must be noted that Tam's actions were filtered to Robert through not only Alida's perception but also that of the "High Dutch woman," a woman (likely a Palatine) who lived either on the estate or nearby to whom Alida outsourced Tam's surveillance. She also had a vested interest in projecting a

CHAPTER 5

particular image of the manor operations. Alida wanted Robert to sell Tam or have him sent away, but regardless, a year later, Tam was still enslaved on the manor tasked with ferrying goods such as lumber, rum, and gunpowder up and down the river and, according to Alida, still resisting. By 1722 he was likely sold away (or had even died), because his name was crossed out in Robert's will.[92]

One man who attempted to escape from the manor was met with violent death. On April 22, 1721, Alida wrote Robert in Albany from New York City while she and her granddaughter were visiting. Alida still received a steady stream of news from the manor, which she had left in Gilbert's hands, a decision she likely regretted as things had already begun to fall apart. Gilbert allowed neighbor Tobias ten Broeck to accompany the land surveyor without Robert's express consent—a significant breach in the protocol as nothing was more important to Robert than maintaining his massive landholdings.[93] He had also lost an enslaved man: "Our Gysbert's negro had run away. Yet they caught him again [and] beat him very much, and in 10 days [he] died from disorder" (*onze gysbert negher was wegh gheloopen doch ze hem weer kreghen sloeg hem heb'n heel veel en in 10 docghen uijt beordigheit gestorven*). The man's harrowing death, which Alida noted only because Gilbert "then suffered so much damage by it" (*en he toen soo veel schod [schade] door*), was at the hands of the patrol—whose captain, Johannes Dyckman, still resided on Manor Livingston—and in direct compliance with the law passed by Robert, which made running away a capital offense.[94]

Some enslaved people turned to mitigation and everyday survival to endure the perils of enslavement. Out of all those enslaved by the Livingstons, Dego's name appears with most frequency and for the longest duration. Although he was described as laboring in the bakehouse with Palatines in 1711, by 1717 he piloted the Livingstons' sloop down the Hudson. On November 16, 1717, Alida notified Robert that Dego was waylaid by a daylong rainstorm, which caused him to reroute to the Esopus (Kingston) where he was waiting to find transport down to the city.[95] Several weeks later, Dego was on the move again, sent down to New York to toil for Robert.[96] By 1721 he was listed in Robert's will as being a father to a little girl named Alida.[97] Was her name a choice, an appeal to make her sale a little harder, or was it compelled by the Livingstons as a show of fealty or even complete mastery? That same year, the elder Alida wrote to Robert: "Give Deko your old hat if it is outdated."[98] The reason for the gift is unclear. While enslaved domestics were often clothed in the old apparel of their enslavers, it arguably could have been a gift given to commemorate years of service as a valet. The gift also communicated Dego's place in the world, for the hat was not new, but old, not his own, but his enslaver's. In August 1722, Dego was aboard a ship that transported the governor, William Burnett, with whom Robert was actively trying to curry favor.[99] Dego's duties afforded him considerable freedom of movement.

Even those who did not defy their enslavers could be subjected to abuse and limitations. After that mention, Dego's name abruptly disappears from the Livingstons' correspondence for four years, save for one letter. On March 10, 1724, Joanna's husband, Cornelius van Horne wrote his father-in-law Robert Livingston a letter which, uncharacteristically briefly covered the family's intricate trade dealing, though he did offer space to mention that "only two or three vessels arrived from Curaçao and St. Thomas" and that returns for Robert's flour, corn and butter were down.[100] The rest of his letter concerned Robert's claim on Dego. A Londoner, named Thomas Cardle claimed that he owned Dego. Thomas recently returned to Long Island, after a between "15 and 16 years" stay in England. In the intervening time, he claimed to have loaned Dego to Mr. Falconer who then subsequently sold Dego to Robert because he was in "want of money." Cornelius believed Thomas's claim to be strong enough to council his father-in-law to "Ceap him Home as Much as possible," a change of mobility that would have drastically altered Dego's life. Cornelius was highly motivated to support his father-in-law's claim to Dego, as he stood to inherit both Dego and his daughter upon Robert's death. Dego was effectively subjected to house arrest.

Dego's life of ports and waterways changed suddenly with the threat of capture by Thomas Cardle. Robert's granddaughter, Alida Vetch, wed Stephen Bayard on March 12, 1724, in New York, just two days after Cornelius warned Robert of Thomas's claim on Dego.[101] The chaos of wedding preparations was arguably just the sort of opportunity that Thomas was hoping for "to send up a cupple of men by Land in order to Decoy and Delude" Dego "away from" Robert or to "take him by force when at a Distance from home." There would have certainly been opportunity. After the nuptials, Alida Vetch moved into the Dock Street house her grandfather offered as her dowery (the same one he had purchased from his betrayed friend William Kidd) with her new husband, who was the grandson of Nicholas Bayard and Judith Varlet and great grand-nephew of Petrus Stuyvesant. The marriage united the Livingston and Stuyvesant-Bayard dynasties. Little Diana would have traveled along with her as part of Alida's dowry. Dego would have normally piloted the sloop on such an occasion. Cornelius believed that even the close family associate Rip van Dam, of New York, might use the opportunity to capture Dego, but he promised to "Inquire further In the Matter" and then to "advise" Robert "by the first opertunity or as soon as I knew the certenty."

CHAPTER 5

Thus, shut away, Dego's world shrank to the Dock Ward property. Stephen, whose family had forged slaveholding ties throughout the Atlantic world, was quickly incorporated into the Livingston family's slave dealings. By November 1725, just one year after becoming Robert's son-in-law, Stephen informed Robert of the death of half of the enslaved people on the ship *Onckell Philips*. The slave ship's name *Onckell* evoked the double meaning of *onkelijc* or "bountiful," conjuring a Dutch linguistic heritage and the more familiar and family-evoking *onkel*, or "uncle" to English-speaking ears. Stephen blamed a shortage of food and provisions for the human losses and because they went "trough the fatigue of a 17 weeks Voyage obliged to Divide their bread 14 Days—before they came in; Each man then having 12 Bisketts for their share & Just so much meath Lft as served them the Day they came in."[102] Dego, always in close proximity to his enslavers but now unable to travel as he once could, would have likely had to suffer the angry conversations of his enslavers who mourned the loss of profits rather than human beings.

Meanwhile on the manor, while the captive people on the *Onckell Philips* were dying in the middle of the Atlantic, Alida demanded that Robert sell her ladies' maid Mary. He responded: "I am not minded to sell Mary under 70 pounds—and [for] cash. I do not know yet how to get a negro woman who is able to do housework and who has command for the language (*Ick niet gein negrin noch to kopen die huys werk kan doen en die Taaal heft*). Let us first try to get another, else we might be in want."[103] Hannibal and Joe were listed alone in Robert's final will, evidence of the violence and forced loss of a mother, wife, and lover. They were not the only ones. Flora and Diana only appeared in relation to their parceled-out children, and not as part of the bequests of the Livingston households. Dego's daughter, Alida, was also missing from the final will, her loss a death, whether to sale or the grave.

Dego remained with the Livingstons, as Thomas Cardle, consumed by debts, eventually committed suicide in prison—"in the hole" (*in't gat*) is written the lower right margin of the letter.[104] With their remaining years on earth, the Livingstons would mark the passage of Dego's life by the labor they could extract. On May 17, 1726, Robert wrote to Alida that he expected Dego would bring a weathered saddle to be repaired in New York.[105] A few months later, Alida tasked Dego with taking their broken buccaneer gun down to Robert in New York to get it fixed (*Deko heft[heft] de boeka[-]nier om te laete maken*).[106] But such proximity to the Livingstons invited censure as well. On May 20, 1726, Robert wrote to Alida complaining in the left margin of the letter's first page that those enslaved on Manor Livingston were still sabotaging the flour and called them "our mischievous people" (*onse ondeugende volk*). He assigned Joe the task of overseeing these laborers, expecting the enslaved miller would do this after his own work was completed; Robert instructed Alida to "let Jos see to it afterwards" (*laat Jos daarna bekijken*). He reserved his outrage against Dego for the main body of his letter. Robert grumbled that Dego "bought a leg of mutton for 3 sh. (shillings) 9d. (pence), without order, in the place of some ox-meat," continuing "had there been no ox-meat, I could have bought him a ham for the same amount of money. And now I must also buy him a ham."[107] Still upset, he scrawled in the right margin of the letter's third page, "I have not bought Dego a ham for I cannot spare 6d (pence) for a pound of ham for a negro. He can eat butter and bread until he comes home."[108] Despite years of unrelenting service, Dego was worth neither "a leg of mutton" (*een Shaps Beit* [*schaapbeen*]) nor "a pound of ham" (*een Pond ham*) in Robert's estimation. One wonders what awaited Dego when he arrived "home" at Manor Livingston.

The last mention Robert made of Dego in his correspondence was scathing. After asking Alida to send a "Spanish chair" from their own collection to give to Cornelius for his writing desk, he complained that he had not received news of their creditors or progress reports from Albany about his political efforts. Chafing at living so far away from the political center of the colony, Robert asked both their vendor and Dego for the intelligence but ended his discussion derisively, writing: "The shipper and the dumb negro Dego do not know anything and say nothing" (*Het Shipper ende Domms Negir Dego Wedten nirgens oft, en zeggen niets*).[109] "Dumb negro"—the same phrase Jeremias van Rensselaer applied to his despised enslaved laborer was joined by "cunning" (*slim*), "godless gits" (*godtloos guyts*), and "slick" (*gladt*) to form a constellation of pejoratives that elites like the Livingstons, locked into a cold war with their enslaved people, regularly used. But Jeremias, who dwelled on the individual slights of enslaved people, never used group language, possessive or otherwise, uncovering that much had changed in nearly a century. The Hudson Valley's enslaved populace were politically savvy and used the instabilities of the borderlands, mitigation, work slowdowns, sabotage, escape, and their own physicality to challenge their captors. The Livingstons never used the term *family* (*gezin* or *familie*) when referring to the enslaved in their correspondence or wills, although they did for themselves and their local coterie of friends. Instead, they used the term *our folk* (*onse volk*) for the enslaved, substituted their households as "home" (*thuis*), allowed enslaved people access to their own families only on sanctioned excursions. They possessively referred to those they held in bondage as "our negros" (*onse negers*) or obliquely evoked dependence with "our Indians" (*onse wilde*). Violence on the manor, however, was both public and intimate—directed at enslaved people and their closest kin.

Dego's voice remains silenced. No known account of his life exists written in his own hand. No towns or monuments wear his name. His daughter Alida's life likewise disappears into the tissue of the past, a stark contrast to the narratives of those who held them in bondage. The Livingstons cultivated their image and maintained their trading networks by beating, burning, trading, and bequeathing the lives of those enslaved among them. The violence of that rupture remains.

The stories of the enslaved offer an alternate portrait of the Northeastern merchant families. Robert's final will ensured through entail that the manor would descend to Philip and "the male heirs of his body carefully begottin in Free Tail for ever, not to be by him or his heirs sold or alienated in part or in whole."[110] But in the preceding paragraph, even before ensuring the future of the estate lands, Robert gifted Philip "Ceaser and his Son Daniel," passing down the third generation of Diana's children. While Robert's family was centered on the upper Hudson Valley, it was cross-colonial in nature, with members shifting locales throughout the Northeast to support growth in trade or kinship. The people whom they held in bondage were caught up in these transitions. Caesar and Daniel may have remained in the Hudson Valley with Philip, but Isabel was forced to relocate to Boston with Margaret, and other enslaved people were sent to far corners of the Livingstons' familial empire.

Insurrections exacerbated this trend, with elites increasingly viewing "onze neggers" with suspicion after the 1712 New York Slave Revolt. Tenants and other nonelite whites were caught in the middle of such tension—not elite themselves, but still attempting to carve out mastery over their own lives, environment, and enslaved people. Elites seeking to send a message of dominance to the community used their legal power to make examples of the enslaved of nonelites—as Robert did to Tom earlier in this chapter. Nonelites, like Johannes Dyckman, could then find their own efforts at mastery overwritten, though they remained a crucial force of daily enforcement and control. Throughout the first decades of the long eighteenth century, elite families like the Livingstons traded, married, and grew across the Northeast in pursuit of their ambitions, but were themselves hounded by fears of violence, rebellion, and insurrection, and these compounding forces upended the lives of those they held in bondage.

CHAPTER 6

Market

Creating Kinship-Based Empires United by Slaveholding (1730s–50s)

By the middle of the eighteenth century, orchards and fields dotted the landscape of the Out Ward, evidence of a production cycle that began under Dutch rule a century earlier. By then, the pear tree planted during Petrus's lifetime, would have netted nearly a hundred harvests for the bowery. The majority of the land owned by free Black people had decades earlier been swallowed up to expand elite white families' property footprint, though a few families managed to hold onto their houses.[1] But not everything had changed. Enslaved laborers still brought produce to bustling marketplaces where traders of every walk of life mingled, shouted, haggled, and bartered. Such markets could not be confined to "the lower end of the Wall Street, near the East River," but spilled into the "houses, outhouses & yards."[2] There, such enslaved Out Warders would have seen slave traders selling human beings and encountered other enslaved people who sold "Boiled Indian Corn, Pears Peaches, Apples and other kind of fruit," as side hustles, grasping any available opportunity to grow their meager resources.

Gerardus Stuyvesant, Petrus's grandson, spied danger in their numbers. Not the danger of conspiracy but of contagion. On August 20, 1740, presiding over the Common Council as deputy mayor, he passed "A Law to Prohibit Negroes and Other Slaves Vending Indian Corn, Peaches or Any other Fruit within this Ceity." Ostensibly alarmed by the "great Numbers of Negros, Indians and Molatto Slaves" who traded in the city, Gerardus and the council

CHAPTER 6

FIGURE 10. Cross section of Stuyvesant pear tree. On August 20, 1740, while Gerardus Stuyvesant served as deputy mayor, he and the other assemblymen introduced "A Law to Prohibit Negroes and Other Slaves Vending Indian Corn, Peaches, or Any other Fruit Within this City." The law linked such enterprise to "encreasign if not Occasioning Many and Dangerous Fevours, and other Distmpers & Diseases" in New York City. Perpetrators were ordered "publickly Whiped" at the "Public Whipping post of this city at the Discretion of the Mayor." Image courtesy of the New York Historical Society.

blamed these traders for "Encreasing if not Occasioning Many and Dangerous Fevours, and other Distempers & Diseases in the inhabitants in the Same City."[3] Lawbreakers would be subjected to whipping at the "Public Whipping post of this city at the Discretion of the Mayor, Recorder & Alderman." Despite a veneer of concern for public health, Gerardus and his compatriots sought not to cease but to corner the trade. They excepted enslaved vendors "Coming to Markett from the County or the Outward of this City by Order of their Masters or Mistresses."

For such regional elites, public displays of mastery over markets and enslaved people were crucial to their wider ambitions. Four summers before the passage of the council's law, in the Dock Ward, two Black men toiled as part of the crew that constructed the *Oswego*, a ship owned by Philip

Livingston and his sons. The Livingstons planned for the ship to travel the world, trading goods which included human beings. Ships like the *Oswego* were constructed and commissioned even as news of slave rebellion and fears of conspiracy poured into New York harbor carried by ships from across the Atlantic world. Between 1729 and 1740, Livingston-owned ships imported 238 documented people into New York.[4] Slave trading and the profit gained from enslaved and bonded labor underwrote elite expansion into worldwide markets during this period. Their vessels bore monikers that traced the reach of their family's dynastic ambitions. They actively built an Atlantic world replete with floating Oswegos and Rhode Islands that were no longer tethered to the geography of the Northeast, but rather traveled with the family as part of their evolving bid for a kinship-based empire.

Control

By the middle of the eighteenth century, many wealthy Anglo-Dutch families had publicly eschewed "Dutchness" for a generalized regional elite status. While their letters were only rarely written in Dutch, the language remained prevalent in certain areas and in the spoken language of a number of enslaved people across the region.[5] Despite such changes, elite Dutch-descended families maintained some ties to the Dutch colonial past. The diversifying interests that characterized elite Anglo-Dutch families' portfolios did not entail any lessening grip on the enslaved, but rather an increased commitment to the expansion of slavery. The Bayard and Stuyvesant families' reach extended far beyond the island of Manhattan as they continued to be a major regional presence, maintaining their considerable landholdings in Hoboken and Kingston, areas with sizeable enslaved populations. The Bayards and the Livingstons had confederated together by marriage for a decade. Alida's husband, Stephen, continued to promote the slave trade work he had previously done for their family when Philip took on the mantle of "Lord of the Manor" (the first of the Livingstons to consistently style himself using the title). The two men co-owned the ships *Francis* and *Byam* which traveled from Antigua to New York with sixty-one human beings between 1730 and 1731.[6] Meanwhile, the Bayards' Maryland branch benefited from a centuries-old formally Labadist network. Couple James and Susannah Bayard enlisted the slaver Joseph de la Montagne to trade in human beings between Barbados and Maryland.[7] Susannah's stepfather, Henry Sluyter was part of the Bohemia community's leadership, a group which counted Nicholas de la Montagne, Joseph's father and the son of Johannes de la Montagne, as well as Samuel Bayard, James's father. Her co-ownership signaled the continuance of an active female presence in the family slave trade.⁸ But even as the Dutch language faded from the tongues of such moneyed colonials, they continued to intermarry those whose lineage dated back to the Dutch era and to own and traffic in human beings.

The Livingstons plied old trade routes that had been enriching the broader family network for generations. Curaçao remained a vital port of call in the Livingstons' portfolio, and while the port's importance as an exclusive slaving depot to the northern colony had faded with time, merchant ships would not fail to bring up several enslaved people to trade along with the tea that they purchased from the island.⁹ On January 30, 1739, Pedro de Wolf, the family's Amsterdam factor, wrote to Robert Livingston, updating him on the conditions of trade in Curaçao.¹⁰ In a series of letters sent during the late summer of 1740, Philip Livingston wrote to Robert Jr.: "I hope that the Duty of Some of the Negros be savd if any become. I could sell severall young negros now."¹¹ Three days later, he followed up with Robert Jr, writing, "I wish you could Engage some trusty Capt who goes to Curaçao to bring some tea."¹² Smuggled Dutch tea and the trope of slavery would in later decades come to define some family member's protest rhetoric.¹³

The Livingstons and other Northeastern trader families would connect their profits in human beings to the broader world market. While a portion of the grain and bread produced on Manor Livingston was earmarked for Curaçao, Jamaica would quickly emerge as their key West Indian market for luxury goods and enslaved people.¹⁴ During the summer of 1732, the Livingstons traded fifty men women and children from Jamaica to New York aboard the *Katherine*. Additionally, they imported goods totaling more than 76 pounds, among which included a box of China and three large bins of China Dishes.¹⁵ Another ship, named the *Jamaica Packet*, arrived in late October 1734 with a "cargo" that included casks of rum and three enslaved people.¹⁶ While such people were often sold out of the New York warehouse by Robert Jr., who resided in the city, the manor house was sometimes used as a staging ground for sales. On July 14, 1735, Philip complained to Dirk van Veghten Jr. that he had sent "a negro boy which Johnathan Wheelor promist [*sic*] to take down to the Manor, and so did Swits, but they have both deceivd me in it. I suppose we shall not gett a chapman for this boy being very Lean; he has been sick, and is on his recovery."¹⁷ The boy likely hailed from Jamaica as Dirk was Philip's partner in the Jamaica trade, where they "sourced" most of the human beings they intended to sell. He was likely sent up to New York by Philip with the hopes that he might have more success selling him among his neighbors or in Albany rather than New York. On November 27, 1739, Philip instructed Robert Jr.: "When you have opportunity send the remainder of my flour & bread to Jamaica Curaçao or where you think it will render the best acct meet ye quickest sale and remittances."[18] Black servers would present food on China dishes and the manor's enslaved workforce would harvest and mill flour to provision the Caribbean.

During the 1730s Nicholas Bayard added sugar refining to the family's trading ventures, diversifying his Out Ward–based grain exports to the Caribbean with a product whose raw form was harvested by slave labor. Other New York merchants quickly followed, including the Van Cortlandts and Livingstons.[19] Such refined sugar would sweeten teas and the fruit pies made by the pears, apples, and peaches of the Out Ward, Long Island, New Jersey, and Hudson Valley orchards.[20] Just as the trees themselves served as markers of claimed and colonized land, so too the products made from their bounty would evoke a cultural hearkening back to a remembered colonial past.[21] Such elites made a show of brutally executing any enslaved person who targeted their profits, as was the case of the execution of a man named Jack in Ulster County, who was burned alive for "Burning a barne and a Barrack of wheat."[22] New York's provincial elite expanded their wealth through commodities, exploitation, and death.

But New York's most powerful families also broadened their influence through mass communication, drawing for ever-expanding audiences the social and racial tropes they had cultivated for a century. William Bradford's *New-York Gazette* was founded in 1725, and its back pages ran advertisements for a myriad of products including human beings.[23] On October 1, 1733, New York merchant Jacobus van Cortlandt ran an advertisement for Andrew Saxon, a man he described as "a tall lusty fellow" and "very black," who fled from his Dock Street home with a "broad-Axe" a "two-foot rule" and a "Howell-hovel," equipped with training as a "carpenter and a cooper."[24] Two days later, Samuel Bayard's name appeared in a runaway slave advertisement, as the New York contact for would-be slave catchers sent on behalf of "Robert Piersen of Notinham near Tentown" to apprehend "a Negro man named Jack." Such notices would be continued in the *New York Weekly Journal*, edited by Peter Zenger. Bradford's former apprentice and onetime business partner, Peter had emigrated to New York as a child along with his widowed mother during the Palatine resettlement in 1710, before quickly being apprenticed out to the printing business. By the 1730s, he opened his own rival paper, which became a key conduit for news and controversy in the city, providing an outlet for regional information from Manor Livingston in the same way that the *Boston-News-Letter* did at the turn of the eighteenth century.[25]

Just as the Bayards were doing in New York City, the Livingstons sought to expand their own trading portfolios, family influences, and physical footprint in the Hudson Valley. Robert Sr.'s eldest surviving sons settled on landed estates of their own. Even Robert's youngest son, Gilbert, ended up on the massive Beekman lands in Kingston with his marriage into that family. Robert Jr. (who came to be termed Robert of Clermont in later histories) inherited the southern part of the manor and erected a stately house he named Ancram, evoking his father's Scottish birthplace. He would eventually come to rename the house Clare Mount and, after the destruction of the original house during the American Revolution, its successor was called Clermont. Robert Jr. did not abandon the name Ancram, and used that name for other projects, blending the family's European origins with enslavement, just as his father's choice of *Onckell Philips* for a slaver had done a generation earlier. The Scottish identity the two brothers conjured, during a time when Scottish ports spewed slaving voyages, would become the primary identity assigned to the Livingstons in later histories. On November 18, 1741, the *Ancram* arrived from Jamaica, carrying three enslaved people aboard.[26] The name Robert Jr. chose for the ship evoked his father's Scottish birthplace as a floating statement of mastery, one his elder brother could not control. And yet the two brothers' aims were intertwined. Philip had been given charge of the ironworks business from his father, who had only begun to scope the project; *Ancram* ironworks would ultimately grow it to profitability. White laborers of varying degrees of unfreedom, in addition to a group of African-descended enslaved laborers, toiled in the Ancram ironworks.[27] The Livingstons' entry into the iron market must be viewed within a broader perspective: their Schuyler cousins in New Jersey were also heavily involved in copper and silver mining, and the turn was part of a diversification strategy that other elite families like the Rhode Island–based Browns pursued.[28]

Three generations of Livingstons—Robert Sr., brothers John and Philip Sr., and Robert Jr.—all imagined a manor workforce of mixed labor where enslaved workers—while not, on the surface, strictly needed—were nevertheless a vital part of their business plans. Their wide-ranging family and business contacts would have afforded them numerous models of ironworks worked solely by enslaved labor, had they chosen to go that direction. The first of such ironworks were begun in the Chesapeake at the turn of the eighteenth century. Indeed, one scholar has argued early success turned most southern ironworks solely to enslaved laborers and "helped to establish slavery as the dominant labor system within most antebellum southern industries." In middle colony ironworks, enslaved labor was deployed precisely to "discipline white waged workers."[29] Robert Sr. and John Livingston's own nascent designs at building a successful ironworks in their lifetimes were challenged by the continued state of warfare that marked the sociopolitical landscape at the turn of the eighteenth century. Robert Sr.'s tenants were continually being called up for service, first in King William's and then for Queen Anne's War, a destabilization that some of their enslaved people exploited to self-emancipate. Their heirs determined to profit from the dispossession of Indigenous peoples by dotting the landscape with markers of possession: grain, ironworks, tenants, bonded and enslaved laborers.

While working on the iron project, Philip was also scouting new markets. In December 1740, he wrote to his brother Robert Jr., that he was "very well Satisfied" that the "Ship Oswego" is "designed for South Carolina and Amsterdam." He explained that their Amsterdam-based factor Pedro de Wolf informed him that rice "was up again" and that he "expected it would advance higher." Philip hoped that it would not "be too late" to send the ship directly "to South Carolina in order to be one of the first Ships, in the spring, at Market."[30] In naming the ship *Oswego*, the Livingstons symbolically transported a landscape borne out of dispossession and brutality from the Northeast to the wider Atlantic World as a controllable commercial family product. The name also expressed an aspirational domination in a regional market over which they had little control. The trading post of Oswego had been created to directly counter French competition, but these English efforts also undercut Albany's fur trade market of which Philip was a major fur trader. But the ship represented Philip's diversification in slaving where he became a major actor both in the Caribbean and direct African markets.[31]

Such ships traced the routes other earlier vessels had traveled bearing enslaved Native people southward in the aftermath of brutal wars of dispossession in the seventeenth and eighteenth centuries. The Livingstons' confederation with the South Carolina trading firm Yeomans & Escott was one that connected their bonded world in the Hudson Valley to the misery of captured, brutalized, and exploited African and African-descended people in Charleston and Barbados. The thirteen years that the firm's trading business was advertised in the *South-Carolina Gazette* exposes the misery their "profit" was built on. In August 1732, they listed Rum and Madera Wines—most likely sourced from the Livingstons—alongside "a Negro house Wench and two children."[32] Two years later, in 1734 they advertised "a choice parcel of Gold Coast Negroes, just arriv'd." In the fall of 1736, they listed "a Small Parcel of likely young new Negroes lately imported," as well as choice "Barbados Rum, Lime-juice & Muscovado Sugar."[33] In 1739 they sold a "plantation belonging to Mr. *Lake*, on the Ashley-River, within 3 Miles of *Charlestown*," replete with "7 Negroes, among which is a very good Sempstress and House Negroes."[34] That same year, an enslaved man named Cato, who was enslaved nearby along the Ashley River, joined by other Kongolese enslaved people mounted an armed response against their enslavement. News of this uprising would be carried on such elite-owned ships, manned in part by African-descended people whose presence would fill New Yorkers with fear.[35]

On April 11, 1741, a year after he worked to pass a law to reassert a semblance of elite control over the bustling New York marketplaces, Gerardus Stuyvesant, acting in concert with his fellow councilmen passed a resolution requesting that Lieutenant Governor George Clark issue a proclamation offering monetary rewards for any white persons, enslaved person, and free "Negro, Mulatto or Indian" with information on persons of interest related to the series of fires that had broken across the city a month earlier. Clarke's own residence was completely destroyed, and popular opinion had shifted in support of a wide-ranging conspiracy.[36] For the enslaved, an added incentive of freedom was proffered with a cash reparation of twenty-five pounds, given to the bondsperson's enslaver.[37] As an alderman representing the Out Ward, Gerardus hoped to gain information from the population of enslaved and free people who lived near the bouweries.

A little over a month later, on May 30, the executions began with the public burning at the stake of Quack and Cuffee. After the men desperately confessed at the stake with a rowdy crowd pressing in, a dragnet resulted in the arrest of numerous enslaved people. The testimony of two enslaved men—Adam and Braveboy—extracted under coercion, placed much of the "frolic" at sites that would have been very familiar to Gerardus and his Bayard cousins. They mentioned "the new Dutch Church," the Out Ward's "fields," and a "free negroes' house in Bowery-Lane," which was located "between Mr. Bayard's land and Greenwich's land." Such sites were places where Black people congregated together to relax, dance, and mingle with one another.[38] The court was not interested in investigating these locations—while the Out Ward bouweries were sites of Black community life, they were also claimed land and, as such, were protected by the elites whose property had been wrested from the free Black community. Despite owning a considerable number of human beings, the Stuyvesant and Bayard families maintained their wealth in captive people and none enslaved to them were executed, though one was transported.

Philip Livingston remained detached from the hysteria gripping the city. This silence stood in stark contrast to the involved network of contacts and cousins living in New York: his friend and business partner John Cruger was mayor of the City of New York, his cousin James Livingston was called as part of the grand jury, and the enslaved man of another cousin, Captain Robert Livingston Jr. was implicated (Tom, who was ultimately sentenced to transportation). In a break with the events of 1712, fears of conspiracy did not sweep through his correspondence with family members at either the manor or Clermont in 1741. Instead, his focus was trained toward tending and expanding the Livingstons' cross-colonial trading connections, and if he harbored fears that those enslaved on Manor Livingston might thwart his designs it left no trace in his letters. Instead, as Craig Wilder asserts, Philip, his wider family, and merchant network invested in the slave trade.[39] The biggest crisis that appeared in Philip's correspondence was the May 9 news that his South Carolina contact, Gabriel Escott, died after having gotten sick in Barbados on a business trip, an event that delayed the sale of the Livingstons' wine.[40] Meanwhile, Philip was obsessed with the ironworks as a retirement project, writing to his son, Robert, during the summer of 1741: "I hope to live more at my Ease and have more time to Enjoy my Brook and find and lay up an Everlasting treasure."[41] Philip held plans to develop the estate into a vision of landed leisure: "I wish you would inquire for Some Timothy Seed & Clover seed I intend to make a fine English Farm at Ankram."[42] Despite his "ease" and vision for a "fine English Farm," Ancram would develop in the midst of a Hudson Valley riven by tenant uprising and slave resistance. The Livingstons may have claimed the upper Hudson as their domain of mastery where they could pursue diverse economic interests, but slavery remained central to their pursuits.

Factors

The global reach of these families was also underwritten by the forced labor of subjugated family members. By the middle of the eighteenth century, the Livingstons sent their grain milled by enslaved workers, iron forged in part by enslaved smiths, and Madeira wine in wooden "pipes" made by Black coopers to global markets. Caesar, Diana's son, and Isabel's brother, who had been bequeathed to Philip by Robert Sr. nearly two decades earlier, had been working as a cooper on Manor Livingston. Caesar was a vital member of Philip Livingston's business empire. For every good listed in Philip and Robert Livingston's correspondence—for flour, corn, molasses, and rum—Caesar's labor would have created the wooden containers that stored them. He had learned his trade well, as Philip Livingston grudgingly conceded by noting, "He is a good working fellow." Caesar had lost much. His family had been scattered across the Northeast. His mother, Diana, did not appear in the list of enslaved people parceled out among the Livingston children, and thus could have died or been sold. His half-sister, Isabel, had lived out her life in Boston and was either sold or had died, given that she too did not appear in Robert's final will. Caesar's own white father's identity remains shrouded in mystery, but could well have been one of the Livingston sons, given the timing of his birth and the fact that Robert Sr. was in Europe at the most likely times of conception.

A few months after the collapse of the Livingstons' South Carolina contacts, the *Oswego* netted a shortfall. Philip used the loss as a teachable moment for his adult son, Robert: whom he counseled not to "murmur" and "grumble," but rather "patiently Submitt" to the will of God. Such pious suffering, Philip hoped, was not without reward, but rather the catalyst for future blessing. He framed Robert's trading ventures with religious imagery and presented them as a "Just Endeavor for ye future." In the following paragraphs, he turned to a discussion of Caesar, who either consciously or unconsciously emerged as the very antithesis of submission. He was according to Philip, "discontented," displaying "wimsecall humors" and acting "quarlesome."[43] These attributes are the very opposite of the sober submission that he wished for Robert to embrace. That he was relying on gossip about Caesar's actions, admitting "the fellow *I hear* is discontented" offered him no cognitive dissonance.

Caesar had earlier requested to be "sold out of the Country," an appeal that could suggest a personal tragedy.[44] Caesar had been listed as the father of a little boy named Daniel, whom the Livingstons owned completely. There is no record of his fate. Caesar was also ostracized from the community of Manor Livingston's enslaved people. Philip noted that "he has been troublesome & quarrelsome with our Negroes."[45] The details behind the strife in the enslaved community are lost, but it was enough that Philip sent Caesar down to New York and counseled that Robert "sell him" or "send him to Madera." Failing that, he told Robert to "put him on board of any vessel at what you can agree for [several] months." Robert was clearly in no hurry to comply with any of his father's suggestions, and Caesar remained with him by the time that his father wrote of the *Oswego* and his continuing plans for Ancram, as Philip was clearly responding to an earlier letter from Robert arguing for retaining Caesar when he responded: "I can't advice you to keep ye Negro Ceasar." Philip had planned to "put out" Caesar "to a Smith" so that he might labor at Ancram, but never entertained allowing Caesar to stay with Robert on a permanent basis: "Try this fellow, how he may prove and then Send him after or sell him."[46]

Philip posited "Madera" as the location for the "discontented" Caesar, one that would have taken him off the coast of Africa and far from all he had known and loved. It was where several of those enslaved accused of conspiracy and sentenced to transportation had been sent.[47] Madeira was organized around one of the oldest, brutal sugar slave regimes in the Atlantic world. But Philip's desire to send Caesar to the island—and the indication that it was offered to Caesar as a choice—hints at a possible familial relationship between the two men. Philip and his by-then-widowed elder sister Margaret imported wine from Madeira—the only Albany merchant family to do so— and arguably he had plans to install Caesar as a kind of contact on the island.[48] Philip trained each of his sons with specialized skills so that they might serve as family contacts in a truly Atlantic empire.[49] If Caesar had requested to be "sold out of the Country," then going to sea would allow him to get away from the suffocating reality of Manor Livingston, the place where he spent his childhood but had lost his family. He could have already spent some of his time as a cooper on Philip's local ships because Philip advised Robert, Jr. to essentially hire him out by putting "him on board of any vessel at what you can agree for [per] month." Caesar's future was debated, like that of Andries nearly a century earlier, by two people with power to change his circumstances completely. His protest was juxtaposed against the religiously infused business identity Philip hoped to instill in Robert Jr. The banishment Philip planned for Caesar mirrored the exile Robert had imposed on Isabel, and Caesar's son would, like his father before him, feel the pain of lost family.

The shift to such diversification was regional, mirrored by the Schuylers in New Jersey and the Brown family of Providence, Rhode Island. Philip Sr. likewise envisioned a labor organization at Ancram that used enslaved laborers: "I want to buy two negro boys of 16 or 18 years to put to a Smith or a hammerman."[50] Such a smith would have worked in sweltering conditions, in front of a blast furnace, manipulating molten metal, the purest of which was poured into castings with the less pure made into iron bars, known as "pig iron."[51] These bars would be transferred to the second forge at Ancram. The hammerman at this second forge would then be tasked with refining the pig iron bars.[52] These men would have spent hot days marked by the sound of the percussive hammer powered by the Livingstons' watermill, blending with the sounds of their own efforts to work the melted pig iron bars—called the bloom—into iron quality enough to fashion the Livingstons' export products.[53] The Livingstons' laborers would have kept a gang-style yearlong schedule that closely hewed to the type of labor arrangements found on a Chesapeake plantation devoted to staple crop agriculture.[54] Arguably Philip hoped that among the African captives that his slave ships brought back were some that brought knowledge of metalworking, though such a person would have also received instruction from white forge men as well.[55] Skilled African and African-descended artisans, who had forged and fashioned the gated mansions of Charleston, had been brought along with Barbadian planters to South Carolina. Such considerations likely guided Philip's investment in slave-trading ventures.[56]

White supervision was the norm when it came to enslaved ironworks. Just as tenants on the Livingstons' estate were also enslavers, ironworkers could have had their own enslaved people who worked alongside them at Ancram. The specter of violence would also rule the lives of enslaved workers on ironworks across the region. The iron that they manipulated was shaped into shackles, manacles, and other devices designed to torture the enslaved into submission.[57] The enslaved presence could also tip the balance of power toward business owners in regards to white labor. Iron entrepreneurs in New Jersey and Pennsylvania used enslaved labor to solve the labor shortage, thus creating a surplus within the free labor population, which weakened white workers' bargaining position.[58] Some of the iron produced on mid-Atlantic and southern forges was destined to construct slaving vessels owned by Northeastern elites.

The Livingston-owned *Rhode Island* departed alongside the *Storke* in November 1748 bound for the Gold Coast and their missions were entwined from the start.[59] Although the Livingstons, like most Northeastern merchants who invested in the slave trade, focused on lighter vessels to cut the time across the Atlantic, they settled on a strategy of clustering such slave voyages together to mitigate the risk. The *Rhode Island's* name conjured the family's dense political and personal connections to the colony. In 1732, a decade before the *Rhode Island* departed from New York bound for Africa, Philip Livingston Sr. presided as president over a committee of twenty commissioners drawn from New York, New Jersey, Rhode Island, and Nova Scotia.[60] His sons Philip and Henry had slave-trading deals with the Channing and Lopez families of Rhode Island.[61] Perhaps the ship's name had been meant as an enduring legacy to Philip's own political accomplishments in negotiating the colony's southern and eastern boundary lines, or an homage to the family's Rhode Island slaving associates, one that hoped for continued collaboration. Family, slavery, and diversified interests emerged as a regional trend that was part of claiming the land and expanding a newly generic elite power that was intended to be legible far beyond the Northeast. Although situated by later scholars as provincial elites, these Northeastern families of traders had global ambitions of mastery.

Global Identities

Northeastern slaveholders' households, warehouses, wharves, and slave ships were never distinct spaces; they served as nodes of connection and expanding familial identity that superseded imperial allegiances. Before the slave ships returned to New York, Philip Sr. would be dead, but not before ensuring a smooth transition of his lands and operations, which would be doled out to his sons whom he had meticulously placed across the Atlantic world. In 1748 Philip left "unto my said son Robert Livingston Junior his Executors and assigns my Negro Man Tom and his wife Mary and my Negro Man Benjamin, Twelve horses Six Gildons, six mares, six melch Cows, Six Sheep, Six hoggs my Chariot and Gold watch." He further gave his eldest son Robert the remainder of my "slaves," and to his wife, Catrine, bequeathed "the half of my silver plate, three negro men & three negro women."[62]

While Tom, Mary, and Benjamin, were named in Philip's will, other people held captive by the Livingstons appear fleetingly in his personal correspondence. John Livingston (Philip's third son), described the gathering of his parents, cousins, and extended family on the Manor, a portrait that included a family moment between an enslaved couple in the postscript: "People Came her[e] to call Jack our Jenna's husband."[63] Benjamin drove Philip's sled between Albany and Kingston and, on one occasion, was sent to "accompany" Philip's daughters after their visit to the community.[64] Of those named in Philip's will, Tom would appear in the family correspondence with some degree of frequency. At a time when the family turned to slave trading, their correspondence also evidences the indispensability of Tom's function within the family in the wake of Philip's death. On March 6, 1749, overseer Petrus de Witt closed his favorable report to Robert Jr. concerning the ironworks: "I now send Gysbert Voogterhoneth & Thom the Negroe in order to fetch the Boate, about which I have wrote Mr. Peter at Lange. The Grist Mill begun to Grind last fryday."[65] Tom would navigate a world of ever-proliferating Livingston-owned slave ships that would have been different in degree but not character to the one inhabited by Ben and Dego a generation earlier.

By the summer, the *Rhode Island* had returned to New York, full of sick and dying captives and one-half of the enslaved people and goods traded by the *Storke* on the Guinea Coast. On July 29, 1749, Robert Jr. wrote to Petrus DeWitt of the voyage. The *Rhode Island* had disembarked the African coast with 120 captive people aboard, a number that could have only been accommodated by the tight packing method. Robert Jr. noted that the additional days at sea caused the deaths of thirty-seven peoples whose corpses were thrown unceremoniously into the sea, or "bumped." One more person did indeed die of the voyage, which brought the death toll up to thirty-eight human beings.[66] Their deaths moved Robert Jr. only as financial loss.[67] It was one that Robert Jr. was determined to turn to his favor and make "a savering voyage" out of one that had seemed to him at the start, "golden." Ignoring the weak condition of those survivors who made it to New York, Robert Jr. was eager to have his overseer inspect and price the arrivals. While he had planned to purchase several people for the manor, forwarding Petrus cash for that reason, he also was pricing them to sell in the northern New York Market. He had his eye on one particular captive whom he described as "a negro man I judge not to be above 20 years of age," whom he priced as "worth £56" and instructed Petrus not to sell him for "under £54."[68]

Of those remaining that were not sent up the Hudson to Manor Livingston, they were put up for sale, and advertised in the July 31, 1749, edition of the *New York Evening Post*: "A Fine Parcel of Men, Women, Boys and Girls Slaves, imported direct from Africa, to be sold on board the sloop Rhode Island, at Mr. Scuyler's Wharf."[69] While the fates of those captives lay off the weathered pages of the Livingston Family Papers, Tom's life appears in fragments and passing references. On his trips up and down the river, Tom was given cash to purchase provisions and might have also ferried the captive peoples up the Hudson. On June 12, 1751, Peter van Brugh opened his letter to his older brother Robert Jr. noting, "Your Letter by Tom I have rec'd," and closed it with a supplies list given for the journey, including two line items amounting to six dollars and labeled "Cash to Tom for Provisions"[70]

The New York traversed by Tom was much different than the city experienced by the Livingston brothers. When the Livingston-owned *Rhode Island* arrived in New York, two years after its first African voyage, on Monday, May 27, 1751, it was the day after Pentecost. In its holds were sixty-nine enslaved men, women, and children. Tom left an upper Hudson abuzz with Pinksterday celebrations, to make the journey down to New York. The traditionally Dutch holiday had become an important cultural event in the Black community, though as Andrea Mosterman notes, this was also a time of surveillance.[71] When Tom reached the city, carrying a letter meant for Peter van Brugh, did he pass the *Rhode Island* or witness the men, women and children who had survived the voyage only to be sold? The specter of the trading vessel shaped and determined the lives of enslaved people, existing as a conjured threat, or a place of work. It functioned within the entangled lives of those enslaved by the Livingstons to shape the terms by which they worked, struggled, lived, and died.

At the beginning of the eighteenth century, white Livingston children settled as slaveholders in Connecticut, New York, and Massachusetts. By midcentury, Livingston heirs migrated southward but still maintained their ties to the Northeastern regional elite. Henry, the youngest of Philip's sons, relocated to Jamaica and conducted the family's trade from the island, eventually becoming a plantation owner on a large scale. He maintained friendships with slaveholding peers across the Atlantic world. On February 26, 1752, his brother, Peter van Brugh, noted to Robert that their sloop the *Diamond* "coming from Jamaica bound for South Carolina in the windward passage near Cap Nicholas she had above £3,000 Jamaica money on board £200 of which was shipped by Brother Henry for his Carolina friends."[72] While Henry created a Caribbean life, he—like Balthazar Stuyvesant had nearly a century earlier—became an Atlantic arm of his Northeastern family's slaveholding dynasty. By the time of his relocation, such Atlantic identities were commonplace. But Henry would ultimately attempt to expand his family's aspirations beyond the Atlantic world.

On October 24, 1753, Henry faced John Channing and Walter Chaloner in a Jamaican court. The two men accused Henry of shorting them "£2,470 current money of Jamaica" in the form of the lives of "80 Negroes" who had never arrived to be "disposed of at the Island of Jamaica."[73] Where did these enslaved people end up? Had they been promised and then sold in New York? Had some of their number been part of those enslaved on the Livingstons' many holdings in the Hudson Valley and in New York City? Were some included in that number as a punishment for running away? Henry spent most of his adult life away from New York in Jamaica, but he would be far from the only Livingston to have active ties to the island. In 1750 and 1751, Henry's brother, Philip, was the principal investor in the slave ship *Stork*, which landed in St. John, Antigua, after leaving Anomabu on Africa's Gold Coast. A month before, Henry stood in court in Jamaica to answer for shorting his Newport business partners the lives of eighty people. On July 13, 1754, Henry angrily wrote to the Rhode Island owners of the slave ship *Elizabeth*, which had arrived in Kingston on July 7, characterizing the sixty-two enslaved people who arrived—fifteen men, nineteen women, seventeenth boys, and eleven girls—as "no better than refuse."[74] The majority of the ship's inhabitants had been sold to Dias and Gutteres, enslavers in Kingston, Jamaica.

Henry's ambitions for a global family presence went far beyond the older markets plied by his grandfather and colonials like the Stuyvesants. By 1764, Henry was trading in Aleppo, Syria, in an attempt to expand his sugar trade ventures from the Caribbean to the Middle East.[75] That same decade he purchased a plantation in Jamaica along with his nephew, Philip Philip which he named Aleppo. Upon settling in Jamaica, Philip Philip married Sarah Johnson, who had been born in St. Andrew's parish on the island, and by early 1770, he acquired the Friendship sugar estate and another he named Albany Estate in Saint Mary's upon the death of its previous owner George Paplay Esquire.[76] At his death, Henry Livingston had settled in the Parish of St. Mary's, Jamaica, and was a large slaveholder with landholdings in New York and Jamaica. In his will dated 5 February 1772, Henry left all his "lands and

CHAPTER 6

> Hamlet, Billy, Little Quashey, Simon, Ned, Yorkshire, Otho, Coom, Quaco, Diego, Guy, Purrier, Mars, Jamaica, Giddy, Quashy, Quaco, Quaco, Coom, Cuffee, John, Calamantee, Quashy, Simon, Dan, Rueban, Phore, Attagua, Hero, Benjamin, Joseph, Dick, Frank, Ishmael, July, Mercury, Cupid, Bacchus, Beaus, Toribble, Bristol, York, Dublin, Cork, Oxford, Windsor, Kent, little Simon, Sancho, Cuffee, Sam, Bull, Jack, Gunner, Jeimy, Quamino, Dover, Peter, Ned, James, Scipio, Cuffee, Quashey, Totness, John, George, Cudjoe, Quaco, Jemmy, Jupiter, Adrien, Apollo, Bronoco, August, Chelsea, Hercules, Dick, Femola, John, Peter, Simon, Billy, Quamin, Perrin, Duke, Towerhill, Tom, Alexander, Johnny, Cudjoe, Pollydore, Pallanhie, Joe, Aporto, William, Prince, Ventura, Caesar, Quamina, Quamin, Britton, Mintas, Otter, Love, Margarett, Daphny, Maria, Priscilla, Judy, Sunury, Sylvia, Sarah, Yahow, Old Phebe, Old Doll, Old Diana, Cretia, Young Phebe, Benny, Dido, Phillis, Mary, Abba, Nanny, Isabba, Quasheba, Mintas, Joan, Mimba, Betsy, Nancy, Margritta, June, Violet, Hannah, Phillis, Flora, Diana, Phebe, Marinda, Celia, Rose, Molly, Quasheba, Fanny, Lucy, Cindah, Betty, Lilly, Pink, Ruth, Daisy, Prue, Juba, Venus, Daphney, Mimba, Nancy, Lucy, Quasheba, Chamba, Juba, Cuba, Cuba, Bess, Patience, Bech,, Katy, Old Kate, Savannah, Friday, Juba, Fanny, Lucy, Venus, Sabin a Eboe, Sarah, Dutchess, Rose, Phillis, Nanny, Molly, Linda, Mornimba, Hannah, Nancy, Katy, Regna, Mary, Grace, Congo, Sarah Creole, Sarah, Kelly, Quasheba, Chloe, Prince, Judith, Diana, Congo, Mimba, Candris, Mary, Quasheba, Myrtilla, and Elenora.
>
> …and the Issue and Increase of the Females of the said slaves born since ethe Execution of the said Indenture of Mortgage or such of them as are now alive together with the future Issue, Offspring and Increase of the Females of them…

FIGURE 11. Names of enslaved people listed on Friendship Indenture.

tenements, and all real and personal property in the Province of New York" to his brother, John Livingston, naming him executor. He left a "silver punch bowl," all "books and real and personal estate in Jamaica" to his nephews, the sons of John Livingston. Henry's last wishes also uncovers the extensive network of Livingstons living throughout the empire, including "John Livingston, son of Captain Gilbert Livingston, of Bermuda and Captain Muscor Livingston of Great Britain, mariner."[77]

By the middle decades of the eighteenth century the Stuyvesants would grow in wealth and power, expanding their regional influence through ties of enslavement. By midcentury, Petrus, Gerardus Stuyvesant's eldest, wed Margaret "Peggy" Livingston, and lived in an imposing hilltop Georgian mansion on Eighth Street. His business ties with his Bayard and Livingston cousins would include tracking down runaways and managing the sale of estates advertised with "negroes" and "negro houses," even throughout the Revolutionary War. Nicholas William, Gerardus's youngest son, established himself as a player in regional trade and educated circles. Possessing a degree from Kings College (now Columbia University), he operated a trading shop in the city, was a Trinity church vestryman and a mentee of King's College president Samuel Johnson.[78] He had spent time in Connecticut and maintained contacts in New England. He lived in a house in the city and was attended by a pregnant enslaved woman named Sarah whose family resided in Connecticut.[79] Like his great grandfather before him, he traded the lives of enslaved human beings to cement ties of friendship, networking with New England families such as the Willets that his ancestor Petrus had pioneered, and expanding his own ambitions. In 1765 he advertised a "negro wench and child" to be sold at his shop on King Street, along with a few Pieces of Plate.[80]

His cousins were united in similar purpose. In 1752 William Bayard posted an advertisement in search of a man demeaningly named Crook, who he described as "a likely Mulatto fellow" and estimated was twenty-two years old. William noted that he "pretends to be free" but wore signs of his subjugation including the detail that he was barefoot."[81] William's advertisement was meant to appeal to his network of contacts, and the entire region teamed with an interconnected kin network united in singular purpose from Maine to the southern banks of the Delaware. Yet, one practice that they had decidedly abandoned since the days of New Amsterdam was manumission of any sort. Instead, by the mid-eighteenth century, such elites were committed to closing off avenues of emancipation.

A month before William Bayard posted his advertisement, Philip Livingston was called on to witness the manumission of an enslaved woman named Ann. Her two hundred pound bond was paid, not by the wealthiest members of New York society, but by tradespeople—John Vanduersen, a cordwain, and Peter Burger, a cooper—in order to enact the manumission given to Ann as a stipulation of the will of Eve Surlock, a New York City tavern keeper. The exorbitant price was levied in accordance with the Conspiracy Act, which was explicitly laid out in Ann's manumission papers. The document promised that despite the payment of the extraordinary fine, if Ann did not "live or Reside according to the tenor Effect and true Intent and meaning of the said Recited act then the above bond or Recognizance shall be Void and of none Effect," a condition that linked her moment of freedom to Mayken van Angola nearly a century before. But while Petrus had wanted to keep Mayken's labor for himself, even as he agreed to emancipate her after decades of service, Philip and his ilk had no interest in profiting from Ann's continued bonded labor—they were there to enforce a race-based control that formed the foundation of their efforts to expand in a global market that incorporated slavery.

CHAPTER 7

Identity

*Navigating Racial Expectations to
Escape Slavery (1750s–60s)*

When a group of men escaped from Monmouth County, New Jersey, during the early summer of 1734, they set out together in a canoe, traversing the expanse of water that serves as the imaginary boundary between the mid-Atlantic and New England. Their lives each held separate and entwined geographies and genealogies, and their enslaver attempted to read their intentions like a map to aid in their capture. On June 24, 1734, Judith Vincent ran a runaway slave advertisement in the *New-York Gazette* that presented a portrait of three confederates with varied skills, a violin, and a canoe.[1]

Although the three surely pulled the oars together away from New Jersey across the sound bound for "Connecticut or Rhode Island," Judith had her sights trained on only one, "an Indian Man named Stoffels." He had a command of English and in his four decades on earth, had mastered a diverse set of skills, serving as a "House Carpenter, a Copper, a Wheelwright" and was even "a good Butcher." She offered to pay "forty shillings" for his capture and return in addition to "all reasonable charges." As to the others, she offered the barest of details. One of them was a musician who "plays upon the violin" and brought his instrument with him during the flight. The skills of the other remained undetailed in the advertisement, their names, and identities erased in favor of generic racial monikers "one being half Indian and half Negro and the other a Mulatto." Who they were is lost to time, but they certainly knew the route or the sea. They also had some familiarity with one another. The intimacies of their lives were deemed unimportant to their pursuer who intended only to track them down.

Uncovering networks that were by necessity either intended to be hidden or were not privileged in a historical record designed by those with vested interests to undermine such confederacies is a difficult endeavor.[2] Nevertheless, scholarly attempts at such reconstruction serve to uncover—however contingent—the lives of people discoverable only in such fragments. Struggling with recalcitrant sources is not only the hallmark of studies about the lives of the enslaved: women, the poor, children, and marginalized likewise present difficulties to any reconstruction of a past whose contours are reliant on available sources. Recently works have begun to question notions like what it meant to escape to "freedom" and the values that determined the lives and desires of eighteenth-century actors.[3] The multicultural social world of those enslaved within Northeastern family networks necessitates a reimagining of not only the social expectations of slavery but the shifting cultural experiences of the enslaved.

Enslaved people maintained a vast network of associations that created a geographical map of the broader region that crossed colonial boundaries. Scholars most frequently emphasize the disconnections of enslavement in the Northeast, but the region was knit together by connections held between the enslaved. Such avenues of cross-colonial networking within the enslaved community bore fruit: supporting freedom cases, regional flights away from slavery, and by creating identities that challenged the power of elite hegemonic ambitions. Mixed-raced members of elite networks presented specific challenges to the structure of slaveholding that shaped not just the southern colonies and the Caribbean but also the Northeast, challenging the gendered and racial underpinnings of enslavement, and uncovering the sexual violence of such networks.

Manipulating Identity

Knowledge of enslaved networks (as well as the desire to gather more intelligence on them) culturally united enslavers of different means. Nonelite enslavers expanded their dragnets through their association with powerful, elite families, who in turn expanded the reach of their slaveholding networks. Judith Vincent was a nonelite enslaver, and she was not isolated. She was embedded within a network of women who benefited from their proximity to Anna Pritchard, Petrus Stuyvesant's long-widowed granddaughter. By the time that she placed the advertisement, Judith had already been widowed once, had remarried the mariner Samuel Vincent, who traded in merchandise and enslaved people from the Caribbean to Perth Amboy, had at least one son named John by her first husband and a young daughter named Phoebe.[4] Judith appeared in Anna's 1759 will. Anna, who was the granddaughter of Petrus and Judith Stuyvesant by their son, Nicolaes Willem, left "Judith Vincent, of Monmouth County, East New Jersey, and her daughter Phebe, £20."[5] She also left a bequest to other elite widows, including Cornelia Schuyler (Alida Schuyler Livingston's great-niece by marriage and the granddaughter-in-law to Arent Schuyler.) Judith was one of a group of widows of varying statuses folded into the Stuyvesants' broader orbit.

Judith's life depended on the forced labor of others, which also created a forced intimacy and knowledge of the wider worlds of those she held in bondage. Stoffels was clearly indispensable. As a house carpenter, he would have maintained the house structure and outbuildings, an essential task.[6] Such woodworking knowledge complemented his skill as a wheelwright and would have made him vital to the household.[7] His skills as cooper would have supported any type of trading that Judith wished to conduct on her property in making casks.[8] But with this skill, he could have also been hired out to other merchants bringing in additional income for Judith.[9] As a butcher, he would have kept food on Judith's table.[10] Judith placed the advertisement highlighting clues that she believed would aid in the capture of the group of men. Stoffels's diverse set of skills would have distinguished him, as would the instrument of one of the runaway men but, alongside skills, she prominently highlighted race, language, and geography in her pursuit of the men.

Unlike Alida Livingston before her, Judith Vincent immediately widened the dragnet for Stoffels beyond her personal network to the readership of the *New-York Gazette* and posited that the three men were headed toward New England. Their destination could have been determined by Indigenous geographies as much as it was by the boundaries of European settlement. Rhode Island certainly seemed an odd choice for freedom, given Providence's prominent place as a center for the trade in human beings, and the colony, like New Jersey, featured a high proportion of slave plantations.[11] Likewise, Connecticut would have offered perils for runaway enslaved people, as nearly fifty years earlier, Alida Livingston had mobilized her own personal contacts to pursue an enslaved man who ran away in that colony.[12]

These inherent dangers suggest that such places were not the final destinations for the group. If they were making their way northward through Massachusetts and New Hampshire, then Fort Chambly in French territory offered a potential destination.[13] Traveling by canoe, they were comfortable on the water and could have headed for work on a ship, particularly if we assume they had other skills that would have made it easy to adapt to the life of a seafarer. Knowledge of the sea and tidal marshes could have offered the men a vital defense against any pursuers.[14] Although Judith did not provide any more specificity to Stoffels and his compatriots' identities beyond the generalized monikers of "Indian," "half Indian and half Negro," and "Mulatto," the men certainly held the asset of their own personal cultural histories as they ran. That Stoffels "speaks good English" suggests that another local language was his native tongue, an asset that would have allowed the group to fluidly converse across cultural boundaries. When they set off together, they encountered geography that would have been both familiar and wholly different from that experienced by Judith. Although scholarly treatments of the geographical and social world inhabited by self-emancipators largely privileges the unique understandings of their pursuers and enslavers, such sources can be read to reveal an alternate experience of the geographical avenues of escape and evasion open to the enslaved.[15]

The geography of the Northeast was connected by routes traversed by the enslaved that were created by navigating regional racial expectations and histories as much as physical environments. Six years after Stoffels and his compatriots ran away from Judith Vincent, on October 1, 1740, Galloway, a man enslaved to New York City leather dresser, John Breese, headed toward North Tarrytown, New York, and away from bondage. On October 27, 1740, his enslaver ran an advertisement in the *New-York Weekly Journal*, seeking his capture.[16] For an enslaved person, the route north from New York City was far from safe, as it took Galloway into an area marked by large slaveholding estates. As a stranger clad in a hodgepodge of clothing that included a "dark gray homespun Jacket," "a pair of Linnnen Breeches," and a pair of "new Shoes," Galloway would have seemed suspicious. Indeed, he was "seen and challenged at Coll. *Phillipse's* Mill," located in Philipsburg Manor.[17] Nevertheless, displaying a canniness that reflected a sophisticated knowledge of not only the geographical terrain but the expectations of his interrogator, he "escaped by asserting he was sent in pursuit of a *Cuba* Man Run away."

Constructions of social, ethnic, and racial identity were crucial to Galloway's flight. When his enslaver ran an advertisement in the *New-York Weekly Journal* twenty-seven days later, it included Galloway's ethnic identity— "mullato *Indian*"—the direction that he was headed "towards *New England*," his nativity—"born in the Fort at *Albany*" and that he "lived many Years with *Paul Richards*, Esq; some Years Mayor of this City." Galloway's life had been spent in the two urban centers of New York, learning the intricacies, networks, and expectations of slaveholding society. He had a command of Dutch and had lived "many years" encountering the elite of New York

CHAPTER 7

society, through his enslavement to Paul Richards. Galloway manipulated the expectations of his society to aid in his escape. In so doing, his flight illuminates the cross-ethnic and cross-colonial networks that made up the physical and social geography of those enslaved by elite Northeasterners.

John Breese clearly employed his network to gather the details of Galloway's flight. He maintained an ongoing enough friendship with Paul Richards that he named him an executor in his will two years later.[18] The advertisement gives no timeframe beyond "a long while" for Galloway's time spent enslaved to Paul, but the former mayor had been a slaveholder for decades.[19] Paul Richards was also deeply embedded in the slaveholding elite of New York. He served as mayor of the city from 1735 to 1739 and was succeeded by John Cruger. Paul subsequently served as a representative from New York in the Twenty-fifth Assembly from February 12, 1747/8 until November 12 the following year alongside Cornelius van Horne and Henry Cruger.[20] The representative from Livingston Manor was Robert Livingston, with Frederick Philipse and Lewis Morris representing Westchester. Paul's household also stood at the heart of the New York slave conspiracy, as his enslaved woman Maria was married to Quack, the man who allegedly declared his intention to burn the city down if he were not allowed to see his wife.[21]

Galloway could have spent much of his time working for Florah, John's wife. When John died, Florah inherited the Breese estate, along "with power to sell."[22] Flora passed on a thriving leather-dressing business to her son—who was still plying the trade twenty years later—leveraging skills that she either learned as a widow or gathered by co-running the shop.[23] Giving her such broad powers in the future of the business indeed argues that Florah had skills in her own right. Notwithstanding laws that made enslaving local Indigenous people illegal, the lines between bonded labor and enslavement were thin and deployed against Indigenous people.[24] If Galloway descended from one of the local Haudenosaunee peoples, he could have been familiar with leatherworking before being enslaved to the Breese household. Yet, this detail also includes a clue to the process of cultural alienation Galloway's bondage would have enacted on his societal identity. In Haudenosaunee societies, leatherworking was a female task, and thus Galloway's work within the leather shop—an inversion of gender norms—would have, like the work of male African captive people on the rice fields, enacted a specific form of social alienation.[25]

Galloway's broader regional map came from his earlier experiences and connections among bonded people and slaveholders. His life had not begun in New York City but, instead in Albany. He held onto that past in his knowledge not only of Dutch but also of the "Road to New-England," which led away from Albany. Although Galloway had endured the dislocation of slavery, moving from Albany to New York City, and changing hands from the political and merchant-minded Richards family to the leather-dressing Breese family, according to the runaway slave advertisement he had spent some time in New York. A member of Paul's household, he would have had daily interactions with Maria and known her husband Quack, as well as his childhood friend, Adam, the enslaved man of lawyer Joseph Murray.[26] He would have come into contact with many more enslaved people who served the elite politicians and families that frequented the Breese's tannery. Richards was among the elite slaveholding New Yorkers who sent his enslaved people to Elias Neau's catechism class.[27] If Galloway had been among them, he could have made useful contact with people who helped him hatch the specifics of his escape.

Galloway's escape route depended not just on understanding geographical landmarks of New York but the racial ones as well: it required he invent an enslaved "Cuba man" to evade capture. Elites across the Atlantic World employed Indigenous slave catchers, a reality that Galloway both noted and used to his advantage. Perhaps this is why he did not make for Quebec, where Haudenosaunee served as both slave guides and slave catchers, but instead took the road to New England. Perhaps he sought to establish himself as a leather dresser in Hartford or in Boston.[28]

Galloway was clearly running away from John's wrath. The advertisement noted that "whoever Secures the said Slave so that his Master or Attorney may dispose of him shall have *Forty* Shillings, Reward and reasonable Charges paid by." Eschewing the phrase "so that his master might have him again" for the more ominous "may dispose of him," John gave little doubt of what awaited Galloway, should he be recaptured. A year later, John was called to sit on a jury to decide the fate of Quack, Maria's husband, an enslaved man that Galloway and—through his friendship with Paul Richards—John had likely encountered on numerous occasions. Any familiarity he had with Quack—who protested his innocence—did not move John or the others who sat on the jury to mercy. On May 30, 1741, they convicted Quack of conspiracy and sentenced him to burn at the stake.[29]

John Breese's description of Galloway's escape route and strategies demonstrate that a skillful manipulation of environmental and social geographies, so central to enslaved escape plans, was to at least some extent understood by enslavers. The similarity and centrality of networks—between kin, friends and customers, religious and secular communities—was a language that both enslaver and enslaved held in common. Ten years later, a man named Tom ran away from the estate of Nicholas Everson in Perth Amboy,

New Jersey. In 1751, Nicholas posted a runaway slave advertisement, highlighting that Tom had a command of both English and Dutch as well as knowledge of a skilled trade—shoemaking—and a saleable talent—"can play well upon the fiddle."[30] Like Galloway before him, Tom planned to use a cross-colonial network and Native racial identity in his bid for freedom. He was described as "a mulatto Negroe" who "intends to cut his watchcoat, to make him Indian stockings, and to cut off his hair, and get a blanket, to pass for an Indian." He also "enquired for one John and Thomas Nutus, Indians at Susquehanna, and about the Moravians, and the way there." Tom's potential destination was advertised by his pursuing enslaver to aid in his capture, but it can offer a glimpse into the alternative geography that made up the landscape of his flight. He set out with not only a destination in mind but also contacts with whom he networked before crossing the border from New Jersey into Pennsylvania. Nicholas's estate was merely "two miles from Perth-Amboy ferry," offering Tom an opportunity to gather information from the multitudes of people arriving from New York. From there, Tom could have clandestinely followed the stagecoach route from Perth Amboy to Bordentown.[31] If he had the proper papers to travel, as some skilled enslaved people would undoubtedly have had, then he would have even been able to board the stagecoach unmolested. In as much as Nicholas's information can be trusted, Tom believed that he could convincingly "pass for an Indian."

Unlike John Breese, Nicholas Everson did not give specific details of where his informants caught Tom's trail, but the advertisement is not devoid of clues. Tom escaped from Nicholas in Perth Amboy. If Tom made his enquiries for "one John and Thomas Nutus, Indians at Susquehanna" before he left his hometown, he would have been able to access a local well of knowledge from those who could help him in his flight. The enslaved community in Perth Amboy was multiethnic.[32] In 1737 another enslaved man named Wan fled his Perth Amboy enslaver Samuel Leonard, with abilities that allowed him to cross not only colonial but cultural borders. Like Tom, he was a musician. Despite his enslaver's racialized presentation of Wan as "as black as most Negroes," he spoke "good English and this country Indian."[33] He was also headed for Pennsylvania. Tom's own destination of the Susquehanna, as well as enquiring for specific people by name, argues for familial or other close ties to Indigenous homelands of the Northeast. Moravian missions were a crucial feature of Nicholas' advertisement, and such missions were sprouting up in towns and cities across New Jersey.[34] Although Everson claimed that Tom was a "mulato" attempting to pass for an Indigenous person, Tom clearly had an inroad into Indigenous social networks that went beyond clothing. Moravians enjoyed such missionary success because they used Native missionaries as cultural go-betweens.³⁵ Perhaps Thomas and John Nutus were Native missionaries. If that was the case, then Tom could have learned of them from community members who frequented the shop and attended one of their meetings. Tom's flight, like Galloway's, shows that regional networks and geographies were as present as local ones for enslaved people.

If he followed (or even rode) the stagecoach to Bordentown, Tom could have caught a ferry from his last destination in New Jersey to Philadelphia. Everson pursued Tom for a year before resorting to publishing his search in the *Pennsylvania Gazette*. His posting suggests that his network of informants gathered the information about Tom in Pennsylvania. During his journey down the Delaware River, the ferry could have passed slave ships heading toward Philadelphia as well.³⁶ Upon arriving in Philadelphia, the urban environment would have aided in his attempts to shed his past.³⁷ Tom was not just in possession of the skilled trade of shoemaking—Nicholas noted that he was a "good" shoemaker. An Indigenous identity would have allowed him to avoid the racial antipathy that was directed toward skilled workers of African descent. But the Susquehanna and not a colonial city was Tom's intended destination. Tom's passage through colonized spaces toward the Susquehanna highlights the continued importance of Indigenous geographies to Northeastern enslaved networks and regional conceptions.

Tom's world was also shaped by contemporary demographic shifts, revolts, and slave ship arrivals, showing that enslaved networks, social circles, and geographic worlds were dynamic. Tom's past was not used to aid in his capture and thus is shrouded in silence. Were his parents descended from the group of enslaved people from Madagascar sold in 1683?³⁸ If the age Nicholas supplied was roughly accurate, then he would have been a young man during the slave revolt that broke out in Perth Amboy in 1734.³⁹ His bilingual abilities and cultural fluency point to a past rooted in the area, but the makeup of the enslaved population of Perth Amboy was changing considerably during Tom's lifetime. Although the period witnessed an influx of enslaved people from the Caribbean into Perth Amboy, there were also several slave ships destined for Perth Amboy from the "coast of Guinea."⁴⁰ Among those was the *Catherine*, a hundred-ton vessel with five mounted guns that arrived in 1731 and was co-owned by Alida Livingston's nephew, Arnot Schuyler (the son of her younger brother Arent who had settled in Bergen County) and New York trader, John Watts.⁴¹ Three years later, the *Catherine* arrived again in Perth Amboy, this time co-owned by more of Alida's family: her nephews Peter, Arnot, and Adoniah, as well as New York trader John Walter.⁴²

Perhaps it was the shifting demographics that offered Tom the opportunity for escape, and once he made it to the city, he would have been harder to track. The dragnet, widened by the reach of print culture, would have pulled in any man of African or Indian descent who met the physical description. Tom's life disappears from view—if it ever appeared as more than a negative of his enslaver's priorities—with the publication of the runaway advertisement. If Nicholas continued his practice of owning human beings after Tom's escape, that too is lost to the historical record: when he placed his estate of Chesequkes up for sale he did not feature it as having enslaved people or outbuildings, and by the time of his will in 1783, Everson did not explicitly mention any enslaved people as part of his estate.[43] One year before Nicholas Everson died, Moravian Indians near Gnadenhutten were attacked and massacred by the Pennsylvania militia.[44] The expansive geographies of enslaved people bound the Northeast together, offering an alternative map of the region that presents it as linked by the social, ethnic, and racial realities of bonded people as much as by colonial boundaries.

Fighting against the Networks

Archival records starkly illuminate the scope of elite slaveholding networks, and as scholars have shown, they are not just a record of what happened, but a part of the violence. Centralizing enslaved people as historical actors by reading such documents "against the grain" highlights the human struggles of bonded people underpinning the generational wealth cultivated by Northeastern slaveholding networks. Even partial reconstructions of the narratives of enslaved people sharpen a fuller picture of the varied human beings whose lives underpinned the wealth of Northeastern elites. Philip Livingston Jr. owned the *Wolf*, which was captained by Gurney Wall and set sail for the coast of Africa in 1749, an event that ran in the *New-York Gazette*.[45] On May 13, 1751, the *Wolf* arrived back in New York, and Philip advertised a "publick Vendue" to sell "a Number of Likely Negro Slaves."[46] His advertisement collapsed into "likely" the hopes and dreams, nightmares, and sufferings of the women and children who disembarked the fetid sloop, whose tight holds, chosen to maximize Philip's profits while minimizing his overhead, had offered them 112 days of torture.[47]

Some enslaved networks were forged by language and cultural affinities between captive peoples. Such confederations represent alternative maps of the region woven by landmarks of African belonging, not alienation. Two months after the arrival of the *Wolf*, Philip ran another advertisement, pursuing a man he described as "lately imported from Africa."⁴⁸ The man, with "His Hair . . . curled in Locks, in a very remarkable Manner . . . was seen last Monday on New-York Island, and is supposed now to be in the Woods near Harlem." He could not "speak a Word of English, or Dutch, or any other Language but that of his own Country." Newly arrived, he would have carried the still-fresh memory of the stench of the hold, and the chains that had held him. If he arrived on the *Wolf*, he would have seen numerous children die, their bodies full of worms.⁴⁹ The ship began its trade in Africa on November 15, 1749, and who knows how long the man was forced to endure the ship's coasting. Before the ship departed Africa for New York, a slave rebellion broke out on board. The memory of that event, although ultimately unsuccessful, would have lingered in the man's mind and could have encouraged his flight.

Despite Philip's contention that the man was unable to "speak a Word of English, or Dutch, or any other Language but that of his own Country" he managed to evade capture for a week without communicating in a European or Creole tongue. Slave ships arrived from the Gold Coast to New York with rapidity, and the man would not have been at a loss to find people taken from the Asante empire who were conversant in Anyi-Baule and Abrone.⁵⁰ Or he could have encountered others brought several decades earlier who spoke Asante and Fante, who would have been able to decipher shared words and phrases.

Gendered markers of belonging physically linked the cultural landscapes of West and West Central Africa to the geographies of the Northeast. Several months before the man escaped Philip's grasp, during the winter of 1750, a woman named Nell, who toiled for Robert James Livingston's household in New York, ran away. Robert James did not descend from the elder Robert and Alida, but rather from Robert's nephew, who had also immigrated to Albany following his uncle during the late seventeenth century. He subsequently married into the Schuyler family, beginning a pattern that would keep the cousins closely related for a century. Robert James placed an advertisement in the *New-York Gazette*, describing "a tall likely Negro Wench, named Nell, about 36 Years of Age . . . mark'd with nine Spots on each Temple, and nine on her Forehead."⁵¹ At some point in the ensuing months, Nell was tracked down and brought back to Robert James. During that time, did she encounter the man who was pursued by Philip? Perhaps as punishment for her flight, Robert James sold her away from the city to Isaac Kingsland, who resided in Bergen County, East New Jersey. If the move was intended to chasten her, it proved no deterrence, because by April 12, 1753, she had escaped again. On April 23, Isaac posted an advertisement looking for "a Negro wench named Nell, who formerly belonged to Robert J. Livingston, Merchant in New York; she is a tall slim Wench, has three Diamonds on her face, one on each side and the other on her Forehead."[52]

Read together the advertisements give some portrait, albeit distorted, of Nell. In Robert James's advertisement she "had on when she went away, a blue Penniston Petticoat"; during her second flight she took along "three Petticoats" with one described as "old" and "quilted" and the "other two homespun." "A short blue and white homespun gown" makes an appearance in both advertisements paired "with a short blue duffils Cloak." Both men described her as "tall" with Robert James offering "likely" while Isaac described her as "slim." Life for an enslaved person in rural New Jersey would have been one of want, and thus her frame, once "likely," was now hollowed out by the harsh work routines. They both noted her facial markings, a detail that argues for an African birthplace. Perhaps she had been brought into the colony aboard one of Robert Livingston's ships. Isaac Kingsland was willing to pay twice the bounty that Robert James had offered for her recapture. Nell's body was read by her enslavers as a map to recapture her, but her facial markers and three petticoats could also have gained her shelter and aid from others who read cultural meaning in the signs of belonging she carried on her journey.

Such social and cultural connections were used by an array of people entrapped within the Bayards' network of enslavement in New York. In 1749 a free Black North Carolina man named Simon Moore, who was apprenticed to a merchant named William Paxton, requested to be included as part of a crew on a sloop bound for New York.[53] Upon arriving in New York, he was captured and held as a slave by the sloop's co-owner, Samuel Bayard, as collateral against his business partner, William Payton, whom Samuel claimed had shorted him his payment. When in 1753, Simon faced the court in New York protesting his free status, he was a stranger far from anyone who might corroborate his story, challenging a powerful man with connections in the political and merchant slaveholding community and whose family roots dated back to New Netherland. Samuel Bayard's father had been a judge in New York City, and his enslaved man named Pompey had been convicted during the New York Conspiracy and sentenced to transportation, though Pompey protested his innocence.[54] Stephen Bayard, Samuel's older brother, dispassionately handled the slave-trading affairs of his father-in-law, Robert Livingston.[55] Samuel Bayard had the time, money, and resources to hold Simon Moore for life.

Although isolated far from home, Moore was not without defense. By mobilizing his own network, Simon Moore won the case against Samuel

Bayard. He secured testimony from the captain of the sloop, Captain Samuel Dunscomb, and a man named "John Brown" identified as "a Sailor." Samuel Dunscomb testified that "he well knows Simon Moor a Negro now residing with Samuel Bayard of New York Merchant, that he well knew him, his Mother and several of his Brothers in North Carolina and that they were all free people."[56] He named his place of indenture as Bath Town in North Carolina, and the man to whom he was indentured as William Peyton.

Simon depended on white testimony to verify his free status, but it was a testimony that he had to wait five years to receive. Nevertheless, the fact that his case made it to the court reflects that Simon mobilized far more than merely the word of the sloop captain. Did he network with other enslaved men on the dock to look out for Samuel Dunscomb's return? Did his family in North Carolina begin the search from Bath, asking about where their son and brother had gone? Simon Moore did write "to his friends in North Carolina for certificates of his Freedom," but the court official noted that he "never has received an answer."[57] Even in the face of frustration and failure, Simon was able to extricate himself from the clutches of Samuel Bayard, but not before spending five years of his life enslaved to the connected New York merchant. By 1758 he was back in Beaufort County, North Carolina, purchasing three hundred acres of land along with his brother Abram "on the south side of Terts Swam and Durham's Creek."[58]

Simon's voice was distanced from his testimony, as were those of the men he amassed to testify on his behalf. Their statement was written down to be delivered later, and evidence of the interaction and assumptions of the scribe remain on the surviving record. The transcript of Simon's testimony verifies this process, indicating that "this informant says he was born at Bath Town in North Carolina, the son of Abraham and Mary Moore, that his Father was Mother was a free Woman and born so, that his Father was not."[59]

The clerk initially wrote that his father, rather than his mother, was free and then later crossed it out. *Partus sequitur ventrum*, which based one's enslaved status on the free or enslaved status of his or her mother, made such a slip potentially costly indeed. It is unlikely that Simon would have made this mistake in his testimony, as the free-born status of his mother was his only claim to freedom. Thus, its addition begs the question, was the subsequent clarifying statement "that his Father was not" added by the transcriber to make it clear to the person tasked with reading the testimony? Everything rested on the voice of one man and the words that made it from the testimony page to the ears of the court. Simon Moore, Captain Duncombe, and Smith's voices were all erased, replaced by that of the court clerk who was

CHAPTER 7

tasked with reading their testimony. What moved the court to back Simon against Samuel Bayard? Perhaps political considerations held some force in this case. Simon Moore had protested his freedom for five years, written letters to amass documentation of his free-born status, and yet there was little indication that he made any leeway. His case was finally heard after the tenure of Samuel's father as mayor came to a close, suggesting that he waited to file, demonstrating political acumen.

While Simon Moore was resuming his life in Beaufort County, North Carolina, other enslaved people struggled against Samuel Bayard, using their feet, rather than the courts, to emancipate themselves from his grasp. On July 31, 1758, Samuel Bayard advertised in the *New York-Mercury* for "a Negro Fellow named Robin, lusty, and well-made, talks good Dutch and English, smooth-skin'd, and is about 36 Years old" who had run away from Hobuck.[60] Robin's bilingual capacity would have served him, as it had Galloway, to more easily maneuver his way through the colony. His choice of two coats—"one of Ratteen, with red Lining, and the other of Bearskin"—suggests a few possibilities about his flight. Either he was confident in his ability to evade Samuel because, although leaving in the summer, he planned to need such coats for the colder seasons, or he was industrious in keeping one and selling another on the market. Samuel eyed the same waterways that brought Simon Moore into his dragnet as a potential avenue for Robin's escape, and in light of Simon's ability to marshal evidence from several colonies away, he had reason to worry.

The following year, on August 13, 1759, Samuel Bayard ran another advertisement, this time in pursuit of a woman named Flora, who escaped "the 24th of July last, from Capt. Samuel Bayard, of the City of New-York . . . [she] has lived several Years with Ellias Ellis, near Oswego-Market, and used to go out a cleaning Houses and Washing, and is very well known in Town."[61] If Flora had not been purchased from Ellias by Samuel, then she arguably had been hired out as a house cleaner and washer to him. To Samuel, her potential network of connections—the fact that she was "very well known in Town," coupled with her ability to readily change her physical appearance through fashion, as "she changes her Apparel very often" and "dresses very gay"—were crucial markers in identifying Flora to would-be slave catchers. Like Robin, her physicality was central as well: Samuel described Robin as "smoothed skinned" and Flora as "a strong, tall likely Wench." With the breadth of his dragnet, Samuel acknowledged the geographical reach of Flora's potential network, which, like Robin's, could have taken her outside the limits of New York City. The enslaved strategized carefully, mobilizing robust and wide-ranging networks of their own in order to evade the grasp of their enslavers' networks.

Identity in Black and White

In 1748 a little boy named Philip arrived in Somerset County, New Jersey, wrapped in a blanket.[62] He was passed from the hands of James van Horne into those of Van Horne's housekeeper, a woman named Margaret Wiser, who resided at the Rocky Hill plantation year round. Tasked with finding a wet nurse for the infant, Margaret decided on Jane Furman, a local woman of Welsh descent. Jane was at home with her niece Abigail when Margaret arrived with the baby, an event notable enough that Abigail relayed the detail of the encounter to her husband, Gabriel.[63] After asking Jane if she "would be good enough to suckle the child," Margaret pulled back the blanket that covered the child, and they "found he was a Blacke."[64] While a Black woman might serve as a wet nurse to her white enslaver's children, especially within elite Dutch slaveholding networks in New York and New Jersey, the opposite was extremely rare.[65] Margaret stressed the pedigree of Philip's mother and that (perhaps as proof) she would visit her newborn child shortly. Despite Margaret's case, Jane required "some persuasion" before she finally consented. James van Horne and his wife corroborated the story in person. Philip's story would have been forgotten had he not used his nativity narrative in his successful bid for freedom. His subtle knowledge of the performativity of the courtroom and the way notions of gender and race would be read gives some insight into Philip's own intellectual world, the shape of his community, and the resources available to nonwhite people within such elite networks who lived on the margins of freedom.[66]

The narrative had been carefully chosen and crafted to make a specific claim to freedom that would convince the court that Philip was indeed deserving of manumission. It conjured a time, nearly four decades earlier, and represents a rare glimpse into the everyday life of the denizens of the Raritan Valley. Most such reconstructions rely on reading moments of Black life from the margins. But, when combined with another account of life among the Van Hornes, written by an African man named Ukawsaw Gronniosaw, which had been published in England in 1772, a compelling picture of the conditions that surrounded African-descended people caught within such elite family networks emerges.

Two decades before Philip's birth, a young captive man named Ukawsaw Gronniosaw arrived in the Raritan Valley. He had been purchased from a Barbados slaver by Cornelius van Horne, a New York merchant whose first cousin with the same name was the slave-trading factor married to Joanna Livingston. This Cornelius was married to Elizabeth French, whose massive landholdings in New Jersey augmented the property that Cornelius had inherited from his father Johannes. The properties that bordered the large plantation where Ukawsaw would be held in bondage belonged to Cornelius's brothers Abraham and James. Although the Van Horne wills dwell on the division of the land, Ukawsaw's narrative unfolds within the manor home: where he was "dress'd" in the Van Hornes' livery, and put to the "chief business" of waiting "at table, and tea, and clean knives."[67] His subsequent description chronicles a domestic world of resentment and violence.

The "servants us' to cus and swear surprisingly," he described and it was "almost the first English I could speak." He recounted a world filled with china and cursing in the rooms of the Van Horne house. He foregrounded the piety of an elderly enslaved man named "Ned," who told him not to swear at an enslaved maid in the house by warning him of "a wicked man call'd the Devil, that liv'd in hell, and would take all that said these words, and put them in the fire and burn them." Ned's story easily contained two meanings: the image of Black people being thrown in the fire and burned was seared into the consciousness of the enslaved, who like Ned would have lived through 1712, the torture and burning of the Halletts' enslaved people, and the executions of many others, designed to leave trauma on the community.

Despite describing Elizabeth French as "a fine young lady and very good to me," he featured Elizabeth's tyranny in the home. When Elizabeth cursed as she berated her enslaved maid for accidentally sprinkling the wainscotting with water while cleaning, Ukawsaw entreated her to stop, saying that "there is a black man call'd the Devil that lives in hell, and he will put you in the fire and burn you, and I shall be very sorry for that." When asked who told him that, Ukawsaw identified Ned, who was ultimately "tyed up and whipp'd, and was never suffer'd to come into the kitchen with the rest of the servants afterwards."[68]

Old Ned's punishment was intended as an example, and he was banished from the house. The story became a lark that Elizabeth told at table to "many of her acquaintance that visited her," which would have certainly included Johanna Livingston, Cornelius's sister Catharine, and Cornelius's brother James's wife Margaret Bayard. The story became the means whereby Ukawsaw was ultimately purchased by the Dutch Calvinist firebrand minister Theodorus Frelinghuysen. In the year before Philip's birth George Whitefield preached at Theodorus's invitation to a massive crowd at Six Mile Run in New Jersey. That crowd would make up a good portion of the neighborhood of Philip's childhood, members of whom were relatives, others that would lay claim to Philip's body, and a few who would witness on his behalf.

Ukawsaw and Philip's worlds intersected, illuminating a diverse community within the Van Hornes' elite slaveholding orbit. In the latter decades of the seventeenth century, East New Jersey had, like Carolina, been settled by several Barbadian transplants and had only strengthened its ties to the institution of slavery during the eighteenth century. The Van Horne family profited from both the slave trade and from the bondage of people of African descent.[69] One year after Philip's birth, James's sons, David and Samuel van Horne became co-owners of the slave ship *Revenge*, along with their cousins William, Gerard, and G. G. Beekman, and two other New York merchants.[70] The ship left New York for the Sierra Leone estuary and the set sail for Jamaica, unloading 150 of its original 172 captive people as well as taking on additional slaves. It then embarked for New York, its final port of call, where 45 enslaved human beings were sold.

Gabriel, Philip's witness, had lived in Somerset County for years and had some standing in the community but was by no means elite. He held only secondhand knowledge of the details as it was his aunt Jane who had been used as a wet nurse. Yet, according to his testimony, he had plenty of time to interact with Philip, who grew up and remained in the neighborhood after spending five years living with Jane. The Furman family were "near neighbors" of the Van Hornes and served other community functions. On July 12, 1735, Gabriel Furman and Nowell Furman acted as witnesses for the will of Ethan Field who lived in Newton, New Jersey. In 1739, Gabriel and Nowell, along with family members and friends were deeded land from Jacobus Springsteen south of Newton in order to build a school. They were described as "all farmers residing thereabouts."[71] The "neighborhood" where Gabriel and Philip lived roiled with racial tensions. Court cases within the Rocky Hill community, which would have certainly qualified as a society with slaves, reflected the violence and tension of slavery. Gabriel Furman would have likely been involved in policing the enslaved population and his wife Abigail, or aunt Jane might well have wielded direct control over enslaved people. In 1739, an enslaved man was tried for the murder of his overseer's son and for burning their barn down, although his original target had been the overseer's wife. He was publicly burned at the stake.[72]

Philip was by no means the only child of mixed racial heritage with links to the elite of New York and New Jersey, but his position in the community was apparently met with unease. The Furmans clearly understood that they were being tasked with safeguarding a certain degree of Philip's elite familial

CHAPTER 7

identity. They recognized that whiteness and, by extension, blackness was not absolute. James van Horne, although leaving the couple with instructions to raise the child with an elite education in keeping with his lineage, did not need to explain that the child's color would make him subject to intense discrimination. He would not grow up with his mother and among the rest of his elite household. He would experience such a separation that, in his adult years, a relative would claim him as property in court. His freedom would ultimately hinge on appealing to the blood of the elite Dutch-descended woman who gave him up and invoking whiteness reinforced by Jane's milk.

Just as the actions of slaveholding women like Judith Stuyvesant were, at the very beginning of such Dutch-descended families' American experiences, both buttressed and limited by the slave system, so too was Philip's mother constrained from taking a public, active role in his early life. Philip's mother, whose name remains a mystery, visited eighteen months after James dropped off her son, around the time that Jane weaned Philip.[73] Now a toddler, young Philip would have changed dramatically. Nursed and cared for by Jane, his early words would have been English (or even a bit of Welsh) but not the Dutch words and idioms his mother would have no doubt heard as a child in the primarily Dutch elite community that surrounded Rocky Hill and the Van Hornes' wider familial networks. Nevertheless, Philip's later appeal would rest on his maternal blood tie to that elite Dutch community. Philip's mother was prevented from breastfeeding her son, not due to biological fault or some disease of the breast, but to hide her nonmarital sexuality and her son's race from elite society. Despite her status or personal wishes, she was pushed to the margins of his life, so far that her name and identity remain a mystery.

Several young women were the right age to have been Philip's mother, including Johanna Livingston's daughter Alida, who was born in 1724 and would have been twenty-four in 1748. Her parents would have been among the region's "first rank."[74] Gabriel's testimony details only that she arrived in the "company of Mrs. Van Horne." The Van Hornes were closely linked to the Bayards through ties of trade and slavery. On February 4, 1751, an advertisement for the sale of James van Horne's property ran in the *New-York Gazette*, which highlighted it as "containing between 13 and 14 Hundred Acres of choice Land . . . a good Dwelling House, Barn, Waggon and Negro Houses" and saying that any interested parties should "apply to William Bayard, Merchant in New York, or to the said James Vanhorne."[75]

The advertisement was repeated four times in the *New-York Gazette* between February and May 1751.[76] By June 16, 1755, James van Horne was on the market again, this time represented by Nicholas Bayard, advertising "four farms or plantations" that made up his Rocky Hill holdings, including the previous lands which were distinguishable by their "negro and waggon-house."[77] This advertisement was repeated eight times between 1755 and 1756.[78] The Bayards and the Van Hornes' merchant and slaveholding ties in East Jersey occurred during a time of both increased commitment to slavery and unrest. On March 10, 1757, the *Pennsylvania Gazette* ran a news story featuring the deaths of enslavers at the hands of the enslaved in Bergen County. Perhaps such tensions were behind James van Horne's desire to sell his lands and his difficulty in so doing. The next year, December 18, 1758, James, working with Nicholas Bayard, ran yet another advertisement for his lands in Rocky Hill in the *New-York Mercury*, repeating the call another four times into the new year. James's Rocky Hill plantation contained numerous enslaved women, and many could have also been lactating.[79] So there had to be a specific reason for his and, by extension, Margaret Wiser's choice of a white wet nurse.

James clearly intended that some vestige of Philip's elite pedigree be passed down. According to Gabriel Furman, Jane's nephew, James left an explicit directive that Philip be educated genteelly and took pains to emphasize the station of Philip's mother.[80] Philip's freedom claim rested on his mother's whiteness because freedom was intrinsically linked to gender in the colonial context with *partus sequitur ventrum*, which mandated that slavery followed the condition of the womb.[81] New York, with its large contingent of seventeenth-century Virginia transplants, was the only other English colony that formally adopted *partus* before the middle of the eighteenth century, enacting the law in 1706.[82] Two years earlier, in 1704, the New Jersey council passed the *Act for Regulating Negro, Indian and Mallatoo slaves*, which included a clause that mandated castration for any slave convicted of attempting "to Ravish or have carnal Knowledge of any White Woman, Maid or Child." It also encouraged the departure of manumitted enslaved people by refusing them or their children the right to pass down or inherit property.[83] In 1709, the Crown vacated New Jersey's castration clause, arguing that it fell outside of the norm of English law but only because it mandated castration for rape; the Crown did not vacate Carolina's law that mandated castration for repeat cases of running away.[84] New Jersey strengthened its slave law again in response to a 1712 uprising of a biracial coalition of Black and Native enslaved people in New York, replacing the call for castration with the authorization "to inflict such Corporal Punishment (not extending to Life or Limb) . . . [as] shall seem meet," in cases of assault against free persons "professing Christianity." They replaced a trial by jury with summary en banc processes before two justices.[85]

Elite family networks ensnared African-descended members. By 1783, Philip was enslaved to John van Horne and Dierck Ten Broeck. If he was the child of Alida Livingston, then John, James's eldest son, would have also been Philip's first cousin. He grew up in a county with a considerable number of enslaved people whose economy was devoted to slavery. Dierck Ten Broeck was not only a member of the colonial elite, but kinship connected him to other members of the elite who sat on the court, including Philip Livingston (signer of the Constitution), who had married his daughter Christina. Unmoved by the language of liberty, these two men devoted considerable time and financial resources to hindering the freedom of people they counted their property.

But Philip appealed to maternity and pedigree. Gabriel Furman testified that, later, James van Horne directly asked for Jane's consent to nurse Philip, arriving a second time in the company of his wife, and adding that the child's grandparents were "some of the greatest people in New York." Perhaps in this, he was not so obliquely signaling that the child was a close family member. The little boy's name Philip was a family name, one that he shared with Cornelius's eldest son. Further, James insisted that the child "was free-born and could not be made a slave" and "that he was determined to educate him genteelly." As Craig Wilder has shown, the Van Hornes had, along with other elite New York and New Jersey families, been founding benefactors of the newly formed colonial schools such as Kings College in New York City. James's instructions to Jane would have been in line with the educational opportunities he wished for his own children. Philip won his freedom. His erstwhile enslavers' (and perhaps relatives') claim was deemed illegitimate against the community testimony, maternal and social status conjured in Philip's defense.

The geographic and genealogical realities of the enslaved steered not just the rudder of their own lives, but also those of their enslavers. In the middle decades of the eighteenth century, a diverse group of people found themselves ensnared by overlapping and robust networks of bondage but utilized their own networks to traverse the landscapes that others like them had crisscrossed for a century. They deployed their knowledge of the foundations of race as well as the social and family bonds that undergirded the realities of their enslavers to create alternatives to the lives chosen for them by those whose freedom was built on their bondage.

Conclusion
Gentry

When John Bayard attempted to retrace the route of a man named Toby, the trail was already nine months cold. The expanse that he conjured for Toby's potential whereabouts was a map that traced nodes on the wider Bayard family's own centuries-old slaveholding network and included Philadelphia, New York, the West-Indies, Albany or New England. John Bayard ran the advertisement four times, twice in the *Boston Gazette*, on March 25 and April 8, 1771, and another two times in the *New York Journal*, on March 28 and April 11, respectively. In the time between when Toby fled and when John ran the advertisement, John Bayard had already tapped his own personal network—evident in the fact that he offered intelligence of Toby's whereabouts two months after he had run away— a web of connections that included the leading merchants, politicians, and slaveholders in the Northeast. Widening the dragnet across the major metropolitan centers of the Northeast, he hoped to add the eyes of a watchful public to apprehend Toby.[1]

John and his twin brother James had been born in the Great House of a sprawling plantation in Bohemia Manor, Maryland, on August 11, 1738.[2] Their father Samuel had, like their grandfather Petrus before him, been drawn to relocate to Maryland from New York. But, far from pursuing a life of retreat from the corrupting influences of the riches of the world, Samuel Bayard had transformed his father's "neck" of the Labadie tract, building a

CONCLUSION

> *Philadelphia, Feb. 26, 1771.*
>
> ### Twenty Dollars Reward.
>
> RAN away from the Subscriber, (living in Second-Street, between Market and Arch Streets) about the latter end of laſt June, a negro fellow named Toby, about 24 years of age, 5 feet 6 or 8 inches high, a likely well ſet fellow, very talkative and complaiſant, eſpecially when in liquor, has been brought up to houſe work. He was taken up at New-York, the 19th of Aug. laſt, and made his eſcape from gaol the ſame day. It is ſuppoſed he is there got on board ſome Veſſel bound to the Weſt-Indies, or went towards Albany or New-England. Any Perſon who ſhall take up ſaid Negro, ſo that his maſter may get him again, ſhall be entitled to the above reward and all reaſonable charges.   · JOHN BAYARD.
>
> N. B. His clothing are not deſcribed, as he took nothing but his common apparel, which it is ſuppoſed, by this time he has worn out or changed. He can write and perhaps he may change his name and pretend to be a free negro.

FIGURE 12. Runaway Slave Advertisement in search of Toby posted by John Bayard in *New-York Journal; or, the General Advertiser*, March 14, 1771.

brick mansion known as the Great House, and along with his brother-in-law, Hendrick Sluijter, became a planter.[3] While his cousins expanded their political influence, business contacts, lands, and property—including property in human beings—in New York City and New Jersey, Samuel became enmeshed in the burgeoning community of Bohemia Manor, which included the Herman family who had relocated from New Netherland. By the time that Samuel joined the community at the turn of the eighteenth century, the original Labadist community had vanished and in its place was one devoted to profiting off of the regional tobacco trade.

Despite these changes, the tension between profit and piety did not fade away. In 1740, two years after the brothers' births, the evangelist George Whitefield toured the area and was hosted by the Bayards. The conditions that he observed in the region induced him to write his "Letter to the Inhabitants of Maryland, Virginia, North and South Carolina," which admonished the slaveholders of the region to Christianize their slaves and improve their conditions but did not, ultimately, advocate abolition.[4] He warned the "rich Men" to "Behold the Provision of the poor Negroes . . . the Cries of them which reaped, are entered into the Ears of the Lord of *Sabaoth*!"[5]

If Samuel was personally chastened by Whitefield's admonition, it left no evidence in the historical record. He, like his slaveholding cousins across the Northeast, remained committed to the institution and the benefits it bestowed on his family. John and James, like their Bayard cousins in New York and New Jersey, were sent to a local institution of higher learning, attending Maryland's Nottingham Institute whose headmaster, the Reverend Samuel Finley, would go on to become the president of Princeton.[6] After the death of both their parents, John split his inheritance of his family's plantation with his brother.[7] In 1756, both brothers left Bohemia Manor and moved to Philadelphia, where John was trained as a merchant, apprenticing at the counting-house of John Rhea, while James studied medicine. Less than a decade after moving to Philadelphia, John had married and profited as a merchant. He found success in a time of expansion for Philadelphia.[8] Yet, the Townshend Acts threatened that success. In October 1765, John signed the nonimportation agreement. John maintained personal and trading contacts with his cousins across the Northeast, traveling to visit William Bayard in New York and Balthazar Bayard, who lived in Boston after his marriage to Mary Bowdoin. But he was not the only member of his household who maintained wide-ranging contacts that could be leveraged.[9]

At the dawn of 1770, Philadelphia's social climate was undergoing a revolution. Numerous enslavers were freeing the human beings they held in bondage, a manumission impetus that was not solely connected to Quakerism. Among some of Philadelphia's urban professional elite, antislavery had become fashionable, especially with those who, like John Bayard, employed enslaved domestics.[10] Due to an influx of white workers after the Seven Years War, the demand for slavery lessened, alleviating the economic incentive. John did not follow the trend. Instead, like his cousins across the Northeast, he remained comfortable with holding Toby in lifelong heritable bondage. On January 8, 1770, James died, an event which one chronicler reported, "produce[d] a serious illness which confined [John] to his bed for several days."[11] Just three weeks later, on January 30, 1770, Benjamin Franklin published "A Conversation on Slavery" in the *Public Advertiser*, where he placed the debate over slavery in the mouths of an Englishman, a Scotchman, and an American. In a nod to transatlantic debates, it opened with the Englishman questioning American hypocrisy over slavery opining: "You Americans make great Clamour upon every little imaginary Infringement of what you take to be your Liberties; and yet there are no People upon Earth such Enemies to Liberty, such absolute Tyrants, where you have the Opportunity, as you yourselves are."[12] Six months later, Toby made his escape. Might he have read those lines and felt personal outrage at his own enslavement? As the advertisement noted, he was literate.

More likely, Toby was influenced by other enslaved people, or perhaps newly emancipated friends, and wished to ameliorate the condition of perpetual servitude into which he found himself serving a lifelong sentence. John Bayard's grief at the loss of his twin brother and the chaos of the funerary arrangements would have provided Toby additional space to plot his plan for escape. Toby, John advertised, had been "brought up to housework" and could "write." John predicted that "he may change his name and pretend to be a free negro." Toby's choice of June offered him adequate cover. Perhaps he used the festival days allotted African Americans in the mid-Atlantic to blend into the crowd and disappear.[13] Such public celebrations were also surveilled and might have been the reason that he landed in the jail mentioned in John's advertisement. Toby's plan likely involved a maritime network, a fact that John highlighted in the advertisement, one that reached beyond the city of Philadelphia well into New York, and Albany. He may have held kinship ties in northern New York, been sold, or given to John from a New York member of the extended Bayard family network.[14] John at least imagined that he had ridden the regional waterways of the Delaware Bay into New York harbor and then up the Hudson toward Albany or perhaps skirted around Long Island, and into the heart of New England. He may have followed the route that Tom took two decades earlier, through New Jersey, into Perth Amboy and using the ferries to cross into New York City. Or, a fully committed mariner, with a new name and the highly useful ability to write, could freely sail down to the West Indies—a direction that scores of slaveholders used as the ultimate weapon against their slaves—toward freedom.

Before the first rumblings of dissent and displeasure at the imperial policies of metropolitan Great Britain began to become a roar within the networks of elites, these same elites had already enjoyed nearly a century and a half of slaveholding and mastery. In that time, they had hammered out legal codes that were both reactionary and a part of a larger scheme for empire. While never the main source of wealth of the Northeastern families who retained their home base in New York, New Jersey, and Connecticut, slavery was part of the family's broader portfolio of activities, and the members who made their homes in the Chesapeake, South Carolina, Curaçao, and Jamaica practiced slaving policies in step with their neighbors. These families maintained a remarkably strong network that drew them together as an economic and social whole. Despite the unity that such an intertwined system might deploy, local conditions and individual actors did cause division within the whole. While individuals might make different choices in terms of their personal relationship to slavery, the family identity was firmly invested in the proliferation and continuation of Atlantic slavery.

New Netherland's leadership was deeply enmeshed in the burgeoning Atlantic slave system. Reflected in personal and administrative correspondence, colonial elites built their conceptions of status and social hierarchies on racial sensibilities, which were first forged in South America and the Caribbean before being tempered in the Northeast. The regional aspect of slavery became a key unifying force behind the emergence of blended Anglo-Dutch elite networks in the years after New Netherland fell to the English and assumed its New York moniker. Indeed, those elite networks were marshaled for a dual purpose—not just to grow power and connection among other elites across the Northeast, but also to constrain and marginalize those they enslaved, particularly as fears of rebellion and threats of violence became more widespread in the aftermath of Queen Anne's War and the 1712 Slave Revolt. Slave laws, culture, and society became increasingly rigid and surveillance of enslaved people increased as expansion-minded Anglo-Dutch elites leveraged slave regimes, racial, and gendered claims to grow their trade and kinship networks cross-colonially. Enslaved people's struggles for personal freedom and family cohesion rippled through the Northeast, impacting regional and local histories. Similarly, a heritage of Dutch slaveholding formed an important, but overlooked, part of the identity of elites like the Livingstons as they created regional networks of kinship and influence from the Northeast southward through the Chesapeake, the Carolinas, and the Caribbean. Running alongside those elite networks lay a broad web of connections between a diverse group of enslaved, bonded, and free people, knitting together the region along alternate pathways.

The ancestors of Samuel Bayard's gentry class relied on familial networks borne of marriage and blood to expand zones of trade and influence. Fur, timber, wheat, sugar, and enslaved people were traded to their fellow colonists and across transatlantic routes in a bid to increase their wealth and power. Interconnected family units provided them with access to markets and resources, and provided a vector along which they could exert mastery. The enslaved people who served them were viewed as engines of growth, providing much-needed skills and labor that fueled their burgeoning empires, but were also signifiers of class who provided members of the gentry opportunities to unite in the expression of a common language of control. Mastery and slavery defined the gentry's approach to trade, growth, and connection, with ships named for colonial locales, built by enslaved people, and used to trade goods that included other enslaved people.

Enslaved laborers, acting on behalf of their captors, had access to these same familial and trade networks, and often established their own shadow networks alongside them. Coordinated moments of violence and rebellion, like the Slave Revolt of 1712 and the Slave Conspiracy of 1741, were obvious but infrequent displays of the value of these networks. Less obvious but more frequent was the use of these networks to foster resistance and escape. Robin, Galloway, and Toby each used their facility with multiple languages and networks of contacts to navigate Anglo-Dutch, African, and Indigenous environments and escape their enslavers. Enslaved people were political actors who leveraged the vagaries of diplomacy to assert their autonomy.

Elites made sense of the changes wrought by a century of colonization using the language of racial slavery: a frame as old as their families' settlement in the Americas. Over the years, much had changed about the circumstances the families found themselves in: they no longer lived under the rule of the Dutch Republic, or ultimately by the end of the eighteenth century even Great Britain, they no longer conversed—even at church—in Dutch, and they reckoned their estates following the English custom; some had traded in old religious convictions for new ones. They shifted market interest from dairy to wheat, and from privateering to iron, but slavery remained a constant aspect of their everyday lives and their larger portfolios. Bondage was both foundational and fundamental. It shaped their self-identities and the societies that they sought to build—either on a small or large scale. Strategies of mastery changed with time, and as a result of local and market conditions, but the fact of bondage reigned supreme. Elites did inhabit societies built on the assumption of overlapping inequalities, but chattel slavery was a new experiment for British and Dutch societies and the colonial societies that they spawned, and it was one that such families not only vigorously took on but actively shaped. Such interconnected elites created a network of bondage that had been birthed and nurtured simultaneously in the Northeast, the Southern colonies, and the Caribbean. It was a legacy that would continue to expand in the nineteenth century, even as members of dynastic slaveholding families joined the antislavery effort.

Appendix A

The state against Tiercke Tenbroecke
New Jersey Supreme Court
The State against Tiercke Tenbroecke
On Habeas Corpus of Negro Philip.[1]

Gabriel Furman, of full age, being duly sworn, says that in the year 1748 he was a near neighbour of Mr. James van Horne, that in part of the winter season Mr Van Horne frequently resided in New-York, and in the summer season came up to his Plantation at Rocky-hill in Somerset County where Mr. John van Horne *now lives*. That one Margaret Wiser lived constantly at the Plantation as his Mr. Van Horne's housekeper. That in the month of March 1748 she came to the house of the Deponent in the dusk of the evening with a small child in her arms; said she had received a [present] from New-York and did not know what to do with it; asked Deponent's wife, in his Deponent's Hearing, if she would be good enough to suckle the child, as she then gave the Breast of; that his wife opened the Blanket in which the Child was wrapped and found it was a Blacke; Deponent then observed to Mrs. Wiser that the Mother of the Child must certainly be a white woman, or they would not take so much pains to conceal it from the eyes of the world; her answer was that the mother of the child *was* a white woman, and further said that the Father and mother of the young woman who was the mother of the child were people of almost the first Rank in New-York; and that it was a Free-Born child and never could be made a slave; that she had received a letter from Mr. Van Horn, then in New-York, desiring her that if she could not have it taken care of in his house, to apply to one of the neighbouring women to keep it till he came up; Deponent's wife consented and kept the child till Mr. Van Horne came; When Mr Van Horne came up he interceded further with Deponent's wife to keep the child a year longer; she agreed to nurse it for some time after some persuasion; that Mr. Van Horne requested the Deponent that if should be inconveneint to keep the child here the Deponent would provide another nurse; which the Deponent accordingly did after a little time; That the said Child was a male; that the next time Mr. Van Horne came up from New-York, Deponent saw him, and in Conversation observed to him that the mother of the child must be of Family, or so much pains would not be taken to conceal the matter; that Mr. Van Horn answered her Parents were some of the greatest people in New York, that he (the child) was free born and could not be made a slave; and further, that he was determined to educate him genteely; That Jane Furman, sister of Nowell Furman, was the nurse, he, the Deponent, procured for the child. That the said Jane Forman was aunt to the Deponent lived part of the time while the child was brought up, within two miles of Deponent, and at no time more than three miles and a half from him; that the Child was with the said Jane Forman five years, or about that time, that he saw him frequently and has frequently seen him since he, the said child, after he was grown up having continued in the same neighborhood; and that he verily believes the person called Negro Philip, now before the Court, is the same—Deponent further says, that in a conversation which happened between Mrs. Wiser and the Deponent, while the Child was at Deponent's House, Mrs. Wiser told him the mother of the child would come up to see it; that about eighteen months after, or thereabouts, the Lady came up who was said to be the mother that Deponent saw her; and that some little time after this, the Deponent's aunt said Forman and also Nowell Forman's wife, told him that Lady had been there to see the child in company with Mrs. Van Horne, wife of the said James van Horne. That the Child was always called by the name of Philip, and that it was always the general opinion and report of the neighborhood that the said Philip was the child of a Lady in New York. And further saith with.

Gabriel Furman

Sworn 17 May 1783 before
Mr. Isaac Smith

Superior Court
The State against Tiercke TenBroeck
On Habeus Corpus of Negro Philip

Affidavit of Gabriel Furman—
Agreed by the attornies on both sides to be read in evidence

Filed May From 1783
Houstou

Judgement give in September 1783

The court's judgement handed down in September 1783, was:

> The Court having fully considered the Evidence, and the Arguments of Counsel in the Cause, *are unanimously of Opinion*, and do adjudge, that the said Negro *Philip* be discharged and set at Liberty from the said Tierck Tenbroeck, and also from John Vanhorne of Rocky-Hill, in the Couny of Somerset, who hath appeared and claimed the said Negro Philip, On Motion of Mr. Paterson for the State.[2]

Appendix B

The Case of Simon Moore a free Negro[1]

This informant says he was born at Bath Town in North Carolina the son of Abraham and Mary Moore, that his ~~Father was~~ Mother was a free Woman and born so, that his Father was not. That at the age of 11 years this Informant was bound apprentice to one William Peyton Merchant at Bath Town aforesaid for Ten years. That about five years ago William Peyton upon this Informant's request, sent him to New York to help man a sloop under the command of Samuel Dunscomb (of which sloop Mr. Peyton was half owner) which was consigned to Captain Samuel Bayard of this City Merchant.

That he was to return back in the sloop, but Captain Bayard under pretense of some Money owing to him from the said Mr. William Peyton kept the sloop here and never sent her back and she has been broke to Pieces since at Hell Gate, and has ever since kept this Complainant in Slavery, and says he shall not go home to Carolina, till Mr. Peyton pays him the Money which he owes him, insisting that this Complainant is a slave and that he has a Right to detain him for the money due to him from William Payton.

That this Complainant's time for which he was bound to the said Mr. Peyton is expired he being twenty two years of age being bound out till he arrived at the age of Twenty One. That he has often sent to his Friends in North Carolina for Certificates of his Freedom but Never has received an answer.

Mr. Peyton by the Indenture was to have him taught the Trade of a Cooper and during the apprenticeship was to give him two years schooling at writing and reading and was to give him two Suits of cloaths, none of which covenants have been performed, but this Complainant believes they would had not his Mistfortunes compelled to stay here.

Captain Dunscomb and John Brown a Sailor both now in Town can prove his freedom.

Samuel Dunscomb of the city of New York mariner maketh oath that about four years since he commanded a sloop or vessel of which Samuel Bayard of the city merchant and William Peyton of Bath Town in North Carolina Merchant were the owner, as this Deponent then understood and believes to be true that about five years since and better this Deponent went as Master of aforesaid sloop from New York aforesaid to Bath Town aforesaid with cargo of goods consigned to the said William Peyton. Which sloop was there loaded again with goods by the said William Peyton consigned to the said Samuel Bayard, and that this Deponent wanting hands to carry the said sloop from Bath Town aforesaid to New York, Simon Moore a free Negro youth then an apprentice of the said William Peyton as this Deponent then understood and believes to be true told this Deponent that the said Sloop was as he understood to return soon again to Bath Town, he would go the voyages if the said William Peyton his master would give leave; and thereupon this Deponent saith that by his the said William Peyton the master's leave the said Simon Moore did provide in the said vessel from Bath Town aforesaid to New York to help man the said vessel. And this Deponent further saith that upon the said sloop's arrival at New York on her return from Bath Town aforesaid the said Samuel Bayard kept the said sloop to his own use and never sent her back and also took and detained the said Simon Moore on pretense of a debt which he claimed as due to him from the said William Peyton, and on that pretense still keeps and detains the said Simon Moore as a slave as this Deponent has heard and believes . . .

> Witnesses his Hand this 19th Day of November 1753 Samuel Dunscomb
> Testimony of Simon More
> Sworn this 20th day of December 1753 before me.

And this Examenant further says that near five years ago, he was commander of a Sloop which belonged to the said Mr. Bayard and Mr. Peyton, and sailed about that time from the Port of New York to Bath Town in North Carolina,

APPENDIX B

with Goods consighted to the Peyton by William Bayard and afterwards from there with Goods consigned from William Peyton to Mr Bayard, that whilst he was at Carolina wanting hands to man his sloop for her return to New York th said Simon Moore desird his Mastr Wm Payton that the might go the Voyage, the said sloop being to return to Carolina which his Master William Peyton consented to and sent him to help man the sloop to New York and when the Sloop arrived at New York Mr. Bayard sold her and has ever since kept the said Simon Moore as his slave. 19 November 1753

Appendix C

Table 1 Household composition and slaveholding by family member according to the 1790 census

STATE	COUNTY	TOWN	FIRST NAME	LAST NAME	ENSLAVED PEOPLE
SC	Charleston	Charleston	H.	Livingston	42
MD	Cecil	Bohemia Manor	Benjamin	Bayard	10
MD	Cecil	Bohemia Manor	Samuel	Bayard	10
NY	Montgomery	Caughnawaga	James	Livingston	3
NY	Columbia	Clermont	Robert R.	Livingston	9
NY	Columbia	Clermont	Margaret	Livingston	15
NY	Columbia	Livingston	Robert	Livingston	44
NY	Columbia	Livingston	Walter	Livingston	10
NY	Columbia	Livingston	Peter B.	Livingston	14
NY	Columbia	Livingston	Robert I.	Livingston	1
NY	Columbia	Livingston	Peter W.	Livingston	0
NY	Columbia	Livingston	James I.	Livingston	0
NY	Albany	Stillwater	John	Livingston	6
NY	Albany	Stillwater	Abraham	Livingston	1
NY	Albany	Watervliet	Moncrief	Livingston	1
NY	Albany	Watervliet	William	Livingston	[Destroyed]

(Continued)

APPENDIX C

Table 1 (Continued)

STATE	COUNTY	TOWN	FIRST NAME	LAST NAME	ENSLAVED PEOPLE
NY	Dutchess	Poughkeepsie	Henry Jr.	Livingston	1
NY	Dutchess	Poughkeepsie	Gilbert	Livingston	1
NY	Dutchess	Poughkeepsie	Henry Sr.	Livingston	5
NY	Dutchess	Poughkeepsie	Gilbert I.	Livingston	0
NY	Dutchess	Rhinebeck	Henry G.	Livingston	13
NY	Dutchess	Rhinebeck	Robert G.	Livingston	5
NY	Dutchess	Rhinebeck	Henry B.	Livingston	11
NY	Dutchess	Beekman	Beekman	Livingston	0
NY	Dutchess	Beekman	Gilbert R.	Livingston	3
NY	Westchester	Greenburgh	Philip	Livingston	6
NY	Westchester	Westchester	Samuel	Bayard	5
NY	Westchester	Westchester	Philip I.	Livingston	3
NY	Queens	South Hampstead	John	Livingston	1
NY	New York	Dock Ward	Samuel	Bayard	3
NY	New York	Dock Ward	Sarah	Livingston	9
NY	New York	Dock Ward	Robert C.	Livingston	3
NY	New York	Dock Ward	Peter B.	Livingston	2
NY	New York	East Ward	John	Livingston	1
NY	New York	Montgomery Ward	Edward	Livingston	1
NY	New York	Out Ward	Nicholas	Bayard	5
NY	New York	Out Ward	Peter	Stuyvesant	14
NY	New York	West Ward	Philip P.	Livingston	3
NY	New York	West Ward	Brocholst	Livingston	4
NY	New York	West Ward	Robert R.	Livingston	6
NY	New York	West Ward	Walter	Livingston	10
NY	New York	West Ward	William I.	Livingston	1
NY	New York	West Ward	John H.	Livingston	3

Source: Census Bureau, *Historical Statistics of the United States, Colonial Times to 1957*, July 1960, 756. https://www.census.gov/library/publications/1960/compendia/hist_stats_colonial-1957.html.

Appendix D

Table 2 Extended Stuyvesant-Bayard family slaveholding: Counts of enslaved people by enslaver name and ward—1703 New York City Census

FIRST NAME	DOCK	EAST	OUT	WEST	HOUSEHOLD TOTAL
Balthazar Bayard				6	6
Colonel Nicholas Bayard	3				3
Peter Bayard				1	1
Samuel Bayard	2				2
Capt. Sidmen			10		10
Capt. Baker		1			1
Ward total	**5**	**1**	**10**	**7**	**23**

Abbreviations

CHMANY	O'Callaghan, Edmund Bailey, ed. *Calendar of Historical Manuscripts in the Office of the Secretary of State Albany New York*. 2 vols. Albany, NY: Weed, Parsons, 1865–66.
CJVR	Van Laer, A.J.F., trans. and ed. *Correspondence of Jeremias van Rensselaer, 1651–1674*. Albany: University of the State of New York, 1932.
Clermont	Clermont State Historic Site Manuscript Collection, Germantown, New York.
CLNY	Northrup, A. Judd, et al., eds. *The Colonial Laws of New York: From the Year 1644 to the Revolution*. Albany, NY: James B. Lyon, 1894.
CMARS	Van Laer, A.J.F., trans. and ed. *Minutes of the Court of Albany, Rensselaerswyck and Schenectady*. 3 vols. Albany: University of the State of New York, 1926–28.
CMVR	Van Laer, A.J.F., ed. and trans. *Correspondence of Maria van Rensselaer, 1669–1689*. Albany: University of the State of New York, 1935.
Correspondence 1654–1658	Gehring, Charles T., trans. and ed. *Correspondence 1654–1658*. Syracuse, NY: Syracuse University Press, 2003.
Council Minutes 1652–54	Gehring, Charles T., trans. and ed., *New York Historical Manuscripts: Dutch, Council Minutes, 1652–1654*. Vol. 5. Baltimore, MD: Genealogical Publishing, 1976.
CP	Gehring, Charles T., trans. and ed. *Curaçao Papers, 1640–1665: Translation*. Albany, NY: New Netherland Institute, 2011.
DCAC, 1646–1664	New York State Archives. Dutch colonial administrative correspondence, 1646–1664.

ABBREVIATIONS

	Series A1810-78. Volume 12, document 39, page 1, side 1.
DCB	*Dictionary of Canadian Biography.* Vol. 2. Toronto: University of Toronto/Université Laval, 2003.
DECPR	Manwaring, Charles William, comp. *A Digest of the Early Connecticut Probate Records.* Hartford, CT: R. S. Peck & Co., 1904.
DHSNY	O'Callaghan, E. B. *The Documentary History of the State of New-York.* Vol. 2. Albany: Weed & Parsons, 1850.
DHSNY1	O'Callaghan, E. B. *The Documentary History of the State of New-York.* Vol. 1. Albany: Weed & Parsons, 1850.
DIHSTA	Donnan, Elizabeth. *Documents Illustrative of the History of the Slave Trade to America.* 4 vols. Washington, DC: Carnegie Institution of Washington, 1930–35.
DRCHNJ	Nelson, William, and Abraham van Doren Honeyman, ed. *Documents Relating to the Colonial History of the State of New Jersey.* 29 vols. Paterson, NJ: The Press Printing and Publishing, 1894.
DRCHNY	O'Callaghan, E. B., and Berthold Fernow, eds. *Documents Relative to the Colonial History of the State of New York.* 15 vols. Albany, NY: Weed, Parsons, 1853–87.
EAN	America's Historical Newspapers: Early American Newspapers, Readex.
EEBO	Early English Books Online, Readex.
ERNY	Hastings, Hugh, et al., eds. *Ecclesiastical Records of the State of New York.* 7 vols. Albany, NY: J. B. Lyon, 1901–16.
FFY	Hunt, Gaillard, ed. *The First Forty Years of Washington Society, Portrayed by the Family Letters of Mrs. Samuel Harrison Smith (Margaret Bayard) from the Collection of her Grandson J. Henley Smith.* New York: Charles Scribner's Sons, 1906.

ABBREVIATIONS

FOR	Gehring, Charles T., trans. and ed. *Fort Orange Records 1656–1678*. Syracuse, NY: Syracuse University Press, 2000.
GL	Gilder Lehrman Collection on Deposit at the New-York Historical Society.
IAVoyages	*Voyages: The Intra-American Slave Trade Database*.
inv. nr.	Inventory Number (*Inventarisnummer*).
Kingston Papers	Dingman Versteeg, trans., Peter R. Christoph, Kenneth Scott, and Kenn Stryker-Rodda, eds., *Kingston Papers: Kingston Court Records, 1668–1675 and Secretary's Papers, 1664–1675*. Baltimore: Genealogical Publishing, 1976.
LFP-Trans	Livingston Family Papers in Dutch, translated by Adrian van de Linde, Franklin D. Roosevelt Library, Hyde Park, NY.
Liber A-2	Sypher, Jr., Francis J., trans. and ed. *Liber A of the Collegiate Churches of New York*. Part 2. Grand Rapids, MI: William B. Eerdmans, 2015.
LP	Livingston Family Papers, The Gilder Lehrman Collection on deposit at the New-York Historical Society.
LR-MSS	Livingston-Redmond Manuscripts, Franklin D. Roosevelt Library, Hyde Park, NY.
MCARS	Van Laer, A.J.F., trans. and ed. *Minutes of the Court of Albany, Rensselaerswyck and Schenectady*. . . . Vol. 2. Albany: University of the State of New York, 1928.
MCCCNY	*Minutes of the Common Council of the City of New York, 1675–1776*. 8 vols. New York: Dodd, Mead, 1905.
MCR	Van Laer, A.J.F., trans. and ed. *Minutes of the Court of Rensselaerswyck: 1648–1652*. Albany: University of the State of New York, 1922.
Memoranda van Klaverack	Undated "Memoranda van Klaverack" signed by Elis [Elizabeth] Stuyvesant. New-York Historical Society. Mss Collection AHMC—Stuyvesant Family Non-circulating.
NAN	Nationaal Archief (National Archives of the Netherlands) The Hague, The Netherlands.

ABBREVIATIONS

NEQ	*New England Quarterly.*
NJEJD	New Jersey State Archives. East Jersey Deeds.
NNCCR	New York State Archives. New York (Colony). Council. Curaçao records, 1640–1665. Series A1883-78. Vol. 17.
NNCM	New York State Archives. New Netherland. Council. Dutch Colonial Council Minutes, 1638–1665. Series A1809. Vol. 9.
NNDR	New York State Archives. New Netherland Council. Dutch Delaware River Settlement Administrative Records, 1646–1664. Series A1878. Vol. 19.
Notarial Papers	Van Laer, A.J.F., ed. *Notarial Papers 1 and 2, 1660–1696.* Translated by Jonathan Pearson. Vol. 3. *Early Records of the City and County of Albany and Colony of Rensselaerswyck.* Albany: University of the State of New York, 1918.
NYCMA	New York City Municipal Archives.
NYHM	Gehring, Charles T., and Venema, Janny trans. and ed. *New York Historical Manuscripts: Dutch, Vol. 8, Council Minutes, 1656–1658.* Syracuse, N.Y.: Syracuse University Press: 2018.
NYHME	Christoph, Peter, and Florence A. Christoph, eds. *New York Historical Manuscripts English: Books of General Entries of the Colony of New York.* Baltimore: Genealogical Publishing, 1982.
NYHMRCB	Van der Linde, A.P.G. Jos, trans. and ed. *New York Historical Manuscripts, Dutch: Old First Dutch Reformed Church of Brooklyn, New York First Book of Records, 1660–1752.* Baltimore: Genealogical Publishing, 1983.
NYHS	New-York Historical Society, New York, NY.
PGCANY	*Proceedings of the General Court of Assizes held in the City of New York, October 6, 1680 to October 6 1682.* New York: Printed for the New York Historical Society, 1912.
PRCC	Hoadly, Charles J., ed. *The Public Records of the Colony of Connecticut.* Hartford, CT: Press of Case, Lockwood and Brainard, 1868.

ABBREVIATIONS

RONA	Fernow, Berthold, ed. *The Records of New Amsterdam: From 1653 to 1674*. 7 vols. New York: Knickerbocker Press, 189*7.
RRDCA	Duermyer, Louis, ed. *Records of the Reformed Dutch Church of Albany, New York, 1689–1809: Marriages, Baptisms, Members, etc. Excerpted from Year Books of the Holland Society of New York*. Baltimore, MD: Genealogical Publishing, 1978.
SAA	Stadsarchief Amsterdam (Municipal Archives of Amsterdam). Amsterdam, The Netherlands.
TAVoyages	*Voyages: The Trans-Atlantic Slave Trade Database.*
UCADR	Ulster County Archives. Dutch Records Index.
VCM	Van Cortlandt. Manuscripts Collection. New-York Historical Society.
VRBM	Van Laer, Arnold J. F., trans. and ed. *Van Rensselaer Bowier Manuscripts, Being the Letters of Kiliaen Van Rensselaer, 1630–1643, and Other Documents Relating to the Colony of Rensselaerswyck*. Albany: University of the State of New York, 1908.
VRMP	New York State Library. Van Rensselaer Manor Papers. Correspondence of Jeremias van Rensselaer. Letter books of Jeremias van Rensselaer SC7079 Box 4, Folder 42.
VSSJAA	O'Callaghan, Edmund Bailey, trans. and ed. *Voyages of the Slavers St. John and Arms of Amsterdam, 1659, 1663*. Albany, NY: J. Munsell, 1867.
Wills	Pelletreau, William S., ed. *Abstracts of Wills on File in the Surrogate's Office: City of New York with Appendix and Miscellaneous Documents*. 17 vols. New York: Printed for the Society, 1893–1913.
WMQ	*William and Mary Quarterly.*

NOTES

Introduction: Manhunt

1. Across the Atlantic World, the family has been used as a way of reimagining the bounds of slave networks. Jane E. Mangan, *Transatlantic Obligations: Creating the Bonds of Family in Conquest-Era Peru* (Oxford: Oxford University Press, 2016); Gloria Whiting, "Power, Patriarchy, and Provision: African Families Negotiate Gender and Slavery," *Journal of American History* 103, no. 3 (2016): 583–605, https://doi.org/10.1093/jahist/jaw325; Gretchen Holbrook Gerzina, *Mr. and Mrs. Prince: How an Extraordinary Eighteenth-Century Family Moved Out of Slavery and into Legend* (New York: Amistad, an imprint of HarperCollins Publishers, 2008); Elise Lemire, *Black Walden: Slavery and its Aftermath in Concord, Massachusetts* (Philadelphia: University of Pennsylvania Press, 2009); Randy J. Sparks, *The Two Princes of Calabar: An Eighteenth-Century Atlantic Odyssey* (Cambridge: Harvard University Press, 2004); Lisa A. Lindsay, *Atlantic Bonds: A Nineteenth-Century Odyssey from America to Africa* (Chapel Hill: The University of North Carolina Press, 2017). For the connection of enslaved networks to Black genealogy, see Saidiya Hartman, *Lose Your Mother: A Journey Along the Atlantic Slave Route* (New York: Farrar, Straus and Giroux, 2007).

2. The citation includes the detail that it was on manuscript page 48. Since this transcription in the late nineteenth century, the original has been burned. "A Warrant for Mr. Stuyvesants 4 Negroe Servant's lost," 6 October 1664, j.d., in *New York State Library Annual Report* (Albany: University of the State of New York, 1899), 81: 117; Graham Russell Hodges and Alan Edward Brown, eds., *"Pretends to Be Free": Runaway Slave Advertisements from Colonial and Revolutionary New York and New Jersey* (New York: Garland, 1994), 324. For a discussion of the document's destruction, see Peter Christoph, "Books from Ashes: A Project of Recreating Lost Documents," *De Halve Maen: Quarterly Magazine of the Dutch Colonial Period in America*, 56, no. 2 (fall 1981): 17–18.

3. "A warrant for Mr. Stuyvesants 4 Negro servants lost," 6 October 1664, in *New York State Library Annual Report* 81: 117.

4. James Lydon asserted that slave trading was a minimal feature of New York's economy before 1748, and James Rawley and Stephen Behrendt argued that "Van Cortlandt's slaving ventures were a minor part of his commercial activities, just as were his occasional sales of a slave in New York or in the coasting trade." James G. Lydon, "New York and the Slave Trade, 1700–1774," *WMQ* 35, no. 2 (April 1978): 384, http://www.jstor.org/stable/1921840; James A. Rawley and Stephen D. Behrendt, *The Transatlantic Slave Trade, A History*, rev. ed. (1981; reprint Lincoln, NE: University of Nebraska Press, 2005), 339. For works that challenge the contention that slavery was a minor part of Northeastern life, see Wendy Warren, *New England Bound: Slavery*

and Colonization in Early America (New York: Liveright/W. W. Norton, 2016); Margaret Ellen Newell, *Brethren by Nature: New England Indians, Colonists, and the Origins of American Slavery* (Ithaca, NY: Cornell University Press, 2015); John Wood Sweet, *Bodies Politic: Negotiating Race in the American North, 1730–1830* (2003; reprint Philadelphia: University of Pennsylvania Press, 2006); Craig Steven Wilder, *Ebony and Ivy: Race, Slavery, and the Troubled History of America's Universities* (New York: Bloomsbury Press, 2013).

5. Julia Adams argued convincingly that the family, not the state, was the driver of Dutch continental politics, linking patrimonial families to the rise of Dutch influence in the "Golden Age" and also crediting them with its downfall. For the sake of familial prestige, according to Adams, Dutch ruling families sabotaged the success of the West India Company and accelerated the state's decline. Julia Adams, *The Familial State: Ruling Families and Merchant Capitalism in Early Modern Europe* (2005; reprint Ithaca, NY: Cornell University Press, 2007). Such a focus on colonial elite families has proved particularly useful in reconstructing the lives of both enslaver and enslaved in many early colonial contexts. See Jennifer L. Palmer, *Intimate Bonds: Family and Slavery in the French Atlantic* (Philadelphia: University of Pennsylvania Press, 2016); Daniel Livesay, *Children of Uncertain Fortune: Mixed-Race Jamaicans in Britain and the Atlantic Family, 1733–1833* (Chapel Hill: Published for the Omohundro Institute of Early American Culture, Williamsburg, Virginia, by the University of North Carolina Press, 2018); Allegra di Bonaventura, *For Adam's Sake: A Family Saga in Colonial New England* (New York: Liveright/W. W. Norton, 2013); Annette Gordon-Reed, *The Hemingses of Monticello: An American Family* (New York: W. W. Norton, 2008); Catherine Kerrison, *Jefferson's Daughters: Three Sisters, White and Black in a Young America* (New York: Ballantine Books, 2018).

6. Jaap Jacobs, *New Netherland: A Dutch Colony in Seventeenth-Century America*, The Atlantic World: Europe, Africa and the Americans, 1500–1830, vol. 3 (1999; reprint Leiden: Brill, 2005), 381. For lower estimates, see Patricia Bonomi, "'Swarm of Negroes Comeing about My Door': Black Christianity in Early Dutch and English North America," *Journal of American History*, vol. 103, no. 1 (June 2016), 40–41, https://doi-org.proxy.library.cornell.edu/10.1093/jahist/jaw007. Joyce D. Goodfriend, *Before the Melting Pot: Society and Culture in Colonial New York City, 1664–1730* (Princeton, NJ: Princeton University Press, 1994), 61. For a recently updated estimate of the population, see Michael J. Douma, "Estimating the Size of the Dutch-Speaking Slave Population of New York in the 18th Century," *Journal of Early American History* (forthcoming).

7. *TAVoyages*. Calculated as the total of all enslaved people imported on ships between 1601 and 1664 as a proxy for total population.

8. Andrew Lipman, *The Saltwater Frontier: Indians and the Contest for the American Coast* (New Haven, CT: Yale University Press, 2015), 96–97.

9. The yacht *Bruynvisch* departed from Texel on January 13 for the Caribbean. It met up with other Dutch yachts, from the chamber Zeeland, which had taken a Portuguese ship coming from São Tomé with 225 enslaved people. As the prize ship was quite leaky and the crew couldn't handle a number that size, they took twenty-two enslaved people on board, and let the ship go with the remainder. The Zeeland yachts and the *Bruynvisch* met up near Hispaniola in June 1627. It is very likely, though not specified by De Laet, that a number of the enslaved from the Portuguese

ship were transferred to the *Bruynvisch*. The *Bruynvisch* sailed along the Florida coast to New Netherland, anchoring there on August 20. It left the Noordt Rivier at the end of September and arrived at Texel on October 25. Jaap Jacobs, email message to author, 27 May 2021, based on Johannes De Laet, *Iaerlyck verhael van de verrichtinghen der Geoctroyeerde West-Indische Compagnie in derthien boecken* (Den Hague, NL: Martinus Nijhoff, 1937), https://resolver.kb.nl/resolve?urn=KONB10:000019207:00015), 114–19.

10. Jean R. Soderlund, *Lenape Country: Delaware Valley Society Before William Penn* (Philadelphia: University of Pennsylvania Press, 2015), 112.

11. New York has had more studies devoted to slavery than other regions of the Northeast. Shane White, *Somewhat More Independent: The End of Slavery in New York City, 1770–1810* (Athens: University of Georgia Press, 1991); Craig Steven Wilder, *A Covenant with Color: Race and Social Power in Brooklyn 1636–1990* (New York: Columbia University Press, 2000); Wilder; *In the Company of Black Men: The African Influence on African American Culture in New York City* (New York: New York University Press, 2001); Leslie M. Harris, *In the Shadow of Slavery: African Americans in New York City, 1626–1863* (Chicago: The University of Chicago Press, 2003); Vivienne Kruger, "Born to Run: The Slave Family in Early New York, 1626–1827" (PhD diss., Columbia University, 1985); Jill Lepore, *New York Burning: Liberty, Slavery and Conspiracy in Eighteenth-Century Manhattan* (2005; reprint New York: Vintage Books, 2006); David N. Gellman, *Emancipating New York: The Politics of Slavery and Freedom, 1777–1827* (Baton Rouge: Louisiana State University Press, 2006); Margaret Washington, *Sojourner Truth's America* (Chicago: University of Illinois Press, 2009); Thelma Wills Foote, *Black and White Manhattan: The History of Racial Formation in Colonial New York City* (New York: Oxford University Press, 2004); Jeroen Dewulf, "Emulating a Portuguese Model: The Slave Policy of the West India Company and the Dutch Reformed Church in Dutch Brazil (1630–1654) and New Netherland (1614–1664) in Comparative Perspective," *Journal of Early American History* 4 (2014): 3–36; Dewulf, *The Pinkster King and the King of Kongo: The Forgotten History of America's Dutch-Owned Slaves* (Jackson: University Press of Mississippi, 2017); Oscar Williams, "Slavery in Albany, New York, 1624–1827," *Afro-Americans in New York Life and History* 34, no. 2 (July 2010): 154–68. For New York merchant families' connection to slavery, see Wilder, *Ebony and Ivy*; Sean D. Moore, *Slavery and the Making of Early American Libraries: British Literature, Political Thought, and the Transatlantic Book Trade, 1731–1814* (Oxford: Oxford University Press, 2019); Paul J. Polgar, *Standard-Bearers of Equality: America's First Abolition Movement* (Chapel Hill: Published for the Omohundro Institute of Early American History and Culture by the University of North Carolina Press, 2019); Andrea Mosterman, *Spaces of Enslavement: A History of Slavery and Resistance in Dutch New York* (Ithaca, NY: Cornell University Press, 2021). For slavery in the Hudson Valley, see A. J. Williams-Myers, *Long Hammering: Essays on the Forging of an African American Presence in the Hudson River Valley to the Early Twentieth Century* (Trenton, NJ: Africa World Press, 1994); Michael E. Groth, *Slavery and Freedom in the Mid-Hudson Valley* (Albany: State University of New York Press, 2017).

12. Such an approach marked most of the early work devoted to slavery in New Netherland, due to an emphasis differences in slavery's formal legal structure between the Dutch and English eras. Edgar J. McManus, *A History of Negro Slavery in New York* (Syracuse, NY: Syracuse University Press, 1966), 1–22; Morton Wagman, "Corporate Slavery in New Netherland," *Journal of Negro History* 65, no. 1

(winter 1980): 40, http://www.jstor.org/stable/3031546; Peter R. Christoph, "The Freedmen of New Amsterdam," in *A Beautiful and Fruitful Place*, 1:157. For a tempering of the view of the exceptionalism of New Netherland's slavery, see Goodfriend, "Burghers and Blacks," 125–44; Jaap Jacobs, *New Netherland*, 173–74, 173n80; Susanah Shaw Romney, *New Netherland Connections: Intimate Networks and Atlantic Ties in Seventeenth-Century America* (Chapel Hill: Published for the Omohundro Institute of Early American History and Culture by the University of North Carolina Press, 2014), 191–93. For a refutation of this view using spatial analysis see Mosterman, *Spaces of Enslavement*, introduction.

13. Eliga H. Gould, "Entangled Histories, Entangled Worlds: The English-Speaking Atlantic as a Spanish Periphery," *American Historical Review* 112, no. 3 (June 2007): 764–86, http://www.jstor.org/stable/40006670; Wim Klooster, *The Dutch Moment, War, Trade and Settlement in the Seventeenth-Century Atlantic World* (Ithaca, NY: Cornell University Press, 2016); Wim Klooster and Gert Oostindie, *Realm between Empires: The Second Dutch Atlantic, 1680–1815* (Ithaca, NY: Cornell University Press, 2018).

14. For the broader interpenetration of the English and Scottish worlds into Dutch and Dutch Atlantic communities, see Keith L. Sprunger, *Dutch Puritanism: A History of English and Scottish Churches of the Netherlands in the Sixteenth and Seventeenth Centuries* (Leiden: Brill, 1983); Alexander Murdoch, *Scotland and America, c.1600–c.1800* (Basingstoke, UK: Palgrave Macmillan, 2010); T. M. Devine, ed., *Recovering Scotland's Slavery Past: the Caribbean Connection* (Edinburgh, UK: Edinburgh University Press, 2015).

15. For Anglo-Dutch European networks and their influence, see Lisa Jardine, *Going Dutch: How England Plundered Holland's Glory* (New York: Harper, 2008); and Steve Pincus, *1688: The First Modern Revolution* (New Haven, CT: Yale University Press, 2009).

16. Diverse networks of Dutch intercolonial connections shape the work of Christian Koot, Linda Rupert, Mark Meuwese, and Susanah Shaw Romney. For the importance of Anglo-Dutch trade see Christian J. Koot, *Empire at the Periphery: British Colonists, Anglo-Dutch Trade, and the Development of the British Atlantic, 1621–1713* (New York: New York University Press, 2011). For intercultural trade alliances between Dutch and Native peoples, see Meuwese, *Brothers in Arms, Partners in Trade: Dutch-Indigenous Alliances in the Atlantic World, 1595–1674* (Leiden and Boston: Brill, 2011). For the creation of a vibrant Atlantic trading culture see Linda Rupert, *Creolization and Contraband: Curaçao in the Early Modern Atlantic World* (Athens: The University of Georgia Press, 2012). For an expansive early modern trading world linked by "intimate networks," see Romney, *New Netherland Connections*.

17. Bernard Bailyn's prolific work on the burgeoning seventeenth- and eighteenth-century merchant culture of colonial New England set the tenor for a field of studies focused on the importance of merchant families to the settlement and rise of the Northeast. The fortunes of New York merchant families have long dominated the historiography of the region. Their lives and fortunes have produced works examining the economic, social, political, and cultural histories of the region and are so ubiquitous that their dominance in the field has only recently been challenged by historians. Bernard Bailyn, *The New England Merchants in the Seventeenth Century*

(Cambridge, MA: Harvard University Press, 1955); Bailyn, *Voyagers to the West: A Passage in the Peopling of American on the Eve of the Revolution* (1986; reprint New York: Vintage Books, 1988); and *The Peopling of British North America: The Barbarous Years, The Conflict of Civilizations, 1600–1675* (2012; reprint New York: Vintage Books, 2013). For more on the wider field devoted New England's merchant culture, see Marsha L. Hamilton, *Social and Economic Networks in Early Massachusetts: Atlantic Connections* (University Park: Pennsylvania State University Press, 2009); for more on colonial New York's merchant culture, see Michael G. Kammen, *Colonial New York: A History* (1975; reprint Oxford, UK: Oxford University Press, 1996); Cynthia A. Kierner, *Traders and Gentlefolk: The Livingston of New York, 1675–1790* (Ithaca, NY: Cornell University Press, 1992); Cathy D. Matson, *Merchants & Empire: Trading in Colonial New York* (Baltimore, MD: Johns Hopkins University Press, 1998); Thomas M. Truxes, *Defying Empire: Trading with the Enemy in Colonial New York* (New Haven, CT: Yale University Press, 2008).

18. For more on slavery and maritime culture, see Jeffrey Bolster, *Black Jacks: African American Seamen in the Age of Sail* (Cambridge, MA: Harvard University Press, 1997); Charles Foy, "Ports of Slavery, Ports of Freedom: How Slaves Used Northern Seaports' Maritime Industry to Escape and Create Trans-Atlantic Identities, 1713–1783" (PhD diss., Rutgers, 2008)," 36; Maria Vann, "Sirens of the Sea: Female Slave Ship Owners of the Atlantic World, 1650–1870," *Coriolis: the Interdisciplinary Journal of Maritime Studies* 5, no. 1 (winter 2015): 22–33; Peter Linebaugh and Marcus Rediker, *The Many Headed Hydra: Sailors, Slaves, Commoners, and the Hidden History of the Revolutionary Atlantic* (Boston, MA: Beacon Press, 2000); Marcus Rediker, *Villains of All Nations: Atlantic Pirates in the Golden Age* (Boston: Beacon Press, 2004); Marcus Rediker, *The Slave Ship: A Human History* (New York: Viking Penguin Group, 2008); Kevin P. McDonald, *Pirates, Merchants, Settlers, and Slaves* (Berkeley: University of California Press, 2015); Kevin Dawson, *Undercurrents of Power: Aquatic Culture in the African Diaspora* (Philadelphia: University of Pennsylvania Press, 2018).

19. Massachusetts Body of Liberties, 1641, in *DIHSTA* 3: 4; Wendy Warren, *New England Bound*; 12–13; Newell, *Brethren by Nature*, 6; Sweet, *Bodies Politic*; William D. Piersen, *Black Yankees: The Development of an Afro-American Subculture in Eighteenth-Century New England* (Amherst: The University of Massachusetts Press, 1988).

20. For merchant connections to slavery, see Karen Ordahl Kupperman, *Providence Island, 1630–1641: The Other Puritan Colony* (1993; reprint Cambridge: Cambridge University Press, 1995); Robert K. Fitts, *Inventing New England's Slave Paradise: Master/Slave Relations in Eighteenth-Century Narragansett, Rhode Island* (New York: Garland, 1998); Charles Rappleye, *Sons of Providence: The Brown Brothers, the Slave Trade, and the American Revolution* (New York: Simon & Schuster Paperbacks, 2006); Cynthia Mestad Johnson, *James DeWolf and the Rhode Island Slave Trade* (Charleston, SC: History Press, 2014); Christy Clark-Pujara, *Dark Work: The Business of Slavery in Rhode Island* (New York: New York University Press, 2016). Several scholars have noted that the lack of ready cash due to the glut of sewant on the New Netherland market due to the establishment of a mint in Boston was one of the factors that led to the fall of New Netherland. See Edwin G. Burrows and Mike Wallace, *Gotham: A History of New York City to 1898* (1999; reprint New York: Oxford University Press, 2000), 47–48; and Lynn Ceci, "The First Fiscal Crisis in New York," *Economic Development and Cultural Change* 28, no. 4 (July 1980): 846–47, http://www.jstor.org/stable/1153524.

21. W.E.B. Du Bois, *The Souls of Black Folk* (1903; reprint New York: Oxford University Press, 2009), 7–8; Thomas C. Holt, "Du Bois, W. E. B.," *African American National Biography*, Henry Louis Gates Jr. and Evelyn Brooks Higginbotham, eds. (New York: Oxford University Press, 2008).

22. For more on the broader impact of Anglo-Dutch rivalries and wars on contests for empire, see Benjamin Schmidt, "Mapping an Empire: Cartographic and Colonial Rivalry in Seventeenth-Century Dutch and English North America," *WMQ* 54, no. 3 (July 1997): 549–78, http://www.jstor.org/stable/2953839; Koot, "The Merchant, the Map, and Empire: Augustine Herrman's Chesapeake and Inter-imperial Trade," 1644–73, *WMQ* 67, no. 4 (October 2010): 603–44, https://www.jstor.org/stable/10.5309/willmaryquar.67.4.0603; Christian J. Koot, *A Biography of a Map in Motion: Augustine Herrman's Chesapeake* (New York: New York University Press, 2017), 51, 133, chapter 3. See also Donna Merwick, *Death of a Notary: Conquest and Change in Colonial New York* (Ithaca: Cornell University Press, 1999); Merwick, *Stuyvesant Bound: An Essay on Loss Across Time* (Philadelphia: University of Pennsylvania Press, 2013). For studies that foreground Dutch and Anglo-Dutch networks in the Caribbean, South America, and Atlantic Africa, see Rupert, *Creolization and Contraband*; Klooster, *The Dutch Moment*; Koot, *Empire at the Periphery*. Although there are works devoted to the impact of Dutch transplants on Chesapeake trade, and even their influence on religious groups, only Hatfield and Natalie Zemon Davis connect their presence to the emergence of slavery in the regions. April Lee Hatfield, *Atlantic Virginia: Intercolonial Relations in the Seventeenth Century* (Philadelphia: University of Pennsylvania Press, 2005), 137–68; Natalie Zemon Davis, *Women on the Margins: Three Seventeenth-Century Lives* (Cambridge, MA: Harvard University Press, 1995), 170–71. For more on Dutch trade and religious connections in the Chesapeake, see Victor Enthoven and Wim Klooster, "The Rise and Fall of the Virginia-Dutch Connection in the Seventeenth Century," in *Early Modern Virginia: Reconsidering the Old Dominion*, eds. Douglas Bradburn and John C. Coombs (Charlottesville: University of Virginia Press, 2011), 90–127; Claudia Schnurmann, "Atlantic Trade and American Identities: The Correlations of Supranational Commerce, Political Opposition, and Colonial Regionalism," in *The Atlantic Economy during the Seventeenth and Eighteenth Centuries: Organization, Operation, Practice, and Personnel*, ed. Peter A. Coclanis (Columbia: University of South Carolina Press, 2005), 186–204; Bartlett Burleigh James, *The Labadist Colony in Maryland* (Baltimore: The Johns Hopkins Press, 1899).

23. Romney, *New Netherland Connections*, 16–19.

24. Vincent Brown, *Tacky's Revolt: The Story of an Atlantic Slave War* (Cambridge, MA: The Belknap Press of Harvard University Press, 2020), 4.

25. Roper argues convincingly for the Connecticut colony's centrality to New Netherland's fall. L. H. Roper, "The Fall of New Netherland and Seventeenth-Century Anglo-American Imperial Formation, 1654–1676," *NEQ* 87, no. 4 (2014): 666–708. Jaap Jacobs centralizes the importance of linguistic battles in "'It Has Pleased the Lord that We Must Learn English': Dutch New York After 1664," his epilogue to *The Colony of New Netherland: A Dutch Settlement in Seventeenth-Century America* (Ithaca: Cornell University Press, 2009). This is theme that Merwick likewise engages in *Death of a Notary*. For more on Jacob Leisler, see Adrian Howe,

"The Bayard Treason Trial: Dramatizing Anglo-Dutch Politics in Early Eighteenth-Century New York City," *WMQ* 47, no. 1 (January 1990): 57–89, http://www.jstor.org/stable/2938041; David William Voorhees, "'To assert our Right before it be quite lost': The Leisler Rebellion in the Delaware River Valley," *Pennsylvania History: A Journal of Mid-Atlantic Studies,* 64, no. 1 Regional Perspectives on Early American History (winter 1997): 5–27, https://www.jstor.org/stable/27773953; Evan Haefeli, "A Scandalous Minister in a Divided Community: Ulster County in Leisler's Rebellion, 1689–1691," *New York History* 88, no. 4 (fall 2007): 357–89, http://www.jstor.org/stable/23185822; Hermann Wellenreuther, ed., *Jacob Leisler's Atlantic World in the Later Seventeenth Century: Essays on Religion, Militia, Trade, and Networks by Jaap Jacobs, Claudia Schurmann, David W. Voorhees and Herman Wellenreuther* (Münster, Germany: LIT Verlag, 2009).

26. Robert S. Grumet, *The Munsee Indians: A History* (Norman: University of Oklahoma Press, 2009); Juliana Barr and Edward Countryman, *Contested Spaces of Early America* (Philadelphia: University of Pennsylvania Press, 2014); Tom Arne Midtrød, *The Memory of All Ancient Customs: Native American Diplomacy in the Colonial Hudson Valley* (Ithaca, NY: Cornell University Press, 2012); Lipman, *The Saltwater Frontier.* For Native slavery, see Alan Gallay, *The Indian Slave Trade: The Rise of the English Empire in the American South, 1670–1717* (New Haven: Yale University Press, 2002); Brett Rushforth, *Bonds of Alliance: Indigenous and Atlantic Slaveries in New France* (Chapel Hill: Published for the Omohundro Institute of Early American History and Culture, Williamsburg, Virginia by the University of North Carolina Press, 2012); Katherine Howlett Hayes, *Slavery Before Race: Europeans, Africans, and Indians at Long Island's Sylvester Manor Plantation, 1651–1884* (New York: New York University Press, 2013); Newell, *Brethren by Nature.* Kim Hall, Kathleen Brown, Jennifer Morgan, and Londa Schiebinger linked the hardening of racial categories to changing understandings of gender. Kim Hall, *Things of Darkness: Economies of Race and Gender in Early Modern England* (Ithaca, NY: Cornell University Press, 1996); Kathleen Brown, *Good Wives, Nasty Wenches, and Anxious Patriarchs: Gender, Race, and Power in Colonial Virginia* (Chapel Hill, NC: University of North Carolina Press, 1996); Jennifer L. Morgan, *Laboring Women: Reproduction and Gender in New World Slavery* (Philadelphia: University of Pennsylvania Press, 2004); Londa L. Schiebinger, *Nature's Body: Gender in the Making of Modern Science* (1993; reprint New Brunswick, NJ: Rutgers University Press, 2004).

27. Mosterman, *Spaces of Enslavement*; Romney, *New Netherland Connections,* 191–244; Romney, "Reytory Angola, Seventeenth-Century Manhattan (US)," in *As If She Were Free: A Collective Biography of Women and Emancipation in the Americas,* eds. Erica Ball, Tatiana Seijas, and Terri Snyder (Cambridge: Cambridge University Press, 2020), 58–78; Romney, "Intimate Networks and Children's Survival in New Netherland in the Seventeenth Century," *Early American Studies: An Interdisciplinary Journal* 7, no. 2 (fall 2009): 270–79; Mosterman, "Nieuwer-Amstel, stadskolonie aan de Delaware" in *De slavernij in Oost en West* (Amsterdam: Uitgeverij Het Spectrum, 2020), 164–71; Dennis Maika, "To 'experiment with a parcel of negros': Incentive, Collaboration, and Competition in New Amsterdam's Slave Trade," in *Journal of Early American History* 10, no. 1 (2020): 33–69.

28. Carolyn Steedman, *Dust: The Archive and Cultural History* (2001; reprint New Brunswick, NJ: Rutgers University Press, 2002), 68.

29. For more works that centralize the Livingston family's regional power, see Edwin Brockholst Livingston, *The Livingstons of Livingston Manor* (New York: Knickerbocker Press, 1910); Lawrence H. Leder, *Robert Livingston 1654–1728 and the Politics of Colonial New York* (Chapel Hill: University of North Carolina Press, 1961); G.M. Waller, *Samuel Vetch: Colonial Enterpriser* (Chapel Hill: Published for the Omohundro Institute of Early American History and Culture, Williamsburg, Virginia, by the University of North Carolina Press, 1960). For this theme in studies that highlight the Livingston women, see Linda Biemer, ed., "Business Letters of Alida Schuyler Livingston, 1680–1726," *New York History* 63, no. 2 (April 1982): 182–207; Linda Biemer, *Women and Property in Colonial New York: The Transition from Dutch to English Law, 1643–1727* (1979; reprint Ann Arbor, MI: UMI Research Press, 1983); Mary Lou Lustig, *Privilege and Prerogative: New York's Provincial Elite, 1710–1776* (Madison, NJ: Fairleigh Dickinson University Press, 1995); Cynthia A. Kierner, *Traders and Gentlefolk: The Livingston of New York, 1675–1790* (Ithaca, NY: Cornell University Press, 1992); Serena R. Zabin, *Dangerous Economies: Status and Commerce in Imperial New York* (Philadelphia: University of Pennsylvania Press, 2009). For works that examine the Livingstons in other contexts, see Philip Otterness, *Becoming German: The 1709 Palatine Migration to New York* (2004; reprint Ithaca, NY: Cornell University Press, 2006); Robert C. Ritchie, *Captain Kidd and the War against the Pirates* (Cambridge, MA: Harvard University Press, 1986); Jennifer van Horn, *The Power of Objects in Eighteenth-Century British America* (Chapel Hill: Published for the Omohundro Institute of Early American History and Culture, Williamsburg, Virginia by the University of North Carolina Press, 2017), 273–76, 302–3; Caroline Frank, *Objectifying China, Imagining America: Commodities in Early America* (Chicago: The University of Chicago Press, 2011), 97–99, 102, 106–11, 126, 151, 161; Sara S. Gronim, *Everyday Nature: Knowledge of the Natural World in Colonial New York* (New Brunswick, NJ: Rutgers University Press, 2007). Several studies have highlighted Manor Livingston as a site for bonded and enslaved labor. See Philip Otterness, *Becoming German: The 1709 Palatine Migration to New York* (2004; reprint Ithaca, NY: Cornell University Press, 2006); Roberta Singer, "The Livingstons as Slaveholders: The 'Peculiar Institution' on Livingston Manor and Clermont," in *The Livingston Legacy: Three Centuries of American History*, ed. Richard T. Wiles (Annandale, NY: Bard College Office of Publications, 1987), 67–97; di Bonaventura, *For Adams Sake*. Wilder, *Ebony and Ivy*, 48–49, 51–52, 60–61, 64–70, 74–76, 96–97, 104–5, 122, 132, 172–73, 181–82, 204, 228, 263; Philip Misevich, "In Pursuit of Human Cargo: Philip Livingston and the Voyage of the Sloop 'Rhode Island,'" *New York History* 86, no. 3 (summer 2005): 184–204, http://www.jstor.org/stable/23185791; Darold D. Wax, "A Philadelphia Surgeon on a Slaving Voyage to Africa, 1749–1751," *Pennsylvania Magazine of History and Biography* 92, no. 4 (Oct 1968): 465–93; https://www.jstor.org/stable/20090230.

30. Di Bonaventura, *For Adam's Sake*; Whiting, "Power, Patriarchy, and Provision"; Mary Beth Norton, *In the Devil's Snare: The Salem Witchcraft Crisis of 1692* (New York: Alfred Knopf, 2002); Serena Zabin, *The Boston Massacre: A Family History* (Boston: Houghton Mifflin Harcourt, 2020).

31. Graham Russell Hodges, *Slavery and Freedom in the Rural North: African Americans in Monmouth County, New Jersey, 1665–1865* (Madison, WI: Madison House Publishers, 1997); Graham Russell Hodges, *Root and Branch: African Americans in New York and East Jersey 1613–1863* (Chapel Hill: The University of North Carolina Press,

1999); Marisa J. Fuentes and Deborah Gray White, eds., *Scarlet and Black: Slavery and Dispossession in Rutgers History* (New Brunswick, NJ: Rutgers University Press, 2016); Wilder, *Ebony and Ivy*; Graham Russell Hodges, *Black New Jersey: 1664 to the Present Day* (New Brunswick, NJ: Rutgers University Press, 2019).

32. Goodfriend, *Who Should Rule at Home*, 2. In "'The Cause of her Grief'" Wendy Warren offered, "Given such paltry evidence, perhaps only indefinite articles capture the indefinite nature of this narrative." Wendy Anne Warren, "'The Cause of Her Grief': The Rape of a Slave in Early New England," *Journal of American History* 93, no. 4 (March 2007): 1031; 1049, http://www.jstor.org/stable/25094595; Natalie Zemon Davis and John Demos have both filled in such gaps with historical questions and Catherine Kerrison has made educated assumptions about a life lived behind a purposeful veil of passing by creating a tableau using available historical evidence. Such evidence beautifully illuminates the biases of history: that the call for more evidence silences the lives of so many people. Natalie Zemon Davis, *The Return of Martin Guerre* (Cambridge, MA: Harvard University Press, 1983); John Demos, *The Unredeemed Captive: A Family Story from Early America* (1994; reprint New York: Vintage Books Edition, 1995); Kerrison, *Jefferson's Daughters*.

33. In *Alabi's World* examining eighteenth-century Dutch Suriname, Richard Price deploys conditional terminology to illuminate a slaveholding world. Price foregrounds his methodological justification, writing, "Without such attempts at empathy, ethnographic or historic interpretation risks being empty and soulless." Richard Price, *Alabi's World* (Baltimore, MD: The Johns Hopkins University Press, 1990), xvii. Additionally, more recently, Marisa Fuentes constructed *Dispossessed Lives*, to challenge "the overdetermining power of colonial discourses" by "changing the perspective of a document's author to that of an enslaved subject, questioning the archives' veracity and filling out miniscule fragmentary mentions or the absence of evidence with spatial and historical context." Fuentes, *Dispossessed Lives*, 4. Saidiya Hartman has written several academic works justifying critical fabulation in scholarly historical study. Hartman, "Venus in Two Acts," *Small Axe* 12, no. 2 (June 2008): 1–14, https://muse-jhu-edu.proxy.library.cornell.edu/article/241115/pdf.

34. Romney, *New Netherland Connections*, xviii; Evert Wendell, *"To Do Justice to Him & Myself": Evert Wendell's Account Book of the Fur Trade with Indians in Albany, New York, 1695–1726*, ed. and trans. Kees-Jan Waterman (Philadelphia: American Philosophical Society, 2008); Linda Biemer, ed. "Business Letters of Alida Schuyler Livingston, 1680–1726," *New York History* 63, no. 2 (April 1982), 199.

35. The importance of local geographies to the experience of slavery has gained renewed interest alongside the rise of digital humanities. Efforts to explore and map the geographies of slavery have proliferated in an attempt to inhabit a more fully tactile world of colonial slavery. On mapping the enslaved world, see Simon Newman, "Hidden in Plain Sight: Long-Term Escaped Slaves in Late-Eighteenth and Early-Nineteenth Century Jamaica," *WMQ* (June 2018), https://blog.oieahc.wm.edu/the-wmq-on-the-oi-reader/; Dienke Hondius, "Mapping Slavery," https://clue.vu.nl/en/projects/current-projects/mapping-slavery/index.aspx, which maps places important to slavery across the Dutch Empire, including in New York; Billy Smith and Paul Sivits, "Mapping Historic Pennsylvania," http://www.mappinghistoricphiladelphia.org/; Diana di Zerega Vall and Anne-Marie Cantwell, *Touring*

Gotham's Archaeological Past: 8 Self-Guided Walking Tours through New York City (New Haven: Yale University Press, 2004), 29.

36. Antonio T. Bly, *Escaping Bondage: A Documentary History of Runaway Slaves in Eighteenth-Century New England, 1700–1789* (Lanham, MD: Lexington Books, 2012). Hodges and Brown, eds., *"Pretends to Be Free"*; Billy Smith and Richard Wojtowicz, *Blacks Who Stole Themselves: Runaway Slaves in the 19th Century Mid-Atlantic* (Philadelphia: University of Pennsylvania Press, 2015). Likewise, digital archives that contain runaway slave advertisements have flourished, such as Simon Newman's database on runaway slaves in the United Kingdom, and Freedom on the Move, Cornell University's digital database of fugitive slave advertisements.

37. For an alternate view to the centrality of the elite narrative that dominates New York history, see Patricia U. Bonomi, *A Factious People: Politics and Society in Colonial New York* (1971, reprint Ithaca, NY: Cornell University Press, 2014); Goodfriend, *Before the Melting Pot*; Goodfriend, *Who Should Rule at Home? Confronting the Elite in British New York City* (Ithaca, NY: Cornell University Press, 2017).

38. Advertisement, New-York Gazette, and Weekly Mercury, 13 October 1777, no. 1355, page 3, EAN.

39. United States Census, 1790, database with images, FamilySearch, https://familysearch.org/ark:/61903/3:1:33SQ-GYB6-7LL?cc=1803959&wc=3XT9-92F%3A1584070828%2C1584071633%2C1584071639, New York > New York > New York City Out Ward > image 11 of 12; citing NARA microfilm publication M637 (Washington DC: National Archives and Records Administration, n.d.); Will of Gerardus Stuyvesant, 26 Oct 1774, Probate court records, wills and administrations, Ulster County, New York, 1662–1783, Image 67, Family Search, https://www.familysearch.org/ark:/61903/3:1:3QSQ-G99K-R99L-8?i=66&wc=Q7PB-BZQ%3A213302401%2C221314701&cc=1920234. Petrus inherited the entire original bowery when his brother Nicholas William died in 1780.

Chapter 1 *Neger*

1. Jeremias to Jan Baptist van Rensselaer, 2 June 1661, VRMP, NYSL_sc7079-b04-f42_ncn, https://digitalcollections.archives.nysed.gov/index.php/Detail/objects/18522; for another translation, see *CJVR*, 255. Jeremias was recounting an event that happened six months earlier. Stuyvesant traveled on the yacht of Jacob Jansz Flodder in November 1660. Report of Stuyvesant's visit to Esopus and Fort Orange, 27 November 1660, NNCM, NYSA_A1809-78_V09_0451, https://digitalcollections.archives.nysed.gov/index.php/Detail/objects/53644.

2. Jeremias to Jan Baptist van Rensselaer, 2 June 1661, VRMP, NYSL_sc7079-b04-f42_ncn, https://digitalcollections.archives.nysed.gov/index.php/Detail/objects/18522; See also *CJVR*, 255. I have noted only where my own translation differs in meaning from Van Laer's translation.

3. Jeremias to Jan Baptist van Rensselaer, 2 June 1661, VRMP, NYSL_sc7079-b04-f42_ncn, https://digitalcollections.archives.nysed.gov/index.php/Detail/objects/18522; See also *CJVR*, 116–17, 255.

4. Jeremias to Jan Baptist van Rensselaer, 2 June 1661, VRMP, NYSL_sc7079-b04-f42_ncn, https://digitalcollections.archives.nysed.gov/index.php/Detail/objects/18522. See also *CJVR*, 116–17, 255.

NOTES TO PAGES 18–19

5. Jan Baptist first mentions purchasing an enslaved man from Trijntjen Rodenborch, referring to her as Rodenborch's widow (which he spelled Roodenburgh). Jan Baptist to Jeremias van Rensselaer, 1 September 1657, VRMP, NYSL_sc7079-b01-f20_ncn, https://digitalcollections.archives.nysed.gov/index.php/Detail/objects/18337; see also *CJVR*, 59. Rodenborch is the most frequent variant of the family name that appears in the records, although it is alternately spelled, Roodenburgh, Rodenburch, Rodenborh, Rodenborg, Rodenburg, Rodenborgh, and Rodenburgh.

6. Letter form the WIC Directors to Petrus Stuyvesant, 14 June 1656, DCAC, 1646–1664, NYSA_A1810-78_V12_39, https://digitalcollections.archives.nysed.gov/index.php/Detail/objects/45224; letter from the WIC Directors to Petrus Stuyvesant, 14 June 1656, *Correspondence 1654–1658*, 92.

7. Petition of Catrina Roeloffs, widow of Lucas Rodenborch, for permission to raise money on account of the salary due her husband as vice director of Curaçao, 17 April 1657, NYSA_A1809-78_V08_0518a, https://digitalcollections.archives.nysed.gov/index.php/Detail/objects/56122; NYHM, https://iarchives.nysed.gov/xtf/view?docId=tei/A1809/NYSA_A1809-78_V08_0518a.xml.

8. Jeremias to Jan Baptist van Rensselaer, 6 September 1657, VRMP, NYSL_sc7079-b04-f06_p1_ncn, https://digitalcollections.archives.nysed.gov/index.php/Detail/objects/18467; *CJVR*, 60–61.

9. Jan Baptist to Jeremias van Rensselaer, 20 December 1659, VRMP, NYSL_sc7079-b02-f29_ncn, https://digitalcollections.archives.nysed.gov/index.php/Detail/objects/18386; *CJVR*, 195–97.

10. Jeremias van Rensselaer to Anna Wyly van Rensselaer, 23 August [September] 1658, VRMP, NYSL_sc7079-b04-f12_p1_ncn, https://digitalcollections.archives.nysed.gov/index.php/Detail/objects/18478. In *CJVR* the date is given as 23 September 1658, but the manuscript date listed at the New York State Archives is 23 August. Since the portion of the letter containing the date is burned, I have not been able to determine which is correct. *CJVR*, 109–10, 110n258.

11. Jan Baptist to Jeremias van Rensselaer, Amsterdam, 25 April 1659, VRMP, NYSL_sc7079-b02-f15_ncn, https://digitalcollections.archives.nysed.gov/index.php/Detail/objects/18372; see also *CJVR*, 152–53; Jaap Jacobs, *New Netherland*, 118. Johannes, Kiliaen van Rensselaer's eldest son by his first wife, Hillegond van Bijlaer, was named the first patroon of Rensselaerswijck after his father's death, but he remained in Holland. Instead, his half-brother Jan Baptist traveled to New Netherland to manage the patroonship.

12. Jan Baptist van Rensselaer, 20 February 1659, VRMP, NYSL_sc7079-b02-f07_ncn, https://digitalcollections.archives.nysed.gov/index.php/Detail/objects/18364. *CJVR*, 136. Jan Baptist to Jeremias van Rensselaer, Amsterdam, 25 April 1659, VRMP, NYSL_sc7079-b02-f15_ncn, https://digitalcollections.archives.nysed.gov/index.php/Detail/objects/18372; see also *CJVR*, 152–53.

13. When Andries was enslaved to the Van Rensselaers, Jeremias lived in the patroon's house, which lay inside Beverwijck—an administrative slight intended to assert the colony's control over the power of the patroonship. Venema, *Beverwijck*, 206–7.

14. "New Project of Freedoms and Exemptions," in *DRCHNY*, 1:99. In the 1629 Charter, article XXX, the company promised to try "to supply the colonists with as many blacks as it possibly can [*om aen de Coloniers soo veel Swarten toe te stellen / als*

haer moghelijck wesen], on the conditions hereafter to be made, [*sal / op de ordre daer van te maecken*] without however being bound to do so to a greater extent or for a longer time than it shall see fit [*sonder nochtans daer in ghehouden of verbonden te zijn*]." Charter of Freedoms and Exemptions, 7 June 1629, in *VRBM*, 152, 161. Jaap Jacobs offers a detailed reading of this document as it related to the establishment of the patroon system. Jacobs, *New Netherland*, 113–15. See also Venema, *Beverwijck*, 6. For an exploration of the "Freedoms" as a brainchild of Kiliaen van Rensselaer's ambitions for settlement, see Janny Venema, *Kiliaen van Rensselaer (1586–1643): Designing a New World* (Hilversum, NL: Verloren published with financial support of the New Netherland Institute, 2010), 224.

15. For a detailed discussion of the place of these two documents within the broader Dutch colonization project vis-à-vis enslavement, see Dewulf, *The Pinkster King*, 38, 37n6; See also, Linda M. Heywood and John K. Thornton, *Central Africans, Atlantic Creoles, and the Foundation of the Americas, 1585–1660* (2007; reprint Cambridge: Cambridge University Press, 2011), 252, Foote, *Black and White Manhattan*, 37, Hodges, *Root and Branch*, 289; Goodfriend, "Burghers and Blacks," 127, A. Leon Higginbotham Jr., *In the Matter of Color: Race and the American Legal Process: The Colonial Period* (Oxford: Oxford University Press, 1978), 109–10.

16. For a comprehensive overview of the wider Dutch cultural context of New Netherland's patroonships, see Jaap Jacobs, "Dutch Proprietary Manors in America: The Patroonships in New Netherland," in *The Atlantic World: Europe, Africa and the Americas, 1500–1830*, eds. Benjamin Schmidt and Wim Klooster, vol. 11, *Constructing Early Modern Empires: Proprietary Ventures in the Atlantic World, 1500–1750* (Leiden, NL: Brill, 2007), 301–26.

17. Evan Haefeli, *New Netherland and the Dutch Origins of American Religious Liberty* (Philadelphia: The University of Pennsylvania Press, 2013), 126. For the patroon model in Caribbean and the contrasting example of Brazil, see Klooster, *The Dutch Moment*, 208. Wim Klooster offers a fascinating exploration of the importance of the "freedoms and exemptions" granted by the WIC to Jewish settlers in the Caribbean, Brazil, and the Wild Coast in the early to mid-seventeenth century as "the culmination of the privileges Jewish settlers had obtained since the first Dutch overseas colonies had been carved out." Klooster, "The Essequibo Liberties: The Link between Jewish Brazil and Jewish Suriname," *Studia Rosenthaliana* 42–43 (210–11): 78, doi: 10.2143/SR.43.0.2175920.

18. Oliver Rink, *Holland on the Hudson: An Economic and Social History of Dutch New York* (Ithaca, NY: Cornell University Press, 1986), 196; Daniel J. Weeks, *Gateways to Empire: Quebec and New Amsterdam to 1664* (Bethlehem, PA: Lehigh University Press, 2019), 243.

19. Such a mixed work regime is evident in Kiliaen's further instructions: "This being done, your honor can issue an order in my name, that his farm [Notelman] and that of *Bijlevelt* shall be worked in my interest by a foreman and a boy or a negro and the animals which can be dispensed with may be sent up the river." Kiliaen van Rensselaer to Wouter van Twiller, 23 April 1634, in *VRBM*, 276. Thomas E. Burke, Jr., *Mohawk Frontier: The Dutch Community of Schenectady, New York, 1661–1710*, 2nd ed. (1991; reprint Albany: State University of New York Press, 2009), xx, 139. Jacobs, *New Netherland*, 79. Jan Folkerts posited that enslaved people were introduced into the workforce as a solution to the high wages demanded by farmworkers in New

Netherland, but that their numbers have not been fully accounted for in the documentary record. Folkerts, "Kiliaen van Rensselaer and Agricultural Productivity in His Domain: A New Look at the First Patroon and Rensselaerswijck before 1664," in *A Beautiful and Fruitful Place: Selected Rensselaerswijck Seminar Papers*, eds. Nancy Anne McClure Zeller and Charles Gehring (Albany, NY: New Netherland Publishing, 1993), 302–3; See also Heywood and Thornton, *Central Africans*, 252–53.

20. Venema, *Kiliaen van Rensselaer (1568–1643)*, 276n15; Jacobs, *New Netherland*, 70, 118.

21. Jacobs, *New Netherland*, 431, 118. For a description of the lifestyle led by Jeremias in America, see Joanne Reitano, *New York State: Peoples, Places, and Priorities, a Concise History with Sources* (New York: Routledge, 2016), 16, 16n9.

22. Domine Henricus Selijns to the Classis of Amsterdam, 9 June 1664 Amsterdam Correspondence, Box 1, No. 46. Gardner A. Sage Library, New Brunswick Theological Seminary. The older translation entitled "Two Letters Written by Domine Henricus Selijns during his Ministry in Breuckelen, 1660–1664," Second letter, New Netherland, 9 June 1664, has been shown by Jaap Jacobs, to be faulty when used to estimate the makeup of the Black population, as it was created out of nineteenth-century racial and social conventions rather than seventeenth-century norms. Jaap Jacobs, "Slavery in Stuyvesant's World," St. Mark's Church in-the-Bowery, 31 January 2021; cf. *NYHMRCB*, 231. Godefridus Udemans in *'t Geestelijck Roer van 't Coopmans Schip* (The Spiritual Rudder of the Merchant Ship) had argued that baptism should not emancipate the enslaved from earthly bondage. Godefridus Udemans, *'t Geestelijck Roer van 't Coopmans Schip* (Dordrecht, NL: Francois Boels, 1640), 183. The shift against baptism has been analyzed as a religious struggle waged within the Dutch oversees empire as well as a cultural shift where the Dutch Republic was imagined as a Protestant, free white zone. Danny Noorlander, *Heaven's Wrath: The Protestant Reformation and the Dutch West India Company* (Ithaca, NY: Cornell University Press, 2019), chapter 5, footnote 8. Jacobs, *New Netherland*, 316–17. Dienke Hondius, *Blackness in Western Europe: Racial Patterns of Paternalism and Exclusion* (New Brunswick, NJ: Transaction Publishers, 2014), 111–62.

23. Jeremias flipped the paper on its side and wrote the details about the house through his comments about Volckert Jansz, from left to right in the left margin. From the New York State Education Department, Jeremias to Jan Baptist van Rensselaer, 4 September 1659, NYSL_sc7079-b04-f19_ncn, http://digitalcollections.archives.nysed.gov/index.php/Detail/objects/18490; See also *CJVR*, 177.

24. Venema, *Beverwijck*, 233.

25. Venema, *Kiliaen van Rensselaer (1586–1643)*, 156, 158, 268; Venema, *Beverwijck*, 45, 220.

26. Venema, *Beverwijck*, 228.

27. Jeremias to Jan Baptist van Rensselaer, 20 August 1659, VRMP, NYSL_sc7079-b04-f17_ncn, https://digitalcollections.archives.nysed.gov/index.php/Detail/objects/18487; See also *CJVR*, 167.

28. Mosterman, *Spaces of Enslavement*, 26.

29. I have used Van Laer's translation, which includes words no longer visible due to continuing damage from the 1911 fire, as only the words "your neger Andries" are legible today. For the original see Jeremias to Jan Baptist van Rensselaer, 11 May 1659, NYSL_sc7079-b04-f25_p2-f26_p1_ncn, https://digitalcollections.archives.nysed.gov/index.php/Detail/objects/18506; *CJVR*, 159.

30. Jeremias to Jan Baptist van Rensselaer, 11 May 1659, NYSL_sc7079-b04-f25_p2-f26_p1_ncn, https://digitalcollections.archives.nysed.gov/index.php/Detail/objects/18506; *CJVR*, 159. See also Venema, *Beverwijck*, 222, 222n284.

31. Jan Baptist to Jeremias van Rensselaer, 25 April 1659, NYSL_sc7079-b02-f15_ncn, https://digitalcollections.archives.nysed.gov/index.php/Detail/objects/18372. The relevant section is midway down the second of four pages of the letter: *"Ick ^hebbe hem noodtsaeckelijck op Cralo vand . . . om op mij paerdt te passen, Ick hebben een blauwbont . . . een spaense merrie van 3 jaer op gedaen is vol ws[ ]schrijft hoe mij aenteelinghe van paerden."* "Blauwbont," translated as roan piebald, is a change from Van Lear's translation of dappled blue-black. When *-bont* is added to a horse color, it is an indication that the animal is multicolored—"piebald" in English—but dapples are slight patterns of the same color. The *blauw* indicates genetically black horses that contain a high mixture of white in the coat, or "blue roan" horses in English—in this case "roan piebald." Susanah Shaw Romney, email message to author, 13 May 2021; cf. *CJVR*, 152–53.

32. For Petrus Stuyvesant's restriction of access to horses on Curaçao, see INSTRUCTIONS given by Petrus Stuyvesant to Matthias Beck, vice-director of Curaçao, 8 June 1655, NNCCR, NYSA_A1883-78_V17_019, https://digitalcollections.archives.nysed.gov/index.php/Detail/objects/19384; *CP*, 76 81n75.

33. Karwan, Fatah-Black and Matthias van Rossum, "Slavery in a 'Slave Free Enclave': Historical Links Between the Dutch Republic Empire and Slavery, 1580s–1860s," *Werkstatt Geschichte* 66–67 (2015): 58–59; Dienke Hondius, "West-European Urban Networks in the History of Slavery and the Slave Trade: New Research Perspectives from the Netherlands," in *Serfdom and Slavery in the European Economy 11th–18th Centuries*, ed. Simonetta Cavaciocchi (Florence, Italy: Firenze University Press, 2014), 585. For an excellent treatment in Dutch see Leo Balai, *Geschiedenis van de Amsterdamse slavenhandel: over de belangen van Amsterdamse regenten bij de trans-Atlantische slavenhandel* (Zutphen, NL: Walburg Pers, 2013).

34. The presence of the enslaved within the Dutch Republic, brought by their enslavers from others parts of the empire, was captured by Dutch painters and writers. For more on this subject, see Mark Ponte, "1656 'Twee mooren in een stuck van Rembrandt,'" in *Wereldgeschiedenis van Nederland*, eds. Karel Davids, Karwan Fatah-Black, Marjolein 't Hart, Leo Lucassen, Jeroen Touwen, and Lex Heerma van Voss (Den Hague, NL: Huygens Instituut Voor Nederlandse Geschiedenis, 2018), 265–69; Ponte, "'Al de swarten die hier ter stede comen' Een Afro-Atlantische gemeenschap in zeventiende-eeuws Amsterdam," *TSEG/ Low Countries Journal of Social and Economic History* 15, no. 4 (2018): 33–61; Dienke Hondius, "Access to the Netherlands of Enslaved and Free Black Africans: Exploring Legal and Social Historical Practices in the Sixteenth-Nineteenth Centuries," *Slavery and Abolition* 32, no. 3 (2011): 377–95, https://doi.org/10.1080/0144039X.2011.588476; Hondius, *Blackness in Western Europe*; Nicole Saffold Maskiell, "Elite Slave Networks in the Dutch Atlantic," in *Shifting the Compass: Pluricontinental Connections in Dutch Colonial and Postcolonial Literature*, eds. Jeroen Dewulf, Olf Praamstra, and Michiel van Kempen (Newcastle, UK: Cambridge Scholars Publishing, 2013), chap. 10.

35. Jan Baptist to Jeremias van Rensselaer, Amsterdam, 20 February 1659, VRMP, NYSL_sc7079-b02-f07_ncn, https://digitalcollections.archives.nysed.gov/index.php/Detail/objects/18364; Jeremias to Jan Baptist van Rensselaer, 11 May 1659, VRMP, NYSL_sc7079-b04-f25_p2-f26_p1_ncn, https://digitalcollections.archives.nysed.gov/index.php/Detail/objects/18506; See also *CJVR*, 136, 159.

36. Jeremias to Jan Baptist van Rensselaer, 20 August 1659, VRMP, NYSL_sc7079-b04-f17_ncn, https://digitalcollections.archives.nysed.gov/index.php/Detail/objects/18487; See also *CJVR*, 167.

37. Jeremias to Jan Baptist van Rensselaer, 2 June 1661, VRMP, NYSL_sc7079-b04-f42_ncn, https://digitalcollections.archives.nysed.gov/index.php/Detail/objects/18522; Jan Baptist to Jeremias van Rensselaer, 20 December 1659, NYSL_sc7079-b02-f29_ncn, http://digitalcollections.archives.nysed.gov/index.php/Detail/objects/18386; see also *CJVR*, 167, 196–97.

38. Jaap Jacobs, email message to author, 23 May 2021; Dutch National Archives, 1.01.02, inv.nr. 12564.46; *DRCHNY*, 2:31.

39. Jeremias to Jan Baptist van Rensselaer, 20 August 1659, VRMP, NYSL_sc7079-b04-f17_ncn, https://digitalcollections.archives.nysed.gov/index.php/Detail/objects/18487; See also *CJVR*, 167.

40. Venema, *Beverwijck*, 221.

41. Jacobs, *New Netherland*, 256.

42. Hondius, *Blackness in Western Europe*, 213–20.

43. Jeremias to Jan Baptist van Rensselaer, 2 June 1661, VRMP, NYSL_sc7079-b04-f42_ncn, https://digitalcollections.archives.nysed.gov/index.php/Detail/objects/18522; See also CJVR, 255–56.

44. Venema, *Beverwijck*, 227.

45. *CJVR*, 255n568. According to a memorandum, the man was sent down in the summer of 1661 by skipper Symon Janzen de Vries.

46. East Jersey Proprietors to Petrus Stuyvesant, NJEJD, Vol. 1 Part A, Folio 66; Lease of Farm at Wiltwyck, in the Esopus from Petrus and Judith Stuyvesant to Willem Beekman, 1666, UCADR, Book 2, 157-9, https://archives.ulstercountyny.gov.

47. Henricus Selijns, Letter to Amsterdam Classis, 4 October 1660, Amsterdam Correspondence, Box 1, No. 41. Gardner A. Sage Library, New Brunswick Theological Seminary.

48. Rev. Samuel Drisius to the Classis of Amsterdam, 5 August 1664, in *ERNY*, 1:555.

49. Petition. Juan Gallardo Ferrara, praying for the restoration of his negro slaves, and order thereupon, 6 September 1656, NYCM, NYSA_A1809-78_V08_0166, https://digitalcollections.archives.nysed.gov/index.php/Detail/objects/55860; Resolution, director and council, on receipt of letters from the States-General, the burgomasters of Amsterdam, and an extract from a memorial of the Spanish ambassador, relative to the case of the aforesaid Juan Gallardo vs. captain Sebastiaen Raeff and his lieutenant, Jan van Campen, 6 September 1656, NYCM, NYSA_A1809-78_

V08_0168b, https://digitalcollections.archives.nysed.gov/index.php/Detail/objects/55862; Resolution, director and council adhering to their previous resolution of September 6, on the claim of Juan Gallardo Ferara for the restitution of certain negroes. 31 October 1656, NYCM, NYSA_A1809-78_V08_0258, https://digitalcollections.archives.nysed.gov/index.php/Detail/objects/55926. For a translation with the missing list of enslaved people, see "Sundry Papers in relation to the Case of Juan Gallardo and his Negro Slaves," in *DRCHNY*, 2:31.

50. Resolution granting a petition presented by the Nine men, 12 February 1652, NYCM, NYSA_A1809-78_V05_0017a, http://digitalcollections.archives.nysed.gov/index.php/Detail/objects/54639.

51. Freedom Petition of Mayken van Angola, Lucretia Albiecke van Angola and the wife of Peter Tamboer, 28 December 1662, NYCM, NYSA_A1809-78_V10_pt1_0296, https://digitalcollections.archives.nysed.gov/index.php/Detail/objects/55199; translation by Eric Ruijssenaars, https://wams.nyhistory.org/early-encounters/dutch-colonies/fighting-for-freedom-in-new-amsterdam/; Certificate of manumission of Domingo Angola and Maykie, his wife, 17 April 1664, NYCM, NYSA_A1809-78_V10_pt3_0170, http://digitalcollections.archives.nysed.gov/index.php/Detail/objects/55635. Eekhof, A. *De Hervormde Kerk in Noord-Amerika* ('s-Gravenhage, Netherlands: M. Nijhoff, 1913), 2: 159.

52. Resolution to charter to Frederick Phillipse, late the director's carpenter, the company's sloop for a voyage to Virginia, 20 September 1660, NNCM, NYSA_A1809-78_V09_0416, http://digitalcollections.archives.nysed.gov/index.php/Detail/objects/53620. Russell Shorto and Len Tantillo, "In Search of Stuyvesant's Bowery," *New Netherland Matters* (spring 2020), 5–9.

53. Henricus Selijns, Letter to Amsterdam Classis, 4 October 1660. Amsterdam Correspondence, Box 1, No. 41. Gardner A. Sage Library, New Brunswick Theological Seminary. Overall shape for the island and the roadways in the settlement of New Amsterdam are based on the *Castello Plan of 1660* from The New York Public Library. Location of the House for the Company Blacks was further informed by discussion in Isaac Newton Phelps Stokes, *The Iconography of Manhattan Island, 1498–1909* (New York: Robert H. Dodd, 1915). Location of Free Negro Lots based on a letter from Petrus Stuyvesant to Secretary Cornelis van Ruyven in 1660. Petrus Stuyvesant to Secretary Van Ruyven, 18 March 1660, NNCM, NYSA_A1809-78_V09_0131, https://digitalcollections.archives.nysed.gov/index.php/Detail/objects/53433; DRCHNY, 13:151–52; Lionel Pincus and Princess Firyal Map Division, The New York Public Library, "Redraft of the Castello Plan, New Amsterdam in 1660," New York Public Library Digital Collections, https://digitalcollections.nypl.org/items/510d47e4-7369-a3d9-e040-e00a18064a99; Stokes, *Iconography*, 207, 297.

54. For Jeremias van Rensselaer's early life, see Janny Venema, *Kiliaen van Rensselaer (1586–1643)*, 270. Nicolaes Willem Stuyvesant was baptized on 2 December 1648. *Liber A-2*, 42. Jeremias van Rensselaer married Maria van Cortlandt (recorded as Marritje Cortlant), 27 April 1662. *Liber A-2*, 507.

55. Joanne van der Woude and Jaap Jacobs, "Sweet Resoundings: Friendship Poetry by Petrus Stuyvesant and Johan Farret on Curaçao, 1639–45," *WMQ* 75, no. 3 (2018), 510, https://www.jstor.org/stable/10.5309/willmaryquar.75.3.0507.

56. *CP*, 25.

57. *CP*, 41.

58. Dutch Colonial Council Minutes, 27 May 1647, NYSA_A1809-78_V04_p287, https://digitalcollections.archives.nysed.gov/index.php/Detail/objects/11684. Petrus and Judith were wed in Breda on 13 August 1645. "Netherlands, Noord-Brabant, Church Records, 1473–1965," Image 302, Family Search, https://www.familysearch.org/ark:/61903/3:1:3QS7-99QX-5FJ1?i=507&cc=2037960, NAN. Jacobs, *Petrus Stuyvesant*, 43.

59. Jacobs, *Petrus Stuyvesant*, 27.

60. Instruction for Hendrick van Dijck, Fiscal of the General Incorporated West India Company in New Netherland and adjoining places, in *DRCHNY*, 1:505.

61. For a concise analysis of the economic impact of the Dutch slave trade, see Karwan Fatah-Black and Matthias van Rossum, "Beyond Profitability: The Dutch Transatlantic Slave Trade and its Economic Impact," *Slavery & Abolition* 36, no. 1 (2015), 63–83, http://dx.doi.org/10.1080/0144039X.2013.873591. The *Bonte Koe*, which left the Bight of Biafra (Gabon-Cape Lopez) captained by Mathias Henrique, was the first slave ship recorded in the Slave Trade database to arrive in Curaçao directly from Africa and carried 281 captured human beings aboard. Sixty-six people died on the voyage. *TAVoyages*, Voyage ID no. 11362. Linda Rupert posits some origins of Curaçao's enslaved population can be garnered from the extant names, with surnames such as Van Angola or Creole. Rupert, *Creolization and Contraband*, 61–62, 61n128. Linda Rupert highlights a Sephardic trading diaspora with nodes in Dutch West Africa, Brazil, and Curaçao; Rupert, *Creolization and Contraband*, 47–48, 51–52; 57, 61–62.

62. After Stuyvesant's decision to repatriate, Lucas Rodenborch was chosen as an interim replacement by a plurality of votes. Resolution drafted the 22 of August 1644 at Fort Amsterdam Curaçao. Resolution, Providing for the government of the island of Curaçao, in consequence of director Stuyvesant being obliged to return home on account of a wound he received at St. Martin, 22 August 1644, NYCCR, NYSA_A1883-78_V17_009d, https://digitalcollections.archives.nysed.gov/index.php/Detail/objects/19371; Resolution, Appointing Lucas Rodenborche provisional director of Curaçao and dependencies. 22 August 1644, NYCCR, NYSA-A1883-78_V17_010a, https://digitalcollections.archives.nysed.gov/index.php/Detail/objects/19372; *CP*, 46–47. For Trijntjen Roelofs's marriage information see Willem Frijhoff, *Fulfilling God's Mission: The Two Worlds of Dominie Everardus Bogardus, 1607–1647*, translated by Myra Heerspink Scholz, vol. 14 in *The Atlantic World: Europe, Africa and the Americas, 1500–1830*, eds. Benjamin Schmidt and Wim Klooster (Leiden, NL: Brill, 2003–), 599n3; See also Romney, *New Netherland Connections*, 260. Her daughter Elizabeth was born ca. 1652 on Curaçao, and another daughter Lucretia was born five years later and baptized on July 1, 1657, in New Amsterdam. *Liber A-2*, 91. For the end of Lucas Rodenborch's term see *CP*, 74–81. Elizabeth married Ephraim Herrman, Augustine Herrman's son, 10 August 1679. *Liber A-2*, 538.

63. Most servants in the seventeenth-century United Provinces were women. Martha Hollander posits that "the majority of households in the Netherlands included one or two maidservants." Martha Hollander, *Structures of Space and Society in the Seventeenth-Century Dutch Interior* (PhD diss., University of California, Berkeley, 1990), 53, 53n61. Schama gives an extended examination of the trope of the lascivious Dutch maidservant. Simon Schama, *The Embarrassment of Riches: An Interpretation of Dutch Culture in the Golden Age* (1987; reprint New York: Vintage Books, 1997), 158, 316, 438; Romney traces this cultural expectation from the United Provinces to colonial

America. Romney, *New Netherland Connections*, 66, 77n13,87. Although Curaçao would have been the Stuyvesant-Bayards' first encounter with Atlantic slavery, Black maidservants were in Amsterdam. Dienke Hondius and Linda Rupert point to the presence of Black servants among the seventeenth-century Jewish communities in Amsterdam during the 1640s. Rupert, *Creolization and Contraband*, 48; Dienke Hondius, "Black Africans in Seventeenth-Century Amsterdam," *Renaissance and Reformation/Renaissance et Réforme* 31, vol. 2 (2008): 94–95. See also Hondius, *Blackness in Western Europe*; Allison Blakely, *Blacks in the Dutch World: The Evolution of Racial Imagery in a Modern Society* (Bloomington: Indiana University Press, 1993); Heike Raphael-Hernandez, ed., *Blackening Europe: The African American Presence* (New York: Routledge, 2004); Hans Werner Debrunner, *Presence and Prestige: Africans in Europe, A History of Africans in Europe before 1918* (Basel: Basler Afrika Bibliographien, 1979).

64. Petrus Stuyvesant's commitment to the spread of slavery has been noted by numerous historians and is supported by a record of slave requests and correspondence highlighting the centrality of the trade; see Hodges, *Root & Branch*, 25–26; Rupert, *Creolization and Contraband*, 64; Dewulf, "Emulating a Portuguese Model," 28.

65. Rupert, *Creolization and Contraband*, 66. Lucas Rodenburch, vice director of Curaçao, to the directors at Amsterdam, 2 April 1654, NNCCR, NYSA_A1883-78_V17_014, https://digitalcollections.archives.nysed.gov/index.php/Detail/objects/19379; *CP*, 62. Instructions given by Petrus Stuyvesant to Matthias Beck, 8 Jun 1655, NYSA_A1883-78_V17_019, https://digitalcollections.archives.nysed.gov/index.php/Detail/objects/19384; *CP*, 76 81n75.

66. Susan Scott Parrish, "Richard Ligon and the Atlantic Science of Commonwealths," *WMQ* 67, no. 2 (April 2010): 209–48.

67. De Laet, *Iaerlyck verhael*, https://resolver.kb.nl/resolve?urn=KONB10:000019207:00015), 114–19.

68. Bonomi, "Swarms of Negroes Coming about My Door, 41–43; Hodges, *Root & Branch*, 10–13.

69. Warren Milteer, *Beyond Slavery's Shadow: Free People of Color in the South* (Chapel Hill: University of North Carolina Press, 2021), 23; Jennifer Morgan, *Reckoning with Slavery: Gender, Kinship, and Capitalism in the Early Black Atlantic* (Durham, NC: Duke University Press, 2021), 177–80. Innes, Stephen, and T. H. Breen, *Myne Owne Ground: Race and Freedom on Virginia's Eastern Shore, 1640–1676* (1980; reprint New York: Oxford University Press, 2004), 4.

70. Copy of Resolutions of the Amsterdam chamber of the West India Company regarding Wouter van Twiller's farm, 24 May 1642, NNCM, NYSA_A0270-78_V3_061d, https://digitalcollections.archives.nysed.gov/index.php/Detail/objects/19141; A.F. Van Laer, trans., K. Stryker-Rodda, eds., *New York Historical Manuscripts: Dutch, Register of the Provincial Secretary, 1648–1660* (Baltimore: Genealogical Publishing, 1974), 3: 174

71. For more on the respective roles of private individuals and the WIC in funding, chartering, and operating slaving voyages, see Maika, "To 'experiment with a parcel of negros,'" 33–69.

72. Instruction to the Director General and Council of New Netherland in *DRCHNY*, 1:162.

73. For a compelling analysis of Maurits's time as a slaveholder in Brazil, see Carolina Monteiro and Erik Odegard, "Slavery at the Court of the 'Humanist

Prince': Reexamining Johan Maurits van Nassau-Siegen and his Role in Slavery, Slave Trade, and Slave-smuggling in Dutch Brazil," *Journal of Early American History* 10, 1 (2020): 3–32, https://doi.org/10.1163/18770703-01001004.

74. Letter from the Directors in Amsterdam to the council of New Netherland, 26 June 1647, in *Correspondence 1654–1658*, 5.

75. Directors to Petrus Stuyvesant, April 7, 1648, NNCAC, NYSA_A1810-78_V11_12, https://digitalcollections.archives.nysed.gov/index.php/Detail/objects/45078; Letter from the Directors in Amsterdam to Petrus Stuyvesant, 7 April 1648, in *Correspondence 1654–1658*, 55.

76. *Correspondence 1654–1658*, 59.

77. *Liber A-2*, 35.

78. *MCR*, 12, 12n2; Dewulf, *The Pinkster King*, 41; Hodges, *Root and Branch*, 15. Romney, *New Netherland Connections*, 209

79. Jan Francisco had been advanced thirty-five florins for clothes received "in the service of the patroon," in *VRBM*, 834; Venema, *Beverwijck*, 114.

80. Romney, *New Netherland Connections*, 216–17.

81. Romney, *New Netherland Connections*, 216–17.

82. Ira Berlin, *Many Thousands Gone: The First Two Centuries of Slavery in North America* (Cambridge, MA: Harvard University Press, 1998), 17–24, 52.

83. Patent. Domingo Antony, negro; 5 morgens of land on the island of Manhattan, and 505 rods behind Bouwery No. 5, near the Fresh water, 13 Jul 1643, NNCPD, NYSA_A1880-78_VGG_0080, https://digitalcollections.archives.nysed.gov/index.php/Detail/objects/51177; Patent, Catelina, widow of Jochim Antony, negro; 4 morgens and 91 rods of land on the island of Manhattan, next the above, a common double wagon road remaining between both, 13 Jul 1643, NNCPD, NYSA_A1880-78_VGG_0081, https://digitalcollections.archives.nysed.gov/index.php/Detail/objects/51178; Land grant from Willem Kieft to Paulo de Angola, 14 July 1645 in Stokes, *Iconography*, 74. Patent, Anthony Portuguese, negro; 6 morgens, 425 rods of land (Manhattan Island), 5 Sept 1645, NNCPD, NYSA_A1880-78_VGG_0117, https://digitalcollections.archives.nysed.gov/index.php/Detail/objects/51214; Patent, Big Manuel, negro; 4 morgens, 380 rods land on the island of Manhattan, east of the above last-mentioned lot, 19 Oct 1645, NNCPD, NYSA_A1880-78_VGG_0125, https://digitalcollections.archives.nysed.gov/index.php/Detail/objects/51222; Patent, Francisco, a negro; piece of land on the public wagon road, Manhattan Island, containing 200x335 paces, 25 March 1647, NNCPD, NYSA_A1880-78_VGG_0199a, https://digitalcollections.archives.nysed.gov/index.php/Detail/objects/51297; Patent, Bastiaen, a negro; piece of land on Manhattan Island, adjoining the above, 200x300 paces, 26 Mar 1647, NNCPD, NYSA_A1880-78_VGG_0200, https://digitalcollections.archives.nysed.gov/index.php/Detail/objects/51299; Patent, Jan, a negro, who came with the privateer; piece of land on the public wagon road, Manhattan Island, at the end of Mr. Hans (Kierstede's) house and plantation, 200x225 paces, 26 Mar 1647, NNCPD, NYSA_A1880-78_VGG_0201, https://digitalcollections.archives.nysed.gov/index.php/Detail/objects/51300; Patent, Peter van Campen, negro; 3 morgens 225 rods of land on the island of Manhattan, adjoining the negroes' land, 8 Apr 1647, NNCPD, NYSA_A1880-78_VGG_0209, https://digitalcollections.archives.nysed.gov/index.php/Detail/objects/51309; Deed, Paulo de Angola and Clara Crioole, negroes, to Symon Joosten, of a lot

of land on the east side of the Kolck, Manhattans. [1651], NNCPD, NYSA_A0270-78_V3_075a, 7 Apr 1648, https://digitalcollections.archives.nysed.gov/index.php/Detail/objects/19172. For a comprehensive overview of the community of free Africans and creoles who lived along the wagon road see Michael A. Gomez, *Black Crescent: The Experience and Legacy of African Muslims in the Americas* (Cambridge: Cambridge University Press, 2005), 120–30, 129m4.

84. Dutch Colonial Council Minutes, 25 February 1644, NNCM, NYSA_A1809-78_V04_p183-184, https://digitalcollections.archives.nysed.gov/index.php/Detail/objects/11580.

85. Petrus and Judith were married in Breda on 13 August 1645. Jaap Jacobs includes details of Judith's early life in *Petrus Stuyvesant*, 43.

86. *Liber A-2*, 36.

87. *Liber A-2*, 37.

88. Indenture of service of Maria, a young Negro girl, to Nicolaes Coorn, 25 May 1644, NNRPS, NYSA_A0270-78_V2_111b, http://digitalcollections.archives.nysed.gov/index.php/Detail/objects/11106.

89. See multiple baptisms of enslaved people, including the children of Andries, Emanuel, Anthony, Paulus in Sypher, *Liber A-2*.

90. Sypher, *Liber A-2*, 42.

91. Certain foods were served during the lying-in period and may well have been prepared for Judith by enslaved hands. For an image of a Dutch lying in which features the food served intended to bring the milk down, see Matthijs Naiveu, "The Newborn Baby," in *Matters of Taste: Food and Drink in Seventeenth-century Dutch Art and Life*, eds. Donna R. Barnes and Peter G. Rose (Syracuse, NY: Syracuse University Press, 2002), 94. Food culture was a central form of seventeenth-century Dutch identity. Linda Civitello, *Cuisine and Culture: A History of Food and People* (Hoboken, NJ: Wiley, 2008), 158–61.

92. For Selijns's wedding poem entitled "Bridal Torch," written to celebrate Ægidius Luyck and Judith van Isendoorn's wedding and its allusions to the slavery he encountered in New Amsterdam, see Nicole Saffold Maskiell, "Elite Dutch Slave Networks," 192. Stuyvesant doubtlessly invited Ægidius to his *bouwerij*, where Ægidius likely met Henricus Selijns. Henry Cruse Murphy, trans. and ed., *Anthology of New Netherland, Or, Translations from the Early Dutch Poets of New York, With Memoirs of Their Lives* (1865; reprint Amsterdam: N. Israel, 1966), 171.

93. Esther J. Lee et al., "MtDNA Origins of an Enslaved Labor Force from the 18th Century Schuyler Flatts Burial Ground in Colonial Albany, NY: Africans, Native Americans and Malagasy?" *Journal of Archaeological Science* 36, no. 12 (December 2009): 2805–10, https://doi.org/10.1016/j.jas.2009.09.008.

94. Jennifer L. Morgan, "'Some Could Suckle over Their Shoulder': Male Travelers, Female Bodies, and the Gendering of Racial Ideology, 1500–1700," *WMQ* 54, no. 1 (January 1997): 183–84.

95. Jeremias to Jan Baptist van Rensselaer, 2 June 1661, VRMP, NYSL_sc7079-b04-f42_ncn, http://digitalcollections.archives.nysed.gov/index.php/Detail/objects/18522; Susanah Shaw Romney, email messages to the author, 31 May 2021, 1 June 2021.

96. Stuyvesant to the vice director of Curaçao, NNCAC, NYSA_A1810-78_V13_070, https://digitalcollections.archives.nysed.gov/index.php/Detail/objects/54453; *DIHSTA*, 3:421; Jaap Jacobs, email message to the author, 28 May 2021.

97. Letter from the Director-General to the Nine men, 15 November 1651, NNCM, NYSA_A1809-78_V05_0019c, https://digitalcollections.archives.nysed.gov/index.php/Detail/objects/54646; *Council Minutes 1652–54*, 13–14.

98. Instruction for Hendrick van Dijck, in *DRCHNY*, 1:505. For a clear explanation of the governance structure of the colony, specifically the difference between the positions of fiscael and schout, see Jaap Jacobs, "'To Favor this New and Growing City of New Amsterdam with a Court of Justice.' The Relations between Rulers and Ruled in New Amsterdam," in *Amsterdam—New York: Transatlantic Relations and Urban Identities Since 1653*, eds. George Harinck and Hans Krabbendam (Amsterdam: VU University Press, 2005), 17–29, herein 24–26.

99. Instruction for Hendrick van Dijck, in *DRCHNY*, 1:505.

100. Journal of New Netherland; Written in the years 1641, 1642, 1643, 1644, 1645 and 1646, in *DRCHNY*, 1:187.

101. Jacobs, *New Netherland*, 95.

102. Instruction for Hendrick van Dijck, 1652 in *DRCHNY*, 1:504. For documents concerning the broader fight between Petrus and Hendrick, see Petition of Fiscal Van Dijck to change the phrasing of the resolution on The Bride, 6 February 1652, NNCM, NYSA_A1809-78_V05_0014, https://digitalcollections.archives.nysed.gov/index.php/Detail/objects/54637; Letter from Director-General to the council, 27 March 1652, NNCM, NYSA_A1809-78_V05_0036, https://digitalcollections.archives.nysed.gov/index.php/Detail/objects/54659; Minute approving the suspension of Hendrick van Dijck, 28 March 1652, NNCM, NYSA_A1809-78_V05_0037a, https://digitalcollections.archives.nysed.gov/index.php/Detail/objects/54660; Minute of the appearance of Hendrick van Dijck before the council, 28 March 1652, NNCM, NYSA_A1809-78_V05_0037b, https://digitalcollections.archives.nysed.gov/index.php/Detail/objects/54661; Order to the secretary to furnish Van Dijck with a copy of the lampoon, 28 March 1652, NNCM, NYSA_A1809-78_V05_0037c, https://digitalcollections.archives.nysed.gov/index.php/Detail/objects/54662; Order to Hendrick van Dijck to vacate the company's house which he occupies, 15 October 1652, NNCM, NYSA_A1809-78_V05_0078, https://digitalcollections.archives.nysed.gov/index.php/Detail/objects/54704.

103. The year 1647 marked a transitional period for the Dutch in the Atlantic slave trade. With the loss of Brazil and control of São Tomé the Portuguese turned their attention on recapturing Luanda. Cornelis C.H. Goslinga, *The Dutch in the Caribbean on the Wild Coast 1580–1689* (1971; reprint Gainesville: Library Press@UF and imprint of the University of Florida Press, 2017), 106, 308, 312, 315. Klooster offers a detailed analysis of the multicultural identities of slave ship captains who plied the Dutch Atlantic and the varied ports they frequented. Klooster, *The Dutch Moment*, 146, 195. *TAVoyages*, Voyage ID no. 11353. *Eendracht* (1647). This ship was flying under a French flag but captained by Dutchman Pieter Mijnerts. It arrived in São Tomé on July 1, 1647, after a shipboard rebellion and a voyage during which 85 captive people died. Another such example was the *Prince van Denemarcken*, captained by Maarten Honnich, which lost 72 people in its voyage to the Caribbean; the remaining 320 would be sold into the regional slaving market. The year also marked a peak in investment in Barbados. Pieter Cornelis Emmer, *The Dutch Slave Trade, 1500–1850* (Oxford, UK: Berghahn Books, 2006), 24. Russell R. Menard, *Sweet Negotiations: Sugar, Slavery, and Plantation Agriculture in early Barbados* (Charlottesville: University of Virginia Press, 2006), 52.

104. On Barbados, during the mid-1640s, sugar was still worked in part by European servants but it was quickly being racialized. Ligon gives an example of a group enslaved people attacking with fire the sugar processing plant, although others thwart the effort by informing their enslavers. Richard Ligon, *A True and Exact History of the Island of Barbados*, ed. Karen Ordahl Kupperman (1657; reprint Indianapolis, IN: Hackett, 2011), 101–6. By the late seventeenth century, the association of sugar and blackness informed Aphra Behn's *Oroonoko*. Aphra Behn, *Oroonoko*, in *Versions of Blackness: 'Oroonoko', Race, and Slavery*, ed. Derek Hughes (1688; reprint Cambridge: Cambridge University Press, 2007), 127. For a discussion of the breakdown of tasks such as tending hogs and building fortification, see Foote, *Black and White Manhattan*, 38; See also Romney, *New Netherland Connections*, 207–8; For the racialization of dishonorable work like serving as an executioner, see Venema, *Beverwijck*, 114. Menard, *Sweet Negotiations*, 45, 98.

105. Gabriel de Haes vs. Nicolaes Meyer, 15 November 1655, in *Minutes of the Court of Burgomasters and Schepens of New Amsterdam, Sept. 1654–Nov. 15, 1655*, NYCMA, http://nycma.lunaimaging.com/luna/servlet/s/51qx5e. A published English translation of the case included in *RONA*, 1:398.

106. Benjamin Schmidt, *Innocence Abroad: The Dutch Imagination and the New World, 1570–1670* (Cambridge: Cambridge University Press, 2001), 113–15, 301.

107. Ulrich Lupoldt, *fiscael*, vs. Gijsbert Cornelissen Beyerlandt, New Amsterdam, 3 February 1639, NNCM, NYSA_A1809-78_V04_p031, https://digitalcollections.archives.nysed.gov/index.php/Detail/objects/11428. For another version of the translation see *Council Minutes, 1638–1649*, 37.

108. For the public and humiliating nature of punishment in medieval and early modern Amsterdam, see Geert Mak, *Amsterdam: A Brief Life of the City*, trans. Philipp Blom (London: Vintage Books, 2001), 46; Steven Nadler, *A Book Forged in Hell: Spinoza's Scandalous Treatise and the Birth of the Secular Age* (Princeton, NJ: Princeton University Press, 2011), 37.

109. Proclamation annulling ordinances in Rensselaerswyck prohibiting the cutting and hauling of firewood for Fort Orange, 27 January 1652, NNCM, NYSA_A1809-78_V05_0004, https://digitalcollections.archives.nysed.gov/index.php/Detail/objects/54626; For another translation, see *Council Minutes 1652–54*, 2.

110. See "BON – BOR" in Henry Hexham *A copious English and Netherduytch dictionaire Composed out of our best English Authours. With an appendix of the names of Beasts, Fowles, Birds, Fishes, Hunting, and Hawking and also a compendious grammar for the instruction of the learner. Het groot woorden-Boeck, etc.* (Rotterdam, NL: Aernout Leers, 1647).

111. Hondius, *Blackness in Western Europe*, 81–82.

112. Remonstrance of The Director—General and Council of New—Netherland to the States—General, Exposing the Bad Conduct of the Barbarous Indians towards the Dutch, 31 Oct 1655, NNCM, NYSA_A1809-78_V06_0130, https://digitalcollections.archives.nysed.gov/index.php/Detail/objects/52388; *DRCHNY*, 13:49–51.

113. Jean R. Soderlund, *Lenape Country: Delaware Valley Society Before William Penn* (Philadelphia: University of Pennsylvania Press, 2015), 93–94; Lipman, *The Saltwater Frontier*, 187–88.

114. Extract from a Letter of the Directors in Holland to Stuyvesant and Council: They Accuse the (Former) Fiscals Van Tienhoven and Van Dijk as Being the Cause of the Late Indian Massacre, in *DRCHNY*, 13:70.

115. April 20/30 1665. Certificate. That sundry grant of land, near Stuyvesant's bouwery, had been made in the years 1659 and 1660 to divers negroes' with the names of said negroes and a description of their lands, NNCM, NYSA_A1809-78_V10_pt3_0329, https://digitalcollections.archives.nysed.gov/index.php/Detail/objects/55731; See also https://www.newnetherlandinstitute.org/files/2814/0681/8946/Stuyvesantmanumission.

116. Letter from Petrus Stuyvesant to Secretary Van Ruyven. The Esopus Indians have been Attacked and Defeated; the Out Settlements are to be Put on their Guard, 18 March 1660, NNCM, NYSA_A1809-78_V09_0131, https://digitalcollections.archives.nysed.gov/index.php/Detail/objects/53433; *DRCHNY*, 13:151–52.

117. Letter to Jan Baptist Van Rensselaer, 3–6 June 1660, VRMP, NYSL_sc7079-b04-f32_p1-f36_p2_ncnin, https://digitalcollections.archives.nysed.gov/index.php/Detail/objects/18514. *CJVR*, 220.

118. Transport of Esopus Indians to Curaçao, 12 July 1660, NNCM, NYSA_A1810-78_V13_0117, https://digitalcollections.archives.nysed.gov/index.php/Detail/objects/54501.

119. For the use of Black people as enslaved labor to build and protect New Netherland before Stuyvesant's tenure see Romney, *New Netherland Connections*, 191–99, 203.

120. Jeremias to Jan Baptist van Rensselaer, 25 April 1664, VRMP, NYSL_sc7079-b05-f15_p2-f16_p1_ncn, https://digitalcollections.archives.nysed.gov/index.php/Detail/objects/18546; Jaap Jacobs, email message to author, 28 May 2021; cf. *CJVR*, 353.

Chapter 2 *Kolonist*

1. Names of the purchasers of slaves, 29 May 1664, NNCM, NYSA_A1809-78_V10_pt3_0228, https://digitalcollections.archives.nysed.gov/index.php/Detail/objects/55671.

2. Nicolaes Verlet, wed^e. van Susanna Jillis, en Anna Stuijvesants, wed^e. van Samuel Baijarts. Banns of Nicolaes Verlet and Anna Stuyvesant, 14 October 1656, in *Liber A-2*, 494.

3. Jaap Jacobs, *Petrus Stuyvesant* (Amsterdam: Uitgeverij Bert Bakker, 2009), 41.

4. Ariadne Schmidt argues that despite the personal financial resources of a woman at the time of her widowhood or civic structures in place to maintain widows, early modern Dutch widows experienced "social polarization." Ariadne Schmidt, "Survival Strategies of Widows and Their Families in Early Modern Holland, c. 1580–1750," *History of the Family* 12, no. 4 (2007), 268–81.

5. Jacobs, *Petrus Stuyvesant*, 41.

6. Joanne van der Woude and Jaap Jacobs detail the dense connections of friendships that surrounded the Stuyvesant/Bayards. Such ties were cultivated and maintained while living abroad, such as his relationship with Johan Farret, who lived near Alphen in Woerden. Jacobs, *Petrus Stuyvesant*, 42; Joanne van der Woude and Jaap Jacobs, "Sweet Resoundings: Friendship Poetry by Petrus Stuyvesant and Johan Farret on Curaçao, 1639–45," *WMQ* 75, no. 3 (July 2018), 507–40, http://www.jstor.org/stable/10.5309/willmaryquar.75.3.0507.

7. See chapter 1, note 53, for an extended discussion of Dutch maidservants. Schama, *The Embarrassment of Riches*, 103, 319, 458.

NOTES TO PAGES 40-42

8. Her decision to emigrate was not unique but part of a larger pattern uncovered by Romney of Dutch widows through the seventeenth-century Atlantic World who weathered "frequent uprootings" and "repeatedly formed new intimate relationships" to reinvent themselves anew far away from continental Europe. Romney, *New Netherland Connections*, 23.

9. Varlet is also spelled Varleth, Varlet, Varleet, Verlett, and Verleth in colonial documents. April Lee Hatfield, "Dutch Merchants and Colonists in the English Chesapeake: Trade, Migration, and Nationality in 17th-century Maryland and Virginia," in *From Strangers to Citizens: The Integration of Immigrant Communities in Britain, Ireland, and Colonial America, 1550–1750*, ed. Randolph Vigne and Charles Littleton (London: Sussex Academic Press, 2001), 299–300, 304n.

10. April Lee Hatfield, "Dutch Merchants and Colonists in the English Chesapeake," 299–300, 304n. Hatfield noted that the Varlet daughters were particularly robust traders of tobacco and slaves. Anna Varlet Hack established a plantation in Virginia, and some of her slaves, Hatfield posited, were brought from New Netherland.

11. Jacobus Backer, van Amsterdam, en Margariet Stuijvesant, van Delfsziel. Banns of Jacobus Backer and Margrietje Stuyvesant, 30 Oct 1655, *Liber A-2*, 492. Letter from Willem Beeckman to Director Stuyvesant (mentions "Bycker's place in Virginia"), NNDR, NYSA_A1878-78_V18_0064, https://digitalcollections.archives.nysed.gov/index.php/Detail/objects/50750.

12. Hatfield, *Atlantic Virginia*, 97; Cor Snabel and Elizabeth Johnson, "The Hack and Varlet Families of Amsterdam and America," in *The Varlet Family of Amsterdam and Their Associated Families in the American Colonies and in the Netherlands* (2008), chapter 7, http://varletfamily.pbworks.com.

13. Snabel and Johnson, "The Hack and Varlet Families of Amsterdam and America."

14. Hatfield, *Atlantic Virginia*, 97–100; Koot, *Empire at the Periphery*, 78.

15. Nicholaes Boot v. Teunis Kraey, Mr. Jacob Huges and Mr. Scharborgh, 13 September 1655, New Amsterdam Records, RNA_v1_bk3, image 132, page 398. NYCMA, https://nycma.lunaimaging.com/luna/servlet/s/8n6k04; cf. *RONA*, 1:362–63.

16. Dennis Maika, "Commerce and Community: Manhattan Merchants in the Seventeenth Century" (Ph.D. diss., New York University, 1995), 124.

17. Nicholaes Boot v. Teunis Kraey, Mr. Jacob Huges and Mr. Scharborgh, 13 September 1655, New Amsterdam Records, RNA_v1_bk3, image 132, page 398, NYCMA, https://nycma.lunaimaging.com/luna/servlet/s/8n6k04; cf. *RONA*, 1: 362–63.

18. Nicholaes Boot v. Teunis Kraey, Mr. Jacob Huges and Mr. Scharborgh, 13 September 1655, New Amsterdam Records, RNA_v1_bk3, image 132, page 398, NYCMA, https://nycma.lunaimaging.com/luna/servlet/s/8n6k04; cf. *RONA*, 1: 362–63.

19. Myndert Lourisen v. Nicolaes Boot, 6 September 1655, New Amsterdam Records, RNA_v1_bk3, image 122, page 388, NYCMA, https://nycma.lunaimaging.com/luna/servlet/s/8n6k04. RONA, 1:354.

20. Deposition in the Protocol of Amsterdam Notary Hendrick Schaef, 1656, SAA, 5075/54.2.28/A32698000044, https://archief.amsterdam/inventarissen/scans/5075/54.2.28/start/0/limit/50/highlight/44.

21. Hatfield, "Dutch and New Netherland Merchants in the Seventeenth-Century English Chesapeake," in *The Atlantic Economy during the Seventeenth and Eighteenth Centuries: Organization, Operation, Practice, and Personnel*, ed. Peter A. Coclanis (Columbia: University of South Carolina Press, 2005), 215, 214n.

22. Hatfield, "Dutch Merchants and Colonists in the English Chesapeake," in Vigne and Littleton, *From Strangers to Citizens*, 300.

23. The Directors at Amsterdam to the Director and Council of New Netherland, 20 January 1664, NNCAC, NYSA_A1810-78_V15_0097, https://digitalcollections.archives.nysed.gov/index.php/Detail/objects/50613; Audit. Account of Nicolas Varleth and Jacobus Backer, for expenses incurred by councillor de Decker's mission to Virginia, 28 January 1664, NNCM, NYSA_A1809-78_V10_pt3_0026, https://digitalcollections.archives.nysed.gov/index.php/Detail/objects/55539. See also *DIHSTA*, 3:462.

24. Caspar Varlet was an Amsterdam silk merchant who used colonial intermediates to diversify his portfolio. Jacobs, *New Netherland*, 298; Snabel and Johnson, "The Caspar Varlet Family," in *The Varlet Family of Amsterdam*, chapter 2, http://varletfamily.pbworks.com. For a detailed examination of how the Stuyvesants leveraged their Atlantic kin connections to the Varlets and others see Romney, *New Netherland Connections*, 105–10.

25. Bill of lading for the "Rensselaerswijck." 26 August 1636, Notarissen ter Standplaats Amsterdam, SAA, notaris Jacob Jacobs en Nicolaes Jacobs, 5075.17.414A.173, KLAB09445000226-227, https://archief.amsterdam/inventarissen/inventaris/5075.nl.html#KLAB09445000420; Shipment for the "Wapen van Leeuwarden," 12 December 1639, Notarissen ter Standplaats Amsterdam, Stadsarchief Amsterdam, notaris Jacob Jacobus en Nicolaes Jacobus, 5075.17. 420B. For a guide to these voyages along with more resources housed at the Amsterdam archives on the early tobacco trade, see Jan Kupp, comp., "Calendar to Amsterdam and Rotterdam Notarial Acts Relating to the Virginia Tobacco Trade," https://www.uvic.ca/library/locations/home/spcoll/documents/Kupp_calendar.pdf.

26. Such an argument was pioneered by historians such as Ira Berlin, Philip D. Morgan, Stephen Innes, T. H. Breen and others. Berlin, *Many Thousands Gone*, 10, 109–15; Philip D. Morgan, *A Slave Counterpoint: Black Culture in Eighteenth-Century Chesapeake and Low Country* (Chapel Hill: Published for the Omohundro Institute of Early American Culture, Williamsburg, Virginia, by University of North Carolina Press, 1998), 1–27; Innes and Breen, *Myne Owne Ground: Race and Freedom on Virginia's Eastern Shore, 1640–1676* (New York: Oxford University Press, 2004), x, 31–45. The importance of Atlantic currents in shaping the chronology of enslavement in the Chesapeake, specifically with regards to the Dutch context, is explored by April Lee Hatfield. Hatfield, *Atlantic Virginia*, 137–68. Hatfield also details that the Varlet/Hack, Hermans and Volckert émigrés were granted headrights alongside "Domingo, a Negro, George, a Negro, Kathrine, a Negro, Ann, a Negro," 99n64.

27. See note 22 in the Introduction for more on the state of research into the impact of Northeastern transplants.

28. James H. Kettner, *The Development of American Citizenship, 1608–1870* (Chapel Hill: Published for the Omohundro Institute of Early American History and Culture, Williamsburg, Virginia by the University of North Carolina Press, 2014), 91–92; Hatfield, *Atlantic Virginia*, 97.

29. Christian J. Koot, "The Merchant, the Map, and Empire: Augustine Herrman's Chesapeake and Interimperial Trade, 1644–73," *WMQ* 67, no. 4 (October 2010): 635–36, https://www.jstor.org/stable/10.5309/willmaryquar.67.4.0603; *Proceedings and Acts of the General Assembly January 1637/8-September 1664*, reproduced in William Hand Browne, Edward C. Papenfuse et al., eds., Archives of Maryland, 215+ volumes (Baltimore and Annapolis, Md., 1883–), 1:462, https://msa.maryland.gov/megafile/msa/speccol/sc2900/sc2908/000001/000001/html/am1--462.html.

30. Snabel and Johnson, "The Hack and Varlet Families of Amsterdam and America."

31. Koot, "The Merchant, the Map, and Empire," 613; Hatfield, *Atlantic Virginia*, 97.

32. Resolution to charter to Frederick Philipse, late the director's carpenter, the company's sloop for a voyage to Virginia, 20 September 1660, NNCM, NYSA_A1809-78_V09_0416, http://digitalcollections.archives.nysed.gov/index.php/Detail/objects/53620.

33. *Partus sequitor ventrem*, or progeny follows the womb, was first applied in the colonial context in Virginia in 1662 in the wake of the successful freedom case of Elizabeth Key, but beyond the reference of maternal descent as prerequisite for heritable slavery, was an entirely new invention, holding little in common with ancient law. "A Report of a Committee from an Assembly Concerning the Freedome of Elizabeth Key," in *The Old Dominion in the Seventeenth Century: A Documentary History of Virginia, 1606–1689*, ed. Warren M. Billings (Chapel Hill: Published for the Omohundro Institute of Early American History and Culture, Williamsburg, Virginia by the University of North Carolina Press, 1975), 167–69. Jonathan Bush offers a great roadmap to colonial legal precedent and its only vague relation to Roman Law. Jonathan A. Bush, "Free to Enslave: The Foundations of Colonial American Slave Law," *Yale Journal of Law and the Humanities* 5, no. 2 (summer 1993), 425, 425n22, https://digitalcommons.law.yale.edu/yjlh/vol5/iss2. For a complete analysis of this law's effect on enslaved women's lives see, Jennifer Morgan, "*Partus sequitur ventrem*: Law, Race, and Reproduction in Colonial Slavery," *Small Axe* 22, no. 1 (March 2018), 1–17, doi: https://doi-org.proxy.library.cornell.edu/10.1215/07990537-4378888.

34. Willem Beeckman to Petrus Stuyvesant, 18 and 20 March 1662, NNDR, NYSA_A1878-78_V19_0023, https://digitalcollections.archives.nysed.gov/index.php/Detail/objects/51114; Gehring, *Delaware Papers*, 264–65. In Samuel Hazard's edited version, the date is given as 18 March 1662 and the quote is rendered: "A company of *negroes*, as I am very much in want of them in many respects." *Annals of Pennsylvania, 1609–1682*, ed. Samuel Hazard (Philadelphia: Hazard and Mitchell, 1850), 331. For a fantastic treatment of Dutch presence in Delaware see William H. Williams, *Slavery and Freedom in Delaware, 1639–1865* (Wilmington, DE: Scholarly Resources, 1996), chapter 1.

35. According to his replacement, Adriaen Beaumont, Michiel had allowed all manner of licentiousness to flourish during his tenure in Curaçao, but he was also controversial because of his baptism of Black people, a practice that Beaumont himself followed before being censured. Adriaen Beaumont to the Classis of Amsterdam, 17 April 1660, 5 Dec 1662, SAA, Archief van de Classis Amsterdam van de Nederlandse Hervormde Kerk, 379/224:11–13, 17–21. https://archief.amsterdam/inventarissen/scans/379/2.1.1.1/start/210/limit/10/highlight/4 and 5.

36. Matthias Beck to Petrus Stuyvesant, 23 August 1659, NNCCR, NYSA_A1883-78_V17_041, https://digitalcollections.archives.nysed.gov/index.php/Detail/objects/19408; *CP,* 131.

37. Classis of Amsterdam to Samuel Drisius, 5 December 1661, SAA, 379/2.1.1.1/217 https://archief.amsterdam/inventarissen/scans/379/2.1.1.1/start/210/limit/10/highlight/7; *ERNY,* 1:514.

38. Samuel Drisius to the Classis of Amsterdam relating the departure of Domine Selijns for the Netherlands and speculating on Samuel Megapolensis as his replacement; the French on Staten Island request a minister; 5/14 August 1664 Amsterdam Correspondence, Box 1, No. 47. New Brunswick Theological Seminary; *ERNY,* 1:555.

39. Commission of Rev. Samuel Drisius to be ambassador to Virginia, 16 December 1653, NYCM, NYSA_A1809-78_V05_0187, https://digitalcollections.archives.nysed.gov/index.php/Detail/objects/54783.

40. "Notes and Queries," *New York Genealogical and Biographical Record* 13, no. 1 (January 1882): 49; Hatfield, "Dutch Merchants and Colonists in the English Chesapeake," in *From Strangers to Citizens,* ed. Vigne and Littleton, 299, 301.

41. Resolution adopted at the meeting of the Director General and council of New Netherland, 31 May 1664. Extract included in John Romeyn Brodhead, *Documents Relative to the Colonial History of the State of New York: Procured in Holland, England and France* (Albany, NY: Weed, Parsons, 1858), 2:474; Contract with Thomas Willett for a quantity of beef and pork, payable in negroes, 31 May 1664, NYCM, NYSA_A1809-78_V10_pt3_0232b, https://digitalcollections.archives.nysed.gov/index.php/Detail/objects/55674.

42. Petrus Stuyvesant to Matthias Beck, 28 October 1659, NYCM, NYSA_A1810-78_V13_0049, http://digitalcollections.archives.nysed.gov/index.php/Detail/objects/54428; Order to allow Thomas Willet 3 or 4 slaves with permission to remove them wherever he likes, 30 September 1660, NYCM, NYSA_A1809-78_V09_0427, http://digitalcollections.archives.nysed.gov/index.php/Detail/objects/53629. For more on the *St Jan,* see the Journal of the *St Jan,* 4 March 1659, 135–38; "List of the slaves who died aboard the ship *St. Jan* from the 30th of June to the 29th of October in the year 1659," *CP,* 138–40, Matthias Beck to the Directors of the WIC, 5 January 1660, *CP,* 167; Matthias Beck to the Directors of the WIC, 4 February 1660, in *CP,* 170; Matthias Beck to Petrus Stuyvesant, 23 August 1659, NNCCR, NYSA_A1883-78_V17_041, https://digitalcollections.archives.nysed.gov/index.php/Detail/objects/19408. *CP,* 133.

43. Stuyvesant's July 8, 1664 loan request of Jeremias van Rensselaer and Johannes La Montagne is partially reproduced in *Documents of the Senate of the State of New York* (Albany, NY: James B. Lyon, State Printer, 1901), 13:253.

44. For more on Captain Thomas Willet, see Hodges, *Root and Branch,* 31; Romney, *New Netherland Connections,* 205.

45. A detailed overview of Thomas Willet's biography is included in a footnote in George William Ellis and John Emery Morris' *King Philip's War,* although his wife Mary is erroneously listed as the sister of James Brown, and not his daughter. George William Ellis and John Emery Morris, *King Philip's War: Based on the Archives and Records of Massachusetts, Plymouth, Rhode Island and Connecticut, and Contemporary Letters and Accounts, with Biographical and Topographical Notes* (New York: Grafton

NOTES TO PAGE 46

Press, 1906), 60–61n6. A pdf document entitled "A Genealogical Profile of Thomas Willett," included on the website of Plimoth Plantation offers considerable detail about Willet's life, including residing in Leiden on the Jacobsgracht, his marriage to Mary Browne, which produced thirteen children, and details about his life in New England. It also includes a short bibliography of works that contain biographical details on Willet. Despite his trading past with New Netherland, Willet was a member of the English force that invaded New Netherland when the colony fell in 1664. Plimoth Plantation and New England Genealogical Society, "A Genealogical Profile of Thomas Willett," https://blogs.plimoth.org/sites/default/files/media/pdf/willett_thomas.pdf. For more on Thomas Willett, see Elizur Yale Smith, "CAPTAIN THOMAS WILLETT First Mayor of New York," New York History 21, no. 4 (1940): 404–17, http://www.jstor.org/stable/23134735.

46. From the New York State Education Department. Court proceedings: Allert Anthony vs. Thomas Willet . . . Willem Beeckman vs. Adriaen van Tienhoven, 9 September 1652, NYCM, NYSA_A1809-78_V05_0053, http://digitalcollections.archives.nysed.gov/index.php/Detail/objects/54675. The certificate for the spoiled flour also was signed by Oloff Stevensz and Cornelis van Tienhoven. Certificate of Thomas Willet and others, respecting the condition and value of flour landed from the *Shark*, 23 November 1654, NYCM, NYSA_A1809-78_V05_0389, http://digitalcollections.archives.nysed.gov/index.php/Detail/objects/54933; minute that 1,500 guilders was borrowed from Thomas Willet by the director-general for the public service, 31 August 1655, NYCM, NYSA_A1809-78_V07_pt1_0081b, http://digitalcollections.archives.nysed.gov/index.php/Detail/objects/56708; note to Thomas Willet for 1,500 guilders wampum, payable in merchandise or beaver, 31 August 1655, NYCM, NYSA_A1809-78_V06_0087a, http://digitalcollections.archives.nysed.gov/index.php/Detail/objects/52341; Thomas Willet was Petrus Stuyvesant's creditor. Minute that 1,500 guilders was borrowed from Thomas Willet by the director-general for the public service, 31 August 1655, NYCM, NYSA_A1809-78_V06_0087b, http://digitalcollections.archives.nysed.gov/index.php/Detail/objects/52342; note To Thomas Willet, for 1,500 guilders wampum, payable in merchandise or beaver, 31 August 1655, NYCM, NYSA_A1809-78_V07_pt1_0081a, http://digitalcollections.archives.nysed.gov/index.php/Detail/objects/56707; minute of communication to Thomas Willet of complaints presented by the Mohawks against the Northern Indians, for transmission to Boston, 24 July 1664, NYCM, NYSA_A1809-78_V10_pt3_0284a, http://digitalcollections.archives.nysed.gov/index.php/Detail/objects/55707; Mitigation of the seizure of Mr. Willet's beavers, 27 October 1673, NYCM, NYSA_A1881-78_V23_0139, http://digitalcollections.archives.nysed.gov/index.php/Detail/objects/51845; receipt of John Safflin, curator of the estate of Thomas Willet, for a lot of peltries seized by the government and now released, 1 October 1674, NYCM, NYSA_A1881-78_V23_0405, http://digitalcollections.archives.nysed.gov/index.php/Detail/objects/52130.

47. Misevich, "In Pursuit of Human Cargo," 187. By the middle of the eighteenth century the slave population of New York was second only to Charleston, South Carolina. Lepore, *New York Burning*, xii.

48. Thomas Willet kept up a brisk trade with New Netherland. When he was living in New Plymouth he served as security for the sale of the ship *Amandare*. From

the New York State Education Department. "Bill of Sale of the Ship Amandare from Directors Stuyvesant and Kieft to Thomas Broughton," 31 May 1647, NNRPS, NYSA_A0270-78_V2_156a, http://digitalcollections.archives.nysed.gov/index.php/Detail/objects/11302. This is the same ship noted as the slaver *Tamandare* (or *T'Amandare*) in the Voyages slave-trading database, *TAVoyages*, Voyage ID no. 107713. *Tamandare* (1646). Governor Bradford welcomed Petrus to the area, recommended the services of Thomas Willet and William Peddie, and hoped to continue to "Carrie on theyre trade with as much freedom & saufetie" as had been enjoyed under Kieft. William Bradford to Petrus Stuyvesant, 3 August 1647, NNCAC, NYSA_A1810-78_V11_03a, http://digitalcollections.archives.nysed.gov/index.php/Detail/objects/45108.

49. In the same letter in which Petrus relayed the trade of supplies from Boston to Curaçao for salt, and discussed the interests of Thomas Willet and William Davids in New England, Stuyvesant requested more "negroes." From the New York State Education Department. Petrus Stuyvesant to Matthias Beck, 20 July 1663, NNCM, NYSA_A1810-78_V15_0046, http://digitalcollections.archives.nysed.gov/index.php/Detail/objects/50557.

50. From the New York State Education Department. "Minute. Information furnished to director Stuyvesant by Thomas Willett, of the receipt of news at Boston of the sailing of an English fleet for the reduction of New Netherland with one "Nicles" on board who has been appointed governor," 8 July 1664, NNCM, NYSA_A1809-78_V10_pt3_0251, http://digitalcollections.archives.nysed.gov/index.php/Detail/objects/55686. For more on the fall of the colony, see L. H. Roper, "The Fall of New Netherland and Seventeenth-Century Anglo-American Imperial Formation, 1654–1676" *NEQ* 87, no. 4 (2014): 666–708, http://www.jstor.org/stable/43286385.

51. The first explicit mention of Balthazar Stuyvesant by name is in the letter written by Matthias Beck to Petrus Stuyvesant, where he also reports on the accidental sale of Stuyvesant's slaves. Matthias Beck to Petrus Stuyvesant, 5 November 1664, NNCCR, NYSA_A1883-78_V17_094, https://digitalcollections.archives.nysed.gov/index.php/Detail/objects/19465; *CP*, 182, 210.

52. Stuyvesant's original letter inquiring about the enslaved children was sent on 29 July 1664, and does not survive. Beck's reply, dated 5 November 1664, responds to that letter. *CP*, 211.

53. "One girl" is listed as going to Petrus Stuyvesant with the *Speramundij* in 1659, "six boys and five girls" were delivered to Stuyvesant with *den Nieuw Netherlandsen Indiaan*, 21 July 1661. Bill of Lading for the Speramundij Jan Pietersen, 24 August 1659, NNCCR, NYSA_A1883-78_V17_051a, https://digitalcollections.archives.nysed.gov/index.php/Detail/objects/19420; *CP*, 155; Bill of Lading for Den Nieuw Netherlandsen Indiaan, Dierck Jansz, 21 July 1661, NNCCR, NYSA_A1883-78_V17_073, https://digitalcollections.archives.nysed.gov/index.php/Detail/objects/19444; *CP*, 187. Such trade consistently shaped Stuyvesant's actions throughout the end of his tenure. Director Stuyvesant to Vice-Director Beck, 30 January 1664, in *DIHSTA*, 1:431.

54. As Wim Klooster argued in *The Dutch Moment*, the continued state of warfare shaped Dutch colonial ideas of empire. Matthias Beck's statement about the Stuyvesants' lost slaves follows directly a paragraph detailing English actions against Dutch possessions in Cabo Verde and their plans to attack Dutch Coastal forts along Guinea. Matthias

Beck to Petrus Stuyvesant, 5 November 1664, NNCCR, NYSA_A1883-78_V17_094, https://digitalcollections.archives.nysed.gov/index.php/Detail/objects/19465; *CP*, 210–11; Klooster, *The Dutch Moment*, 3.

55. *Liber A-2*, 36, 42, 53, 55, 69, 98, 108, 115, 121, 141, 143, 148, 151, 190. Standing as baptismal witness was, as Joyce Goodfriend argued, one central role that women played in the Dutch Reformed Church and some women even provided for godchildren in wills. Joyce Goodfriend, "Incorporating Women into the History of the Colonial Dutch Reformed Church: Problems and Proposals" in *Patterns and Portraits: Women in the History of the Reformed Church in America*, eds. Renée S. House and John W. Coakley (Grand Rapids, MI: Eerdmans, 1999), 27–28.

56. Genesis 17:7 "Ende ick sal mijn verbont oprichten tusschen my ende tusschen u / ende tusschen uwen zade na u in hare geslachten / tot een eeuwich verbont: om u te zijn tot eenen Godt / ende uwen zade na u," http://www.statenvertaling.net/bijbel/gene/17.html. Judith Stuyvesant would have likely heard these versus intoned from the new Dutch translation of the Bible, the *Statenvertaling*, or States Bible, published in 1637, which grew out of a call for a new translation during the Synod of Dordrecht. For a detailed study of the new Dutch translation of the Bible, see Frits G.M. Broeyer, "Bible for the Living Room: The Dutch Bible in the Seventeenth Century," in *Lay Bibles in Europe 1450–1800*, eds. Mathijs Lamberigts and A. A. den Hollander (Leuven, Belgium: Leuven University Press, 2006), 207–15.

57. The form of baptism was included within the *formulierboek*. "Forme om den heylighen Doop uyt te richten," *Catechismus ofte Onderwijsinghe inde Christelicke Leere* . . . (Middelburg, 1611), Archief van de Nederlandse Hervormde Kerk, Classis Amsterdam, Inventaris 379, Algemeen, 1.2.2.1.1, 32 Formulierboek, bestaande uit een catechismus . . ., KLAD02048000039-43; https://archief.amsterdam/inventarissen/scans/379/1.4.2/start/30/limit/10/highlight/9, Stadsarchief Amsterdam. Danny Noorlander discusses the importance placed on the consistency of liturgy and the high bar for baptism throughout the Dutch WIC enforced by church leaders in Holland. Noorlander, "Serving God and Mammon: The Reformed Church and the Dutch West India Company in the Atlantic World, 1621–1674" (PhD diss., Georgetown University, 2011), 133–34, 134n48, 312, 312n46; Noorlander, *Heaven's Wrath*, 114n8.

58. Jaap Jacobs, *New Netherland*, 315–18, 315n92, 316n93. For baptism under Bogardus's tenure, see Willem Frijhoff, *Fulfilling God's Mission: The Two Worlds of Dominie Everardus Bogardus, 1607–1647*, trans. Myra Heerspink Scholz, The Atlantic World: Europe, Africa and the Americas, 1500–1830, vol. 14 (1995; reprint Boston: Brill, 2007), 542.

59. Domine Henricus Selijns to the Classis of Amsterdam, 9 June 1664 Amsterdam Correspondence, Box 1, No. 46. Gardner A. Sage Library, New Brunswick Theological Seminary. Cf. *NYHMRCB*, 231.

60. Jacobs, *Petrus Stuyvesant*, 41–42.

61. Names of enslaved people and their locations based on lawsuit by Portuguese slaver Juan Gaillardo Ferera who claimed that his "property" had been illegally sold in New Netherland in 1659. Dutch National Archives, 1.01.02, inv.nr. 12564.46. *DRCHNY*, 2:31.

62. Letter from Matthias Beck, vice director of Curaçao to the directors in Amsterdam, 4 February 1660, NYSA_A1883-78_V17_057, https://digitalcollections.archives.nysed.gov/index.php/Detail/objects/19427. *CP*, 172.

63. Gehring, "Introduction," in *Curaçao Papers, 1640–1665*, ed. and trans. Charles T. Gehring and J. A. Schiltkamp (Interlaken, NY: Heart of the Lakes, 1987), xviii–xv. For evidence of Matthias's presence in Brazil in the 1630s, see C. J. Wasch, "Een dooppregister der Hollanders in Brazilië," in *Algemeen Nederlandsch Familieblad*, vol. 5 (Netherlands: Bureau Groenendaal, 1888), 143.

64. Marcus P. Meuwese, "'For the Peace and Well-Being of the Country': Intercultural Mediators and Dutch-Indian Relations in New Netherland and Dutch Brazil, 1600–1664" (PhD diss., University of Notre Dame, 2003), 297, https://curate.nd.edu/show/6m311n81g6m.

65. Matthias Beck to Petrus Stuyvesant, 23 August 1659, NYSA_A1883-78_V17_041, https://digitalcollections.archives.nysed.gov/index.php/Detail/objects/19408. *CP*, 131–32. Matthias Beck to Petrus Stuyvesant, 28 July 1657, NYSA_A1883-78_V17_028. https://digitalcollections.archives.nysed.gov/index.php/Detail/objects/19393. *CP*, 108–9.

66. For evidence of the reciprocal relationship between the Becks and Stuyvesant, see Matthias Beck to Petrus Stuyvesant, 4 February 1660, NNCR, NYSA_A1883-78_V17_056, https://digitalcollections.archives.nysed.gov/index.php/Detail/objects/19426; *CP*, 169; Matthias Beck to Petrus Stuyvesant, 21 July 1664, NNCR, NYSA_A1883-78_V17_087, https://digitalcollections.archives.nysed.gov/index.php/Detail/objects/19458; *CP*, 200; Matthias Beck to Petrus Stuyvesant, 5 November 1664, NNCR, NYSA_A1883-78_V17_094, https://digitalcollections.archives.nysed.gov/index.php/Detail/objects/19465; *CP*, 212; "Register of goods loaded at Curaçao for New Netherland," 1665, NNCR, NYSA_A1883-78_V17_108, https://digitalcollections.archives.nysed.gov/index.php/Detail/objects/19477; *CP*, 232.

67. Names of the purchasers of slaves, 29 May 1664, NNCM, NYSA_A1809-78_V10_pt3_0228, https://digitalcollections.archives.nysed.gov/index.php/Detail/objects/55671.

68. Newell, *Brethren by Nature*, 45, 48, 54.

69. Certificate that the half-slaves who petitioned for manumission had been fully emancipated and made free, 21 December 1664, NNCM, NYSA_A1809-78_V10_pt3_0327, http://digitalcollections.archives.nysed.gov/index.php/Detail/objects/55730. For an earlier petition made in September of the same year, see Petition of several half slaves to be manumitted and made entirely free, 4 September 1664, NNCM, NYSA_A1809-78_V10_pt3_0317, http://digitalcollections.archives.nysed.gov/index.php/Detail/objects/557260. Romney offers a well-considered overview of this moment in *New Netherland Connections*, with a document roadmap that I have followed. Romney, *New Netherland Connections*, 238.

70. Certificate that the half-slaves who petitioned for manumission had been fully emancipated and made free, 11/21 December 1664, NYSA_A1809-78_V10_pt3_0327, http://digitalcollections.archives.nysed.gov/index.php/Detail/objects/55730.

71. Certificate that sundry grants of land near Stuyvesant's bouwery had been made in the years 1659 and 1660 to various negroes, 30 April 1665, NYSA_A1809-78_V10_pt3_0329, http://digitalcollections.archives.nysed.gov/index.php/Detail/objects/55731; Romney, *New Netherland Connections*, 239.

72. For more on this topic, see Edgar McManus, *A History of Negro Slavery in New York*, 22; Rink, *Holland on the Hudson*, 163–64; Goodfriend, "Burghers and Blacks," 126.

NOTES TO PAGES 50-51

73. Trial of Jan Creoly, 25 June 1646, in *Council Minutes 1638–1649*, 4:326–28, https://www.newnetherlandinstitute.org/download_file/view/1584/1240/.

74. Testimony of Fockke Jans, Kier Wolters, and Jan Jansen van de Langestraet, August 6, 1666. Stukken betreffende de bemoeingen van de Staten-General met de beschuldigingen tegen en de verdediging van Pieter Stuyvesant, gewezen directeur-generaal van Nieuw-Nederland, inzake zijn gedrag bij het verlies van Nieuw-Nederland, 1665–1667. Nationaal Archief, Staten-Generaal, inv. nr. 12564.57; See also *DRCHSNY*, 2:474.

75. Romney, *New Netherland Connections*, 245, 294.

76. For more on Stuyvesant's financial status after the fall of the colony, see Johannes Postma, *The Dutch in the Atlantic Slave Trade, 1600–1815* (Cambridge: Cambridge University Press, 1990), 27; Rupert, *Creolization and Contraband*, 62–63; *NYHME*, 1:104, 361–62; *TAVoyages*, Voyage ID no. 11781. *Leonora (a) Leeuwinne* (1669); Will of Nicolaes Stuyvesant, 13 August 1698, in *Wills*, 1:294.

77. Petrus Stuyvesant to States General, 1666, in *DRCHNY*, 2:430; Nationaal Archief, Staten-Generaal, inv. nr. 12564.57.

78. Jaap Jacobs, email message to author, 4 June 2021.

79. Matthias Beck to Petrus Stuyvesant, 5 November 1664, NYSA_A1883-78_V17_094, https://digitalcollections.archives.nysed.gov/index.php/Detail/objects/19465; *CP*, 108. Williams, *Slavery and Freedom in Delaware, 1639–1865*, 7.

80. Matthias Beck to the Directors of the WIC, 21 July 1664, in *CP*, 196. For more on the *Den Gideon*, see Mosterman, "Nieuwer-Amstel, stadskolonie aan de Delaware," 164–71.

81. *VSSJAA*, 222; Letter from the council to the directors at Amsterdam, 17 August 1664, NYSA_A1810-78_V15_0139, https://digitalcollections.archives.nysed.gov/index.php/Detail/objects/50656. Some of those enslaved were traded to Maryland. Williams, *Slavery and Freedom in Delaware*, 7–9.

82. *VSSJAA*, 213, 221–24; cf. Williams, *Slavery and Freedom in Delaware*, 7. Romney, *New Netherland Connections*, 240.

83. Merwick, *Stuyvesant Bound*, 3, 121–35; Russell Shorto, *The Island at the Center of the World: The Epic Story of Dutch Manhattan and the Forgotten Colony that Shaped America* (2004; reprint New York: Vintage, 2005), 306; Mark Reinberger and Elizabeth McLean, *The Philadelphia Country House: Architecture and Landscape in Colonial America* (Baltimore: Johns Hopkins University Press, 2015), 34.

84. Theodore Roosevelt to the New-York Historical Society, 13 September 1895, NYHS-RG 2, Box 66, NYHS; Jan Seidler Ramirez, "Stuyvesant's Pear Tree: Some Interpretive Fruits," *New York Journal of American History* 65, no. 4 (fall 2004): 116–21.

85. Petition, 4 September 1664, in *CHMANY*, 1: 269; certificate, "That sundry grants of land, near Stuyvesant's bouwery, had been made in the years 1659 and 1660 to divers negroes," 20/30 April 1665, vol. 10, pt. 3, *New York Colonial Manuscripts*, 329–32, New York State Archives, https://www.newnetherlandinstitute.org/files/2814/0681/8946/Stuyvesantmanumission.pdf; Conveyance of Judith Stuyvesant to Frans Bastiaensz, 24 September 1674, New York City Deeds, MS 1972, 23, NYHS, https://blog.nyhistory.org/black-history-month-17th-century/. See also Original Book of New York Deeds, January 1st 1672 to October 19th 1675 in *Collections of the New-York Historical Society for the Year 1913: The John Watts De Peyster*

Publication Fund (New York: Printed for the Society, 1914) 46: 42–43. For the proximity of Stuyvesants' land to the community of free Blacks see Romney, *New Netherland Connections*, 239.

86. Matthias Beck to Petrus Stuyvesant, 5 November 1664, NNCCR, NYSA_A1883-78_V17_094, https://digitalcollections.archives.nysed.gov/index.php/Detail/objects/19465; *CP*, 208–9; Matthias Beck to Petrus Stuyvesant, 16 April 1665, in *CP*, 224. For Balthazar Stuyvesant's trade passes, see *NYHME*, 1: 104, 361–62.

87. Matthias Beck to Petrus Stuyvesant, 16 April 1665, NNCCR, NYSA_A1883-78_V17_104, https://digitalcollections.archives.nysed.gov/index.php/Detail/objects/19473; *CP*, 224. "Curaçao as the Centre of the Slave Trade," Kura Hulanda Museum, http://www.kurahulanda.com/slavery/slave-trade, accessed Dec 9, 2010. For information in Dutch on the branding of enslaved Africans when they arrived on Curaçao, see Johannes Hartog, *Curaçao: Van Kolonie Tot Autonomie: Deel 1 (Tot 1816)* (Aruba: D.J. de Witt, 1961), 440–41.

88. Balthazar Lazarus Stuyvesant to Nicolaes Baeyaert op de Manhatans, 2 July 1665, *CP* 232–35.

89. East Jersey Proprietors to Nicholas Bayard, NJEJD, vol. 1, part A, folio 11; Anthony Brockholes to Nicholas Bayard, NJEJD, vol. H, folio 4; "Census of the City of New-York: About the Year 1703," in *DHSNY*, 403; Ordinance of the Director General of New Netherland imposing a Land tax at Esopus, to defray the expense of building a Minister's house there, in E. B. O'Callaghan, ed. *Laws and Ordinances of New Netherland, 1638–1674* (Albany: Weed, Parsons, 1868), 413.

90. *TAVoyages*, Voyage ID no. 44270. *Leonora* (1667). On 9 February 1674 Cornelis Steenwijck was assessed as being the second most affluent resident of New Netherland alongside Nicolaes de Meyer, with both estates worth 50,000 guilders, in DRCHSNY, 2: 699–700. Olof Stevense van Cortlandt, was roughly equivalent in terms of city property with an estate valued at 45,000 guilders. According to that 1674 valuation, Frederick Phillips was the wealthiest, with an estate worth 80,000 guilders; cf., Jacobs, *New Netherland*, 337–38. Cornelis Steenwijck used his fortune to invest in diverse projects, from slave trading to ironworks. In 1652 he signed a petition explaining that "the undersigned Burghers and inhabitants of this city New Amsterdam" were "inclined to a foreign trade, and especially to the coast of Africa" to "fetch thence slaves" so "this city and the entire country would increase and prosper in merchandize, commerce, population and more especially in the tobacco trade." They asked for "permission to trade free and unobstructed in ship or ships, along the whole of the west coast of Africa." Proposed Contract to Import Slaves into New Netherland, 1652, in *DIHSTA*, 3: 412–14, 414n4. For his investment in New Jersey ironworks, see Daniel J. Weeks, *Not for Filthy Lucre's Sake: Richard Saltar and the Antiproprietary Movement in East New Jersey, 1665–1707* (Cranbury, NJ: Associated University Press, 2001), 72. He donated to a fund for the city's defense in 1653. Jacobs, *New Netherland*, 328–29. For Cornelis Steenwijck's trading networks, see Rink, *Holland on the Hudson*, 205.

91. *TAVoyages*, Voyage ID no. 44281. *Leonora* (1667).

92. *TAVoyages*, Voyage ID no. 44281. *Vergulde Posthoorn* (1669).

93. *TAVoyages*, Voyage ID no. 44281. *Vergulde Posthoorn* (1669).

94. *TAVoyages*, Voyage ID 11781. *Leonara (a) Leeuwinne* (1669). Between 1670 and 1674, fifty-nine documented slave ships carrying 24,202 slaves departed from Africa for Dutch Atlantic colonies. Postma, *Dutch in the Atlantic Slave Trade*, 110, table 5.1.

NOTES TO PAGES 52-53

95. Kopie-kontrakt van de vergadering van Negentien met Domingo Grillo, Ambrosio Grillo en anderen inzake de leverantie van slaven door de Compagnie aan hen, en het vervoer van dezen naar Curaçao, 1662 September 15, 1668 Mei 18, 1670 September 20, Nationaal Archief, Den Haag, Netherlands Archief van de Staten-Generaal, 1.01.01.01, inventarisnummer 1362.

96. Edsall in "Queries," 58; Cuyler Reynolds, *Annals of American Families* (New York: National Americana Society, 1916), 2:103. St. Thomas continued to have a planter majority of Dutch heritage, even after the Danish takeover. Jonathan I. Israel, *Dutch Primacy in World Trade, 1585–1740* (1989; reprint Oxford, UK: Clarendon Press, 2002), 326. For more on the development of slavery in the Danish Caribbean, see Neville A. T. Hall, *Slave Society in the Danish West Indies* (1992; reprint Mona, Jamaica: Department of History, University of the West Indies at Mona, Cave Hill, and St. Augustine, 1994).

97. Edsall in "Queries," 58; Reynolds, *Annals of American Families*, 2:103; Rupert, *Creolization and Contraband*, 122, 171; Yda Schreuder, *Amsterdam's Sephardic Merchants and the Atlantic Sugar Trade in the Seventeenth Century* (New York: Palgrave Macmillan, 2019), 240; Koot, *Empire at the Periphery*, 137–39, 187–90.

98. Balthazar Lazarus Stuyvesant to Nicolaes Baeyaert op de Manhatans, 2 July 1665, NNCCR, NYSA_A1883-78_V17_109, https://digitalcollections.archives.nysed.gov/index.php/Detail/objects/19478; *CP* 232–35.

99. Edsall in "Queries," 58; Reynolds, *Annals of American Families*, 2:103; Koot, *Empire at the Periphery*, 125–29; Hall, *Slave Society in the Danish West Indies*, 7.

100. Nicolaes Baijard, jm. van Alphen, en Judith Verlet, j.d. van Amsterdam verk, ingescriven 25 Maij, *Liber A-2*, 516.

101. I. N. Phelps Stokes, *The Iconography of Manhattan Island, 1498–1909*, vol. 6 (New York: Robert H. Dodd, 1915–1928), 123.

102. "Census of the City of New-York: About the Year 1703," in *DHSNY1*, 622.

103. George Johnston's book offers detail about Petrus Bayard's activities among the Labadists and the fact that they were initially antislavery but then became slaveholders. George Johnston, *History of Cecil County, Maryland: And the Early Settlements around the Head of the Chesapeake Bay and on the Delaware River with Sketches of Some of the Old Families of Cecil County* (Elkton, MD: George Johnston, 1881), 84–132; See also Jasper Danckaerts, *The Journal of Jasper Danckaerts, 1679–1680*, eds. Bartlett Burleigh James and J. Franklin Jameson (New York: Charles Scribner's Sons, 1913), 141n1.

104. Henry C. Murphy, "Introduction" to *Journal of a Voyage to New York and a Tour in Several of the American Colonies in 1679–80*, by Jaspar Dankers and Peter Sluyter, trans. and ed. Henry C. Murphy (Brooklyn: Published by the Long Island Historical Society, 1867), xxxiiin1.

105. Murphy, "Introduction," xxxivi–xxxv.

106. T. J. Saxby, *The Quest for the New Jerusalem, Jean de Labadie and the Labadists, 1610–1744* (Dordrecht, Netherlands: Martinus Nijhoff, 1987), 130, 289; Kim Todd, *Chrysalis: Maria Sibylla Merian and the Secrets of Metamorphosis* (London: I. B. Tauris, 2007), 160.

107. For their poor assessment of Maryland, see 15 December 1679, *Journal of Jasper Danckaerts*, 134. For the Labadist shift to enslaved labor see Davis, *Women on the Margins*, 170–71.

108. Petrus Dittelbach details such cruel treatment in *Verval en val der Labadisten* (Amsterdam: Daniel van de Dalen, 1692).

109. David William Voorhees, "'To Assert Our Right before It Be Quite Lost': The Leisler Rebellion in the Delaware River Valley," *Pennsylvania History: A Journal of Mid-Atlantic Studies* 64, no. 1 (1997): 5–27, http://www.jstor.org/stable/27773953.

110. Petrus Baijard, jm. van Alphen, en Blandina Kierstede, j.d. van N. Orangien, beijde wonende alhier den 4 Nov > ingeschreven den 28 Nov > Getrouwt, Liber A-2, 530. In 1697 Blandina purchased land at Rampo in what is now Rockland County, NY, from Indigenous people. Land Sale from Zerickham, Mettissiena, Eghkenem, Onarkommagh, Kraghkon, Saeuwapigh Kim and Nanawaron to Blandina Bayard, 15 October 1697, NYSR88-A936, New York State Library Special Collections.

111. Will of Sara Roeloffse, 29 July 1693, in John O. Evjen, *Scandinavian Immigrants in New York, 1630–1674* (Minneapolis, MN: K. C. Holter, 1916), 107; 1703 census, in W. S. Rossiter, *A Century of Population Growth from the First Census of the United States to the Twelfth, 1780–1900* (Washington, DC: Government Printing Office, 1909), 177. Evidence of the Bayards' domestic life and those of the people they enslaved remains in the trash left behind in their New York privy. The Bayards continued to hold onto their low country origin in the Dutch pipes marked with an "HG," while evidence of gaming pieces pointed to private moments shared among the enslaved that mirrored those found throughout "several plantations in the South and in Jamaica in the West Indies as well as the Almshouse in Albany." Anne-Marie Cantwell and Diana diZerega Wall, *Unearthing Gotham: The Archaeology of New York City* (New Haven, CT: Yale University Press, 2001) 173, 173n11, 174.

112. "Census of the City of New-York: About the Year 1703," in *DHSNY1*, 611–24. See appendix D for Stuyvesant-Bayard family slaveholding in the 1703 New York City Census.

113. James, *The Labadist Colony in Maryland*. 5.

114. Works ranging from family to political and dating from the late nineteenth through the present day have chronicled the Bayard family narrative. Such works present the seventeenth-century origins as an antiquarian prelude to the family's prestige during the Revolutionary and Early national period. James Grant Wilson, *Colonel John Bayard (1738–1807) and the Bayard Family of America* (New York: Trow's Printing and Bookbinding, 1885); Stephen Hess, *America's Political Dynasties: From Adams to Clinton* (Washington, DC: Brookings Institution Press, 2016), 281–306.

Chapter 3 *Naam*

1. Sentence of Tom and Jack, Extraordinary session held in Albany, 31 March 1682, in *CMARS*, 3:228–29.

2. Examination of Tom and Jack, Extraordinary session held in Albany, 31 March 1682, in *CMARS*, 3:225–27.

3. Fuentes, *Dispossessed Lives*, 4.

4. Examination of Tom and Jack, Extraordinary session held in Albany, 31 March 1682, in *CMARS*, 3:225–27; Venema, *Beverwijck*, 458, 463, 473, 477, 480. For Barent Emanuelse birth see Ordinary Session, 26 February 1672/3, *Kingston Papers*, 2: 469–96.

NOTES TO PAGES 58–60

5. Robert was born in Scotland, but spent his formative years in Amsterdam, emigrated to Massachusetts before finally settling in Albany. Leder, *Robert Livingston*, 10–11; Kierner, *Traders and Gentlefolk*, 11–12; Livingston, *The Livingstons of Livingston Manor*, 52–54; Julia Adams, *The Familial State: Ruling Families and Merchant Capitalism in Early Modern Europe* (2005; reprint Ithaca, NY: Cornell University Press, 2007), 66.

6. Adams, *The Familial State*, 65; Power of attorney from Governor Colve to Nicolaes Bayard, in Peter Christoph and Florence A. Christoph, eds. and Charles T. Gehring, trans., *The Andros Papers, 1674–1676* (Syracuse, NY: Syracuse University Press, 1989), 32.

7. Petition of Nicolaes van Rensselaer to be appointed Director of Rensselaerswyck, in Christoph, *The Andros Papers*, 216. Nicolaes is listed as "Minister of N: Albany etc." due to his role as co-minister of the congregation.

8. Linda Biemer, *Women and Property in Colonial New York: The Transition from Dutch to English Law, 1643–1727* (1979; reprint Ann Arbor, UMI Research Press, 1983), 61.

9. Biemer, *Women and Property in Colonial New York*, 59; Venema, *Beverwijck*, 189.

10. Biemer, *Women and Property in Colonial New York*, x.

11. See Kenneth Scott, "Ulster Co., NY Ct. Recs. 1693–1775," *National Genealogical Society Quarterly* (Dec. 1972): 280, quoted in Evelyn Sidman Wachter, *Sidman-Sidnam Families of Upstate New York* (Baltimore, MD: Gateway Press, 1981), 21.

12. Mr Gerrit van Slichtenhorst, plaintiff, against Elisabeth Claese, widow of Jan Burger, deceased, and Maria Ripse, the wife of Claes Ripse, defendants, 6 March 1676/7, in *CMARS*, 2:198; Rob1. Sanders, plaintiff, against Ger^t. van Slichtenhorst, defendant, 6 March 1676/7, in *CMARS*, 2:204–5.

13. Sentence of Claes Croes and Black Barent, 29 August 1679, in *CMARS*, 2:437.

14. Among the court members were listed Captain Philip Schuyler, foreman; the fur and slave trader Johannes Wendell; Pieter Bogardus; and Gerrit Hardenbergh, in *CMARS* 2:436–37.

15. Andrea Mosterman analyzes the relationships and lived experience of both enslaved and enslaver in colonial New York. Mosterman, *Spaces of Enslavement*, chapter 2. See also Oscar Williams, "Slavery in Albany, New York, 1624–1827," *Afro-Americans in New York Life and History* 34, no. 2 (2010): 154–68.

16. The Duke of York's Laws, https://www.nycourts.gov/history/legal-history-new-york/documents/Publications_1665-Dukes-Law.pdf. Sentence of Claes Croes and Black Barent, 29 August 1679, in *CMARS*, 2:437.

17. Sentence of Claes Croes and Black Barent, 30 August 1679, in *CMARS*, 2:437.

18. Robert and Alida were married in the Reformed Church at Albany, 9 July 1679. Jeannie F.J. Robison and Henrietta C. Bartlett, eds., *Genealogical Records: Manuscript Entries of Births, Deaths and Marriages, Taken from Family Bibles, 1581–1917* (New York: Colonial Dames of the State of New York, 1917), 138.

19. William Shaw to Robert Livingston, 8 Oct 1678, Livingston-Redmond Manuscripts, reel 1; cf. Leder, *Robert Livingston*, 21n49; Kierner, *Traders and Gentlefolk*, 19.

20. Nicolaes died on 12 November 1678. Robert and Alida were married on 9 July 1679. For another scholarly readings of their early relationship, see Kierner, *Traders*

and Gentlefolk, 19–24. See also, Biemer, ed. and trans., "Business Letters of Alida Schuyler Livingston, 1680–1726," *New York History* 63, no. 2 (April 1982): 182–207.

21. Sentence of Claes Croes and Black Barent, 29 August 1679, in *CMARS*, 2:437. For more on branding and scars in slavery, see Marisa Fuentes, *Dispossessed Lives: Enslaved Women, Violence, and the Archive* (Philadelphia: University of Pennsylvania Press, 2016), 124.

22. For the full trial records, see *MCARS*, 2: 429–44. Thomas Burke provided a detailed reading of the case, including its broader Native context; Burke, *Mohawk Frontier*, 132; Venema, *Beverwijck*, 189–90.

23. Acknowledgement of Debt by Jacob Jansen Gardinier to Andries Teller, January 22, 1677, in *FOR*, 221–22, https://www.newnetherlandinstitute.org/files/4014/2777/5086/Fort_Orange_Records_16561678.pdf.

24. Stephen van Cortlandt to Robert Livingston, 15 November 1691, LP, GLC03107.00200; See also LFP-Trans; Jacobus van Cortlandt to Mr. Jenkins, 15 April 1698, Letter book of Jacobus van Cortlandt, 1698–1800, BV Van Cortlandt. VCM. In the next decade Stephanus would go on to solidify trading connections with Boston's elite. Samuel Sewall to Jacobus van Courtland, 30 June 1705, in *Collections of the Massachusetts Historical Society* (Boston: John Wilson and Son, 1886), 313. For a discussion of the Van Cortlandts' law, political, and business associates see Leder, *Robert Livingston*, 21, 23–24, 37–38; and Bonomi, *A Factious People*, 63; Venema, *Beverwijck*, 90.

25. Charles Foy offers a detailed overview of the prominent place that Malagasy and Senegambian captive Africans had in New York's mariner culture, noting that enslavers such as Frederick Philipse targeted the Madagascar market searching for experienced mariners. Foy, "Ports of Slavery" (PhD diss., Rutgers University, 2008), 55, 55n61.

26. "An Answer to the Paper given in to the Honble. the Commissioners of the Customs by Mr. William Penn," 27 March 1697, in *The Manuscripts of the House of Lords, 1695–1697* (London: Printed for His Majesty's Stationery Office by Eyre and Spottiswoode, 1903), 504. Patricia Bonomi notes that Albany residents enthusiastically fought against such trading preference for New York. Additionally, the Van Cortlandts used New York placed proxies to capitalize on the trade, Bonomi, *A Factious People*, 52–53. For an overview of the trade laws, see Leder, *Robert Livingston*, 18, 37–38.

27. James Graham to Robert Livingston, 7 April 1679, LP, GLC03107.00037; Leder, *Robert Livingston*, 37.

28. Robert and Alida were married on 9 July 1679. Cynthia Kierner went into significantly more detail about Robert Livingston's financial exploits and his relationship with Alida Livingston. Kierner, *Traders and Gentlefolk*, 10–11; Leder, *Robert Livingston*, 21. See also Biemer, ed. and trans., "Business Letters of Alida Schuyler Livingston, 1680–1726."

29. James Graham to Robert Livingston, 7 April 1679, LP, GLC03107.00037; Leder, *Robert Livingston*, 29.

30. For the Caribbean exploits of Robert Livingston's Van Cortlandt in-laws and financial partners, see Arthur H. Bankoff and Frederick A. Winter, "The Archaeology

of Slavery at the Van Cortlandt Plantation in the Bronx, New York," *International Journal of Historical Archaeology* 9, no. 4 (Dec. 2005): 293–94. See also Firth Haring Fabend, *A Dutch Family in the Middle Colonies: 1660–1800* (New Brunswick, NJ: Rutgers University Press, 1991), 12, 23; and Goodfriend, *Before the Melting Pot: Society and Culture in Colonial New York City 1665–1730* (Princeton, NJ: Princeton University Press, 1992), 112. For the financial and family ties of the Philipse to Barbados and the wider Caribbean during the same time, see Kevin P. McDonald, *Pirates, Merchants, Settlers, and Slaves: Colonial America and the Indo-Atlantic World* (Berkeley: University of California Press, 2015), 111.

31. Robert Livingston traded linens with New York merchant John Sharpe. John Sharpe to Robert Livingston, 7 July 1679, LP, GLC03107.00042; Thomas De Lavalle to Robert Livingston, 22 August 1679, LP, GLC03107.00041. "Accompt of Charges Expended upon the Christian Prisoners," 13 October 1679, LP, GLC03107.01890. James Graham reported to Robert about civil unrest in New York that might slow down the shipment of his goods. James Graham to Robert Livingston, 8 June 1681, LP, GLC03107.00059.

32. The fact that he is referred to in the record as Alida's enslaved man argues that he was owned by her and not by Robert. Alida van Rensselaer appointed administratix of Domine Nicolaes van Rensselaer's estate, 31 December 1678, in *CMARS*, 2:380 (emphasis added). An inventory was taken on January 6, 1678/9, which was mentioned in Robert's request that the estate be appraised, 7 December 1680, in *CMARS*, 3:47–48. The estate paid 12 g sewan "to barent Maynderson for a pair of Shoes for the Maid on May 6, in *CMARS*, 3: 53. There are no enslaved people enumerated in the inventory. A copy of the inventory can be found in *CMARS*, 3:49–57. But if the enslaved person was owned by Alida outright, they would not have appeared in the inventory.

33. For Dutch seventeenth-century estate practices concerning enslaved people, see David E. Narrett, *Inheritance and Family Life in Colonial New York City* (1992; reprint Ithaca, NY: Cornell University Press, 2011), 186. For more on enslaved people as moveable property and as means to increase white women's personal wealth, see Kirsten Denise Sword, *Wives Not Slaves: Patriarchy and Modernity in the Age of Revolutions* (Chicago: University of Chicago Press, 2021), 118-120. Stephanie E. Jones-Rogers, *They Were Her Property: White Women as Slave Owners in the American South* (New Haven, CT: Yale University Press, 2019).

34. Sentence of Tom and Jack, Extraordinary session held in Albany, 31 March 1682, in *CMARS*, 3:218.

35. Sentence of Tom and Jack, Extraordinary session held in Albany, 31 March 1682, in *CMARS*, 3:229; Conveyance of a House and Lot from Stoffell Janse Abell to Claes Janse Stavast, in *FOR*, 196–97, https://www.newnetherlandinstitute.org/files/4014/2777/5086/Fort_Orange_Records_16561678.pdf; A List of the Heads of Families and The Number of Men, Women and Children in Each Household in the City and County of Albany, the 16 June, 1697, *The Annals of Albany* (Albany, NY: Munsell & Rowland, Printers, 1858), 9:81–89.

36. For the enslaved as servants of members, see Allan J. Janssen, *Gathered at Albany: A History of a Classis* (Grand Rapids, MI: William B. Eerdmans, 1995), 18. For a detailed reckoning of the wider Black community of Albany County, which included Schenectady, see Burke, *Mohawk Frontier*, 123–41.

37. Venema, *Beverwijck*, 233.

38. McDonald, *Pirate, Merchants Settlers, and Slaves*, 110; Marvin L. Michael Kay and Lorin Lee Cary, *Slavery in North Carolina, 1748–1775* (Chapel Hill: The University of North Carolina Press, 1995), 139–46. John Thornton's focus on central African naming patterns highlights that some seemingly European sounding names may have been bestowed by Africans in Africa, a point of vital importance to Albany enslaved population's connection to Dutch Atlantic slaving practices. Thornton, "Central African Names and African-American Naming Patterns," *WMQ* 50, no. 4 (October 1993): 727–42; Cheryll Ann Cody, "'There Was No 'Absalom' on the Ball Plantations: Slave-Naming Practices in the South Carolina Low Country, 1720–1865," *American Historical Review* 92, no. 3 (1987): 563–96; Romney, *New Netherland Connections*, 208–12. See also Laura Álvarez López, "Who Named Slaves and Their Children? Names and Naming Practices among Enslaved Africans Brought to the Americas and Their Descendants with Focus on Brazil," *Journal of African Cultural Studies* 27, no. 2 (June 2015): 161–63; Jerome S. Handler and JoAnn Jacoby, "Slave Names and Naming in Barbados, 1650–1830," *WMQ* 53, no. 4 (1996): 689–728; John C. Inscoe, "Carolina Slave Names: An Index to Acculturation," *Journal of Southern History* 49, no. 4 (1983): 527–54. For a recent examination of naming as evidence reflecting the priorities of enslavement and the slave system, see Sharon Block, *Colonial Complexions; Race and Bodies in Eighteenth-Century America* (Philadelphia: University of Pennsylvania Press, 2018), 85–104. See also Trevor Burnard, "Slave Naming Patters: Onomastics and the Taxonomy of Race in Eighteenth-Century Jamaica," *Journal of Interdisciplinary History* 31, no. 3 (2001): 325–46, https://www.jstor.org/stable/207085; Stephen Wilson, *Means of Naming: A Social History* (London: Routledge, 1998), 25–27, 30, 35, 311.

39. Examination of Tom and Jack, Extraordinary session held in Albany, 31 March 1682, in *CMARS*, 3:226.

40. Examination of Tom and Jack, Extraordinary session held in Albany, 31 March 1682, in *CMARS*, 3:225.

41. Conveyance of a House and Lot from Stoffell Janse Abell to Claes Janse Stavast, in *FOR*, 196–97; Bill of Sale of a House and Lot by Thomas Paulussen to Paulus Martense, in *FOR*, 201; Conveyance of a House and Lot from Paulus Martense to Harme Gansevoort, in *FOR*, 223; Conveyance of a House and Lot from Mattheus Abrahamse to Paulus Martensen, in *FOR*, 230–31; Conveyance of a House and Lot from Paulus Martense to Harme Janse, in *FOR*, 250; Conveyance of Lot from Robert Sanders to Paulus Martense, in *FOR*, 255–56, https://www.newnetherlandinstitute.org/files/4014/2777/5086/Fort_Orange_Records_16561678.pdf.

42. Examination of Tom and Jack, Extraordinary session held in Albany, 31 March 1682, in *CMARS*, 3:227.

43. Examination of Tom and Jack, Extraordinary session held in Albany, 31 March 1682, in *CMARS*, 3:226.

44. Andrea Mosterman, *Spaces of Enslavement*, 62.

45. For the spatial geography of Northeastern slavery, see Mosterman, *Spaces of Enslavement*; Mac Griswold, *The Manor: Three Centuries at a Slave Plantation on Long Island* (New York: Farrar, Straus and Giroux, 2013), 165; Alexandra A. Chan, *Slavery in the Age of Reason: Archaeology at a New England Farm* (Knoxville: University of Tennessee Press, 2007), 42–45; Peter Benes, "Slavery in Boston Households, 1647–1770," in *Slavery/Antislavery in New England: The Dublin Seminar for New England Folklife Annual Proceedings 2003*, ed. Peter Benes (Boston: Boston University Press, 2005), 21. Wendy

Warren succinctly lays out the gulf between the archival evidence and the historiographical tradition that New England slaves lived in the same house as their enslavers in *New England Bound*, 316n71.

46. Case of Tom and Jack, Extraordinary Session, 31 March 1682, in *CMARS*, 2:227. Burke, *Mohawk Frontier*, 140–41.

47. Case of Tom and Jack, Extraordinary Session, 31 March 1682, in *CMARS*, 3:227; Hodges, *Root and Branch*, 49.

48. Hodges, *Root and Branch*, 51.

49. "It is RESOVED and ORDERED by this Court and the Authority thereof that From and after the Publication of this Order noe Negro or Indian Slaues within this Government Doe prrsume to Goe or Absent themselves from their Mars Houses or Plantation on the Lords Day or any other Vnseasonable time or times without the said Mars Lycence or Consent Ffirst had and Obtain and Signified by A writing or Tickett under their Hands by the Date thereof, mentioning the time when such Lycence was Given," Slave Law, 4–6 October 1682, in *MCCNY* 93–94.

50. See Linda Biemer, ed. and trans., "Business Letters of Alida Schuyler Livingston, 1680–1726," http://www.jstor.org/stable/23173117; and Biemer, *Women and Property in Colonial New York*.

51. Even though Robert brought the theft case to the court, he was punished in relation to the case, suggesting that he was held at least partially culpable. Sentence of Tom and Jack, 31 March 1682, in *CMARS*, 3:229.

52. Jon Parmenter argued that although such religious divisions existed, the Haudenosaunee were reluctant to attack other members of the confederacy. Jon Parmenter, "After the Mourning Wars: The Iroquois as Allies in Colonial North American Campaigns, 1676–1760," *WMQ* 64, no. 1 (January 2007): 42–44, http://www.jstor.org/stable/4491596?seq=1&cid=pdf-reference#references_tab_contents. See also, in David G. Hackett, ed., *Religion and American Culture; A Reader*, 2nd ed. (New York: Routledge, 2003), 61; Annemarie A. Shimony, "Iroquois Religion and Women in Historical Perspective," in *Women, Religion, and Social Change*, eds. Yvonne Yazbeck Haddad and Ellison Banks Findly (Albany: State University of New York Press, 1985), 399.

53. Colin G. Calloway, *New Worlds for All: Indians, European, and the Remaking of Early America* (Baltimore: The Johns Hopkins University Press, 1997), 42, 45, 66; Gretchen Lynn Green, in her doctoral dissertation, discusses English blankets known as "strouds" and French efforts to curtail their trade to Native communities. Gretchen Lynn Green, "A New People in an Age of War: The Kahnawake Iroquois, 1667–1760" (PhD diss.; College of William & Mary, 1991), 175, 241, 243, https://scholarworks.wm.edu/etd/1539623801/.

54. Leder, *Robert Livingston*, 47.

55. Leder, *Robert Livingston*, 48; Kierner, *Traders and Gentlefolk*, 26, 28.

56. Testimony of Jack, 31 March 1682, in *CMARS*, 3:226.

57. Sentence of Tom, Extraordinary session held in Albany, 31 March 1682, in *CMARS*, 3:229.

58. Leder, *Robert Livingston*, 38–39.

59. Robert kept up trade connections with Amsterdam as well as a network of associates who assisted him in contesting the Van Rensselaer claim in Amsterdam. Gerard Besselz to Robert Livingston, 29 May 1684, LP, GLC03107.00114; Provisions

sent on the pinance *William Voerlandt*. 1684, LP, GLC03107.05059; Inventory for the Account of Robert Livingston, March 1687, LP, GLC03107.05075. This inventory includes line items for European linens. For his Amsterdam factor see: L.V. Schaick to Robert Livingston, 12 August 1697, LP, GLC03107.00357; L.V. Schaick to Robert Livingston, 14 September 1697, LP, GLC03107.00362. Robert was also trading in Barbados flour with his contact Arent van Dyck. Account of Robert Livingston, 10 July 1683, LP, GLC03107.00104; Account of Robert Livingston, 22 October 1683, LP, GLC03107.00105. By 1686 he had turned his sights toward selling his peltries in London on consignment. John Blackall to Robert Livingston, 1 January 1686, LP, GLC03107.00139; Leder, *Robert Livingston*, 46.

60. For evidence of Alida managing the contact between Robert and her brother Brandt, see Alida to Robert Livingston, 7 July 1681, LP, GLC03107.02168. Brant Schuyler to Robert Livingston, 21 November 1681, LP, GLC03107.00055; Brandt Schuyler to Robert Livingston, 19 January 1682, LP, GLC03107.00080; For a discussion of the Schuylers as Robert's way into the beaver economy, see Kierner, *Traders and Gentlefolk*, 21.

61. Warren, *New England Bound*, 95.

62. Warren, *New England Bound*, 109.

63. Kierner, *Traders and Gentlefolk*, 21.

64. Leder, *Robert Livingston*, 41.

65. Esther Mijers, "Scotland, the Dutch Republic, and the Union: Commerce and Cosmopolitanism," in *Jacobitism, Enlightenment and Empire, 1680–1820*, eds. Allan I. Macinnes and Douglas J. Hamilton (New York: Routledge, 2014), 101–3.

66. Examination of Tom and Jack, Extraordinary session held in Albany, 31 March 1682, in *CMARS*, 3:225–27; Jeannie Robison, *Genealogical Record: Manuscript Entries of Births, Deaths and Marriages Taken from Family Bibles, 1581–1917* (New York: The Colonial Dames of the State of New York, 1917), 138.

67. The court record only refers to these two women as the wives of Paulus Martense and Claes Janse Stavast. Their names can be found on other colonial and genealogical documents. For Catharina van Kleeck, see Alvin Seaward van Benthuysen and Edith M. McIntosh Hall, *The Van Benthuysen Genealogy* (Clay Center, KS: Wilson Engraving and Printing Company, 1953), 12–14. For Aefje Gerrits marriage record see Sypher, *Liber A-2*, 424.

68. Erin Kramer, "'That she shall be forever banished from this country': Alcohol, Sovereignty, and Social Segregation in New Netherland," *Early American Studies* (winter 2022): 3–42 (forthcoming).

69. Letter of Maria van Rensselaer to Richard van Rensselaer, October 12 1683, VRMP-MVR, NYSL_sc7079-b07-f32_ncn, https://digitalcollections.archives.nysed.gov/index.php/Detail/objects/18682; To Richard van Rensselaer, October 12, 1683, *CMVR*, 125.

70. Jeremias van Rensselaer, Watervliet, to Oloff Stevensen van Cortlandt, 9 November 1673, VRMP, NYSL_sc7079-b05-f54_p2_ncn, https://digitalcollections.archives.nysed.gov/index.php/Detail/objects/18600; To Oloff Stevensen van Cortlandt, *CJVR*, 450.

71. Will of Gerrit Slichtenhorst, 13 August 1698, in *Wills*, 11:5.

72. April 1, 1679, *CMARS*, 2:401; Untitled, April 30, 1679, and The oath of Volkje van Hoese regarding the negress, Albany, May 2, 1679, *CMARS*, 2:405.

73. Mary Beth Norton, *Founding Mothers & Fathers: Gendered Power and the Forming of American Society* (New York: Vintage Books, 1997), 225–26.

74. Mr Richard Pretty, sheriff, against Cornelis Michielse, defendant and Sentence, Ordinary session held in Albany, June 3, 1679, *CMARS*, 2:417–18.

75. Jennifer L. Morgan, "'Some Could Suckle over Their Shoulder': Male Travelers, Female Bodies, and the Gendering of Racial Ideology, 1500–1770," *WMQ* 54, no. 1 (1997): 171.

76. Kramer, "'That she shall be forever banished from this country'," 4–5, 8–9 (forthcoming).

77. Oath of Claes Janse Stavast and his wife and Paulus Martense and his wife against Tom and Jack, 31 March 1682, in *CMARS*, 3:228.

78. Sentence of Robert Seary and Mingoe, October 1682, in *PGCANY*, 34.

79. Sentence of Robert Seary and Mingoe, October 1682, in *PGCANY*, 34.

80. For an example of enslaved people using waterways for escape, see Resolution drawn up by P. Stuyvesant, Willem Cornelisen Oudemarckt, Jacob Loper, Brian Newton, L. Rodenborch, Jan Klaessan Smal, and Marten Dorne, 26 May 1644, Fort Amsterdam on Curaçao in *CP*, 41–42; Rupert, *Creolization and Contraband*, 96–97. Kevin Dawson situated waterways as alternative geographies for resistance and defiance. Dawson, *Undercurrents of Power*, 19.

81. For sophisticated analysis of naming among New Netherland enslaved and free population, see Linda M. Heywood and John K. Thornton, *Central Africans, Atlantic Creoles, and the Foundation of the Americas* (Cambridge: Cambridge University Press, 2007), 278–85; Romney, *New Netherland Connections*, 208–12; Dewulf, *The Pinkster King*, 37–38. For naming as resistance see Berlin, *Many Thousands Gone*, 188. See also Handler and Jacoby, "Slave Names and Naming in Barbados," 699n5. Dawson, *Undercurrents of Power*, 57–99; Molly A. Warsh, "Enslaved Pearl Divers in the Sixteenth Century Caribbean," *Slavery & Abolition* 31, no. 3 (2010): 345–62, https://doi.org/10.1080/0144039X.2010.504540; Warsh, *American Baroque: Pearls and the Nature of Empire, 1492–1700* (Chapel Hill: Published for the Omohundro Institute of Early American History and Culture, Williamsburg, Virginia by the University of North Carolina Press, 2018), 46.

82. For the ubiquity of Black seamen throughout the Atlantic World by the late seventeenth century, see W. Jeffrey Bolster, *Black Jacks: African American Seamen in the Age of Sail* (Cambridge, MA: Harvard University Press, 1997), 11–13, 51; Dawson, *Undercurrents of Power*, 19.

83. "An Order Concerning Negros and Indian Slaves," October 1682, in *PGCANY*, 37.

84. Higginbotham, *In the Matter of Color*, 116. For similar actions taken by New York City, see Court Minutes, 7 March 1670/71, New York City Municipal Archives, Records of New Amsterdam, vol. 6, book 1, 36, NYCMA, https://nycma.lunaimaging.com/luna/servlet/detail/NYCMA~12~12~52~1206344?page=39.

85. William Beekman to John Collier, 4 May 1683, in *Wills*, 2:436; William B. Aitken, *Distinguished Families in America, Descended from Wilhelmus Beekman and Jan Thomasse van Dyke* (New York: Knickerbocker Press, 1912), 5.

86. Nicolaes Willem Stuijvesant, jm. van N. Jorck en Maria Beeckmans, j.d. als voren, den 5 Maij A°. 1672, in *Liber A-2*, 525.

87. McDonald, *Pirate, Merchants, Settlers, and Slaves*, 114.

88. Inventory of all and Singular the goods, Rights, Chattels, and Credits of the Estate of Mr. Adolph. Phillipse, Deceased, New York, January 24, 1749, Adolph Philipse estate records, 1749–1767, NYPL, https://archives.nypl.org/mss/2412; Tom Lewis, *The Hudson: A History* (New Haven, CT: Yale University Press, 2007), 112.

89. "For the Due Observance of the Lord's Day," 15 March 1683, in MCCNY, 1:134; Higginbotham, *In the Matter of Color,* 117.

90. *DRCHNY*, 3:321–28.

91. List of the members of the Legislative Council in 1683 and "titles of Acts passed at the Second Session of the First Assembly of the Colony of New York" in *Journal of the Legislative Council of the Colony of New York*, ed. E. B. O'Callaghan (Albany: Weed, Parsons & Company, 1861), 1:xii, xiii.

92. "A Bill Concerning Masters Servants Slaves Labourers and Apprentices," 24 October 1684, in, 1:157–58.

93. Frank B. Gilbert, "Early Colonial Charters in Albany," *Proceedings of the New York State Historical Association* 8 (Albany: New York State Historical Association, 1909), 252–61, http://www.jstor.org/stable/42889661.

94. Grant of land to Robert Livingston, 29 April 1667, LP, GLC03107.05423; Land patent for Robert Livingston, 27 August 1685, LP, GLC03107.00129; Land Patent for Robert Livingston, 22 July 1686, LP, GLC03107.00142; Lease between Robert Livingston and Mattheus Abrahamse, 28 March 1687, Livingston-Redmond Manuscripts, Franklin D. Roosevelt Library; Singer, "The Livingstons as Slave Owners," 72.

95. *DRCHNY*, 3:415.

96. Danny Noorlander, *Heaven's Wrath*, 189–190; Romney, *New Netherland Connections*, 226–27.

97. *DRCHNY*, 3:547.

98. Gerret Hendericks, Derick up de Graeff, Francis Daniell Pastorius, Abraham up den Graef, "Quaker Protest Against Slavery in the New World," Germantown, Pennsylvania, 18 April 1688, HC09-10001, manuscript collection 990 B-R, Quakers and Slavery, Haverford College Quaker and Special Collections, http://triptych.bryn mawr.edu/cdm/compoundobject/collection/HC_QuakSlav/id/11.

99. [Anonymous], "A True and exact relation of the Prince of Orange his publick entrance into Exeter," London 1688, Henry E. Huntington Library and Art Gallery, Wing/ 1105:14, EEBO.

100. *The New York Genealogical and Biographical Record*, 2, no. 1 (January 1871): 36.

101. For more on Jacob Leisler within the context of New York and the Glorious Revolution, see David W. Voorhees, "The 'fervent Zeale' of Jacob Leisler," *WMQ*, 51, no. 3 (July 1994): 447–72; Voorhees, "Jacob Leisler and the Huguenot Network in the English Atlantic World," in *Strangers to Citizens, Integration of Immigrant Communities in Great Britain, Ireland and the Colonies, 1550–1750*, eds. Randolph Vigne and Charles Littleton (Sussex Academic Press, 2001), 322–31. Voorhees, "Rotterdam-Manhattan Connections: The Influence of Rotterdam Thinkers upon New York's 1689 Leislerian Movement," in *Rotterdams Jaarboekje* 10, eds. Paul van de Laar, Jan van Herwaarden et al. (Rotterdam, The Netherlands, 2001), 9:196–216; Lawrence H. Leder, "The Unorthodox Domine: Nicholas van Rensselaer," *New York History* 35, no. 2 (April 1954): 166, http://www.jstor.org/stable/23153043.

102. *IAVoyages*, Voyage ID no. 104593 (1677).

103. For an analysis of white/black dialogue with regards to the Jacob Leisler affair, see Dewulf, *The Pinkster King*, 29. For a discussion of the social standing of pro-Leislerians, see Firth Haring Faben, "The Pro-Leislerian Farmer: 'A Mad Rabble' or 'Gentlemen Standing up for Their Rights?'" in *A Beautiful and Fruitful Place*, edited by Nancy Anne McClure Zeller (Albany, NY: New Netherland Publishing, 1991), 2:29–36. For the allegiance of Anti-Leislerians with the merchant ethnically Dutch elite in Ulster County, see Haefeli, "A Scandalous Minister in a Divided Community," 373. See also Bonomi, *A Factious People*, 75–76.

104. "An Account of the Most Remarkable Occurrences in Canada from the Departure of the Vessels, from the Month of November 1689 to the Month of November 1690. My Mons. De Monseignat, Comptroller General of the Marine in Canada," in *DHSNY*, 1:297–302; "Mortgage Book B, in County Clk's Office, Albany," in *DHSNY*, 1:302; "List of Ye People Kild and Destroyed," in *DHSNY*, 1:304–5. "Lyst of ye Persones which ye French and there Indians have taken Prysoners att Skinnechtady and caried to canida ye 9th day of February 1689/90," in *DHSNY*, 1:305–6.

105. Population Return for the City and County of Albany filed by the Sheriff on March 27, 1687 showed "1059: Male, 929: female / Negroes—107: Male. 50: female" for less than 8 percent of the total population "Negro" (using the convention that "Male" and "female" in the first line referred only to white colonists). Peter R. Cristoph, ed., *The Dongan Papers, 1683–1688, Part II: Files of the Provincial Secretary of New York During the Administration of Governor Thomas Dongan* (Syracuse, NY: Syracuse University Press, 1993), 50–51.

106. Norton, *In the Devil's Snare*, 24, 114–16, 305, 313.

107. John Allyn to Robert Livingston, 10 May 1692, LP, GLC03107.00211. The public Hue and Cry was not unprecedented, and had been in use since the English takeover. See Hodges and Brown, eds., *"Pretends to Be Free,"* 323–27.

108. John Allyn to Robert Livingston, 10 May 1692, LP, GLC03107.00211.

109. Leder, *Robert Livingston*, 73.

110. C. S. Manegold, *Ten Hills Farm: The Forgotten History of Slavery in the North* (Princeton, NJ: Princeton University Press, 2010), 97–98.

111. Leder, *Robert Livingston*, 73; John Allyn wrote to Robert Livingston at his residence in Stratford (Fairfield County), Connecticut in November 1690. John Allyn to Robert Livingston re: "sorrowful news of the disaster of the fleet," 18 November 1690, LP, GLC03107.00180.

112. John Allyn wrote to Robert Livingston on several occasions. John Allyn to Robert Livingston re: "sorrowful news of the disaster of the fleet," 18 November 1690, LP, GLC03107.00180; John Allyn to Robert Livingston re: Mrs. Schuyler's slave, Livingston's cattle, 10 May 1692, LP, GLC03107.00211.

113. Approval of Suffield ferry, 1691, in Charles Wilcoxson Whittlesey, *Crossing and Re-crossing the Connecticut River: A Description of the River from its Mouth to its Source, with a History of its Ferries and Bridges* (New Haven, CT: Tuttle, Morehouse and Taylor, 1938), 51.

114. Approval of Suffield ferry, 1691, in Whittlesey, *Crossing and Re-crossing the Connecticut River*, 51.

115. John Allyn to Robert Livingston, 10 May 1692, LP, GLC03107.00211. For Allyn's alliance with the Livingstons see Leder, *Robert Livingston*, 67–69.

116. Sale, William Holmes to Matthew Allyn, 3 May 1638, quoted in William C. Fowler, "The Historical Status of the Negro in Connecticut," in the *Year Book of City of Charleston for 1900 A.D.*, ed. Henry B. Dawson (Charleston, SC: Walker, Evans & Cogswell, 1901), 3.

117. For more on Pequot captives as servants, see Michael L. Fickes, "'They Could Not Endure That Yolke': The Captivity of Pequot Women and Children after the War of 1637," *NEQ* 73, no. 1 (March 2000): 58–81, http://www.jstor.org/stable/366745.

118. Allyn relayed these figures in a report to the Board of Trade and Plantations. Samuel Hart et al., *Connecticut as a Colony and as a State, or, One of the Original Thirteen* (Hartford. CT: Publishing Society of Connecticut, 1904), 2:504.

119. For Petrus's mention of John Allyn as his Connecticut contact see Petrus Stuyvesant to Matthias Beck, 28 October 1659, NYSA_A1810-78_V13_0049, https://digitalcollections.archives.nysed.gov/index.php/Detail/objects/54428. For John Allyn's credit purchase of slaves and horses, see Bond of Captain John Allen securing his debt to Matthias Beck, 7 March 1661, NYSA_A1883-78_V17_075, https://digitalcollections.archives.nysed.gov/index.php/Detail/objects/19446. Also in *CP*, 189.

120. For John Allyn's relation to John Pynchon, see Carl I. Hammer, *Pugnacious Puritans: Seventeenth Century Hadley and New England* (Lanham, MD: Lexington Books, 2018), 16.

121. Graham Hodges notes that posting a hue and cry for an absconded man was among the first acts done by English governor Richard Nicolls. Hodges and Brown, eds., *"Pretends to Be Free,"* xxv. Such notices came with a reward for the slave catcher, one that was written into the New York legal code of 1682. Indians served as slave catchers across the Atlantic world to stem the tide of runaways to free destinations such as Florida. See Sally E. Hadden, *Slave Patrols: Law and Violence in Virginia and the Carolinas* (Cambridge, MA: Harvard University Press, 2001), 15.

122. Leder, *Robert Livingston*, 66–67. Bonomi, *A Factious People*, 151.

123. The Chevalier de Callières to Monseigneur, the Marquis of Seignelay, January 1689, in *DHSNY*, 1:285–86, 290–97; *An Account of the Most Remarkable Occurrences in Canada from the Departure of the Vessels, from the Month of November 1689 to the Month of November 1690. My Mons. De Monseignat, Comptroller General of the Marine in Canada*, in *DHSNY*, 1:297–300; "List of Ye People Kild and Destroyed," in *DHSNY*, 1: 304–5; Jacob Leisler to Maryland, March 4, 1689/90, in *DHSNY*, 1:307; Jacob Leisler to the Governor of Boston, March 4, 1689/90, in *DHSNY* 1:308; Jacob Leisler to the Bishop of Salisbury, March 31, 1690, in *DHSNY* 1:308; Robert Livingston to Sir Edmund Andros, Hartford, April 14, 1690, in *DHSNY*, 1:309; Robert Livingston to Captain Nicholson, June 7, 1690, in *DHSNY*, 1:311–12.

124. Connecticut's position as line of defense for Albany made the geopolitical situations even more heightened in the neighboring colony. The attacks had Atlantic circulation. *New-England's Faction Discovered; or, A Brief and True Account of their Persecution of the Church of England; the Beginning and Progress of the War with the Indians; and other Late Proceedings there, in a Letter from a Gentleman of that Country, to a Person of Quality. Being, an Answer to a most false and scandalous Pamphlet lately Published; Intituled, News from New-England, etc.* in *Narratives of the Insurrections 1675–1690*, ed. Charles M. Andrews (1960; reprint New York: Charles Scribner's Sons, 1915), 261–62, 266–67.

Robert Livingston presented his case for the defense of Albany before Connecticut's court. A General Court Held at Hartford by Special Order of the Governor, 11 April 1690, in *PRCC*, 14–15.

125. Burke, *Mohawk Frontier*, 131.

126. Will of John Olmsted, 20 September 1689, in *DECPR*, 1:343; Will of Philip Moore, A Free Negro. Hartford, 12 April 1695, in *DECPR*, 1: 488–89; Will of Ruth Moore, 27 August 1696, in *DECPR*, 1:574; An Act for Negro and Malatta servants to be maintained by their Masters, 10 October 1700, in *PRCC*, 1: 375–76, 408; 14 May 1704, in *PRCC*, 1:516. Allegra di Bonaventura includes the example of the "Negro Mareah" as "one of few other locals to receive a similar grant" of freedom when her "wealthy master, the British-born merchant Alexander Pygan, released from bondage around 1690 when she was in her forties." di Bonaventura, *For Adam's Sake*, 120.

127. Hodges, *Pretends to be Free*, xxix.

128. Fitz-John's personal and family connection to slavery dated to the seventeenth-century Pequot War. Allegra di Bonaventura offers a detailed analysis of the intertwined lives of the Livingstons, Winthrops, and the enslaved Jackson family. Di Bonaventura, *For Adam's Sake*, 22, 44–46, 76; Livingston, *The Livingstons of Livingston Manor*, 67–68; Kierner, *Traders and Gentlefolk*, 51–52; Warren, *New England Bound*, 94.

129. Di Bonaventura, *For Adam's Sake*, 77.

130. Allegra Di Bonaventura reads John's own slaveholding background on Manor Livingston into his formative time spent in Connecticut. Di Bonaventura, *For Adam's Sake*, 77–83.

131. Kierner, *Traders and Gentlefolk*, 10.

132. Cornelis van Tienhoven's Answer, 1650, in *Narratives of New Netherland 1609–1664*, ed. J. F. Jameson, 2nd ed. (1909; reprint, New York: 1967), 364–65.

133. For an examination of this connection, see the discussion of Whan in Warren, *New England Bound*, 178–80.

134. Peter Hinks, comp., "Slave Population of Colonial Connecticut, 1690–1774," *Yale University Historic Texts & Transcripts*, http://glc.yale.edu/sites/default/files/files/Citizens%20All%20Doc2.pdf.

135. Leder, *Robert Livingston*, 90n35.

136. Case of Tom and Jack, Extraordinary session held in Albany, 31 March 1682, in *CMARS*, 3:226.

137. Alida to Robert Livingston, Albany, 26 September 1698, LP, GLC03107.00424. See also LR-Trans.

138. Alida to Robert Livingston, 14 March 1700, LP, GLC03107.00533. Cf. LFP-Trans.

139. Philip Schuyler v. Aert, the Indian and Wamsahkoo, 24 July 1682, in *CMARS*, 3:275, 281.

140. Alida Livingston to Robert Livingston, 28 March 1698, LP, GLC03107.00405. See also LFP-Trans.

141. Evert mentions "Jan de wilt" putting "3 beavers, and 1 otter and 2 martens," on his account, sixteen days before Alida mentions the same man in her correspondence. Evert Wendell, *"To Do Justice to Him & Myself": Evert Wendell's Account Book*

of the Fur Trade with Indians in Albany, New York, 1695–1726, ed. and trans. Kees-Jan Waterman (Philadelphia: American Philosophical Society, 2008), 100; Tom Arne Midtrød, *The Memory of All Ancient Customs: Native American Diplomacy in the Colonial Hudson Valley* (Ithaca, NY: Cornell University Press, 2012), 85.

142. Midtrød, *The Memory of All Ancient Customs*, 85.

143. Harris, *In the Shadow of Slavery*, 29.

144. Although the Navigation acts past midcentury were intended to halt the clandestine trade in slaves streaming in from the Dutch Atlantic, these were never successfully enforced. Jan de Vries and Ad van der Woude, *The First Modern Economy: Success, Failure, and Perseverance of the Dutch Economy, 1500–1815* (Cambridge: Cambridge University Press, 1997), 465. See also Koot, *Empire at the Periphery*, 127, 197–99. Antiprivateering laws of 1692 and 1699 were passed, in part, to quell the illicit trade in Spanish Indian slaves. Almon Wheeler Lauber, *Indian Slavery in Colonial Times: Within the Present Limits of the United States* (New York: Longmans, Green, 1913), 162–63, 598.

145. Dewulf, *The Pinkster King*, 86–87.

146. Such ethnic diversity in a world of racial contingency offered an important counterpoint to the hardening of difference. Jack D. Forbes, *Africans and Native Americans: The Language of Race and the Evolution of Red-Black Peoples*, 2nd ed. (Urbana: University of Illinois Press, 1993), 5, 56, 86, 199, 221, 230, 260. For an examination of the impact of Native enslaved people within a Long Island enslaved community, see Hayes, *Slavery Before Race*, 168.

147. McManus details that the law was passed in reaction to a feared plot to free the enslaved population in order to fight with the French against Massachusetts. McManus, *Black Bondage in the North*, 127.

148. William Pitkin to Robert Livingston, Hartford, 23 June 1692, LP, GLC03107.00214; William Pitkin to Robert Livingston, Hartford, 29 September 1692, LP, GLC03107.00221.

149. For more, see Kathryn S. LaPrad, "Thinking Locally, Acquiring Globally: The Loockerman Family of Delaware, 1630–1790" (MA thesis, University of Delaware, 2010), 31, https://udspace.udel.edu/handle/19716/5742. By 1691, the tide had turned against Jacob and Balthazar was appointed executor of the Loockermans estate. Will of Balthazar Bayard, 4 March 1699, in *Wills*, 1:416–17.

150. The Trial of Col. Nicholas Bayard in the Province of New York for High-Treason, 19 February 1702, in *A Complete Collection of State-Trials, and Proceedings Upon High-Treason . . .*, ed. Thomas Bayly Howell, 2nd ed. (London: Printed by T. C. Hansard, 1816), 5:427. For a discourse on "antipopery" in Anglo America, see Owen Stanwood, "The Protestant Moment: Antipopery, the Revolution of 1688–1689, and the Making of an Anglo-American Empire," *Journal of British Studies* 46, no. 3 (July 2007): 481–508, doi:10.1086/515441.

151. Burrows and Wallace, *Gotham*, 56; MAAP: Mapping the African American Past, http://maap.columbia.edu/place/22.html; James Trager, *The New York Chronology: The Ultimate Compendium of Events, People, and Anecdotes from the Dutch to the Present* (New York: Harper Resource, 2003), 20, 22.

152. Stephen van Cortlandt to Robert Livingston, 15 November 1691, LP, GLC03107.00200. LFP-Trans.

153. Maria to Richard van Rensselaer, November 1683, in *CMVR*, 135.

154. Stephen van Cortlandt to Robert Livingston, 15 November 1691, LP, GLC03107.00200.

Chapter 4 Bond

1. Benjamin Wadsworth, *Journal, 1694* in *CMHS*, 1:104.
2. Benjamin Wadsworth, *Journal, 1694* in *CMHS*, 1:104.
3. Benjamin Wadsworth, *Journal, 1694* in *CMHS*, 108.
4. "Narrative by John Gardiner of Gardiner's Island, alias Isle of Wight, July 17, 1699," in *LGD*, 98–99.
5. "Narrative by John Gardiner," in LGD, 98–99.
6. Ritchie, *Captain Kidd*, 180.
7. For more on the Gardiner family history, see Lion Gardiner, *Relation of the Pequot Warres* (1660; reprint Hartford, CT: Hartford Press, 1901); Gardiner, ed., *Lion Gardiner*; Steven Gaines, *Philistines at the Hedgerow: Passion and Property in the Hamptons* (New York: Little, Brown, 1998), 63; Richard Dunn, James Savage, and Laetitia Yeandle, eds. *The Journal of John Winthrop, 1630–1649* (Cambridge, MA: The Belknap Press of Harvard University Press, 1996), 189–90, 190n10.
8. Ritchie, *Captain Kidd*, 180; Leder, *Robert Livingston*, 143.
9. Robert Livingston had invested in William Kidd's *Adventure Galley* in 1696 alongside William Blackham whose articles of indenture indicated the mission was to combat piracy against ships from "new England Rode Island, New Yorke & Elsewhere." Articles of Indenture of the *Adventure Galley*, 7 February 1696, LP, GLC03107.00239. William Blackham sued Robert after his losses in relation to the William Kidd affair. Leder, *Robert Livingston*, 198–99.
10. Leder, *Robert Livingston*, 94.
11. Hodges, *Root and Branch*, 41–42.
12. Leder, *Robert Livingston*, 94.
13. Foote, *Black and White Manhattan*, 82.
14. Koot relays from Stephanus's account book that he exported "flower for Suraname, Curaçao and St. Thomas" as part of a broader trade to between New York City, the Caribbean, and Amsterdam, and London. Stephanus van Cortlandt, Ledger, 1695–1701, NYHS, quoted in Koot, *Empire at the Periphery*, 207.
15. Robert Livingston's transcript of conference is in "Propositions by the Sachems of Onondaga and Oneida," 6 February 1699, in *DRCHNY*, 4:492–95.
16. New York Colonial Manuscripts, "Lords of Trade to the Earl of Bellomont," 5 January 1699, in *DRCHNY*, 4:454.
17. For an estimate of New England's seventeenth-century enslaved population, see Warren, *New England Bound*, 10; Margaret Ellen Newell, "Indian Slavery in Colonial New England," in *Indian Slavery in Colonial America*, ed. Allan Gallay (Lincoln: University of Nebraska Press, 2009), 33. For the rise in Boston's eighteenth-century slave population, see Hardesty, *Unfreedom*, 22. Between 1640 and 1650 New Netherland had the largest number of slaves of any North American colony, surpassed by the Chesapeake in 1660. Vivienne Kruger, "Born to Run: The Slave Family in Early New York, 1626–1827" (PhD diss., Columbia University, 1985), 11–12. Beginning in

the 1730s, between 16–18 percent of New York City's population was of African descent, making New York City second only to Charles Town, South Carolina, in the percentage of enslaved people. Evarts Greene and Virginia Harrington, *American Population before the Federal Census of 1790* (1932; reprint Baltimore, MD: Genealogical Publishing, 1993), 91–101; Edwin Vernon Morgan, *Slavery in New York* (New York: G. P. Putnam's Sons, 1898), 28–29.

18. Leder, *Robert Livingston*, 10–14, 18–20; Elizur Holyoke to Robert Livingston re: Holyoke's travel to New York to discuss debt, 3 October 1678, LP, GLC03107.00028.

19. Sewall documented the argument with Mather in the margins of his diary on 20 October 1701. Samuel Sewall, *The Diary of Samuel Sewall*, ed. M. Halsey Thomas (New York: Farrar, Straus and Giroux, 1973), 1:43.

20. Samuel Sewall had published a work on eschatology in 1697 with Bartholomew Green and John Allen, which was sold by Richard Wilkins, the same year that he apprenticed his eldest son, Sam to Wilkins in order to learn the bookseller business. Although the elder Sewall published *The Selling of Joseph* three years later with the same press, he chose to distribute the book privately to a few select friends. Judith S. Graham, *Puritan Family Life: The Diary of Samuel Sewall* (Boston, MA: Northeastern University Press, 2000), table 2, The "Sending Out" of the Sewall Children, 146.

21. Lords of Trade to the Lords Justices, 12 September 1699, DRCHNY, 4:583; Mr. Robert Livingston to the Lords of Trade, 21 June 1701, DRCHNY, 4:883; Duncan Campbell to Robert Livingston re: the arrest of Captain Kidd, 7 March 1700, LP, GLC03107.00549; Advertisement from John Campbell, Postmaster, *The Boston News-Letter*, 24 April 1704, https://www.masshist.org/database/viewer.php?item_id=186&mode=large&img_step=2#page2.

22. Robert E. Desrochers, Jr., "Slave-for-Sale Advertisements and Slavery in Massachusetts, 1704–1781," *WMQ* 59, no. 3, Slaveries in the Atlantic World (July 2002): 1, http://www.jstor.org/stable/3491467; Ritchie, *Captain Kidd*, 180.

23. Kierner, *Traders and Gentlefolk*, 52.

24. Albert J. von Frank, "John Saffin: Slavery and Racism in Colonial Massachusetts," *Early American Literature* 29, no. 3 (1994): 254–72, http://www.jstor.org/stable/25056983. Von Frank detailed Saffin's connection to Virginia and his actions in the domestic and Atlantic slave trade.

25. Diary Entry, 11 September 1701, *Diary of Samuel Sewall*, ed. M. Halsey Thomas (New York: Farrar, Straus and Giroux, 1973), 452; Ann Marie Plane, *Colonial Intimacies: Indian Marriage in Early New England* (Ithaca, NY: Cornell University Press, 2000), 118–22.

26. John Saffin, *A Brief and Candid Answer to a late Printed Sheet Entitled the Selling of Joseph*, 1701, in George Moore, *Notes on the History of Slavery in Massachusetts* (1866; reprint Bedford, MA: Applewood Books, 2008), 251–56.

27. Saffin, *A Brief and Candid Answer*; Lawrence W. Towner, "The Sewall-Saffin Dialogue on Slavery," *WMQ* 21, no. 1 (January 1964): 48–52, http://www.jstor.org/stable/1923355; Newell, *Brethren by Nature*, 242–43.

28. Di Bonaventura, *For Adam's Sake*, 137; Leder, *Robert Livingston*, 175–76.

29. Di Bonaventura, *For Adam's Sake*, 161.

30. John Borland to Robert Livingston, 2 December 1699, LP, GLC03107.00517.

31. Leder, *Robert Livingston*, 68–69.

32. Waller, *Samuel Vetch*, 20.
33. James Livingston to Robert Livingston, 4 January 1700, LP, GLC03107.00539.
34. James Livingston to Robert Livingston, 4 January 1700, LP, GLC03107.00539.
35. For more on Scotland's connection to transatlantic slavery, see T. M. Devine, ed., *Recovering Scotland's Slavery Past: The Caribbean Connection* (Edinburgh, UK: Edinburgh University Press, 2015).
36. See Rosalind Carr's *Gender and Enlightenment* for a discussion of the elite demographics of newspaper readers. Carr, *Gender and Enlightenment Culture in Eighteenth-Century Scotland* (Edinburgh, UK: Edinburgh University Press, 2014), 67.
37. Waller, *Samuel Vetch*, 79–94.
38. Newell, *Brethren by Nature*, 198–99.
39. Minutes of the Common Council, 9 April 1700, in *MCCCNY*, 2:102–3. The ordinance was reinforced seven years later, this time under a different council but one that counted several elite members of the Livingstons' network as members, such as Abraham Keteltas and Paul Droilhet. Minutes of the Common Council, 27 June 1707, in *MCCCNY*, 2:323.
40. Klooster, *The Dutch Moment*, 1–5.
41. Dutch merchants did not necessarily see the fall of New Netherland as an impediment to their efforts to seek out riches and power, but rather as an opportunity. Koot, *Empire at the Periphery*, 153–54.
42. Klooster, *The Dutch Moment*, 1–5.
43. "Patent of Hobocken, granted by Petrus Stuyvesant to Nicholas Varlettt, Esqr.," 5 February 1663, in Charles H. Winfield, *History of the Land Titles in Hudson Country, NJ., 1609–1871* (New York: Wynkoop and Hallenbeck, Printers, 1872), 39.
44. Winfield, *History of the Land Titles in Hudson County, N.J., 1609–1871*, 108n.
45. For Balthazar as schepen in 1673 see *Documents of the Assembly of the State of New York* 23, no. 37 (Albany: J. B. Lyon, 1916), 631. For evidence of his term as alderman see D. T. Valentine, comp., *Manual of the Corporation of the City of New York* (New York: Edmund Jones 7 Co. Printers, 1862), 454.
46. "An Ordr of the Common Councell Prohibiting Negroes to worke as porters &c," 24 July 1686, in *MCCNY*, 1: 179–80; A. Leon Higginbotham, Jr., *In the Matter of Color*, 118, 118n41.
47. United States Department of the Interior National Park Service. The Bowery Historic District, section 8, page 12.
48. "Commission. The Justice and Magistrates of Bergen to try Emmanuel, a negro slave of the family of Capt. Nicolas Verlett dec'd, for arson," 15 March 1669–70, in *Patent and Deeds and Other Early Records of New Jersey, 1664–1703*, ed. William Nelson (1899; reprint Baltimore, MD: Clearfield Company by Genealogical Publishing, 2000), 30–31. On September 12, 1673, and March 8, 1674, and April 18, 1574, Nicholas Bayard was listed as the "secretary" of the colony. He was also present at a council held in Fort James New York on June 20 and September 1, 1686 to determine the boundary line between East and West New Jersey. *DRCHNJ*, 1:131, 142–43, 517–18.
49. Minutes of the Common Council, 25 April 1691, in *MCCCNY*, 1:223–24.
50. Minutes of the Common Council, 29 April 1691, in *MCCCNY*, 1:225–26.

51. An Act for Regulating Negro, Indian and Mallatto Slaves within this Province of New Jersey, in *Civil Rights and African Americans: A Documentary History*, 18–20; Theodore Sedgwick, Samuel Allinson, and New Jersey Court of Chancery, *Acts of the General Assembly of the Province of New-Jersey: from the surrender of the government to Queen Anne...* (Burlington, NJ: Printed by Isaac Collins, Printer to the King, for the Province of New-Jersey, 1776), 5.

52. Representation of the Lords of Trade to the Queen relative an Act passed in 1704 for Regulating Negro, Indian and Mulatto Slaves &c in New Jersey, 18 October 1709, in *DRCHNJ*, 3:473–74.

53. For more on free Black community resistance, see Warren Eugene Milteer Jr., *North Carolina's Free People of Color, 1715–1885* (Baton Rouge: LSU Press, 2020).

54. Kammen, *Colonial New York*, 174.

55. Foote, *Black and White Manhattan*, 63.

56. An alternate published translation without transcription is included in Evelyn Sidman Wachter, *Sidman-Sidnam*.

57. "Census of the City of New-York: About the Year 1703," in *DHSNY*, 405.

58. Memoranda van Klaverack; Wachter, *Sidman-Sidnam*, 55–56.

59. New York Deeds, vol. 23:25, quoted in Wachter, *Sidman-Sidnam*, 28.

60. George Sydenham and Elizabeth Stuyvesant Marriage License, New York Probate Records, 1629–1971, New York Wills 1693–1707 vol 5–6, Image 169. Family Search.

61. Memoranda van Klaverack.

62. "Supplementary agreement between Gerrit van Slichtenhorst and Gerrit Teunissen van Vechten regarding the payment for a negro delivered two months before the appointed time," 25 May 1680. The enslaved man was named Dick. *Notarial Papers*, 3: 491; Bill of sale from Gerrit van Slichtenhorst to Gerrit Teunissen van Vechten of a negro named Harry," 25 May 1680, in *Notarial Papers*, 3: 492.

63. Nicholaes Willem Stuijvensant, wedr. van Maria Beeckman Elisabeth Slechtenhorst, j.d. van N. Albanien, "jn de Esopus," 15 September 1681. Marriage of Nicolaes Willem Stuyvesant to Elisabeth van Slichtenhorst, "in the Esopus." *Liber A-2*, 543; Midtrød, *The Memory of All Ancient Customs*, 74–75; for the Dutch using enslaved people to claim the land, see Mosterman, *Spaces of Enslavement*, 15–17.

64. A survey of lands on the Island of New York in the Bowery Division of the outward of the City on the East side of the Kings Road in the current possession of Gerardus Stuyvesant made by order of Anna Prichard [Pritchard] according to decree of the Supreme Court. New York Historical Society. Mss Collection AHMC—Stuyvesant Family Non-circulating.

65. Will of Gerrit Slichtenhorst, 13 August 1698, in *Wills*, 11:5; See also Wachter, *Sidman-Sidnam*, 15. Wachter's genealogy includes several primary source documents reprinted in their entirety.

66. Memoranda van Klaverack.

67. Wachter, *Sidman-Sidnam*, 28.

68. Pieter van Kampen, wedr. van Susanna Hillarie [ ] wede. van Lovijs Angola, beijde woonende op Stuijvesants bouwerije," 26 July 1682. Marriage of Pieter van Kampen and the widow of Lovijs Angola, married on Stuyvesant's bouwerij, *Liber A-2*, 545.

NOTES TO PAGES 94-98

69. Manuel Pieters, wedr. van Dorothee d'Angola, en Maijken d'Angola, laest wede. van Domingo d'Angola beijde Negroes, en wonende bij Stuyvesants bouwerije, 22 November 1689. Marriage of Manuel Pieters and Maijken d'Angola, and married on Stuyvesant's bouwerij, *Liber A-2*, 568.

70. Pieter Lucaszen, vrijen Neger, jm van Cormeskij, en Marijken Jans, vrijen Negrin, jd. op Stuijvens[ts]. bouwerije beijde wonende alhier, 29 October 1691. Marriage of Pieter Lucaszen (free Black) and Marijken Jans (free Black), *Liber A-2*, 572.

71. *RONA*, 6:286.

72. "Census of the City of New-York: About the Year 1703," in *DHSNY*, 405.

73. Memoranda van Klaverack.

74. Wachter, *Sidman-Sidnam*, 43–46; for more details on the suit, see Chancery Court Clerk of Queens County, New York, *Orders in Chancery, Province of New York, 1701–1802* (Salt Lake City: Genealogical Society of Utah, 1967).

75. Wachter, *Sidman-Sidnam*, 46.

76. Wachter, *Sidman-Sidnam*, 53. This section comes from primary source documents reproduced and included in Wachter's genealogy. While I have been unable to find these documents in another format, I have been able to verify the accuracy of many others reproduced within the work.

77. George Sydenham to Robert Livingston, Claverak, NY, 27 November 1714, LP, GLC03107.01089.

78. For more on the disenfranchisement of white female property owners, see Mary Beth Norton, *Separated by their Sex: Women in Public and Private in the Colonial Atlantic World* (Ithaca, NY: Cornell University Press, 2011); Zabin, *Dangerous Economies*, 34; Sword, *Wives Not Slaves*, 14, 189.

Chapter 5 Family

1. For Ben's duties and those of the Livingstons' other captive people, see Alida to Robert Livingston, 14 March 1700, LP, GLC03107.00533; Alida to Robert Livingston, 1 October 1711, LP, GLC03107.00841; Alida to Robert Livingston, 26 October 1711, LP, GLC03107.00843. For Diana's likely position as a domestic, see Will of Robert Livingston, 25 January 1710, LP, GLC03107.00811; Will of Robert Livingston, 10 Feb 1721, LR-MSS.

2. For Isabel's family, see Leendert Conyn and Kiliaen Winne's oath about the Examination of Joh. Dykeman's negro, 2 February 1715, LP, GLC03107.01103; Will of Robert Livingston, 10 February 1721, LR-MSS; Will of Robert Livingston, 25 January 1710, LP, GLC03107.00811.

3. A map is included in *The Memorial History of Boston Including Suffolk County Massachusetts, 1630–1880*, ed. Justin Winsor (Boston: James R. Osgood, 1881), 2:xxv. The detail about the inhabitants of the neighborhood, including Colonel Vetch and the purchase history of his property, with neighboring properties is included on xxvi. The plot where their property once stood is now home to a bank and a chain coffee shop with a view of Park Street Station, the southernmost section of Boston Common bordering the foot of Beacon Hill.

4. Benjamin Wadsworth, *The Well-Ordered Family or Relative Duties* (Boston, MA: Printed by B. Green for Nicholas Battolph at his Shop in Corn-Hill, 1712), Evans Series I Imprints, America's Historical Imprints.

5. Wadsworth, *The Well-Ordered Family*, 23.

6. Wadsworth, *The Well-Ordered Family*, 104.

7. Will of Robert Livingston Sr., 2 August 1728, transcription of "First Lord's Will" LFP/Box18/Folder 11, CL1988. 38. 18. 11, Clermont; Bequest, December 13, 1729, of a negro girl named Saar by Margarita Schuyler Livingston, Van Rensselaer Family Papers, ca. 1686–1964. SC3282 New York State Library, Box 7 Folder 4, http://www.nysl.nysed.gov/msscfa/sc23282.htm.

8. Williams-Myers, *Long Hammering*, 13–42. A. J. Williams-Myers offers a fantastic overview of labor in the valley during the colonial period in chapter 2, "Hands that Picked No Cotton"; Michael E Groth's recent work on the region has illuminated the intermanorial slaveholding context of the region. See Groth, *Slavery and Freedom in the Mid-Hudson Valley*, chapter 1 (colonial context), 26–27, 38, for his treatment of the Livingston family.

9. Mary Beth Norton, *In the Devil's Snare: The Salem Witchcraft Crisis of 1692* (New York: Alfred Knopf, 2002); Roberto Flores De Apodaca, "'Jethro, Who Saved Taunton': An African Man's Captivity Narrative during King Philip's War," *Journal of American Studies* (2020), 1–24. doi:10.1017/S002187582000136X.

10. Hartman, "Venus in Two Acts," 4.

11. Will of Robert Livingston, 10 February 1721, LR-MSS.

12. Robert to Alida Livingston, 18 October 1710, LP, GLC03107.00819. Cf. LFP-Trans.

13. Leendert Conyn oath about the Examination of Joh. Dykeman's negro, 2 Feb. 1714/1715, LP, GLC03107.01103.

14. Zabin, *Dangerous Economies*, 42.

15. The Hallett murder dragnet widened, stoking fears of a conspiracy and two other enslaved men were put to death. It also occasioned the passage of "An Act for preventing the conspiracy of slaves." *The Boston Weekly News-Letter*, Feb. 9 (detailed the murder) and Feb 23, 1708 [page 2] (detailed the executions), Early American Newspapers; James Riker, Jr., *The Annals of Newtown in Queens County, New-York* (New York: Published by D. Fanshaw, 1852), 142–43.

16. John Winthrop Jr. to Peter Stuyvesant, *Winthrop Family Papers*, vol. 5 (Boston: Massachusetts Historical Society, 1947), 298–99.

17. On November 12, 1707, Samuel Vetch purchased from Col. Tho. Wenham "affd Earthenware and a negro girl," a payment that he made using credit forwarded from his father-in-law Robert Sr. Account of Samuel Vetch, 14 May 1726, LP, GLC03107.00673.

18. *The Manifesto Church: Records of the Church in Brattle Square, Boston, with Lists of Communicants, Baptisms, Marriages and Funerals, 1699–1872*, ed. Ellis Loring Motte, Henry Fitch Jenks, and John Homans, 2nd ed. (Boston: Benevolent Fraternity of Churches, 1902), 130.

19. In his 1710 will Robert Livingston wrote: "I do further give and grant to my sd. Daughter Johanna two negro girls called Eva & Gritta both Daughters of Diana." Will of Robert Livingston, 25 January 1710, LP, GLC03107.00811.

20. Otterness, *Becoming German*, 97–103.

21. Propositions made to the Mohawks, 28 June 1710, Mohawks Answer, 3 July 1710, LP, GLC03107.02098. Midtrød convincingly argues that the Mohawk's resistance against Hunter's planned Schoharie settlement is what led to Manor Livingston as the chosen site. Midtrød, *The Memory of All Ancient Customs*, 161.

22. Robert to Alida Livingston, 21 July 1711, LP, GLC03107.02191. Cf. LFP-Trans.
23. Leder, *Robert Livingston*, 214, 214n7.
24. *DRCHNY*, 5: 238–41; Otterness, *Becoming German*, 100.
25. Robert to Alida Livingston, 21 September 1711, LP, GLC03107.02207. LFP-Trans.
26. Alida to Robert Livingston, 1 October 1711, LP, GLC03107.00841.
27. *DRCHNY*, 5: 238–41; Otterness, *Becoming German*, 100.
28. Alida to Robert Livingston, 29 October 1711, LP, GLC03107.00844. See also LFP-Trans. Alida to Robert Livingston, 7 April 1692, LP, GLC03107.00212. See also LFP-Trans.
29. Alida to Robert Livingston, 5 November 1711, LP, GLC03107.00848: Mr. Dirk Wessels has arrived here and said that Schipper had fled with his whole family from 8 French Indians who were seen there (*hnr. Dirk Wessels blyf heir angekomen en zei doch Schipper met zyn gehele vammelie gevlu[cht] zyn van 8 frocnhe wilden die daar gezien*). Our Negroes have been near the [Schuyler] flats writes Filip (*Onze neggers zijn bij de Vlocckete [Vlackte] geweest sryft [schrijft] Filip*) and he sent Indians after them and did not get them but has Indians out again (*en hy set [zend] wilde daar op hyt en hebben ze niet gekregen maar set [zend] weer wilde uit*) and there is a firewatch going on and there they may catch them if they wanted to get to Canada (*en daar is een brant wocght [brandwacht] uit en daar pakken ze mogen krygen soo[zo] ze naa[r] Kannada wonde [wooden]*). Cf. LFP-Trans.
30. "AN ACT to prevent the running away of Negro Slaves out of the Citty and Couty of Albany to the French at Canada," 4 August 1705, in *CLNY*, 1:582–84.
31. Philip to Alida Livingston, 28 October 1713, LP, GLC03107.02242: I have received his letter from Canada (*heb aen Canada Zijn brief ontfangen*) but I could not convince our negros to go home (*maer [maar] Conde [Kon] niet te weegh brengen [teweeg brengen] om onse [onze] negers die daer zijn te bewillignen om near huys te gaen*) they say that they wanted to stay there (*Sy Seyden dat Sy daer worden blyven*) and as long as they say that there is no means to get them from there (*& so Langh als sy dat Zeggen is daer geen apperceptie om haer daer van daen te Crygen*) but to have them abducted by Indians which will cost quite a bit for the Indians are quite afraid of the French (*als door wilden te laten Steelen & welk vry wast kosten sall want de wilden syn zeer bevreest voor de franse*). Cf. LFP-Trans.
32. In the *Woordenboek der Nederlandse Taal* (Dictionary of the Dutch Language), the word *consenteeren* is defined as "give permission for, agree with, accept or agree with" (*toestemming geven voor, zich akkoord verklaren met, instemmen met*). *Bewilligen* is defined as "to make someone willing, to move them to act, to persuade" (*Iemand tot iets willig maken, hem tot iets bewegen, overhalen*). *Verwilligen* is defined as "to make someone willing or inclined, to acquire a person's permission for something" (*tot iets bereid of genegen vinden of overhalen, iemands toestemming voor iets verwerven*). These terms are no longer in regular use, but have been replaced by the more modern *toestemmen* "to agree or to convince."
33. In the Dutch Act of Abjuration (*Plakkaat van Verlatinge*) of 1581, the notion of consent appears four times. The first in relation to the consent of the king of Spain, and the second in terms of the consent of the people. The term used is *consente* (*by gemeynen accoorde ende consente van heure leden*), which is the closest phrase conceptually to the American Declaration of Independence's "the consent of the

governed." The concept of slavery likewise appears in the text of the document, five times. Plakkaat van Verlatinge, 1581, Nationaal Archief, Den Haag, Netherlands Archief van de Staten-Generaal, 1.01.01.01, inventarisnummer 254G; For an online transcription that retains the original spelling see https://www.law.kuleu ven.be/personal/mstorme/verlating.html; for a modern Dutch transcription see http://www.nederlandseonafhankelijkheidsdag.nl/geschiedenis/placcaat-van-ver latinghe-in-modern-nederlands; for an English translation consult http://www1. umassd.edu/euro/resources/netherlands/25.pdfm. For more on the international influences on the American Declaration of Independence, see David Armitage, *the Declaration of Independence: A Global History* (2007; reprint Cambridge, MA: Harvard University Press, 2008).

34. Waller, *Samuel Vetch*, 234.

35. *DRCHNY*, 5: 238–41; Otterness, *Becoming German*, 100; Robert Livingston to Lawrence Smith, 2 April 1712, in *DHSNY*, 3:681.

36. "An Act for reviving and Continuing an Act, Entituled, an Act to prevent the running away of Negroe Slaves out of the City & County of Albany to the French at Canada," 21 July 1715, in *CLNY*, 1:880–81.

37. Kenneth Scott, "The Slave Insurrection in New York in 1712," *New York Historical Society Quarterly* 45, no. 1 (January 1961), 62–67.

38. Walter Rucker centralized African identity in the planning of the revolt, offering a deep and insightful treatment of the moment's lasting impact for Black communities and as reflective of slaveholders' ethnic prejudices in choosing African captives. Walter C. Rucker, *The River Flows On: Black Resistance, Culture, and Identity Formation in Early America* (Baton Rouge: Louisiana State University Press, 2008), chapter 1; Margaret Newell centralized the Native context of 1712 and how it influenced the passage of legal statues across the region. Newell, *Brethren by Nature*, 207–10.

39. John Borland to Philip Livingston, 14 April 1712, LP, GLC03107.02402.

40. News, *Boston News-Letter*, 21 April 1712, EAN.

41. Hardesty, *Unfreedom*, 22.

42. George Vane to (the Earl of Dartmouth?), Annapolis Royal, 5 May 1712, Co 217/31, British Colonial State Papers, Proquest; Donald F. Chard, "The Impact of Ille Royale on New England, 1713–1763" (PhD diss., University of Ottawa, 1977); Waller, "Vetch, Samuel," in *DCB*, 2.

43. For Robert Livingston's actions following New York's Slave Revolt in 1712 and the subsequent passing of the act, see Kenneth Scott, "The Slave Insurrection in New York in 1712," *New York Historical Society Quarterly* 45, no. 1 (January 1961): 47–52, 58–59, 68, 71; Otterness, *Becoming German*, 147, 147n46.

44. Margaret's letter to her father Robert Sr. details that John had told her about his relationship with Elizabeth Knight while Mary was sick during one of his many trips to Boston. Margaret Livingston Vetch to Robert Livingston, Sr., Boston, 29 June 1713, LP, GLC03107.01015.

45. For Joanna's news concerning Mary's illness, see Joanna Livingston to Robert Livingston, 19 November 1712, LP, GLC03107.00944. She also informed her parents of Mary's death. Joanna Livingston to Robert Livingston, 18 January 1713, LP, GLC03107.00999.

46. Joanna Livingston to Robert Livingston, 13 July 1713, LP, GLC03107.01018.

47. Joanna's letter, addressed to her father, informed her parents she had arrived in Boston safely, but was ill. Joanna to Robert Livingston, 1 June 1713, LP, GLC03107.00964.

48. Joanna to Robert Livingston, 13 July 1713, LP, GLC03107.01022.

49. More than four hundred Bostonians died—about 18 percent of them people of color—at a time when Black people were only 4 percent of the total population. News, "Burials within the Town of Boston, in the Year 1714," *Boston News-Letter*, 7 March 1714, page 2, EAN; Nicole Saffold Maskiell, "Cicely Was Young, Black and Enslaved—Her Death during an Epidemic in 1714 Has Lessons that Resonate in Today's Pandemic," *The Conversation*, December 2, 2020; Nicole Saffold Maskiell, "'Here Lyes the Body of Cicely Negro': Enslaved Women in Colonial Cambridge and the Making of New England History," *NEQ* 94, no. 2 (2022) (forthcoming).

50. Samuel Vetch to Robert Livingston, 28 December 1713, LP, GLC03107.01045; Samuel Vetch to Robert Livingston, 25 January 1714, LP, GLC03107.01043; For mention of the epidemic see John Livingston to Robert Livingston, 1 January 1714, LP, GLC03107.01047; Elizabeth Mather, her newborn twins, and two-year-old daughter died during the epidemic. Cotton Mather, *Diary* (Boston: The Society, 1911), 2: 254–62.

51. Antonio T. Bly, "'Pretends he can read': Runaways and Literacy in Colonial America," *Early American Studies* 6, no. 2 (fall 2008): 261–94, http://www.jstor.org/stable/23546575.

52. Alida to Robert Livingston, 26 October 1711, LP, GLC03107.00843. Cf. LFP-Trans.

53. Leendert Conyn oath about the Examination of Joh. Dykeman's negro, 2 Feb. 1714/1715, LP, GLC03107.01103.

54. Robert to Alida Livingston, 21 April 1714, LP, GLC03107.02249. No negroes procurable that are worth a penny; maybe they will come through (*geen negros te crygen [te krijgen] dat en [een] Stuyver wurt [waard] syn misshien sal dorcomen [door komen]*). Cf. LFP-Trans.

55. Robert to Alida Livingston, 28 April 1714, LP, GLC03107.02251. They are such beautiful negroes as I have yet seen & do not sell them for less than 50£, please, for they are worth it (*Sy syn sulk schoune [schoon] negers als ik yt gesien & [gehandelen] niet minder als 50£ ver copen want zy zyn 't waart*). One, the oldest, speaks good English, has been a sheep herder, was born in Jamaika; the other was born in his land, knows nothing but negro (*De ons de auts [oudste] spraakt gout [good] Engsle [Engels] heft shaap kudde [shaapskudde] geweest, is van Jamaika geborn [geboren], de ander is een uyt zyn Landt geborn [geboren], ken niet als negro*). Cf. LFP-Trans.

56. Alida to Robert Livingston, 21 May 1714, LP, GLC03107.01098. Jeremie got the negro boy who knows English for £50 he shall pay us when you come (*Jeremie got die negher Jonghe die enghels ken voor 50lb ons u komt sal ons naartoe betaeln*) and the other was too small [for] Japick (*en die ander was voor Japick te kliene*) Roelof has the small one for £50 to be paid in winter so that for Japick you should send up a big one like Jeremie's (*Roelof heft het klennige voor 50lb in winter te betalen soo dat u voor Japick de groote van [als] Jeremie hier op moet steur zyn [stuur zijn]*). Cf. LFP-Trans.

57. "A List of the Inhabitants and slaves in the County of Dutchess. 1714," in *Lists of Inhabitants of Colonial New York: Excerpted from the Documentary History of the*

State of New-York, ed. Edmund Bailey O'Callaghan (1979; reprint Baltimore, MD: Clearfield Company by Genealogical Publishing, 2007), 17.

58. Kierner, *Traders and Gentlefolk*, 94.

59. Johannes Dijkeman, Jr. was born in Albany around 1662. Marjorie Dikeman Chamberlain, *Johannes Dyckman of Fort Orange and his Descendants*, vol. 1, *The First Five Generations* (West Rutland, VT: Daamen, 1988), 20.

60. Jaap Jacobs, email message to author, 28 May 2021.

61. Indenture of service of Johannes Dyckman to Tryntie Jochims, the wife of Abraham Staets, 10 April 1676 in *Albany Records*, 3: 339; Chamberlain, *Johannes Dyckman*, 20.

62. Chamberlain, *Johannes Dyckman*, 20.

63. Burke, *Mohawk Frontier*, 140–41. For Johannes's land, see *A History of the Schenectady Patent in the Dutch and English Times; Being Contributions Toward a History of the Lower Mohawk Valley*, comp. Johnathan Pearson, ed. J.W. Mac Murray (Albany: Albany: Joel Munsell's Sons, 1883), 211.

64. Burke, *Mohawk Frontier*, 100–108.

65. "List of People Killed and Destroyed," in *DHSNY*, 1: 304–5.

66. "Lyst of ye Persones whi ye French and there Indians have taken Prysoners at Skinnechtady and carried to canida ye 9th day of February 1689/90," in *DHSNY*, 1: 305–6.

67. "List of the Goods sent from New York and received from Monsr Jan Hendricksen Bruin and Johannes Proofoost to be distributed among the Refugees of Schoonechtede," in Pearson, *A History of the Schenectady Patent*, 266.

68. He was listed as a debtor on Robert Livingston's estate in 1715. In 1715 he was also listed as being a captain in the militia. "The Mills of Livingston Manor," in *The Law Practice of Alexander Hamilton: Documents and Commentary*, ed. Julius Goebel Jr. and Joseph H, Smith, chapter 2 (New York: Columbia University Press, 1 980), 9n19.

69. Leder, *Robert Livingston*, 87, 157.

70. Rucker, *The River Flows On*, 29.

71. Leendert Conyn oath about the Examination of Joh. Dykeman's negro, 2 Feb. 1714/1715, LP, GLC03107.01103.

72. Payment to Jacob Plough from the Supervisors of Dutchess County "upon the Business of a Negro of Johanns Dickman that Wass Burnt," 3 June 1720, in *Book of the Supervisors of Dutchess County, New York, A.D. 1718–1722* (Poughkeepsie, NY: Vassar Brothers' Institute, 1907), 33; Chamberlain, *Johannes Dyckman*, 1: 21, 21n16.

73. Will of Robert Livingston, 10 February 1721, LR-MSS.

74. Jennifer van Horn, *The Power of Objects in Eighteenth-Century British America* (Chapel Hill: Published for the Omohundro Institute of Early American History and Culture, Williamsburg, Virginia by the University of North Carolina Press, 2017), 273–76, 302–3.

75. Maskiell, "'Here Lyes the Body of Cicely Negro.'"

76. Bradish Family of Cambridge and Long Island, http://www.perseus.tufts.edu/hopper/text?doc=Perseus%3Atext%3A2001.05.0228%3Achapter%3D27&force=y.

NOTES TO PAGES 114–117

77. Alida Livingston to Robert Livingston, 7 June 1722, LP, GLC03107.01451: I hear what Naetye thinks granddaughter Veets has said about the negro woman (*Ik hoor wat Naetye denkt dat nichte [kleindochter WDNT] Veets over de negerin heeft gezegd*). Bradis said that the negro woman said she was always ill and he asked Veets about that (*Bradis zei doct de negerin zei dat ze altyd ziek was en dat zij daarover Veets vroeg*). And she sent for the negress and he said he wanted to buy her; and she set a price for her, but the negress said she did not want to be sold and said what illness she had (*En ze stuurde naar de negerin en hij zei dat hij haar wilde kopen; En zij heeft haar geprijzen, maar de negerin zei dat ze niet verkoght wilde en zei welke ziekte ze gaat*). Cf. LFP-Trans.
78. Account of Samuel Vetch, 14 May 1726, LP, GLC03107.00673.
79. Will of Robert Livingston, 2 August 1728, transcription of "First Lord's Will" LFP/Box18/Folder 11, CL1988. 38. 18. 11, Clermont.
80. Roberta Singer's "The Livingstons as Slaveowners" is the only article that provides an extended analysis of the Livingston's slaveholding practices on the Manor. Linda Biemer and Allegra DiBonaventura cover some aspects of their slaveholding practices as well. Roberta Singer, "The Livingstons as Slave Owners: The 'Peculiar Institution' on Livingston Manor and Clermont," in *The Livingston Legacy: Three Centuries of American History*, ed. Richard Wiles (Annandale-on-Hudson, NY: Bard College, 1987), 67–97; Biemer, ed. and trans., "Business Letters of Alida Schuyler Livingston, 1680–1726"; DiBonaventura, *For Adam's Sake*.
81. Alida to Robert Livingston, 3 May 1717, LP, GLC03107.01168. Cf. LFP-Trans.
82. Robert to Alida Livingston, 13 May 1717, LP, GLC03107.02264. Cf. LFP-Trans.
83. Alida to Robert Livingston, 5 November 1720, LP, GLC03107.01347. Cf. LFP-Trans.
84. Alida to Robert Livingston, 13 June 1722, LP, GLC03107.01453. Cf. LFP-Trans.
85. Di Bonaventura, *For Adam's Sake*, 10.
86. Alida to Robert Livingston, 13 June 1722, LP, GLC03107.01453. Cf. LFP-Trans.
87. Robert to Alida Livingston, 19 June 1722, LP, GLC03107.02290: I am sorry to hear that Joe has become so cunning (*Tis my Leedt [Leedt = verdriet, smart, iemand aangedaan. WDNT] om te horren dat Joe so slim is gewordt*). [I] have never found fault with him. (*[ik] heb noijt aan hem kunnis niet*). [I] hope that is may pass off (*[Ik] hoop dat zal ontmagh gaan*). Cf. LFP-Trans.
88. Kathleen Brown noted that Virginians William Byrd II and Landon Carter administered herbal punishments to their captive people. Brown, *Good Wives, Nasty Wenches*, 353.
89. Alida to Robert Livingston, 23 June 1722, in Biemer, ed. and trans., "Business Letters of Alida Schuyler Livingston," 206.
90. Tam (enslaved) and Japick (Palatine) travel delivering goods, described in Alida to Robert Livingston, 3 May 1717, LP, GLC03107.01169; See also LFP-Trans. Alida to Robert Livingston, 22 May 1717, LP, GLC03107.01174. See also LFP-Trans.
91. Alida to Robert Livingston, 5 November 1720, LP, GLC03107.01347: I am having trouble enough here with our folks (*Ik heb hier trobbel genoeg met ons volck.*). Tam does not do anything and does not want to do anything and is fat and slick (*Tam doet niets en wil [niets] mit doen en is vet en gladt ["gladt," heeft ook de betekenis dat hij niet te vertrouwen is]*). He wants to keep his letter himself, he said, or he will do evil (*Hy wil zyn brief zelfs bewaren zei hy, of hy zal quaet [kwaad] doen*). I am afraid he will do something evil—set something on fire—so I am sending him to be sold or to be sent

away (*Ik ben bangs dat hy snigs dings quaet [kwaad] sal doen, om yts[iets] in de brant te steken, soo ik zend hem om te verkoopen of te versonden [verzonden]*) for he is not working and refuses to look after anything (*want hy verbef niet en weigert voor iets te zorgen*). I let him leave (*Ick heb hem laten laten*) And the High-Dutch woman has had him for 4 days (*en de Hoogh duitse vrou heeft hem 4 daghen ghehad*) and she did not get it sorted (*en zy hent hem gesort niet*). She says additionally that he might be willfully doing it in order to get away (*dienchts dat zy zegt hy mocht wil [willens] doet om weg te naartoe*). Have him sold or sent away (*Laat hem verkoght of versonden*). Our people who have brought up the 66 beasts are not at home yet; I hope they will fetch a healthy price (*Ons volck die de 66 beesten opgebrought [opgebracht] hebben, zyn nog niet thuis; Ick hoop dat ze zyn gezonig prys sal beringhen [brengen]*). Cf. LFP-Trans. For the wider meaning of *gladt*, Saskia Coenen Snyder, email message to author, 10 April 2020.

92. Last will and testament (Robert Livingston), 22 September 1722, LP, GLC03107.01366; Alida to Robert Livingston, 7 July 1721, LP, GLC03107.01409. See also LFP-Trans.

93. Tobias was scoping out the land he had inherited from his father that bordered the Roeloff Jansen's Kill. This was one half of a conveyance Robert had sold to his father, Dirck Wesselsz. The inheritance came with farm animals and "one of my negroes." Will of Dirk Wesselsz ten Broeck, 4 February 1715, in *Early Records of the City and County of Albany and Colony of Rensselaerswyck,* Jonathan Pearson, trans. and A.J.F. van Laer, ed. (Albany, 1869–1919), 4:159.

94. Alida to Robert Livingston, 22 April 1721, LP, GLC03107.01392: Our Gysbert's [Gilbert's] negro had run away (*onze gysbert negher was wegh gheloopen [weg gelopen]*). Yet they caught him again [and] beat him very much (*doch ze hem weer kreghen [krijgen] sloeg hem heb'n heel veel*) and in 10 days [he] died from disorder (*en in 10 docghen [dagen] uyt [uit] beordigheit gestorven*). And he then suffered so much damage by it (*en he [hij] toen soo veel schod [schade] door*). Cf. LFP-Trans. For information on Johannes Dyckman's continued life on the manor see Chamberlain, *Johannes Dyckman,* 21–22.

95. Alida to Robert Livingston, 16 November 1717, LP, GLC03107.01218. Cf. LFP-Trans.

96. Alida to Robert Livingston, 3 December 1717, LP, GLC03107.01219. Cf. LFP-Trans.

97. In his 1721 will Robert gave Dego and his daughter to Joanna: "I do give and bequeath to my Daughter Joanna wife of Cornelius van Horn a negro man named Dego who I [illegible] do give and for with negro daughter Alida." Will of Robert Livingston, 10 Feb 1721, LR-MSS.

98. Alida to Robert Livingston, 25 May 1722, LP, GLC03107.01448: Give Deko your old hat if it is outdated (*Gheef [geef] Deko je oude hoed als het is bestant [Bestand: "In staat zijnde, voldoende, toereikend tot datgene wat eene bepaling noemt. Thans verouderd."* WDNT]). Cf. LFP-Trans.

99. Alida to Robert Livingston, 20 August 1722, LP, GLC03107.01487. Cf. LFP-Trans.

100. Cornelius van Horne to Robert Livingston, 10 March 1724, LP, GLC03107.01553.

101. Alida Vetch wed Stephen Bayard, 12 March 1725, RRCNY, 43.

102. Stephen Bayard to Robert Livingston, 12 November 1725, LP, GLC03107.01740.

242 NOTES TO PAGES 120–126

103. Robert to Alida Livingston, 7 September 1725, LP, GLC03107.02347. Cf. LFP-Trans.

104. Robert to Alida Livingston, 15 September 1725, LP, GLC03107.02351.

105. Robert Livingston to Alida Livingston, 27 May 1726, LP, GLC03107.02378: I thought that Dego would bring the old saddle that has been mended (*Ick doght [dacht] dat Dego de ouds Saal [zadle] soud [zou] oft brungen [bringen] and gemaakt is worden*). Then I shall buy a good bridle (*Souds [Zou] d in een goeds Toom Coopon [kopen]*). Cf. LFP-Trans.

106. Alida Livingston, Memorandum for New York, 6 September 1725, LP, GLC03107.01684: Deko has the buccaneer [gun] to get it fixed (*Deko heft [heft] de boeka[-]nier om te laete maken*). Cf. LFP-Trans.

107. Robert to Alida Livingston, 20 May 1726, LP, GLC03107.02373: He bought a leg of mutton for 3 sh. 9d., without order, in the place of some ox-meat (*Coght [Kocht] hij een Shaps Beit [schaapbeen] van 3sh 9d sonder order in 't plats van wat ons vleys*). Had there been no ox-meat, I could have bought him a ham for the same amount of money. And now I must also buy him a ham (*hadden geen ons vleys geweest Ik kon hem een ham gekogt hebben voor hetselfde[de]gelt en nu moet ik hem weer een ham Coupen [kopen]*). Cf. LFP-Trans.

108. Robert to Alida Livingston, 20 May 1726, LP, GLC03107.02373: In the margin: I have not bought Dego a ham for I cannot spare 6d [pence] for a pound of ham for a negro. He can eat butter and bread until he comes home (*Ick heb Dego geen ham gekocght maar [ik] kan niet 6d uitgeven voor en Pond ham voor een neger Hy mogh Butter een Broot eten tot dat thuis comt*). Cf. LFP-Trans.

109. Robert Livingston to Alida Livingston, 31 May 1726, LP, GLC03107.02380. Cf. LFP-Trans.

110. Will of Robert Livingston, Sr., 2 August 1728, transcription of "First Lord's Will" LFP/Box18/Folder 11, CL1988. 38. 18. 11, Clermont.

Chapter 6 Market

1. United States Department of the Interior National Park Service. The Bowery Historic District, section 8, page 12; Stokes, *Iconography*, 6:75–76.

2. News, "A Law Prohibiting the Sale of Meal by Measure," *New-York Weekly Journal*, 6 March 1737, 1, EAN; "A Law to Prohibit Negroes and Other Slaves Vending Indian Corn Peaches or Any other Fruit within this Ceity," *MCCNY*, 4:497–98.

3. *MCCNY*, 4:497–98.

4. Account of Captain Langdon for the Ship Oswego Packet, July 1736–October 1737, LP, GLC03107.02548.

5. Michael J. Douma, "Estimating the Size of the Dutch-Speaking Slave Population of New York in the 18th Century," *Journal of Early American History* (forthcoming).

6. *IAVoyages*, Voyage ID no. 107711 *Byam* (1730); *IAVoyages*, Voyage ID no. 107716 *Byam* (1731); *IAVoyages*, Voyage ID no. 107675 *Francis* (1730); *IAVoyages*, Voyage ID no. 107693 *Francis* (1730); *IAVoyages*, Voyage ID no. 107717 *Francis* (1731); *IAVoyages*, Voyage ID no. 107736 *Francis* (1731).

7. *IAVoyages*, Voyage ID no. 101576 *Bohemia industry* (1731).

8. Saxby, *The Quest for the New Jerusalem*, 314.

9. Between 1718 and 1734, five voyages owned by elite members within the Livingstons' larger circle of family and business associated brought thirteen enslaved people from Curaçao to New York. *DIHSTA*, 3:466, 469, 481, 484, 497. On August 5, 1745, Robert Livingston took out an insurance policy on the sloop *Griffen* in advance of its voyage from New York to Curaçao. On August 7, 1745, Robert Jr. insured the sloop *Deboras* for its voyage between Philadelphia and Curaçao. On June 23, 1746, Robert Jr. purchased an insurance policy for the sloop *Charity* for its voyage between New York and Curaçao. On September 23, 1746, Robert Jr. insured the *Jamaica Packet* for its voyage from New York to Curaçao. On January 22, 1747, Robert Jr. insured the sloop *Stork* in advance of its return voyage from Curaçao to New York; Insurance policy for the sloop *Griffen*, 5 August 1745, LP, GLC03107.02718; Insurance policy for the sloop *Deboras*, 7 August 1745, LP, GLC03107.02719; Insurance policy for the sloop *Charity*, 23 June 1746, LP, GLC03107.02726; Insurance policy for the *Jamaica Packet*, 23 September 1746, LP, GLC03107.02727; Insurance policy for the sloop *Stork*, 22 January 1747, LP, GLC03107.02730.

10. Pedro De Wolf to Robert Livingston & Comp., 30 January 1739, LP, GLC03107.02581.

11. Philip Livingston to Robert Livingston, 2 September 1740, LP, GLC03107.02601.

12. Philip Livingston to Robert Livingston, 5 September 1740, LP, GLC03107.02602.

13. Benjamin L. Carp, "Did Dutch Smugglers Provoke the Boston Tea Party?" *Early American Studies* 10, no. 2 (spring 2021): 340–41, 50–52, https://www.jstor.org/stable/23547671; Robert Parkinson, *The Common Cause: Creating Race and Nation in the American Revolution* (Chapel Hill: Published for the Omohundro Institute of Early American History and Culture by the University of North Carolina Press, 2016), 642.

14. Insurance policy for the brigantine *Ancram*, 23 April 1741, LP, GLC03107.02618; Insurance policy for the brigantine *Ancram*, 16 August 1741, LP, GLC03107.02628; For enslaved people on this voyage of the *Ancram* see *DIHSTA*, 3:508; Insurance policy for brigantine *Ancram*, 17 September 1742, LP, GLC03107.02663; Insurance policy for the brigantine *Ancram*, 15 November 1742, LP, GLC03107.02671.

15. Invoice of sundry goods shipped to Robert Livingston, Jr., 8 June 1732, LP, GLC03107.02503; *DIHSTA*, 3:496.

16. Invoice of goods shipped to Robert Livingston Jr., 28 October 1734, LP, GLC03107.02516.

17. Philip Livingston to Dirk van Veghten Jr., 14 July 1735, LP, GLC03107.02468.

18. Philip Livingston to Robert Livingston, 23/27 November 1739, LP, GLC03107.02589.

19. Michael McMenamin, "Bittersweet: The American Revolution and New York City's Sugar Industry," https://blog.mcny.org/2015/06/30/bittersweet-the-american-revolution-and-new-york-citys-sugar-industry/.

20. Burrows and Wallace, *Gotham*, 119–20.

21. For the importance of agriculture to the settlement of new Netherland, see Ruth Piwonka, "'. . . and I have made good friends with them': Plants and the New Netherland Experience," *New York History* 89, no. 4 (fall 2008): 397–425. For a fantastic treatment of the enslaved and free Black labor extracted toward this effort, see Romney, "Reytory Angola," 58–78, specifically 62n38, which offers an overview of

the heavy toll imposed on these free families to turn over half of the very labor intensive wheat crop. Burrows and Wallace, *Gotham*, specifically the chapter entitled "In the Kingdom of Sugar," 118–37.

22. "An Act to Enable the Justices of the Peace in Ulster County to Build a Court House & Goal for the said County & to Enable them to dispose of the old County house & Goal & the Lott of Gound it stands on & to Enjoine the Supervisors to raise the Charge or Executing ye negore therein Mentioned," passed October 14, 1732, in *CLNY*, 2:763; See also A. J. Williams-Myers, *Long Hammering*, 4n17.

23. Lepore, *New York Burning*, 72; "The New-York Weekly Journal," The News Media and the Making of America, 1730–1865, https://americanantiquarian.org/earlyamericannewsmedia/items/show/109; Rucker, *The River Flows On*, 17–58.

24. *The New-York Gazette*, #415, October 1, 1733, in *"Pretends to Be Free,"* eds. Hodges and Brown, 9.

25. Stanley Nider Katz, Introduction to *A Brief Narrative of the Case and Trial of John Peter Zenger, Printer of the New York Weekly Journal* (Cambridge, MA: Harvard University Press, 2013), 5–9, https://doi.org/10.4159/harvard.9780674730687; List of the Palatines Remaining at New York 1710, *DHSNY*, 339–41; Names of the Palatine Children Apprenticed by Gov. Hunter 1710–1714, *DHSNY*, 341–42.

26. Devine, *Recovering Scotland's Slavery Past: the Caribbean Connection*, 63, 76, 87; *DIHSTA*, 3:508.

27. Singer, "The Livingstons as Slave Owners," 74–75.

28. Wayne Bodle, "'Such a Noise in the World': Copper Mines and an American Colonial Echo to the South Sea Bubble," *The Pennsylvania Magazine of History and Biography* 127, no. 2 (2003): 131–65. http://www.jstor.org/stable/20093617.

29. John Bezís-Selfa, "Slavery and the Disciplining of Free Labor in the Colonial Mid-Atlantic Iron Industry," *Pennsylvania History: A Journal of Mid-Atlantic Studies* 64 (summer 1997): 270, https://www.jstor.org/stable/27774063.

30. Philip Livingston to Robert Livingston, December 1740, LP, GLC03107.02607.

31. Kierner, *Traders and Gentlefolk*, 70–71.

32. Advertisement, *The South-Carolina Gazette*, 12 August 1732. Accessible Archives.

33. Advertisement, *The South-Carolina Gazette*, 16 February 1734, 2 October 1736. Accessible Archives.

34. Advertisement, *The South-Carolina Gazette*, 14 July 1739. Accessible Archives.

35. Mark Smith, ed., *Stono: Documenting and Interpreting a Southern Slave Revolt*, xi–xiii, 55–56.

36. Lepore, *New York Burning*, 50–51.

37. Common Council Meeting, April 11, 1741 in *MCCNY*, 5:17.

38. Lepore, *New York Burning*, 154–55.

39. *DIHSTA*, 3:507–8; Wilder, *Ebony and Ivy*, 57–58.

40. William Yeomans to Robert Livingston, 9 May 1741, LP, GLC03107.02619.

41. Philip Livingston to Robert Livingston, 20 July 1741, LP, GLC03107.02624.

42. Philip Livingston to Robert Livingston, 20 July 1741, LP, GLC03107.02624.

43. Philip to Robert Livingston, Jr., Manor Livingston, 1 June 1745, LP, GLC03107.02715.

44. Philip Livingston to Robert Livingston, 15 May 1745, LP, GLC03107.02714.

45. Philip to Robert Livingston, 15 May 1745, LP, GLC03107.02714.

46. Philip to Robert Livingston, Jr., 1 June 1745, LP, GLC03107.02715.
47. Lepore, *New York Burning*, 175n7.
48. Kierner, *Traders and Gentlefolk*, 51, 51n5, 72.
49. Kierner, *Traders and Gentlefolk*, 70.
50. Philip Livingston to Robert Livingston, 15 May 1745, LP, GLC03107.02714.
51. Bezís-Selfa, "Slavery and the Disciplining of Free Labor," 270–71.
52. Bezís-Selfa, "Slavery and the Disciplining of Free Labor," 270–71.
53. Bezís-Selfa, "Slavery and the Disciplining of Free Labor," 270–71.
54. Bezís-Selfa, "Slavery and the Disciplining of Free Labor," 270–71.
55. Bezís-Selfa, "Slavery and the Disciplining of Free Labor," 270–71.
56. For an analysis of the transport of skilled artisans from Barbados to South Carolina, see Ramona Arlen La Roche, "'Bajan to Gullah' Cultural Capital: Wood, Stone, Iron, and Clay 1670 to 1770" (PhD diss., University of South Carolina, 2017), https://scholarcommons.sc.edu/etd/4454. For the impact of skilled artisans, see Joe William Trotter, *Workers on Arrival: Black Labor in the Making of America* (Berkeley: University of California Press, 2019), 5, 6, 8; see also William S. Pollitzer, *The Gullah People and their African Heritage* (1999; reprint Athens: University of Georgia Press, 2005), 87, 167–68; Emma Hart, *Building Charleston: Town and Society in the Eighteenth-Century British Atlantic World* (Charlottesville: University of Virginia Press, 2010), 78–80.
57. Harry Bischoff Weiss and Grace M. Weiss, *Trades and Tradesmen of Colonial New Jersey* (Trenton, NJ: Past Times Press, 1965), 83.
58. Bezís-Selfa, *Forging America: Ironworkers, Adventurers, and the Industrious Revolution* (Ithaca: Cornell University Press, 2004), 107–12. For the use of overwork and other methods, including the effect of ironworking on disrupting enslaved connections in the North, see Bezís-Selfa, *Forging America*, 112–20.
59. David Lindsey to Robert Livingston, 29 November 1748, LP, GLC03107.02750.
60. Samuel Green Arnold, *History of the State of Rhode Island and Providence Plantations* (1859; reprint Carlisle, MA: Applewood Books, 2015), 2:118.
61. Clark-Pujara, *Dark Work*, 19.
62. Last will and testament of Philip Livingston, 15 July 1748, LP, GLC03107.02493.
63. John Livingston to Robert Livingston, 23 February 1741, LP, GLC03107.02613.
64. Philip Livingston to John DeWitt, 24 February 1741, LP, GLC03107.04431; Philip Livingston to John DeWitt, 27 February 1741, LP, GLC03107.04434.
65. P. DeWitt to Robert Livingston, 6 March 1749, LP, GLC03107.02757.
66. Misevich, "In Pursuit of Human Cargo," 200–201.
67. Misevich, "In Pursuit of Human Cargo," 200.
68. Robert Livingston to Peter DeWitt, 29 July 1749, LP, GLC03107.04449.
69. Advertisement, *New-York Evening Post*, 31 July 1749, EAN; Misevich, "In Pursuit of Human Cargo," 204.
70. Peter van Brugh Livingston to Robert Livingston, 14 June 1751, LP, GLC03107.02798.
71. Mosterman, *Spaces of Enslavement*, 70.
72. Peter van Brugh Livingston to Robert Livingston, 26 February 1752, LP, GLC03107.02840.
73. Jane Fletcher Fiske, *Gleanings from Newport Court Files, 1659–1783* (Boxford, MA: J. F. Fiske, 1998), #845.

74. Henry Livingston to Messrs. Peleg Thurston and Company, 13 July 1754, quoted in *DIHSTA*, 3:145n3.

75. Henry Livingston to Robert Livingston, 10 February 1764, LP, GLC03107.03007.

76. Friendship Estate, "Legacies of British slave ownership," accessed 16 July 2019, https://www.ucl.ac.uk/lbs/estate/view/2524.

77. Will of Henry Livingston, in *Wills,* 31:180.

78. Benjamin Franklin to Samuel Johnson, 2 July 1752, Columbia University Library.

79. Rachel Page, "'A pleasant good Family': Domestic Enslavement in Samuel Johnson's Household, 1723–1772," https://columbiaandslavery.columbia.edu/content/pleasant-good-family-domestic-enslavement-samuel-johnsons-household-1723-1772#/_ftnref79.

80. Advertisement, *New-York Gazette,* 1 April 1765, 3, EAN.

81. Advertisement, *New-York Gazette,* 8 June 1752, 3, EAN.

Chapter 7 Identity

1. Advertisement, *New-York Gazette,* #452, 24 June 24, 1734, in *"Pretends to Be Free,"* eds. Hodges and Brown, 10.

2. Fuentes, *Dispossessed Lives,* 16–17.

3. Jared Hardesty questions the "prism of freedom," as an ahistorical unit of analysis, offering instead that the enslaved defended "a set of customary rights they believed they possessed" but navigated "a world where freedom could be just as fraught as slavery." Thus, Hardesty convincingly argues that "the enslaved became masters of their status." Hardesty, *Unfreedom,* 182. Holly Brewer argues that a turn away from a hierarchal world of inherited status to a more republican ideology occurred in the eighteenth century, and that hereditary slavery was "part of a patriarchal, neo feudal ideology where property and status were, ideally, fixed by lineage." Brewer, *By Birth or Consent: Children, Law, and the Anglo-American Revolution in Authority* (Chapel Hill: Published for the Omohundro Institute of Early American History and Culture, Williamsburg Virginia, by the University of North Carolina Press, 2005), 352, 352n11.

4. Judith wed the mariner Samuel Vincent on December 3, 1717, although she had been married once before to a man named John Smith. On April 10, 1722, Samuel Vincent's Sloop *Adventure,* arrived in Perth Amboy "from St. Domingo." Arrival of the sloop *Adventure, American Weekly Mercury,* 12 April 1722, in *DRCHNJ,* 11:61. On April 30, 1726, his sloop *Anne and Judith* arrived with four enslaved people from the French West Indies. Arrival of *Anne and Judith,* 30 April 1726, in *DIHSA,* 3:511. On November 8, 1726, the *Anne and Judith,* departed Perth Amboy for St. Christopher. Departure of the sloop *Anne and Judith, American Weekly Mercury,* 3–10 November 1726, in *DRCHNJ,* 11:113. Two years before placing the runaway slave advertisement, Judith Vincent attended "a meeting of the Common Council" on October 11, 1734. She was there in order to ensure that "the Water Lott No. 2 on the Dock St. and wharfe fronting to her tenement may be granted to her son John Smith & his heirs on the same conditions as to the other grantees & that the Mayor execute a quitclaim thereto." *Proceedings of the Huguenot Society of America* (1884; reprint New York: Knickerbocker Press, 1899), 254–55. For more on this runaway

slave advertisement see Hodges, *Slavery and Freedom in the Rural North,* 61; Jacqueline Jones, *American Work: Four Centuries of Black and White Labor* (New York: W. W. Norton, 1998), 137.

5. Anna Stuyvesant Pritchard named several Stuyvesant relatives in her will, bequeathing to her nephew, Petrus Stuyvesant "a gold ring, a pair of gloves, and a mourning hat band," and to another nephew, Nicholas William Stuyvesant, her "jewel box, a Tortoise shell box, a shell cup tipped with silver, and all my plate, 2 plain gold rings, 4 damask table cloths, and 2 dozen napkins." Will of Anna Pritchard, 7 June 1759, in *Wills,* 5:323–24.

6. Graham Hodges notes that such skilled enslaved New Jersey men worked in animal husbandry, as "blacksmiths, coopers, carpenters, and farriers; some could also work on privateers and fishing boats." Hodges, *Slavery and Freedom in the Rural North,* 45.

7. Hodges, *Slavery and Freedom in the Rural North,* 45.

8. Hodges, *Slavery and Freedom in the Rural North,* 45. For the public debate over such skilled slave work among New York City's white coopers, see Foote, *Black and White Manhattan,* 77.

9. Hodges, *Slavery and Freedom in the Rural North,* 47–48.

10. Hodges, *Slavery and Freedom in the Rural North,* 45.

11. Rhode Island newspapers were replete with runaway slave advertisements during the eighteenth century. Maureen Taylor and John Wood Sweet have offered edited compendiums of such advertisements. Sweet, *Bodies Politic,* 258n52; Maureen Alice Taylor and Sweet, *Runaways, Deserters, and Notorious Villains from Rhode Island Newspapers* (Camden, ME: Picton Press, 1994). For recent work on slavery in Rhode Island see Clark-Pujara, *Dark Work.*

12. John Allyn to Robert Livingston, 10 May 1692, LP, GLC03107.00211. For slavery in Connecticut, see Di Bonaventura, *For Adam's Sake.*

13. For Canada as a destination for runaway slaves and the policing of the roads from Albany to New England, see chapter 4. For a runaway enslaved person named Simon identified as formally owned by a "rebel" captured by Mohawks and brought to Fort Chambly during the American Revolution, see Frank Mackey, *Done with Slavery: The Black Fact in Montreal, 1769–1840* (Montreal: McGill-Queen's University Press, 2010), 394.

14. Dawson, *Undercurrents of Power,* 19.

15. For a discussion on the challenge to mastery posed by illicit slave movement, see Warren, *New England Bound,* 202, 202n47.

16. Advertisement, *New-York Weekly Journal,* #360, 27 October 1740, in *"Pretends to Be Free,"* eds. Hodges and Brown, 16–17; Advertisement, *New-York Weekly Journal,* 27 October 1740, 4, EAN.

17. The Philipses were the largest slaveholders in the region, with the bulk of the enslaved people located in the "upper mills" in Tarrytown, New York. Kevin McDonald examines a case of a runaway enslaved man named Calico Jack who had been owned by Frederick Philipse over fifty years before Galloway's case. Frederick, like Alida, used his personal networks to track Calico Jack to Connecticut, until losing his trail. For years Frederick continued to pursue the man, extending the dragnet to Madagascar. McDonald, *Pirates, Merchants, Settlers, and Slaves,* 99; Leslie Harris, "The Greatest City in the World? Slavery in New York in the Age of Hamilton,"

in *Historians on Hamilton: How a Blockbuster Musical is Restaging America's Past*, eds. Renee C. Romano and Clare Bond Potter (New Brunswick, NJ: Rutgers University Press, 2018), 82; Harris, *In the Shadow of Slavery*, 28–29.

18. Will of John Breeze, 4 August 1742, in *Wills*, 3:407.

19. This document was advertised for sale in 1909 for five dollars in *The Collector: A Magazine for Autograph and Historical Collectors*. It was described as "a complaint on the case of Paul Richards (Mayor of New York) who says that Johannes de Bryne had enticed away a 'negro woman known as Elizabeth of the value of thirty pounds,' and two other negroes." Sale Notice for Autograph Document Signed, Paul Richards case in *The Collector: A Magazine for Autograph and Historical Collectors* 22 (January 1909): 30.

20. Paul Richards Representative for New York, Twenty-Third Colonial Assembly, 1741–1745, in *Civil List and Constitutional History of the Colony and State of New York*, ed. Edgar A. Werner (Albany: Weed, Parsons, 1889), 405.

21. Jill Lepore noted that "when Adam sent for Quack to come to a plotting meeting, Quack, 'being at Mr. *Richard's* with his Wife, refused to go." Lepore, *New York Burning*, 150.

22. Will of John Breeze, 4 August 1742, in *Wills*, 3:407.

23. Zabin, *Dangerous Economies*, 46, 46n49.

24. Newell, *Brethren by Nature*, 203–4.

25. Maeve Kane argued that such work was gendered and that Haudenosaunee women combined indigenous materials like leather with European goods to create a fashion that changed with cultural interaction. Kane, "Covered with Such a Cappe: The Archaeology of Seneca Clothing 1615–1820," *Ethnohistory* 61, no. 1 (winter 2014): 2, 1–25. For work that discusses gender inversion of norms in the work of enslaved African rice workers, see Judith Ann Carney, *Black Rice: The African Origins of Rice Cultivation in the Americas* (Cambridge, MA: Harvard University Press, 2001), 120.

26. Lepore, *New York Burning*, 8, 17, 25, 28–29, 35, 44, 49, 149–50, 167–69.

27. Foy, "Ports of Slavery, Ports of Freedom," 112–13.

28. Prince Hall was enslaved to leather dresser William Hall from 1749 to 1770. Richard S. Newman, "Prince Hall, Richard Allen, and Daniel Coker: Revolutionary Black Founders, Revolutionary Black Communities," in *Revolutionary Founders: Rebels, Radicals, and Reformers in the Making of the Nation*, eds. Alfred F. Young, Gary B. Nash, and Ray Raphael (2011; reprint Vintage Books, 2012), 307.

29. Daniel Horsmanden, *A Journal of the Proceedings in the Detection of the Conspiracy Formed by Some White People, in Conjunction with Negro and other Slaves, for Burning the City of New-York in America, and Murdering the Inhabitants*, in *The New York Conspiracy Trials of 1741: Daniel Horsmanden's Journal of the Proceedings with Related Documents*, ed. Serena Zabin (Boston, MA: Bedford/St. Martin's, 2004), 87; Lepore, *New York Burning*, 256.

30. Advertisement, *Pennsylvania Gazette* (Philadelphia), #1169, 9 May 1751, in "Pretends to Be Free," eds. Hodges and Brown, 39; See also: Advertisement, *Pennsylvania Gazette*, 9 May 1751, 3, EAN.

31. Before the stagecoach route was established, travelers had to arrange their own methods to traverse the forty miles that separated Bordentown to Philadelphia ferry. Tom might have been compelled to walk the forty miles to Bordentown in order to catch the ferry to Philadelphia. For more on the ferry, see John P. Wall and

Harold E. Pickersgill, *History of Middlesex County, New Jersey, 1664–1920* (New York: Lewis Historical Publishing, 1921), 2:377; "Bordentown City," https://delawareriverheritagetrail.org/Bordentown-City.html.

32. Enslaved Malagasy people traded directly from Madagascar to Perth Amboy in order to avoid the duties levied in New York. Thomas, *The Slave Trade*, 207. For Perth Amboy as being a destination for Akan-descended captive peoples some who came directly from the Gold Coast and many within Caribbean communities of sizeable Akan populations, see Kwasi Konadu, *The Akan Diaspora in the Americas* (Oxford: Oxford University Press, 2010), 193. For more on this multiethnic community see Goodfriend, *Before the Melting Pot*, 114.

33. Advertisement, *American Weekly Mercury* (Philadelphia), #773, 24 October 1734, in *"Pretends to Be Free,"* eds. Hodges and Brown, 11.

34. For the proliferation of Moravian missions, see "Introduction," in *The Moravian Mission Diaries of David Zeisberger, 1772–1781*, eds. Hermann Wellenreuther and Carola Wessel (University Park: Pennsylvania State University Press, 2005). They also include a detailed appendix with the names of such settlements.

35. For Indigenous peoples' actions as go-betweens, see James H. Merrell, *Into the American Woods: Negotiators on the Pennsylvania Frontier* (New York: W. W. Norton, 1999), 88; Jane T. Merritt, *At the Crossroads: Indians and Empires on a Mid-Atlantic Frontier, 1700–1763* (Chapel Hill: Published for the Omohundro Institute of Early American History and Culture, Williamsburg, Virginia, by the University of North Carolina Press, 2003), 103–21; Richard White, *The Middle Ground: Indians, Empires, and Republics in the Great Lakes Region, 1650–1815* (1991; reprint New York: Cambridge University Press, 2011), 389–90. See also, Sherman Day, *Historical Collections of the State of Pennsylvania* (Philadelphia: George W. Gorton, 1843), 138.

36. Darold D. Wax, noted that "as early as 1684" enslaved people had been brought into the region via the Delaware River, although the trade increased exponentially after the 1750s. "Africans on the Delaware: The Pennsylvania Slave Trade, 1759–1765," *Pennsylvania History: A Journal of Mid-Atlantic Studies* 50, no. 1 (January 1983): 38–49, https://www.jstor.org/stable/27772875.

37. Jean Soderlund argues that the slave population of Philadelphia would have been 7.4 percent of the city, with imports steadily rising. See Soderlund, "Black Importation and Migration into Southeastern Pennsylvania, 1682–1810," *Proceedings of the American Philosophical Society* 133, no. 2 (June 1989), table 2, 147, 144–53, https://www.jstor.org/stable/987045. See also Richard Wojtowicz and Billy G. Smith, "Fugitives: Newspaper Advertisements for Runaway Slaves, Indentured Servants, and Apprentices," in *Life in Early Philadelphia: Documents from the Revolutionary and Early National Periods*, ed. Billy G. Smith (University Park: Pennsylvania State University Press, 1995), 92.

38. Thomas, *The Slave Trade*, 207.

39. Elsa A Nystrom, "John Woolman (1720–1772)," in *Slavery in the United States: A Social Political, and Historical Encyclopedia*, ed. Junius P. Rodriguez (Santa Barbara, CA: ABC-CLIO, 2007), 1:520.

40. Hodges, *Slavery and Freedom in the Rural North*, 9.

41. TAVoyages, Voyage ID no. 16633. *Catherine* (1731); Hodges, *Slavery and Freedom in the Rural North*, 9.

42. TAVoyage, Voyage ID no. 25318. *Catherine* (1733).

43. Advertisement, *New-York Gazette, or Weekly Post-Boy*, 27 March 1769, in *EANRJ*, 26:406.

44. White, *Middle Ground*, 389–90.

45. Custom House List, "Outward Entries: Sloop Wolf, Gur. Wall for Coast of Africa," *New-York Gazette*, 14 August 1749, 3, 18 September 1749, EAN.

46. Custom House List, "Inward Entries: Sloop Wolf, Gur. Wall from Coast of Africa," *New-York Gazette*, 13 May 1751, 2, EAN; *TAVoyages*, Voyage ID no. 25340. *Wolf* (1751); Advertisement, *New-York Gazette, or Weekly Post-Boy*, 13 May 1751, 3, EAN; *DIHSTA*, 3:451.

47. For a discussion of the term *likely*, see Sharon Block, *Colonial Complexions*, 49–51.

48. Advertisement, *New-York Gazette, or Weekly Post-Boy*, 6 November 1752, 3; 13 November 1752, 3; 20 November 1752, 4; also run in *New-York Mercury*, 6 November 1752, 3, EAN.

49. Custom House List, "Inward Entries: Sloop Wolf," *New-York Gazette*, 13 May 1751, 2, EAN. Craig Wilder explores the horrid conditions on board the *Wolf*, which were described in the diary of the ship's Harvard-trained surgeon, William Chancellor, and contrasts them with the Livingstons' dispassionate pursuit of prestige. Wilder, *Ebony and Ivy*, 60–65. See also Wax, "A Philadelphia Surgeon on a Slaving Voyage to Africa, 1749–1751," 491.

50. Jacques Arends, *Language and Slavery: A Social and Linguistic History of the Suriname Creoles* (Amsterdam: John Benjamins, 2017), 134. See also Rebecca Shumway, *The Fante and the Transatlantic Slave Trade* (Rochester, NY: University of Rochester Press, 2011).

51. Advertisement, *New-York Gazette, or Weekly Post-Boy*, 12 March 1750, 4; 19 March 1750, 4; March 26, 1750, EAN.

52. Runaway slave advertisement, *New-York Weekly Post-Boy*, #534, 23 April 1753, in *"Pretends to Be Free,"* eds. Hodges and Brown, 45.

53. *Simon Moore v. Samuel Bayard*, John Tabor Kempe Papers, Box 12, Folder 2, NYHS. For a transcription of the document see the appendix.

54. For more details on the examination and fate of Pompey, see Daniel Horsmanden, *The New-York Conspiracy* (1744; reprint New York: Printed and Published by Southwick & Pelsue, 1810), 173, 179, 190, 220, 269. Phaeton, Pompey, and Ben were enslaved by Nicholas, Samuel, and Stephen Bayard respectively and were all implicated in the conspiracy. Phaeton and Ben were released. Lepore, *New York Burning*, 262–63.

55. Stephen Bayard to Robert Livingston, 12 November 1725, LP, GLC03107.01740.

56. *Simon Moore v. Samuel Bayard*, John Tabor Kempe Papers, Box 12, Folder 2, NYHS.

57. *Simon Moore v. Samuel Bayard*, John Tabor Kempe Papers, Box 12, Folder 2, NYHS.

58. Paul Heinegg, *Free African Americans of North Carolina, Virginia, and South Carolina: From the Colonial Period to About 1820* (1992; reprint Baltimore, MD: Printed for Clearfield Company by Genealogical Publishing, 2005), 2:845.

59. *Simon Moore v. Samuel Bayard*, John Tabor Kempe Papers, Box 12, Folder 2, NYHS.

60. Advertisement, *New-York Mercury,* 31 July 1758, EAN.

61. Advertisement, *New-York Mercury,* 13 August 1759, EAN.

62. The *State of New Jersey v. Dierck Ten Broek,* 17 May 1783, box 47, Alexander Court Papers, NYHS.

63. Gabriel Furman was married to Abigail Howard. Arthur Walbridge North, *The Founders and the Founding of Walton, New York: Being an Intimate Historical Sketch of the Making of an American Settlement in the Critical Period Immediately Preceding the Adoption of the Federal Constitution* (Walton, NY: Walton Reporter Company, 1924). 47. The family immigrated to New Netherland when Stuyvesant was director, though their ethnic identity was likely Welsh. James Riker Jr., *Annals of Newtown, Queens County, New York* (New York: D. Fanshaw, 1852), 399n. He was a veteran of the Revolutionary War, had fought during the Battle of Long Island, and was held as a war prisoner. After the freedom case, he became a Federalist and Aldermen of New York City. In 1796 a call by the republican attorney William Keteltas that Furman be removed from office presaged the Keteltas affair and the subsequent loss of power by New York's Federalist Party. For the details of Furman's war service, see "Irving, John Treat," in *The Memorial Cyclopedia of the Twentieth Century: Comprising Memoirs of Men and Women . . .* (New York: Publishing Society of New York, 1906), 94. For more on his role in the Keteltas affair, see Alfred F. Young, *The Democratic Republicans of New-York: The Origins, 1763–1797* (Chapel Hill: University of North Carolina Press, 1967).

64. *The State of New Jersey v. Dierck Ten Broek,* 17 May 1783, box 47, Alexander Court Papers, NYHS. For a full transcription of the case see the appendix.

65. Washington, *Sojourner Truth's America,* 22.

66. The drama of his story and the flourishes added points to the performativity of the testimony as it was read to the court. For scholarship on the development of this performative culture and its links to colonial preaching and revival culture, see Sandra M. Gustafson, *Eloquence Is Power: Oratory and Performance in Early America* (Chapel Hill: Published for the Omohundro Institute of Early American History and Culture, Williamsburg, Virginia by the University of North Carolina Press, 2000), 141. For links to eighteenth-century British theater culture, see *Crime, Courtrooms, and the Public Sphere in Britain, 1700–1850,* ed. David Lemmings (2012; reprint London: Routledge, 2016), 94.

67. James Albert Ukawsaw Gronniosaw, *A Narrative of the Most Remarkable Particulars in the Life of James Albert Ukawsaw Gronniosaw, an African Prince, as Related by Himself,* trans. Walter Shirley (Bath: W. Gye, 1772), 10.

68. Gronniosaw, A *Narrative,* 11.

69. In 1717, his father, also named John van Horne, became a co-owner of the slave ship *Dragon,* along with his brothers Garret and Abraham as well as four other investors. The six-gun brigantine *Dragon* arrived in New York and unloaded 106 enslaved Africans from unspecified areas of Africa which, judging from other slave voyages, were likely the Bight of Benin or the Sierra Leone Estuary, in New York before continuing on to Virginia with six captive people aboard. That same year he also purchased ownership with his family in the *Catherine and Mary,* whose sixty surviving enslaved people were sold in New York. A year later, the *Catherine and Mary* would, like the *Dragon,* sail for New York and then continue on to Virginia, leaving sixty-four and forty-five

enslaved people in each port respectively. *TAVoyages*, Voyage ID no. 25320. *Dragon* (1717); *TAVoyages*, Voyage ID no. 25366. *Catherine and Mary* (1718).

70. *TAVoyages*, Voyage ID no. 27230. *Revenge* (1750).

71. Will of Elnathan Field, 12 July 1735, in *Wills*, 28: 473–74; Riker, *Annals of Newtown*, 159; *The Forman Genealogy: Descendants of Robert Forman of Kent Co., Maryland, Who Died in 1719–20; also Descendants of Robert Forman of Long Island, New York Who Died in 1671: The Forman Family of Monmouth Co., New Jersey; Together with Notices of Other Families of the Name of Forman*, comp. Anne Spottswood Dandridge (Cleveland, OH: The Forman-Bassett-Hatch, 1903), 140.

72. News, "News Report from New-York, January 9," Boston News-Letter, 15 January 1739, EAN.

73. *The State of New Jersey v. Dierck Ten Broek*, 17 May 1783, box 47, Alexander Court Papers, NYHS.

74. Baptism of Alida Vetch, 29 June 1724, Thomas Grier Evans, ed., *Records of the Reformed Dutch Church in New Amsterdam and New York: baptisms from 25 December, 1639, to 27 December, 1730* (New York: New York Genealogical and Biographical Society, 1901) 1:449. Eighty-three other female children were baptized in that church during the year 1724, and many of them to "first rank" families, such as the Van Dams, Beekmans, Schuylers, Van Cortlandts, Ten Eyk, Rutgers, and de Peysters. Evans, *Records of the Reformed Dutch Church in New Amsterdam and New York*, 1:446–54.

75. Advertisement, *New-York Gazette, or Weekly Post-Boy*, 4 February 1751, EAN.

76. Advertisement, *New-York Gazette, or Weekly Post-Boy*, 18 February 1751, 25 February 1751, 25 March 1751, 6 May 1751, EAN.

77. Advertisement, *New-York Mercury*, 16 June 1755, EAN.

78. Advertisement, *New-York Mercury*, 23 June 1755, 30 June 1755, 14 July 1755, 11 October 1756, 18 October 1756, 8 November 1756, 15 November 1756, and 22 November 1756, EAN.

79. Will of John van Horne, 1733, in the *Somerset County Historical Quarterly*, ed. A. Van Doren Honeyman (Somerville, NJ: Somerset County Historical Society, 1915), 4:245–46; Will of James van Horne, 29 October 1760, in *Wills*, 6:123.

80. *The State of New Jersey v. Dierck Ten Broek*, 17 May 1783, box 47, Alexander Court Papers, NYHS.

81. See also the discussion of the emergence of *partus* in chapter 2.

82. Christopher Tomlins, "Transplants and Timing: Passages in the Creation of an Anglo-American Law of Slavery," *Theoretical Inquiries in Law* 10, no. 2 (July 2009), 406–7.

83. "An Act for Regulating Negro, Indian and Mallatto Slaves within this Province of *New-Jersey*," 12 December 1704, *The New Jersey Digital Legal Library*, comp. Paul Axel-Lute, http://njlegallib.rutgers.edu/slavery/acts/A11.html. This act was repealed on October 24, 1709. Sharon Block, *Rape and Sexual Power in Early America* (Chapel Hill: Published for the Omohundro Institute of Early American History and Culture, Williamsburg, Virginia by the University of North Carolina Press, 2006), 151, 151n38; Tomlins, "Transplants and Timing," 413.

84. Tomlins, "Transplants and Timing," 413.

85. An Act for Regulating of Slaves, 11 March 1713/14, NJDLL, http://njlegallib.rutgers.edu/slavery/acts/A13.html; Tomlins, "Transplants and Timing," 414.

Conclusion

1. Advertisement, *New-York Journal; or, the General Advertiser*, 14 March 1771, no. 1471, 291, EAN. This advertisement was rerun three more times in the *New-York Journal; or the General Advertiser,* and appeared four times in the *Boston-Gazette and Country Journal*. Advertisement, *New-York Journal; or, the General Advertiser*, 21 March 1771, no. 1472, 293; 28 March 1771, no. 1473, 303; 11 April 1771, no. 1475, 315; Advertisement, *Boston-Gazette and Country Journal*, 25 March 1771, no. 833, supplement 3; 1 April 1771, no. 834, supplement 4; 8 April 1771, no. 835, supplement 1; 15 April 1771, no. 836, 4; EAN.

2. Biographical information about the Bayards in Maryland and Philadelphia, including John Bayard's journey to visit family in New York and Massachusetts, can be found in Wilson, *Colonel John Bayard*, 410.

3. In his thesis, John Randall Howard argued that Samuel Bayard most likely constructed the Great House and postulates that that would make the Great House "one of the earliest remaining original dwellings in Cecil County, Maryland." John Randall Howard, "Origins and Architecture of Great House Plantation" (MA thesis, University of Pennsylvania, 2004), 4, 42.

4. Thomas Kidd recounts Whitefield's experiences in the Chesapeake and North and South Carolina. Kidd, *George Whitefield: America's Spiritual Founding Father* (New Haven, CT: Yale University Press, 2014), 94–115. Jessica M. Parr focuses on Whitefield's relationship to slavery. Parr, *Inventing George Whitefield: Race, Revivalism, and the Making of a Religious Icon* (Jackson: University Press of Mississippi, 2015), 67, 71, 101, 114. Lepore also notes that slaveowners found Whitefield's reflection on the harsh state of slaves, incendiary, and that "throughout the colonies, men blamed Whitefield for their rebellious slaves." Lepore, *New York Burning*, 187–88.

5. George Whitefield, "Letter to the Inhabitants of Maryland, Virginia, North and South Carolina," 17 April 1740, *Pennsylvania Gazette,* EAN.

6. Wilson, *Colonel John Bayard*, 6.

7. Wilson, *Colonel John Bayard*, 6.

8. Wilson, *Colonel John Bayard*, 6.

9. Wilson, *Colonel John Bayard*, 6.

10. Ira Berlin, "Slavery, Freedom, and Philadelphia's Struggle for Brotherly Love, 1685 to 1861," in *Antislavery and Abolition in Philadelphia: Emancipation and the Long Struggle for Racial Justice in the City of Brotherly Love,* ed. Richard Newman and James Mueller (Baton Rouge: Louisiana State University Press, 2011), 19–24. For the increasing popularity of antislavery sentiment among Franklin's cohort, see David Waldstreicher, *Runaway America: Benjamin Franklin, Slavery, and the American Revolution* (New York: Hill and Wang, 2004), 195–204, 230–36; Soderlund, "Black Women in Colonial Pennsylvania," 58.

11. Wilson, *Colonel John Bayard*, 7.

12. Benjamin Franklin, "A Conversation on Slavery," *The Public Advertiser,* 30 January 1770, in *The Papers of Benjamin Franklin,* vol. 17, *January 1 through December 31, 1770,* ed. William B. Willcox (New Haven, CT: Yale University Press, 1973), 17:37–44, Founders Online, National Archives, https://founders.archives.gov/documents/Franklin/01-17-02-0019.

13. New arrivals to New York noted the broad participation of the African American community in the Pinkster festival. Dewulf, *The Pinkster King,* 58.

NOTES TO PAGES 162–169

14. Antonio Bly posits that Toby may have been from northern New York or New England and "planned to return home" based on the presence of runaway slave advertisements in the *New-York Journal* and *Boston Gazette*, but absence of any runaway slave advertisements in "extant newspapers of Pennsylvania, Virginia, or South Carolina." Antonio T. Bly, "A Prince among Pretending Free Men: Runaway Slaves in Colonial New England Revisited," *Massachusetts Historical Review* 14 (2012), 103, 103n46, 118, https://www.jstor.org/stable/10.5224/masshistrevi.14.1.0087.

Appendix A

1. *The State against Tierck Tenbroeck on Habeas Corpus of Negro Philip for Manumission*, in *Cases Adjudged in the Supreme Court of New-Jersey Relative to the Manumission of Negroes: And Others Holden in Bondage* (Burlington, NJ: Printed for The New-Jersey Society for Promoting the Abolition of Slavery by Isaac Neal, 1794), 13.

2. *The State of New Jersey v. Tierck Tenbroeck*, 17 May 1783, box 47, Alexander Court Papers, NYHS.

Appendix B

1. *Simon Moore v. Samuel Bayard*, John Tabor Kempe Papers, Box 12, Folder 2, New-York Historical Society.

Bibliography

Primary Sources

Manuscript Collections by Archive

FRANKLIN D. ROOSEVELT LIBRARY, HYDE PARK, NY
  Livingston-Redmond Manuscripts.

GILDER LEHRMAN COLLECTION, NEW YORK, NY
  Livingston Family Papers.

NEW JERSEY STATE ARCHIVES
  East Jersey Deeds.

NEW YORK CITY MUNICIPAL ARCHIVES
  New York Probates.
  New York Wills.

NEW-YORK HISTORICAL SOCIETY, NEW YORK, NY
  Van Cortlandt Manuscripts Collection.

NEW YORK STATE ARCHIVES, ALBANY, NY
  Correspondence of Jeremias van Rensselaer.
  New Netherland Council Curaçao records.
  New Netherland Council Dutch colonial administrative correspondence.
  New Netherland Council Dutch colonial administrative records.
  New Netherland Council Dutch colonial council minutes.
  New Netherland Council Dutch Delaware River settlement administrative records.
  New York Colony Council minutes.
  New York Colony Council papers.

BIBLIOGRAPHY

New York State Library, Albany, NY
   Van Rensselaer Manor Papers.

Other Archives

   Boston Public Library, Boston, MA.
   Clermont State Historic Site Manuscript Collection, Germantown, New York.
   Colonial Society of Massachusetts, Boston, MA.
   Gardner A. Sage Library, New Brunswick Theological Seminary, New Brunswick, NJ.
   Historical Society of the New York Courts, White Plains, NY.
   Huntington Library, San Marino, CA.
   Library of Congress, Washington, DC.
   Massachusetts Historical Society, Boston, MA.
   Nationaal Archief Curaçao, Willemstad, Curaçao.
   Nationaal Archief, Den Haag, The Netherlands.
   New York Public Library, New York, NY.
   Stadsarchief Amsterdam, Amsterdam, The Netherlands.
   Ulster County Archives, Kingston, NY.

Online Databases

   America's Historical Imprints, Series I: Evans, 1639–1800.
   America's Historical Newspapers: Early American Newspapers.
   Archives of Maryland Online.
   British Colonial State Papers.
   Early English Books Online.
   Extracts from American Newspapers, Relating to New Jersey, 1704–1775.
   Freedom on the Move.
   The New Jersey Digital Legal Library.
   New York Probate Records, 1629–1971.
   Voyages: The Intra-American Slave Trade Database.
   Voyages: The Transatlantic Slave Trade Database.

Newspapers and Periodicals

   American Weekly Mercury.
   Boston News-Letter.
   Boston Weekly News-Letter.

New-York Evening Post.
New-York Gazette.
New-York Gazette, or Weekly Post-Boy.
New York Mercury.
New-York Weekly Journal.
Pennsylvania Gazette.

Published Primary Sources

Axel-Lute, Paul, comp. *The New Jersey Digital Legal Library.* Accessed February 19, 2019. http://njlegallib.rutgers.edu/slavery/acts/A11.html.

Billings, Warren M., ed. *The Old Dominion in the Seventeenth Century: A Documentary History of Virginia, 1606–1689.* Chapel Hill: University of North Carolina Press, 1975.

Bloomfield, Joseph. *Cases Adjudged in the Supreme Court of New-Jersey Relative to the Manumission of Negroes and Others Holden in Bondage.* 1794. Reprint, Buffalo, NY: Dennis & Co, 1940.

Brodhead, John Romeyn. *Documents Relative to the Colonial History of the State of New York: Procured in Holland, England and France.* Albany, NY: Weed, Parsons, 1858.

Christoph, Peter, Florence A. Christoph, eds., and Charles T. Gehring, trans. *The Andros Papers, 1674–1676.* Syracuse, NY: Syracuse University Press, 1989.

Christoph, Peter, and Florence A. Christoph, eds. *New York Historical Manuscripts English: Books of General Entries of the Colony of New York.* Baltimore: Genealogical Publishing, 1982.

Collections of the Massachusetts Historical Society. Series 4. Vol. 1. Boston: Published by the Society, 1852.

De Laet, Johannes. *Iaerlyck verhael van de verrichtinghen der Geoctroyeerde West-Indische Compagnie in derthien boecken.* Den Hague, NL: Martinus Nijhoff, 1937. https://resolver.kb.nl/resolve?urn=KONB10:000019207:00015.

Dittelbach, Petrus. *Verval en val der Labadisten.* Amsterdam: Daniel van de Dalen, 1692.

Donnan, Elizabeth. *Documents Illustrative of the History of the Slave Trade to America.* 4 vols. Washington, DC: Carnegie Institution of Washington, 1930–35.

Du Bois, W.E.B. *The Souls of Black Folk.* 1903. Reprint, New York: Oxford University Press, 2009.

Duermyer, Louis, ed. *Records of the Reformed Dutch Church of Albany, New York, 1689–1809: Marriages, Baptisms, Members, etc. Excerpted from Year Books of the Holland Society of New York.* Baltimore, MD: Genealogical Publishing, 1978.

Evans, Thomas Grier, ed. *Records of the Reformed Dutch Church in New Amsterdam and New York: baptisms from 25 December, 1639, to 27 December, 1730.* New York: New York Genealogical and Biographical Society, 1901.

Fernow, Berthold, ed. *The Records of New Amsterdam: From 1653 to 1674.* 7 vols. New York: Knickerbocker Press, 1897.

Franklin, Benjamin. "A Conversation on Slavery." *The Public Advertiser,* 30 January 1770. In *The Papers of Benjamin Franklin,* vol. 17, *January 1 through December 31,*

1770, edited by William B. Willcox, 37–44. New Haven, CT: Yale University Press, 1973. Founders Online, National Archives. Accessed January 17, 2019. https://founders.archives.gov/documents/Franklin/01-17-02-0019.

Gehring, Charles T., trans. and ed. *Curaçao Papers, 1640–1665: Translation*. Albany, NY: New Netherland Institute, 2011.

Gehring, Charles T., trans. and ed. *Fort Orange Court Minutes*. Syracuse, NY: Syracuse University Press, 1990.

Gehring, Charles T., trans. and ed. *Fort Orange Records 1656–1678*. Syracuse, NY: Syracuse University Press, 2000.

Gehring, Charles T., trans. and ed., *New York Historical Manuscripts: Dutch, Council Minutes, 1652–1654*. Vol. 5. Baltimore, MD: Genealogical Publishing Company, 1976.

Gehring, Charles T., trans. and ed. "Stuyvesant's Certification that Certain Blacks Had Been Granted Land Near His Farm in the Years 1659 and 1660, with Abstracts of Their Deeds." Transcription and translation from the original in the New York State Archive. https://www.newnetherlandinstitute.org/files/2814/0681/8946/Stuyvesantmanumission.

Gehring, Charles T., and Janny Venema trans. and ed. *New York Historical Manuscripts: Dutch*. Vol. 8, *Council Minutes, 1656–1658*. Syracuse, NY: Syracuse University Press: 2018.

Gronniosaw, James Albert Ukawsaw. *A Narrative of the Most Remarkable Particulars in the Life of James Albert Ukawsaw Gronniosaw, an African Prince, as Related by Himself*. Translated by Walter Shirley. Bath, UK: W. Gye, 1772.

Hastings, Hugh, et al., eds. *Ecclesiastical Records of the State of New York*. 7 vols. Albany, NY: J. B. Lyon, 1901–16.

Hoadly, Charles J., ed. *The Public Records of the Colony of Connecticut*. Hartford, CT: Press of Case, Lockwood and Brainard, 1868.

Horsmanden, Daniel. *A Journal of the Proceedings in the Detection of the Conspiracy Formed by Some White People, in Conjunction with Negro and other Slaves, for Burning the City of New-York in America, and Murdering the Inhabitants*, in *The New York Conspiracy Trials of 1741: Daniel Horsmanden's Journal of the Proceedings with Related Documents*, ed. Serena Zabin (Boston, MA: Bedford/St. Martin's, 2004).

Horsmanden, Daniel. *The New-York Conspiracy*. 1744. Reprint, New York: Printed and Published by Southwick & Pelsue, 1810.

Hunt, Gaillard, ed. *The First Forty Years of Washington Society, Portrayed by the Family Letters of Mrs. Samuel Harrison Smith (Margaret Bayard) from the Collection of her Grandson J. Henley Smith*, ed. Gaillard, Hunt. New York: Charles Scribner's Sons, 1906.

Ligon, Richard. *A True and Exact History of the Island of Barbados*, edited by Karen Ordahl Kupperman. 1657. Reprint, Indianapolis, IN: Hackett, 2011.

The Manuscripts of the House of Lords, 1695–1697. London: Printed for His Majesty's Stationery Office by Eyre and Spottiswoode, 1903.

Manwaring, Charles William, comp. *A Digest of the Early Connecticut Probate Records*. Hartford, CT: R. S. Peck & Co., 1904.

Massachusetts Historical Society. *Collections of the Massachusetts Historical Society*. Boston: John Wilson and Son, 1886.

Massachusetts Historical Society. *Winthrop Family Papers.* Vol. 5. Boston: Massachusetts Historical Society, 1947.
Mather, Cotton. *Diary of Cotton Mather, 1681–1724.* Vol. 2. Boston: The Society, 1911.
Minutes of the Common Council of the City of New York, 1675–1776. 8 vols. New York: Dodd, Mead, 1905.
Nelson, William, and Abraham van Doren Honeyman, ed. *Documents Relating to the Colonial History of the State of New Jersey.* 29 vols. Paterson, NJ: The Press Printing and Publishing, 1894.
Northrup, A. Judd et al., eds. *The Colonial Laws of New York: From the Year 1644 to the Revolution.* Albany, NY: James B. Lyon, 1894.
O'Callaghan, E. B., ed. *Calendar of Historical Manuscripts in the Office of the Secretary of State Albany New York.* 2 vols. Albany, NY: Weed, Parsons, 1865–66.
O'Callaghan, E. B., ed. *The Documentary History of the State of New-York.* Vol. 1. Albany: Weed & Parsons, 1819.
O'Callaghan, E. B., ed. *The Documentary History of the State of New-York.* Vol. 2. Albany: Weed & Parsons, 1850.
O'Callaghan, E. B., ed. *Journal of the Legislative Council of the Colony of New York.* Albany: Weed, Parsons & Company, Printers, 1861.
O'Callaghan, E. B., ed. *Laws and Ordinances of New Netherland, 1638–1674.* Albany: Weed, Parsons & Company, 1868.
O'Callaghan, E. B., ed. *Lists of Inhabitants of Colonial New York: Excerpted from the Documentary History of the State of New-York.* 1979. Reprint, Baltimore, MD: Clearfield Company by Genealogical Publishing, 2007.
O'Callaghan, E. B., trans. and ed. *Voyages of the Slavers St. John and Arms of Amsterdam, 1659, 1663.* Albany, NY: J. Munsell, 1867.
O'Callaghan, E. B., and Berthold Fernow, eds. *Documents Relative to the Colonial History of the State of New York.* 15 vols. Albany, NY: Weed, Parsons, 1853–87.
Pasko, W. W., ed. *Old New York: A Journal Relating to the History and Antiquities of New York City.* 2 vols. New York: W. W. Pasko, 1890.
Pelletreau, William S., ed. *Abstracts of Wills on File in the Surrogate's office: City of New York with Appendix and Miscellaneous Documents.* 17 vols. New York: Printed for the Society, 1893–1913.
Proceedings of the General Court of Assizes held in the City of New York, October 6, 1680 to October 6, 1682. New York: Printed for the New York Historical Society, 1912.
Rossiter, W. S. *A Century of Population Growth from the First Census of the United States to the Twelfth, 1780–1900.* Washington, DC: Government Printing Office, 1909.
Saffin, John. *A Brief and Candid Answer to a late Printed Sheet Entitled the Selling of Joseph,* 1701. In George Moore, *Notes on the History of Slavery in Massachusetts.* 251–56. 1866. Reprint, Bedford, MA: Applewood Books, 2008.
Sedgwick, Theodore, Samuel Allinson, and New Jersey Court of Chancery. *Acts of the General Assembly of the Province of New-Jersey: from the surrender of the government to Queen Anne . . .* Burlington, NJ: Printed by Isaac Collins, Printer to the King, for the Province of New-Jersey, 1776.
Sewall, Samuel. *The Diary of Samuel Sewall,* ed. M. Halsey Thomas. New York: Farrar, Straus and Giroux, 1973.
Stokes, Isaac Newton Phelps. *The Iconography of Manhattan Island, 1498–1909.* New York: Robert H. Dodd, 1915.

Stryker, William S., ed. *Documents Relating to the Revolutionary History of the State of New Jersey.* 42 vols. Trenton, NJ: John L. Murphy, 1901.

Stuyvesant, Petrus. "July 8, 1664 Loan Request of Jeremias van Rensselaer and Johannes La Montagne." In *Documents of the Senate of the State of New York.* Vol. 13, 253. Albany, NY: James B. Lyon, State Printer, 1901.

Sypher Jr., Francis J., ed. and trans. *Liber A of the Collegiate Churches of New York, Part 2.* Grand Rapids, MI: William B. Eerdmans, 2015.

Udemans, Godefridus. *'t Geestelijck roer van 't coopmans schip.* Dordrecht, the Netherlands: Francois Boels, 1640.

Van der Linde, A.P.G. Jos, trans. and ed. *New York Historical Manuscripts, Dutch: Old First Dutch Reformed Church of Brooklyn, New York First Book of Records, 1660–1752.* Baltimore: Genealogical Publishing, 1983.

Van Laer, A.J.F., trans. and ed. *Correspondence of Jeremias van Rensselaer, 1651–1674.* Albany: University of the State of New York, 1932.

Van Laer, A.J.F., trans. and ed. *Correspondence of Maria van Rensselaer, 1669–1689.* Albany: University of the State of New York, 1935.

Van Laer, A.J.F., ed. *Early Records of the City and County of Albany and Colony of Rensselaerswyck: Notarial Papers 1 and 2, 1660–1696.* 4 vols. Albany, NY: University of the State of New York, 1918.

Van Laer, A.J.F., trans. and ed. *Minutes of the Court of Albany, Rensselaerswyck and Schenectady.* 3 vols. Albany: University of the State of New York, 1926–28.

Van Laer, A.J.F., trans. and ed. *Minutes of the Court of Rensselaerswyck: 1648–1652.* Albany: University of the State of New York, 1922.

Van Laer, A.J.F., trans. and ed. *Van Rensselaer Bowier Manuscripts, Being the Letters of Kiliaen Van Rensselaer, 1630–1643, and Other Documents Relating to the Colony of Rensselaerswyck.* Albany, NY: University of the State of New York, 1908.

Wendell, Evert. *"To Do Justice to Him & Myself": Evert Wendell's Account Book of the Fur Trade with Indians in Albany, New York, 1695–1726.* Edited and Translated by Kees-Jan Waterman. Philadelphia: American Philosophical Society, 2008.

Will of John van Horne, 1733. In the *Somerset County Historical Quarterly.* Vol. 4, edited by A. van Doren Honeyman, 245–46. Somerville, NJ: Somerset County Historical Society, 1915.

Secondary Sources

Adams, Julia. *The Familial State: Ruling Families and Merchant Capitalism in Early Modern Europe.* 2005. Reprint, Ithaca, NY: Cornell University Press, 2007.

Aitken, William B. *Distinguished Families in America, Descended from Wilhelmus Beekman and Jan Thomasse van Dyke.* New York: The Knickerbocker Press, 1912.

Álvarez López, Laura. "Who Named Slaves and Their Children? Names and Naming Practices Among Enslaved Africans Brought to the Americas and Their Descendants with Focus on Brazil." *Journal of African Cultural Studies* 27, no. 2 (June 2015): 159–71.

Arends, Jacques. *Language and Slavery: A Social and Linguistic History of the Suriname Creoles.* Amsterdam: John Benjamins, 2017.

BIBLIOGRAPHY

Armitage, David. *The Declaration of Independence: A Global History*. 2007. Reprint, Cambridge, MA: Harvard University Press, 2008.

Arnold, Samuel Green. *History of the State of Rhode Island and Providence Plantations*. 1859. Reprint, Carlisle, MA: Applewood Books, 2015.

Bailyn, Bernard. *The New England Merchants in the Seventeenth Century*. Cambridge, MA: Harvard University Press, 1955.

Bailyn, Bernard. *The Peopling of British North America: The Barbarous Years, The Conflict of Civilizations, 1600–1675*. 2012. Reprint, New York: Vintage Books, 2013.

Bailyn, Bernard. *Voyagers to the West: A Passage in the Peopling of American on the Eve of the Revolution*. 1986. Reprint, New York: Vintage Books, 1988.

Balai, Leo. *Geschiedenis van de Amsterdamse slavenhandel: over de belangen van Amsterdamse regenten bij de trans-Atlantische slavenhandel*. Zutphen, Netherlands: Walburg Pers, 2013.

Bankoff, Arthur H., and Frederick A. Winter. "The Archaeology of Slavery at the van Cortlandt Plantation in the Bronx, New York." *International Journal of Historical Archaeology* 9, no. 4 (Dec. 2005): 291–318.

Barr, Juliana, and Edward Countryman. *Contested Spaces of Early America*. Philadelphia: University of Pennsylvania Press, 2014.

Behn, Aphra. *Oroonoko*, in *Versions of Blackness: 'Oroonoko', Race, and Slavery*, ed. Derek Hughes. 1688. Reprint, Cambridge: Cambridge University Press, 2007.

Benes, Peter. "Slavery in Boston Households, 1647–1770." In *Slavery/Antislavery in New England: The Dublin Seminar for New England Folklife Annual Proceedings 2003*, ed. Peter Benes, 12–30. Boston, MA: Boston University Press, 2005.

Berlin, Ira. *Many Thousands Gone: The First Two Centuries of Slavery in North America*. Cambridge, MA: Harvard University Press, 1998.

Berlin, Ira. "Slavery, Freedom, and Philadelphia's Struggle for Brotherly Love, 1685 to 1861." In *Antislavery and Abolition in Philadelphia: Emancipation and the Long Struggle for Racial Justice in the City of Brotherly Love*, edited by Richard Newman and James Mueller, 19–24. Baton Rouge: Louisiana State University Press, 2011.

Bezís-Selfa, John. *Forging America: Ironworkers, Adventurers, and the Industrious Revolution*. Ithaca, NY: Cornell University Press, 2004.

Bezís-Selfa, John. "Slavery and the Disciplining of Free Labor in the Colonial Mid-Atlantic Iron Industry." *Pennsylvania History: A Journal of Mid-Atlantic Studies* 64, Empire, Society, and Labor: Essays in Honor of Richard S. Dunn (summer 1997): 270–86. https://www.jstor.org/stable/27774063.

Biemer, Linda, ed. "Business Letters of Alida Schuyler Livingston, 1680–1726." *New York History*, 63, no. 2 (April 1982): 182–207.

Biemer, Linda. *Women and Property in Colonial New York: The Transition from Dutch to English Law, 1643–1727*. 1979. Reprint, Ann Arbor, MI: UMI Research Press, 1983.

Billings, Warren M., ed. *The Old Dominion in the Seventeenth Century: A Documentary History of Virginia, 1606–1689*. Chapel Hill: Published for the Omohundro Institute of Early American History and Culture, Williamsburg, Virginia by the University of North Carolina Press, 1975.

Blakely, Allison. *Blacks in the Dutch World: The Evolution of Racial Imagery in a Modern Society*. Bloomington: Indiana University Press, 1993.

BIBLIOGRAPHY

Block, Sharon. *Colonial Complexions; Race and Bodies in Eighteenth-Century America.* Philadelphia: University of Pennsylvania Press, 2018.

Block, Sharon. *Rape and Sexual Power in Early America.* Chapel Hill: Published for the Omohundro Institute of Early American History and Culture, Williamsburg, Virginia by the University of North Carolina Press, 2006.

Bly, Antonio T. *Escaping Bondage: A Documentary History of Runaway Slaves in Eighteenth-Century New England, 1700–1789.* Lanham, MD: Lexington Books, 2012.

Bly, Antonio T. "'Pretends he can read': Runaways and Literacy in Colonial America." *Early American Studies* 6, no. 2 (fall 2008): 261–94. http://www.jstor.org/stable/23546575.

Bly, Antonio T. "A Prince among Pretending Free Men: Runaway Slaves in Colonial New England Revisited." *Massachusetts Historical Review* 14 (2012): 87–118. https://www.jstor.org/stable/10.5224/masshistrevi.14.1.0087.

Bodle, Wayne. "'Such a Noise in the World': Copper Mines and an American Colonial Echo to the South Sea Bubble." *Pennsylvania Magazine of History and Biography* 127, no. 2 (2003): 131–65. http://www.jstor.org/stable/20093617.

Bolster, Jeffrey. *Black Jacks: African American Seamen in the Age of Sail.* Cambridge, MA: Harvard University Press, 1997.

Book of the Supervisors of Dutchess County, New York, A.D. 1718–1722. Poughkeepsie, NY: Vassar Brothers' Institute, 1907.

Bonomi, Patricia U. *A Factious People: Politics and Society in Colonial New York.* 1971. Reprint, Ithaca, NY: Cornell University Press, 2014.

Bonomi, Patricia. "'Swarm of Negroes Comeing about My Door': Black Christianity in Early Dutch and English North America." *Journal of American History*, vol. 103, no. 1 (June 2016): 34–58. https://doi.org/10.1093/jahist/jaw007.

Brewer, Holly. *By Birth or Consent: Children, Law, and the Anglo-American Revolution in Authority.* Chapel Hill: Published for the Omohundro Institute of Early American History and Culture, Williamsburg Virginia, by University of North Carolina Press, 2005.

Broeyer, Frits G.M. "Bible for the Living Room: The Dutch Bible in the Seventeenth Century." In *Lay Bibles in Europe 1450–1800*, edited by Mathijs Lamberigts and A. A. den Hollander, 207–15. Leuven, Belgium: Leuven University Press, 2006.

Brown, Kathleen. *Good Wives, Nasty Wenches, and Anxious Patriarchs: Gender, Race, and Power in Colonial Virginia.* Chapel Hill: Published for the Omohundro Institute of Early American History and Culture, Williamsburg, Virginia by the University of North Carolina Press, 1996.

Brown, Vincent. *Tacky's Revolt: The Story of an Atlantic Slave War.* Cambridge, MA: The Belknap Press of Harvard University Press, 2020.

Burke, Thomas. *Mohawk Frontier: The Dutch Community of Schenectady, New York, 1661–1710.* 2nd ed. 1991. Reprint, Albany: State University of New York Press, 2009.

Burnard, Trevor. "Slave Naming Patterns: Onomastics and the Taxonomy of Race in Eighteenth-Century Jamaica." *Journal of Interdisciplinary History* 31, no. 3 (2001): 325–46. https://www.jstor.org/stable/207085.

BIBLIOGRAPHY

Burrows, Edwin G., and Mike Wallace. *Gotham: A History of New York City to 1898.* Oxford: Oxford University Press, 1998.

Bush, Jonathan A. "Free to Enslave: The Foundations of Colonial American Slave Law." *Yale Journal of Law and the Humanities* 5, no. 2 (summer 1993): 417–70. https://digitalcommons.law.yale.edu/yjlh/vol5/iss2/.

Calloway, Colin G. *New Worlds for All: Indians, European, and the Remaking of Early America.* Baltimore: The Johns Hopkins University Press, 1997.

Cantwell, Anne-Marie, and Diana diZerega Wall, *Unearthing Gotham: The Archaeology of New York City.* New Haven, CT: Yale University Press, 2001.

Carney, Judith Ann. *Black Rice: The African Origins of Rice Cultivation in the Americas.* Cambridge, MA: Harvard University Press, 2001.

Carp, Benjamin L. "Did Dutch Smugglers Provoke the Boston Tea Party?" *Early American Studies* 10, no. 2 (spring 2021): 335–59, https://www.jstor.org/stable/23547671.

Carr, Rosalind. *Gender and Enlightenment Culture in Eighteenth-Century Scotland.* Edinburgh, UK: Edinburgh University Press, 2014.

Ceci, Lynn. "The First Fiscal Crisis in New York." *Economic Development and Cultural Change* 28, no. 4 (July 1980): 846–47. http://www.jstor.org/stable/1153524.

Centre for the Study of the Legacies of British Slavery. "Friendship Estate: Jamaica | St Mary." Accessed July 16, 2019. https://www.ucl.ac.uk/lbs/estate/view/2524.

Chamberlain, Marjorie Dikeman. *The First Five Generations.* Vol. 1 of *Johannes Dyckman of Fort Orange and his Descendants.* West Rutland, VT: Daamen, 1988.

Chan, Alexandra A. *Slavery in the Age of Reason: Archaeology at a New England Farm.* Knoxville: University of Tennessee Press, 2007.

Chancery Court Clerk of Queens County, New York. *Orders in Chancery, Province of New York, 1701–1802.* Salt Lake City, Utah: Genealogical Society of Utah, 1967.

Chard, Donald F. "The Impact of Ille Royale on New England, 1713–1763." PhD diss., University of Ottawa, 1977.

Christoph, Peter R. "Books from Ashes: A Project of Recreating Lost Documents." *De Halve Maen: Quarterly Magazine of the Dutch Colonial Period in America,* 56, no. 2 (fall 1981):17–18, 24–25.

Christoph, Peter R., ed. *The Dongan Papers, 1683–1688, Part II: Files of the Provincial Secretary of New York During the Administration of Governor Thomas Dongan.* Syracuse, NY: Syracuse University Press, 1993.

Christoph, Peter R. "The Freedmen of New Amsterdam." In *A Beautiful and Fruitful Place,* edited by Nancy Anne McClure Zeller, 157–70. Albany, NY: New Netherland Publishing, 1991.

Civitello, Linda. *Cuisine and Culture: A History of Food and People.* Hoboken, NJ: Wiley, 2008.

Clark-Pujara, Christy. *Dark Work: The Business of Slavery in Rhode Island.* New York: New York University Press, 2016.

Cody, Cheryll Ann. "There Was No 'Absalom' on the Ball Plantations: Slave-Naming Practices in the South Carolina Low Country, 1720–1865." *American Historical Review* 92, no. 3 (1987): 563–96.

The Colonial Laws of New York from the Year 1664 to the Revolution. Albany, NY: James B. Lyon, State Printer, 1894.

BIBLIOGRAPHY

Cooper, Afua. *The Hanging of Angélique*. Athens: University of Georgia Press, 2006.

"Curaçao as the Centre of the Slave Trade." Kura Hulanda Museum. Accessed December 9, 2010. http://www.kurahulanda.com/slavery/slave-trade.

Danckaerts, Jasper. *The Journal of Jasper Danckaerts, 1679–1680*, ed. Bartlett Burleigh James and J. Franklin Jameson. New York: Charles Scribner's Sons, 1913.

Dandridge, Anne Spottswood, comp. *The Forman Genealogy: Descendants of Robert Forman of Kent Co., Maryland, who died in 1719–20* . . . Cleveland, OH: Forman-Bassett-Hatch, 1903.

Davis, Natalie Zemon. *The Return of Martin Guerre*. Cambridge, MA: Harvard University Press, 1983.

Davis, Natalie Zemon. *Women on the Margins: Three Seventeenth-Century Lives*. Cambridge, MA: Harvard University Press, 1995.

Dawson, Kevin. *Undercurrents of Power: Aquatic Culture in the African Diaspora*. Philadelphia: University of Pennsylvania Press, 2018.

Day, Sherman. *Historical Collections of the State of Pennsylvania*. Philadelphia: George W. Gorton, 1843.

Debrunner, Hans Werner. *Presence and Prestige: Africans in Europe A History of Africans in Europe before 1918*. Basel: Basler Afrika Bibliographien, 1979.

Delaware River Heritage Trail. "Bordentown City." Accessed July 16, 2019. https://delawareriverheritagetrail.org/Bordentown-City.html.

Demos, John. *The Unredeemed Captive: A Family Story from Early America*. 1994. Reprint, New York: Vintage Books Edition, 1995.

Desrochers, Robert E. "Slave-for-Sale Advertisements and Slavery in Massachusetts, 1704–1781." *WMQ* 59, no. 3 (July 2002): 623–64. http://www.jstor.org/stable/3491467.

Devine, T. M., ed. *Recovering Scotland's Slavery Past: The Caribbean Connection*. Edinburgh, UK: Edinburgh University Press, 2015.

De Vries, Jan, and Ad van der Woude, *The First Modern Economy: Success, Failure, and Perseverance of the Dutch Economy, 1500–1815*. Cambridge: Cambridge University Press, 1997.

Dewulf, Jeroen. "Emulating a Portuguese Model: The Slave Policy of the West India Company and the Dutch Reformed Church in Dutch Brazil (1630–1654) and New Netherland (1614–1664) in Comparative Perspective." *Journal of Early American History* 4 (2014): 3–36.

Dewulf, Jeroen. *The Pinkster King and the King of Kongo: The Forgotten History of America's Dutch-Owned Slaves*. Jackson: University Press of Mississippi, 2017.

Di Bonaventura, Allegra. *For Adam's Sake: A Family Saga in Colonial New England*. New York: Liveright Publishing, 2013.

Douma, Michael J. "Estimating the Size of the Dutch-Speaking Slave Population of New York in the 18th Century." *Journal of Early American History* (forthcoming).

"The Duke's Laws (1665)," Historical Society of the New York Courts. Accessed April 29, 2021. https://www.nycourts.gov/history/legal-history-new-york/documents/Publications_1665-Dukes-Law.pdf.

Dunn, Richard, James Savage, and Laetitia Yeandle, eds. *The Journal of John Winthrop, 1630–1649*. Cambridge, MA: The Belknap Press of Harvard University Press, 1996.

BIBLIOGRAPHY

Eekhof, Albert. *De Hervormde Kerk in Noord-Amerika*. Vol. 2. 'S-Gravenhage, The Netherlands: M. Nijhoff, 1913.

Ellis, George William, and John Emery Morris. *King Philip's War: Based on the Archives and Records of Massachusetts, Plymouth, Rhode Island and Connecticut, and Contemporary Letters and Accounts, with Biographical and Topographical Notes*. New York: Grafton Press, 1906.

Emmer, Pieter Cornelis. *The Dutch Slave Trade, 1500–1850*. Oxford, UK: Berghahn Books, 2006.

Enthoven, Victor, and Wim Klooster. "The Rise and Fall of the Virginia-Dutch Connection in the Seventeenth Century." In *Early Modern Virginia: Reconsidering the Old Dominion*, edited by Douglas Bradburn and John C. Coombs, 90–127. Charlottesville: University of Virginia Press, 2011.

Evjen, John O. *Scandinavian Immigrants in New York, 1630–1674*. Minneapolis, MN: K. C. Holter, 1916.

Fabend, Firth Haring. *A Dutch Family In the Middle Colonies: 1660–1800*. New Brunswick, NJ: Rutgers University Press, 1991.

Fabend, Firth Haring. "The Pro-Leislerian Farmer: 'A Mad Rabble' or 'Gentlemen Standing up for Their Rights?'" In *A Beautiful and Fruitful Place: Selected Rensselaerswijck Seminar Papers*. Vol. 2. Edited by Nancy Anne McClure Zeller and Charles Gehring, 29–36. Albany, NY: New Netherland Publishing, 2011.

Fatah-Black, Karwan, and Matthias van Rossum, "Beyond Profitability: The Dutch Transatlantic Slave Trade and its Economic Impact." *Slavery & Abolition* 36, no. 1 (2015): 63–83. http://dx.doi.org/10.1080/0144039X.2013.873591.

Fatah-Black, Karwan, and Matthias van Rossum, "Slavery in a 'Slave Free Enclave': Historical Links Between the Dutch Republic Empire and Slavery, 1580s–1860s." *Werkstatt Geschichte* 66–67 (2015): 55–74, http://www.werkstattgeschichte.de/.

Fickes, Michael L. "'They Could Not Endure That Yolke': The Captivity of Pequot Women and Children after the War of 1637." *NEQ* 73, no. 1 (March 2000): 58–81. http://www.jstor.org/stable/366745.

Fiske, Jane Fletcher. *Gleanings from Newport Court Files, 1659–1783*. Boxford, MA: J. F. Fiske, 1998.

Fitts, Robert K. *Inventing New England's Slave Paradise: Master/Slave Relations in Eighteenth-Century Narragansett, Rhode Island*. New York: Garland, 1998.

Folkerts, Jan. "Kiliaen van Rensselaer and Agricultural Productivity in His Domain: A New Look at the First Patroon and Rensselaerswijck Before 1664." In *A Beautiful and Fruitful Place: Selected Rensselaerswijck Seminar Papers*, edited by Nancy Anne McClure Zeller and Charles Gehring, 295–308. Albany, NY: New Netherland Publishing, 1993.

Foote, Thelma Wills. *Black and White Manhattan: The History of Racial Formation in Colonial New York City*. New York: Oxford University Press, 2004.

Forbes, Jack D. *Africans and Native Americans: The Language of Race and the Evolution of Red-Black Peoples*, 2d ed. Urbana: University of Illinois Press, 1993.

Fowler, William C. "The Historical Status of the Negro in Connecticut." In the *Year Book of City of Charleston for 1900 A.D.*, ed. Henry B. Dawson, 3–64. Charleston, SC: Walker, Evans & Cogswell, 1901.

Foy, Charles. "Ports of Slavery, Ports of Freedom: How Slaves Used Northern Seaports' Maritime Industry to Escape and Create Trans-Atlantic Identities, 1713–1783." PhD diss., Rutgers, 2008.

Frank, Caroline. *Objectifying China, Imagining America: Commodities in Early America.* Chicago: University of Chicago Press, 2011.

Frijhoff, Willem. *Fulfilling God's Mission: The Two Worlds of Dominie Everardus Bogardus, 1607–1647.* Translated by Myra Heerspink Scholz. Vol. 14 in *The Atlantic World: Europe, Africa and the Americas, 1500–1830*, edited by Benjamin Schmidt and Wim Klooster. Leiden, NL: Brill, 2003–.

Fuentes, Marisa. *Dispossessed Lives: Enslaved Women, Violence, and the Archive.* Philadelphia: University of Pennsylvania Press, 2016.

Fuentes, Marisa, and Deborah Gray White, eds. *Scarlet and Black: Slavery and Dispossession in Rutgers History.* New Brunswick, NJ: Rutgers University Press, 2016.

Gallay, Alan. *The Indian Slave Trade: The Rise of the English Empire in the American South, 1670–1717.* New Haven: Yale University Press, 2002.

Gaines, Steven. *Philistines at the Hedgerow: Passion and Property in the Hamptons.* New York: Little, Brown, 1998.

Gardiner, Curtis, ed. *Lion Gardiner, and His Descendants . . .* [1590–1890]. St. Louis, MO: A. Whipple, 1890.

Gardiner, Lion. *Relation of the Pequot Warres.* 1660. Reprint, Hartford, CT: Hartford Press, 1901.

Gellman, David N. *Emancipating New York: The Politics of Slavery and Freedom 1777–1827.* Baton Rouge: Louisiana State University Press, 2006.

Gerzina, Gretchen Holbrook. *Mr. and Mrs. Prince: How an Extraordinary Eighteenth-Century Family Moved Out of Slavery and into Legend.* New York: Amistad, an imprint of HarperCollins, 2008.

Gilbert, Frank B. "Early Colonial Charters in Albany," *Proceedings of the New York State Historical Association.* Vol. 8. Albany: New York State Historical Association, 1909. http://www.jstor.org/stable/42889661.

Goebel, Julius, Jr. and Joseph H. Smith, ed. *The Law Practice of Alexander Hamilton: Documents and Commentary.* New York: Columbia University Press, 1980.

Gomez, Michael A. *Black Crescent: The Experience and Legacy of African Muslims in the Americas.* Cambridge: Cambridge University Press, 2005.

Goodfriend, Joyce D. *Before the Melting Pot: Society and Culture in Colonial New York City, 1665–1730.* Princeton, NJ: Princeton University Press, 1992.

Goodfriend, Joyce D. "Burghers and Blacks: The Evolution of a Slave Society at New Amsterdam." *New York History* 59, no. 2 (1978): 125–44. http://www.jstor.org/stable/23169655.

Goodfriend, Joyce D. "Incorporating Women into the History of the Colonial Dutch Reformed Church: Problems and Proposals." In *Patterns and Portraits: Women in the History of the Reformed Church in America*, edited by Renée S. House and John W. Coakley, 16–32. Grand Rapids, MI: Eerdmans, 1999.

Goodfriend, Joyce D. *Who Should Rule at Home?: Confronting the Elite in British New York City.* Ithaca, NY: Cornell University Press, 2017.

Gordon-Reed, Annette. *The Hemingses of Monticello: An American Family.* New York: W. W. Norton and Company, 2008.

Goslinga, Cornelis C.H. *The Dutch in the Caribbean on the Wild Coast 1580–1689.* 1971. Reprint, Gainesville: Library Press at the University of Florida, 2017.

Gould, Eliga H. "Entangled Histories, Entangled Worlds: The English-Speaking Atlantic as a Spanish Periphery." *American Historical Review* 112, no. 3 (June 2007): 764–86. http://www.jstor.org/stable/40006670.

Graham, Judith S. *Puritan Family Life: The Diary of Samuel Sewall*. Boston, MA: Northeastern University Press, 2000.

Green, Gretchen Lynn. "A New People in an Age of War: The Kahnawake Iroquois, 1667–1760." PhD diss., College of William & Mary, 1991. https://scholarworks.wm.edu/etd/1539623801/.

Greene, Evarts, and Virginia Harrington. *American Population before the Federal Census of 1790*. 1932. Reprint, Baltimore, MD: Genealogical Publishing, 1993.

Griswold, Mac. *The Manor: Three Centuries at a Slave Plantation on Long Island*. New York: Farrar, Straus and Giroux, 2013.

Gronim, Sara S. *Everyday Nature: Knowledge of the Natural World in Colonial New York*. New Brunswick, NJ: Rutgers University Press, 2007.

Groth, Michael E. *Slavery and Freedom in the Mid-Hudson Valley*. Albany: State University of New York Press, 2017.

Grumet, Robert S. *The Munsee Indians: A History*. Norman: University of Oklahoma Press, 2009.

Gustafson, Sandra M. *Eloquence Is Power: Oratory and Performance in Early America*. Chapel Hill: Published for the Omohundro Institute of Early American History and Culture, Williamsburg, Virginia by the University of North Carolina Press, 2000.

Hackett, David G., ed. *Religion and American Culture: A Reader*. 2d ed. New York: Routledge, 2003.

Hadden, Sally E. *Slave Patrols: Law and Violence in Virginia and the Carolinas*. Cambridge, MA: Harvard University Press, 2001.

Haefeli, Evan. *New Netherland and the Dutch Origins of American Religious Liberty*. Philadelphia, PA: University of Pennsylvania Press, 2013.

Haefeli, Evan. "A Scandalous Minister in a Divided Community: Ulster County in Leisler's Rebellion, 1689–1691." *New York History* 88, no. 4 (fall 2007): 357–89. http://www.jstor.org/stable/23185822.

Hall, Kim. *Things of Darkness: Economies of Race and Gender in Early Modern England*. Ithaca, NY: Cornell University Press, 1996.

Hall, Neville A. T. *Slave Society in the Danish West Indies*. 1992. Reprint, Mona, Jamaica: Published for the Department of History of the University of the West Indies at Mona, Cave Hill and St. Augustine, 1994.

Hamilton, Marsha L. *Social and Economic Networks in Early Massachusetts: Atlantic Connections*. University Park: Pennsylvania State University Press, 2009.

Hammer, Carl I. *Pugnacious Puritans: Seventeenth Century Hadley and New England*. Lanham, MD: Lexington Books, 2018.

Handler, Jerome S., and JoAnn Jacoby. "Slave Names and Naming in Barbados, 1650–1830." *WMQ* 53, no. 4 (1996): 685–728. http://www.jstor.org/stable/2947140.

Hardesty, Jared. *Unfreedom: Slavery and Dependence in Eighteenth-Century Boston*. New York: New York University Press, 2016.

Harris, Leslie M. "The Greatest City in the World? Slavery in New York in the Age of Hamilton." In *Historians on Hamilton: How a Blockbuster Musical is Restaging*

268   BIBLIOGRAPHY

America's Past, edited by Renee C. Romano and Clare Bond Potter, 71–93. New Brunswick, NJ: Rutgers University Press, 2018.

Harris, Leslie M. *In the Shadow of Slavery: African Americans in New York City, 1626–1863.* Chicago: University of Chicago Press, 2003.

Hart, Emma. *Building Charleston: Town and Society in the Eighteenth-Century British Atlantic World.* Charlottesville: University of Virginia Press, 2010.

Hart, Samuel, et al. *Connecticut as a Colony and as a State, or, One of the Original Thirteen.* Hartford. CT: Publishing Society of Connecticut, 1904.

Hartog, Johannes. *Curaçao: Van Kolonie Tot Autonomie: Deel 1 (Tot 1816).* Aruba: D.J. de Witt, 1961.

Hartman, Saidiya. *Lose Your Mother: A Journey Along the Atlantic Slave Route.* New York: Farrar, Straus and Giroux, 2007.

Hartman, Saidiya. "Venus in Two Acts." *Small Axe* 12, no. 2 (June 2008): 1–14. https://doi.org/10.1215/-12-2-1.

Hatfield, April Lee. *Atlantic Virginia: Intercolonial Relations in the Seventeenth Century.* Philadelphia: University of Pennsylvania Press, 2005.

Hatfield, April Lee. "Dutch Merchants and Colonists in the English Chesapeake: Trade, Migration, and Nationality in 17th-Century Maryland and Virginia." In *From Strangers to Citizens: The Integration of Immigrant Communities in Britain, Ireland, and Colonial America, 1550–1750,* edited by Randolph Vigne and Charles Littleton, 299–300, 304n. London: Sussex Academic Press, 2001.

Hatfield, April Lee. "Dutch and New Netherland Merchants in the Seventeenth-Century English Chesapeake." In *The Atlantic Economy during the Seventeenth and Eighteenth Centuries: Organization, Operation, Practice, and Personnel,* ed. Peter A. Coclanis, 205–28. Columbia: University of South Carolina Press, 2005.

Hayes, Katherine Howlett. *Slavery before Race: Europeans, Africans, and Indians at Long Island's Sylvester Manor Plantation, 1651–1884.* New York: New York University Press, 2014.

Hazard, Samuel, ed. *Annals of Pennsylvania, 1609–1682.* Philadelphia: Hazard and Mitchell, 1850.

Heinegg, Paul. *Free African Americans of North Carolina, Virginia, and South Carolina: From the Colonial Period to About 1820.* 1992; Reprint, Baltimore, MD: Printed for Clearfield Company by Genealogical Publishing, 2005.

Hess, Stephen. *America's Political Dynasties: From Adams to Clinton.* Washington, DC: Brookings Institution Press, 2016.

Hexham, Henry. *A copious English and Netherduytch dictionaire Composed out of our best English Authours. With an appendix of the names of Beasts, Fowles, Birds, Fishes, Hunting, and Hawking and also a compendious grammar for the instruction of the learner. Het groot woorden-Boeck, etc.* Rotterdam, NL: Aernout Leers, 1647.

Heywood, Linda M., and John K. Thornton. *Central Africans, Atlantic Creoles, and the Foundation of the Americas, 1585–1660.* 2007. Reprint, Cambridge: Cambridge University Press, 2011.

Higginbotham, A. Leon, Jr. *In the Matter of Color: Race and the American Legal Process: The Colonial Period.* Oxford: Oxford University Press, 1978.

Hinks, Peter, comp. "Slave Population of Colonial Connecticut, 1690–1774." *Yale University Historic Texts & Transcripts.* Accessed October 3, 2017. http://glc.yale.edu/sites/default/files/files/Citizens%20All%20Doc2.pdf.

BIBLIOGRAPHY

Hodges, Graham Russell. *Black New Jersey: 1664 to the Present Day.* New Brunswick, NJ: Rutgers University Press, 2019.

Hodges, Graham Russell. *Root and Branch: African Americans in New York and East Jersey, 1613–1863.* Chapel Hill: University of North Carolina Press, 1999.

Hodges, Graham Russell. *Slavery and Freedom in the Rural North: African Americans in Monmouth County, New Jersey, 1665–1865.* New York: Madison House, 1997.

Hodges, Graham Russell, and Alan Edward Brown, eds. *"'Pretends to Be Free': Runaway Slave Advertisements from Colonial and Revolutionary New York and New Jersey.* New York: Garland, 1994.

Hollander, Martha. "Structures of Space and Society in the Seventeenth-Century Dutch Interior." PhD diss., University of California, Berkeley, 1990.

Holt, Thomas C. "Du Bois, W. E. B." *African American National Biography*, eds. Henry Louis Gates Jr. and Evelyn Brooks Higginbotham. New York: Oxford University Press, 2008.

Hondius, Dienke. "Access to the Netherlands of Enslaved and Free Black Africans: Exploring Legal and Social Historical Practices in the Sixteenth-Nineteenth Centuries." *Slavery and Abolition* 32, no. 3 (2011): 377–95. doi: 10.1080/0144039X.2011.588476.

Hondius, Dienke. "Black Africans in Seventeenth-Century Amsterdam." *Renaissance and Reformation/Renaissance et Réforme* 31, no. 2 (2008): 94–95.

Hondius, Dienke. *Blackness in Western Europe: Racial Patterns of Paternalism and Exclusion.* New Brunswick, NJ: Transaction Publishers, 2014.

Hondius, Dienke. "Mapping Slavery" Accessed October 6, 2020. https://clue.vu.nl/en/projects/current-projects/mapping-slavery/index.aspx.

Hondius, Dienke. "West-European Urban Networks in the History of Slavery and the Slave Trade: New Research Perspectives from the Netherlands." In *Serfdom and Slavery in the European Economy 11th–18th Centuries*, edited by Simonetta Cavaciocchi, 575–92. Florence, Italy: Firenze University Press, 2014.

Howard, John Randall. "Origins and Architecture of Great House Plantation." MA thesis, University of Pennsylvania, 2004.

Howe, Adrian. "The Bayard Treason Trial: Dramatizing Anglo-Dutch Politics in Early Eighteenth-Century New York City." *WMQ*, 47, no. 1 (January 1990): 57–89.

Innes, Stephen, and T. H. Breen, *Myne Owne Ground: Race and Freedom on Virginia's Eastern Shore, 1640–1676.* 1980. Reprint, New York: Oxford University Press, 2004.

Inscoe, John C. "Carolina Slave Names: An Index to Acculturation." *Journal of Southern History* 49, no. 4 (1983): 527–54. https://www.jstor.org/stable/2208675.

"Irving, John Treat." In *The Memorial Cyclopedia of the Twentieth Century: Comprising Memoirs of Men and Women . . .* New York: Publishing Society of New York, 1906.

Israel, Jonathan I. *Dutch Primacy in World Trade, 1585–1740.* 1989. Reprint, Oxford: Clarendon Press, 2002.

Jacobs, Jaap. *The Colony of New Netherland: A Dutch Settlement in Seventeenth-Century America.* Ithaca, NY: Cornell University Press, 2009.

Jacobs, Jaap. "Dutch Proprietary Manors in America: The Patroonships in New Netherland." In *Constructing Early Modern Empires: Proprietary Ventures in the*

Atlantic World, 1500–1750, edited by Louis Roper and Bertrand van Ruymbeke. Vol. 11 of *The Atlantic World: Europe, Africa and the Americas, 1500–1830*, edited by Benjamin Schmidt and Wim Klooster, 301–26. Leiden, NL: Brill, 2003–.

Jacobs, Jaap. "'To Favor this New and Growing City of New Amsterdam with a Court of Justice.' The Relations between Rulers and Ruled in New Amsterdam." In *Amsterdam—New York: Transatlantic Relations and Urban Identities Since 1653*, edited by George Harinck and Hans Krabbendam, 17–29. Amsterdam: VU University Press, 2005.

Jacobs, Jaap. *New Netherland: A Dutch Colony in Seventeenth-Century America*. Vol. 3 of *The Atlantic World: Europe, Africa and the Americas, 1500–1830*, edited by Benjamin Schmidt and Wim Klooster. Leiden, NL: Brill, 2003–.

Jacobs, Jaap. *Petrus Stuyvesant: een levensschets*. Amsterdam: Bert Bakker, 2009.

Jacobs, Jaap. "Slavery in Stuyvesant's World." Presentation given at St. Mark's Church in-the-Bowery, New York, January 31, 2021.

James, Bartlett Burleigh. *The Labadist Colony in Maryland*. Baltimore: Johns Hopkins Press, 1899.

Janssen, Allan J. *Gathered at Albany: A History of a Classis*. Grand Rapids, MI: William B. Eerdmans, 1995.

Jardine, Lisa. *Going Dutch: How England Plundered Holland's Glory*. New York: Harper, 2008.

Johnson, Cynthia Mestad. *James DeWolf and the Rhode Island Slave Trade*. Charleston, SC: History Press, 2014.

Johnston, George. *History of Cecil County, Maryland: And the Early Settlements Around the Head of the Chesapeake Bay and on the Delaware River with Sketches of Some of the Old Families of Cecil County*. Elkton, MD: George Johnston, 1881.

Jones, Jacqueline. *American Work: Four Centuries of Black and White Labor*. New York: W. W. Norton, 1998.

Jones-Rogers, Stephanie E. *They Were Her Property: White Women as Slave Owners in the American South*. New Haven, CT: Yale University Press, 2019.

Kammen, Michael G. *Colonial New York: A History*. Oxford: Oxford University Press, 1996.

Kane, Maeve. "Covered with Such a Cappe: The Archaeology of Seneca Clothing, 1615–1820." *Ethnohistory* 61, no. 1 (winter 2014): 2, 1–25.

Katz, Stanley Nider. "Introduction." *A Brief Narrative of the Case and Trial of John Peter Zenger, Printer of the New York Weekly Journal*, by James Alexander, edited by Stanley Nider Katz, 1–35. Cambridge, MA and London, England: Harvard University Press, 2013. https://doi.org/10.4159/harvard.9780674730687.

Kay, Marvin, L. Michael and Lorin Lee Cary, *Slavery in North Carolina, 1748–1775*. Chapel Hill: University of North Carolina Press, 1995.

Kerrison, Catherine. *Jefferson's Daughters: Three Sisters, White and Black in a Young America*. New York: Ballantine Books, 2018.

Kettner, James H. *The Development of American Citizenship, 1608–1870*. Chapel Hill: Published for the Omohundro Institute of Early American History and Culture, Williamsburg, Virginia by the University of North Carolina Press, 2014.

Kidd, Thomas. *George Whitefield: America's Spiritual Founding Father*. New Haven, CT: Yale University Press, 2014.

BIBLIOGRAPHY

Kierner, Cynthia A. *Traders and Gentlefolk: The Livingston of New York, 1675–1790.* Ithaca, NY: Cornell University Press, 1992.

Klooster, Wim. *The Dutch Moment, War, Trade and Settlement in the Seventeenth-Century Atlantic World.* Ithaca, NY: Cornell University Press, 2016.

Klooster, Wim. "The Essequibo Liberties: The Link between Jewish Brazil and Jewish Suriname." *Studia Rosenthaliana* 42/43 (2010): 77–82. http://www.jstor.org/stable/24388994.

Klooster, Wim, and Gert Oostindie, *Realm between Empires: The Second Dutch Atlantic, 1680–1815.* Ithaca, NY: Cornell University Press, 2018.

Konadu, Kwasi. *The Akan Diaspora in the Americas.* Oxford: Oxford University Press, 2010.

Koot, Christian J. *A Biography of a Map in Motion: Augustine Herrman's Chesapeake.* New York: New York University Press, 2017.

Koot, Christian J. *Empire at the Periphery: British Colonists, Anglo-Dutch Trade, and the Development of the British Atlantic, 1621–1713.* New York: New York University Press, 2011.

Koot, Christian J. "The Merchant, the Map, and Empire: Augustine Herrman's Chesapeake and Interimperial Trade, 1644–73." *WMQ* 67, no. 4 (October 2010): 603–44. https://www.jstor.org/stable/10.5309/willmaryquar.67.4.0603.

Kramer, Erin. "'That she shall be forever banished from this country': Alcohol, Sovereignty, and Social Segregation in New Netherland." *Early American Studies* (winter 2022) (forthcoming).

Kruger, Vivienne. "Born to Run: The Slave Family in Early New York, 1626–1827." PhD diss., Columbia University, 1985.

Kupp, Jan, comp. "Calendar to Amsterdam and Rotterdam Notarial Acts Relating to the Virginia Tobacco trade." Accessed July 28, 2020. https://www.uvic.ca/library/locations/home/spcoll/documents/Kupp_calendar.pdf.

Kupperman, Karen Ordahl. *Providence Island, 1630–1641: The Other Puritan Colony.* 1993. Reprint, Cambridge: Cambridge University Press, 1995.

LaPrad, Kathryn S. "Thinking Locally, Acquiring Globally: The Loockerman Family of Delaware, 1630–1790." MA thesis, University of Delaware, 2010. https://udspace.udel.edu/handle/19716/5742

La Roche, Ramona Arlen. "'Bajan to Gullah' Cultural Capital: Wood, Stone, Iron, and Clay 1670 to 1770." PhD diss., University of South Carolina, 2017. https://scholarcommons.sc.edu/etd/4454.

Lauber, Almon Wheeler. *Indian Slavery in Colonial Times: Within the Present Limits of the United States.* New York: Longmans, Green, 1913.

Leder, Lawrence H. *Robert Livingston 1654–1728 and the Politics of Colonial New York.* Chapel Hill: University of North Carolina Press, 1961.

Leder, Lawrence H. "The Unorthodox Domine: Nicholas van Rensselaer." *New York History* 35, no. 2 (April 1954): 166–76. http://www.jstor.org/stable/23153043.

Lee, Esther J., et al. "MtDNA Origins of an Enslaved Labor Force from the 18th Century Schuyler Flatts Burial Ground in Colonial Albany, NY: Africans, Native Americans, and Malagasy?" *Journal of Archaeological Science* 36, no. 12 (December 2009): 2805–10. https://doi.org/10.1016/j.jas.2009.09.008.

Lemire, Elise. *Black Walden: Slavery and its Aftermath in Concord, Massachusetts*. Philadelphia: University of Pennsylvania Press, 2009.

Lemmings, David, ed. *Crime, Courtrooms and the Public Sphere in Britain, 1700–1850*. 2012. Reprint, London: Routledge, 2016.

Lepore, Jill. *New York Burning: Liberty, Slavery, and Conspiracy in Eighteenth-Century Manhattan*. 2005. Reprint, New York: Vintage Books, 2006.

Lewis, Tom. *The Hudson: A History*. New Haven, CT: Yale University Press, 2007.

Lindsay, Lisa A. *Atlantic Bonds: A Nineteenth-Century Odyssey from America to Africa*. Chapel Hill: University of North Carolina Press, 2017.

Linebaugh, Peter, and Marcus Rediker, *The Many Headed Hydra: Sailors, Slaves, Commoners, and the Hidden History of the Revolutionary Atlantic*. Boston, MA: Beacon Press, 2000.

Lipman, Andrew. *The Saltwater Frontier: Indians and the Contest for the American Coast*. New Haven, CT: Yale University Press, 2015.

Livesay, Daniel. *Children of Uncertain Fortune: Mixed-Race Jamaicans in Britain and the Atlantic Family, 1733–1833*. Chapel Hill: Published for the Omohundro Institute of Early American Culture, Williamsburg, Virginia, by University of North Carolina Press, 2018.

Livingston, Edwin Brockholst, *The Livingstons of Livingston Manor*. New York: Knickerbocker Press, 1910.

Lustig, Mary Lou. *Privilege and Prerogative: New York's Provincial Elite, 1710–1776*. Madison, NJ: Fairleigh Dickinson University Press, 1995.

Lydon, James G. "New York and the Slave Trade, 1700–1774." *WMQ* 35, no. 2 (April 1978): 375–94. http://www.jstor.org/stable/1921840.

MAAP: Mapping the African American Past. Accessed October 21, 2017. http://maap.comumbia.edu/.

Mackey, Frank. *Done with Slavery: The Black Fact in Montreal, 1769–1840*. Montreal: McGill-Queen's University Press, 2010.

Maika, Dennis. "Commerce and Community: Manhattan Merchants in the Seventeenth Century." PhD diss., New York University, 1995.

Maika, Dennis. "To 'experiment with a parcel of negros': Incentive, Collaboration, and Competition in New Amsterdam's Slave Trade." *Journal of Early American History* 10, 1 (2020): 33–69. https://doi.org/10.1163/18770703-010 01005.

Mak, Geert. *Amsterdam: A Brief Life of the City*, translated by Philipp Blom. London: Vintage Books, 2001.

Manegold, C. S. *Ten Hills Farm: the Forgotten History of Slavery in the North*. Princeton, NJ: Princeton University Press, 2010.

Mangan, Jane E. *Transatlantic Obligations: Creating the Bonds of Family in Conquest-Era Peru*. Oxford: Oxford University Press, 2016.

Morgan, Jennifer L. "'Some Could Suckle over Their Shoulder': Male Travelers, Female Bodies, and the Gendering of Racial Ideology, 1500–1700." *WMQ* 54, no. 1 (January 1997): 167–92. http://www.jstor.org/stable/2953316.

Maskiell, Nicole Saffold. "Cicely Was Young, Black and Enslaved—Her Death during an Epidemic in 1714 Has Lessons that Resonate in Today's Pandemic." *The Conversation*, December 2, 2020. https://theconversation.com/cicely-was-young-black-and-enslaved-her-death-during-an-epidemic-in-1714-has-lessons-that-resonate-in-todays-pandemic-147733.

Maskiell, Nicole Saffold. "Elite Slave Networks in the Dutch Atlantic." In *Shifting the Compass: Pluricontinental Connections in Dutch Colonial and Postcolonial Literature*, edited by Jeroen Dewulf, Olf Praamstra and Michiel van Kempen, 186–205. Newcastle, UK: Cambridge Scholars Publishing, 2013.

Maskiell, Nicole Saffold. "'Here Lyes the Body of Cicely Negro': Enslaved Women in Colonial Cambridge and the Making of New England History." *NEQ* 94, no. 2 (2022) (forthcoming).

Matson, Cathy D. *Merchants & Empire: Trading in Colonial New York*. Baltimore, MD: Johns Hopkins University Press, 1998.

McDonald, Kevin P. *Pirates, Merchants, Settlers, and Slaves: Colonial America and the Indo-Atlantic World*. Berkeley: University of California Press, 2015.

McManus, Edgar J. *Black Bondage in the North*. Syracuse, NY: Syracuse University Press, 1973.

McManus, Edgar J. *A History of Negro Slavery in New York*. Syracuse, NY: Syracuse University Press, 1966.

McMenamin, Michael. "Bittersweet: The American Revolution and New York City's Sugar Industry." MCNY Blog: New York Stories. Posted June 30, 2015. https://blog.mcny.org/2015/06/30/bittersweet-the-american-revolution-and-new-york-citys-sugar-industry/.

Menard, Russell R. *Sweet Negotiations: Sugar, Slavery, and Plantation Agriculture in Early Barbados*. Charlottesville: University of Virginia Press, 2009.

Merrell, James H. *Into the American Woods: Negotiators on the Pennsylvania Frontier*. New York: W. W. Norton, 1999.

Merritt, Jane T. *At the Crossroads: Indians and Empires on a Mid-Atlantic Frontier, 1700–1763*. Chapel Hill: Published for the Omohundro Institute of Early American History and Culture, Williamsburg, Virginia, by University of North Carolina Press, 2003.

Merwick, Donna. *Death of a Notary: Conquest and Change in Colonial New York*. Ithaca, NY: Cornell University Press, 1999.

Merwick, Donna. *Stuyvesant Bound: An Essay on Loss Across Time*. Philadelphia: University of Pennsylvania Press, 2013.

Meuwese, Marcus P. *Brothers in Arms, Partners in Trade: Dutch-Indigenous Alliances in the Atlantic World, 1595–1674*. Leiden, NL: Brill, 2011.

Meuwese, Marcus P. "'For the Peace and Well-Being of the Country': Intercultural Mediators and Dutch-Indian relations in New Netherland and Dutch Brazil, 1600–1664." PhD diss., University of Notre Dame, 2003. https://curate.nd.edu/show/6m311n81g6m.

Mijers, Esther. "Scotland, the Dutch Republic and the Union: Commerce and Cosmopolitanism." In *Jacobitism, Enlightenment, and Empire, 1680–1820*, edited by Allan I. Macinnes and Douglas J. Hamilton, 93–108. New York: Routledge, 2014.

Milteer, Warren Eugene, Jr. *Beyond Slavery's Shadow: Free People of Color in the South*. Chapel Hill: University of North Carolina Press, 2021.

Milteer, Warren Eugene, Jr. *North Carolina's Free People of Color, 1715–1885*. Baton Rouge: Louisiana State University Press, 2020.

Midtrød, Tom Arne. *The Memory of All Ancient Customs: Native American Diplomacy in the Colonial Hudson Valley*. Ithaca, NY: Cornell University Press, 2012.

Misevich, Philip. "In Pursuit of Human Cargo: Philip Livingston and the Voyage of the Sloop 'Rhode Island.'" *New York History* 86, no. 3 (summer 2005): 187.

Monteiro, Carolina, and Erik Odegard. "Slavery at the Court of the 'Humanist Prince': Reexamining Johan Maurits van Nassau-Siegen and his Role in Slavery, Slave Trade, and Slave-smuggling in Dutch Brazil." *Journal of Early American History* 10, no. 1 (2020): 3–32. doi: https://doi.org/10.1163/18770703-010 01004.

Moore, Sean D. *Slavery and the Making of Early American Libraries: British Literature, Political Thought, and the Transatlantic Book Trade, 1731–1814.* Oxford: Oxford University Press, 2019.

Morgan, Edwin Vernon. *Slavery in New York.* New York: G. P. Putnam's Sons, 1898.

Morgan, Jennifer L. *Laboring Women: Reproduction and Gender in New World Slavery.* Philadelphia: University of Pennsylvania Press, 2004.

Morgan, Jennifer L. "*Partus sequitur ventrem*: Law, Race, and Reproduction in Colonial Slavery." *Small Axe* 22, no. 1 (March 2018): 1–17. doi:10.1215/07990537-4378888.

Morgan, Jennifer L. *Reckoning with Slavery: Gender, Kinship, and Capitalism in the Early Black Atlantic.* Durham, NC: Duke University Press, 2021.

Morgan, Jennifer L. "'Some Could Suckle over Their Shoulder': Male Travelers, Female Bodies, and the Gendering of Racial Ideology, 1500–1770." *WMQ* 54, no. 1 (1997): 167–92. https://doi.org/10.2307/2953316.

Morgan, Philip D. *A Slave Counterpoint: Black Culture in Eighteenth-Century Chesapeake and Low Country.* Chapel Hill: Published for the Omohundro Institute of Early American Culture, Williamsburg, Virginia, by University of North Carolina Press, 1998.

Mosterman, Andrea. "Nieuwer-Amstel, stadskolonie aan de Delaware." In *De slavernij in Oost en West*, 164–71. Amsterdam: Uitgeverij Het Spectrum, 2020.

Mosterman, Andrea. *Spaces of Enslavement: A History of Slavery and Resistance in Dutch New York.* Ithaca, NY: Cornell University Press, 2021.

Motte, Ellis Loring, Henry Fitch Jenks, John Homans, eds. *The Manifesto Church: Records of the Church in Brattle Square, Boston, with Lists of Communicants, Baptisms, Marriages and Funerals, 1699–1872*, 2d ed. Boston: Benevolent Fraternity of Churches, 1902.

Munsell, Joel. *The Annals of Albany*, Vol. 9. Albany, NY: Munsell & Rowland, Printers, 1858.

Murdoch, Alexander. *Scotland and America, c.1600–c.1800.* Basingstoke, UK: Palgrave Macmillan, 2010.

Murphy, Henry Cruse, trans. and ed. *Anthology of New Netherland, Or, Translations from the Early Dutch Poets of New York, With Memoirs of Their Lives.* 1865. Reprint, Amsterdam: N. Israel, 1966.

Murphy, Henry Cruse. "Introduction." In *Journal of a Voyage to New York and a Tour in Several of the American Colonies in 1679–80*, by Jaspar Dankers and Peter Sluyter, translated and edited by Henry C. Murphy, ix–xlvii. Brooklyn: Long Island Historical Society, 1867.

Nadler, Steven. *A Book Forged in Hell: Spinoza's Scandalous Treatise and the Birth of the Secular Age.* Princeton, NJ: Princeton University Press, 2011.

Naiveu, Matthijs. "The Newborn Baby." In Donna R. Barnes and Peter G. Rose, *Matters of Taste: Food and Drink in Seventeenth-century Dutch Art and Life*, 94. Syracuse, NY: Syracuse University Press, 2002.

Narrett, David E. *Inheritance and Family Life in Colonial New York City*. 1992. Reprint, Ithaca, NY: Cornell University Press, 2011.

Nelson, William, ed. *Patent and Deeds and Other Early Records of New Jersey, 1664–1703*. 1899. Reprint, Baltimore, MD: Reprinted for Clearfield Company by Genealogical Publishing, 2000.

Newell, Margaret Ellen. *Brethren by Nature: New England Indians, Colonists, and the Origins of American Slavery*. Ithaca, NY: Cornell University Press, 2015.

Newell, Margaret Ellen. "Indian Slavery in Colonial New England." In *Indian Slavery in Colonial America*, ed. Allan Gallay, 33–67. Lincoln, NE: University of Nebraska Press, 2009.

"New-England's Faction Discovered . . ." In *Narratives of the Insurrections 1675–1690*, ed. Charles M. Andrews, 251–68. New York: Charles Scribner's Sons, 1960.

Newman, Richard S. "Prince Hall, Richard Allen, and Daniel Coker: Revolutionary Black Founders, Revolutionary Black Communities." In *Revolutionary Founders: Rebels, Radicals, and Reformers in the Making of the Nation*, edited by Alfred F. Young, Gary B. Nash, and Ray Raphael, 305–22. 2011. Reprint, Vintage Books, 2012.

Newman, Simon. "Hidden in Plain Sight: Long-Term Escaped Slaves in Late-Eighteenth and Early-Nineteenth Century Jamaica." *WMQ* (June 2018). https://blog.oieahc.wm.edu/the-wmq-on-the-oi-reader/.

"The New-York Weekly Journal." *The News Media and the Making of America, 1730–1865*. Accessed February 7, 2021. https://americanantiquarian.org/earlyamericannewsmedia/items/show/109.

Noorlander, Danny. *Heaven's Wrath: The Protestant Reformation and the Dutch West India Company*. Ithaca, NY: Cornell University Press, 2019.

Noorlander, Danny. "Serving God and Mammon: The Reformed Church and the Dutch West India Company in the Atlantic World, 1621–1674." PhD diss., Georgetown University, 2011.

North, Arthur Walbridge. *The Founders and the Founding of Walton, New York: Being an Intimate Historical Sketch of the Making of an American Settlement in the Critical Period Immediately Preceding the Adoption of the Federal Constitution*. Walton, NY: Walton Reporter Company, 1924.

Norton, Mary Beth. *Founding Mothers and Fathers: Gendered Power and the Forming of American Society*. New York: Vintage Books, 1997.

Norton, Mary Beth. *In the Devil's Snare: The Salem Witchcraft Crisis of 1692*. New York: Alfred Knopf, 2002.

Norton, Mary Beth. *Separated by Their Sex: Women in Public and Private in the Colonial Atlantic World*. Ithaca, NY: Cornell University Press, 2011.

"Notes and Queries." *New York Genealogical and Biographical Record* 13, no. 1 (January 1882): 49.

Nystrom, Elsa A. "John Woolman (1720–1772)." In *Slavery in the United States: A Social Political, and Historical Encyclopedia*, Vol. 1, edited by Junius P. Rodriguez, 520. Santa Barbara, CA: ABC-CLIO, 2007.

"Original Book of New York Deeds, January 1st 1672 to October 19th 1675." In *Collections of the New-York Historical Society for the Year 1913: The John Watts De Peyster Publication Fund*, 46:42–43. New York: Printed for the Society, 1914.

Otterness, Philip. *Becoming German: The 1709 Palatine Migration to New York*. 2004. Reprint, Ithaca, NY: Cornell University Press, 2006.

Page, Rachel. "'A pleasant good Family': Domestic Enslavement in Samuel Johnson's Household, 1723–1772." https://columbiaandslavery.columbia.edu/content/pleasant-good-family-domestic-enslavement-samuel-johnsons-household-1723-1772.

Paige, Lucius R. *History of Cambridge, Massachusetts, 1630–1877, with a Genealogical Register*. Boston: Houghton and Mifflin. 1877. http://www.perseus.tufts.edu/hopper/text?doc=Perseus%3Atext%3A2001.05.0228%3Achapter%3D27&force=y.

Palmer, Jennifer L. *Intimate Bonds: Family and Slavery in the French Atlantic*. Philadelphia: University of Pennsylvania Press, 2016.

Parmenter, Jon. "After the Mourning Wars: The Iroquois as Allies in Colonial North American Campaigns, 1676–1760." *WMQ*, 64, no. 1 (January 2007): 39–76. https://www.jstor.org/stable/4491596.

Parr, Jessica M. *Inventing George Whitefield: Race, Revivalism, and the Making of a Religious Icon*. Jackson: University Press of Mississippi, 2015.

Parrish, Susan Scott. "Richard Ligon and the Atlantic Science of Commonwealths." *WMQ* 67, no. 2 (April 2010): 209–48. https://www.jstor.org/stable/10.5309/willmaryquar.67.2.209.

Pearson, Johnathan, comp., and J. W. Mac Murray, ed. *A History of the Schenectady Patent in the Dutch and English Times; Being Contributions Toward a History of the Lower Mohawk Valley*. Albany: Albany: Joel Munsell's Sons, 1883.

Pincus, Steven. *1688: The First Modern Revolution*. New Haven, CT: Yale University Press, 2009.

Piwonka, Ruth. "'. . . and I have made good friends with them': Plants and the New Netherland Experience." *New York History* 89, no. 4 (fall 2008): 397–425. https://www.jstor.org/stable/23185849.

Plane, Ann Marie. *Colonial Intimacies: Indian Marriage in Early New England*. Ithaca, NY: Cornell University Press, 2000.

Plimoth Plantation and New England Genealogical Society. "A Genealogical Profile of Thomas Willett." Accessed October 9, 2020. https://blogs.plimoth.org/sites/default/files/media/pdf/willett_thomas.pdf.

Polgar, Paul J. *Standard-Bearers of Equality: America's First Abolition Movement*. Chapel Hill: Published for the Omohundro Institute of Early American History and Culture by University of North Carolina Press, 2019.

Pollitzer, William S. *The Gullah People and Their African Heritage*. 1999. Reprint, Athens: University of Georgia Press, 2005.

Ponte, Mark. "1656 'Twee mooren in een stuck van Rembrandt.'" In *Wereldgeschiedenis van Nederland*, eds. Karel Davids, Karwan Fatah-Black, Marjolein 't Hart, Leo Lucassen en Jeroen Touwen, and Lex Heerma van Voss, 265–69. Den Haag, NL: Huygens Instituut Voor Nederlandse Geschiedenis, 2018.

Ponte, Mark. "'Al de swarten die hier ter stede comen' Een Afro-Atlantische gemeenschap in zeventiende-eeuws Amsterdam." *TSEG—The Low Countries*

Journal of Social and Economic History, 15, no. 4 (2018): 33–62. https://doi.org/10.18352/tseg.995.

Postma, Johannes. *The Dutch in the Atlantic Slave Trade, 1600–1815*. Cambridge: Cambridge University Press, 1990.

Price, Richard. *Alabi's World*. Baltimore, MD: The Johns Hopkins University Press, 1990.

Proceedings of the Huguenot Society of America. 1884. Reprint, New York: Knickerbocker Press, 1899.

Ramirez, Jan Seidler. "Stuyvesant's Pear Tree: Some Interpretive Fruits." *New York Journal of American History* 65, no. 4 (fall 2004): 116–21.

Raphael-Hernandez, Heike, ed. *Blackening Europe: The African American Presence*. New York: Routledge, 2004.

Rappleye, Charles. *Sons of Providence: The Brown Brothers, the Slave Trade, and the American Revolution*. New York: Simon & Schuster, 2006.

Rawley, James A., and Stephen D. Behrendt. *The Transatlantic Slave Trade, A History*. 1981. Reprint, Lincoln: University of Nebraska Press, 2005.

Rediker, Marcus. *The Slave Ship: A Human History*. New York: Viking Penguin Group, 2008.

Rediker, Marcus. *Villains of All Nations: Atlantic Pirates in the Golden Age*. Boston: Beacon Press, 2004.

Reinberger, Mark, and Elizabeth McLean. *The Philadelphia Country House: Architecture and Landscape in Colonial America*. Baltimore: Johns Hopkins University Press, 2015.

Reitano, Joanne. *New York State: Peoples, Places, and Priorities: A Concise History with Sources*. New York: Routledge, 2016.

Reynolds, Cuyler. *Annals of American Families*. New York: National Americana Society, 1916.

Riker, James, Jr. *The Annals of Newtown in Queens County, New-York*. New York: Published by D. Fanshaw, 1852.

Rink, Oliver. *Holland on the Hudson: An Economic and Social History of Dutch New York*. Ithaca, NY: Cornell University Press, 1986.

Ritchie, Robert C. *Captain Kidd and the War against the Pirates*. Cambridge, MA: Harvard University Press, 1986.

Robison, Jeannie F. J., and Henrietta C. Bartlett, eds. *Genealogical Records: Manuscript Entries of Births, Deaths and Marriages, Taken from Family Bibles, 1581–1917*. New York: Colonial Dames of the State of New York, 1917.

Romney, Susanah Shaw. *New Netherland Connections: Intimate Networks and Atlantic Ties in Seventeenth-Century America*. Chapel Hill: Published for the Omohundro Institute of Early American History and Culture by University of North Carolina Press, 2014.

Romney, Susanah Shaw. "Reytory Angola, Seventeenth-Century Manhattan (US)." In *As If She Were Free: A Collective Biography of Women and Emancipation in the Americas*, edited by Erica Ball, Tatiana Seijas and Terri Snyder, 58–78. Cambridge: Cambridge University Press, 2020.

Roper, L. H. "The Fall of New Netherland and Seventeenth-Century Anglo-American Imperial Formation, 1654–1676," *NEQ* 87, no. 4 (2014): 666–708.

Rucker, Walter C. *The River Flows On: Black Resistance, Culture, and Identity Formation in Early America*. Baton Rouge: Louisiana State University Press, 2008.

Rupert, Linda. *Creolization and Contraband: Curaçao in the Early Modern Atlantic World*. Athens: University of Georgia Press, 2012.

Rushforth, Brett. *Bonds of Alliance: Indigenous and Atlantic Slaveries in New France*. Chapel Hill: Published for the Omohundro Institute of Early American History and Culture, Williamsburg, Virginia by the University of North Carolina Press, 2013.

"Sale Notice for Autograph Document Signed, Paul Richards." *The Collector: A Magazine for Autograph and Historical Collectors* 22 (January 1909): 30.

Saxby, T. J. *The Quest for the New Jerusalem, Jean de Labadie and the Labadists, 1610–1744*. Dordrecht, NL: Martinus Nijhoff, 1987.

Schama, Simon. *The Embarrassment of Riches: An Interpretation of Dutch Culture in the Golden Age*. 1987. Reprint, New York: Vintage Books, 1997.

Schiebinger, Londa L. *Nature's Body: Gender in the Making of Modern Science*. 1993. Reprint, New Brunswick, NJ: Rutgers University Press, 2004.

Schmidt, Ariadne. "Survival Strategies of Widows and Their Families in Early Modern Holland, c. 1580–1750." *History of the Family* 12, no. 4 (2007): 268–81. https://doi.org/10.1016/j.hisfam.2007.12.003.

Schmidt, Benjamin. *Innocence Abroad: The Dutch Imagination and the New World, 1570–1670*. Cambridge: Cambridge University Press, 2001.

Schmidt, Benjamin. "Mapping an Empire: Cartographic and Colonial Rivalry in Seventeenth-Century Dutch and English North America." *WMQ* 54, no. 3 (July 1997): 549–78, http://www.jstor.org/stable/2953839.

Schnurmann, Claudia. "Atlantic Trade and American Identities: The Correlations of Supranational Commerce, Political Opposition, and Colonial Regionalism." In *The Atlantic Economy during the Seventeenth and Eighteenth Centuries: Organization, Operation, Practice, and Personnel*, edited by Peter A. Coclanis, 186–204. Columbia: University of South Carolina Press, 2005.

Schreuder, Yda. *Amsterdam's Sephardic Merchants and the Atlantic Sugar Trade in the Seventeenth Century*. New York: Palgrave Macmillan, 2019.

Schwartz, Marie Jenkins. *Ties That Bound: Founding First Ladies and Slaves*. Chicago: University of Chicago Press, 2017.

Scott, Kenneth. "The Slave Insurrection in New York in 1712." *New-York Historical Society Quarterly* 45, no. 1 (January 1961): 43–74.

Scott, Kenneth. "Ulster Co., NY Ct. Recs. 1693–1775." *National Genealogical Society Quarterly* (Dec. 1972): 280, quoted in Evelyn Sidman Wachter, *Sidman-Sidnam Families of Upstate New York*. Baltimore, MD: Gateway Press, 1981.

Shain, Barry Alan, ed. and comp. *The Declaration of Independence in Historical Context: American State Papers, Petitions, Proclamations, & Letters of the Delegates to the First National Congress*. New Haven, CT: Yale University Press, 2014.

Shimony, Annemarie A. "Iroquois Religion and Women in Historical Perspective." In *Women, Religion, and Social Change*, eds. Yvonne Yazbeck Haddad and Ellison Banks Findly, 397–418. Albany: State University of New York Press, 1985.

Shorto, Russell. *The Island at the Center of the World: The Epic Story of Dutch Manhattan and the Forgotten Colony that Shaped America*. 2004. Reprint, New York: Vintage, 2005.

Shorto, Russell, and Len Tantillo, "In Search of Stuyvesant's Bowery." *New Netherland Matters* (spring 2020): 5–9.

Shumway, Rebecca. *The Fante and the Transatlantic Slave Trade.* Rochester, NY: University of Rochester Press, 2011.

Singer, Roberta. "The Livingstons as Slave Owners: The 'Peculiar Institution' on Livingston Manor and Clermont." In *The Livingston Legacy: Three Centuries of American History*, ed. Richard Wiles, 67–97. Annandale-on-Hudson, NY: Bard College, 1987.

"1676 Tax Assessments." *New York Genealogical and Biographical Record* 2, no. 1 (January 1871), 36.

Smith, Billy G., and Paul Sivitz. "Mapping Historic Philadelphia." Accessed October 6, 2020. http://www.mappinghistoricphiladelphia.org/about.html.

Smith, Billy G., and Richard Wojtowicz. *Blacks Who Stole Themselves: Runaway Slaves in the 19th Century Mid-Atlantic.* Philadelphia: University of Pennsylvania Press, 2015.

Smith, Elizur Yale. "CAPTAIN THOMAS WILLETT First Mayor of New York." *New York History* 21, no. 4 (1940): 404–17. http://www.jstor.org/stable/23134735.

Smith, Mark J., ed. *Stono: Documenting and Interpreting a Southern Slave Revolt.* Columbia: University of South Carolina Press, 2005.

Snabel, Cor, and Elizabeth Johnson. *The Varlet Family of Amsterdam and Their Associated Families in the American Colonies and in the Netherlands.* Last Updated, August 2020. http://varletfamily.pbworks.com.

Soderlund, Jean R. "Black Importation and Migration into Southeastern Pennsylvania, 1682–1810." *Proceedings of the American Philosophical Society* 133, no. 2 (June 1989), 144–53. https://www.jstor.org/stable/987045.

Soderlund, Jean R. *Lenape Country: Delaware Valley Society Before William Penn.* Philadelphia: University of Pennsylvania Press, 2015.

Sparks, Randy J. *The Two Princes of Calabar: An Eighteenth-Century Atlantic Odyssey.* Cambridge, MA: Harvard University Press, 2004.

Sprunger, Keith L. *Dutch Puritanism: A History of English and Scottish Churches of the Netherlands in the Sixteenth and Seventeenth Centuries.* Leiden, NL: Brill, 1983.

Stanwood, Owen. "The Protestant Moment: Antipopery, the Revolution of 1688–1689, and the Making of an Anglo-American Empire." *Journal of British Studies* 46, no. 3 (July 2007): 481–508. https://www.jstor.org/stable/10.1086/515441.

Sweet, John Wood. *Bodies Politic: Negotiating Race in the American North, 1730–1830.* 2003. Reprint, Philadelphia: University of Pennsylvania Press, 2006.

Sword, Kirsten Denise. *Wives Not Slaves: Patriarchy and Modernity in the Age of Revolutions.* Chicago: University of Chicago Press, 2021.

Taylor, Maureen Alice, and John Wood Sweet, *Runaways, Deserters, and Notorious Villains from Rhode Island Newspapers.* Camden, ME: Picton Press, 1994.

Thomas, Hugh. *The Slave Trade: The Story of the Atlantic Slave Trade, 1440–1870.* New York: Simon & Schuster, 1997.

Thornton, John. *Africa and Africans in the Making of the Atlantic World, 1400–1800.* Cambridge: Cambridge University Press, 1998.

Thornton, John. "Central African Names and African-American Naming Patterns." *WMQ* 50, no. 4 (October 1993): 727–42. https://www.jstor.org/stable/2947473.

Todd, Kim. *Chrysalis: Maria Sibylla Merian and the Secrets of Metamorphosis*. London: I. B. Tauris, 2007.

Tomlins, Christopher. "Transplants and Timing: Passages in the Creation of an Anglo-American Law of Slavery." *Theoretical Inquiries in Law* 10, no. 2 (July 2009): 389–421. https://doi.org/10.2202/1565-3404.1221.

Towner, Lawrence W. "The Sewall-Saffin Dialogue on Slavery," *WMQ* 21, no. 1 (January 1964): 48–52. http://www.jstor.org/stable/1923355.

Trager, James. *The New York Chronology: The Ultimate Compendium of Events, People, and Anecdotes from the Dutch to the Present*. New York: Harper Resource, 2003.

"The Trial of Col. Nicholas Bayard in the Province of New York for High-Treason, 19 February 1702." In *A Complete Collection of State-Trials, and Proceedings Upon High-Treason . . .*, edited by Thomas Bayly Howell, 2nd ed., 5:427. London: T.C. Hansard, 1816.

Trotter, Joe William. *Workers on Arrival: Black Labor in the Making of America*. Berkeley: University of California Press, 2019.

Truxes, Thomas M. *Defying Empire: Trading with the Enemy in Colonial New York*. New Haven, CT: Yale University Press, 2008.

United States Department of the Interior National Park Service. *National Register of Historic Places Registration Form: The Bowery Historic District*, prepared by Kerri Culhane. NPS Form 10–900. Washington, DC: OMB, 2013. https://www.nps.gov/nr/feature/places/pdfs/13000027.pdf.

Valentine, D. T., comp. *Manual of the Corporation of the City of New York*. New York: Edmund Jones, Printers, 1862.

Van der Woude, Joanne, and Jaap Jacobs. "Sweet Resoundings: Friendship Poetry by Petrus Stuyvesant and Johan Farret on Curaçao, 1639–45." *WMQ* 75, no. 3 (July 2018): 507–40. http://www.jstor.org/stable/10.5309/willmaryquar.75.3.0507.

Van Horn, Jennifer. *The Power of Objects in Eighteenth-Century British America*. Chapel Hill: Published for the Omohundro Institute of Early American History and Culture, Williamsburg, Virginia by the University of North Carolina Press, 2017.

Vann, Maria. "Sirens of the Sea: Female Slave Ship Owners of the Atlantic World, 1650–1870." *Coriolis: the Interdisciplinary Journal of Maritime Studies* 5, no. 1 (winter 2015): 22–33. https://ijms.nmdl.org/article/view/14717.

Venema, Janny. *Beverwijck: A Dutch Village on the American Frontier, 1652–1664*. Albany, NY: State University of New York Press, 2003.

Venema, Janny. *Kiliaen van Rensselaer (1586–1643): Designing a New World*. Hilversum, NL: Verloren, published with financial support of the New Netherland Institute, 2010.

Von Frank, Albert J. "John Saffin: Slavery and Racism in Colonial Massachusetts." *Early American Literature* 29, no. 3 (1994): 254–72. http://www.jstor.org/stable/25056983.

Voorhees, David William. "'To Assert Our Right before It Be Quite Lost': The Leisler Rebellion in the Delaware River Valley." *Pennsylvania History: A Journal of Mid-Atlantic Studies* 64, no. 1 (1997): 5–27, http://www.jstor.org/stable/27773953.

Voorhees, David W. "The 'fervent Zeale' of Jacob Leisler." *WMQ*, 51, no. 3 (July 1994), 447–72.

Voorhees, David W. "Jacob Leisler and the Huguenot Network in the English Atlantic World." In *Strangers to Citizens, Integration of Immigrant Communities in Great Britain, Ireland and the Colonies, 1550–1750*, ed. Randolph Vinge and Charles Littleton, 322–31. Brighton, UK: Sussex Academic Press, 2001.

Voorhees, David W. "Rotterdam-Manhattan Connections: The Influence of Rotterdam Thinkers upon New York's 1689 Leislerian Movement." In *Rotterdams Jaarboekje*, vol. 9, eds. Paul van de Laar et al., 196–216. Rotterdam, The Netherlands, 2001.

Wachter, Evelyn Sidman. *Sidman-Sidnam Families of Upstate New York*. Baltimore, MD: Gateway Press, 1981.

Wadsworth, Benjamin. *The Well-Ordered Family or Relative Duties*. Boston, MA: Printed by B. Green for Nicholas Battolph at his Shop in Corn-Hill, 1712. In Evans Series I Imprints, America's Historical Imprints.

Wagman, Morton. "Corporate Slavery in New Netherland." *Journal of Negro History* 65, no. 1 (winter 1980): 34–42. http://www.jstor.org/stable/3031546.

Wall, Diana di Zerega, and Anne-Marie Cantwell. *Touring Gotham's Archaeological Past: 8 Self-Guided Walking Tours through New York City*. New Haven: Yale University Press, 2004.

Wall, John P., and Harold E. Pickersgill. *History of Middlesex County, New Jersey, 1664–1920*. New York: Lewis Historical Publishing, 1921.

Waller, G. M. *Samuel Vetch: Colonial Enterpriser*. Chapel Hill: Published for the Omohundro Institute of Early American History and Culture, Williamsburg, Virginia, by University of North Carolina Press, 1960.

Warren, Wendy. "'The Cause of Her Grief': The Rape of a Slave in Early New England." *Journal of American History* 93, no. 4 (March 2007): 1031–49. http://www.jstor.org/stable/25094595.

Warren, Wendy. *New England Bound: Slavery and Colonization in Early America*. New York: Liveright, 2016.

Warsh, Molly A. *American Baroque: Pearls and the Nature of Empire, 1492–1700*. Chapel Hill: Published for the Omohundro Institute of Early American History and Culture, Williamsburg, Virginia by the University of North Carolina Press, 2018.

Warsh, Molly A. "Enslaved Pearl Divers in the Sixteenth Century Caribbean." *Slavery & Abolition* 31, no. 3 (Maritime Slavery) (2010): 345–62. https://doi.org/10.1080/0144039X.2010.504540.

Wasch, C. J. "Een doopregister der Hollanders in Brazilië." In *Algemeen Nederlandsch Familieblad*, vol. 5, 169–72. Netherlands: Bureau Groenendaal, 1888.

Washington, Margaret. *Sojourner Truth's America*. Chicago: University of Illinois Press, 2009.

Wax, Darold D. "Africans on the Delaware: The Pennsylvania Slave Trade, 1759–1765." *Pennsylvania history: A Journal of Mid-Atlantic Studies* 50, no. 1 (January 1983): 38–49. https://www.jstor.org/stable/27772875.

Wax, Darold D. "A Philadelphia Surgeon on a Slaving Voyage to Africa, 1749–1751." *Pennsylvania Magazine of History and Biography* 92, no. 4 (October 1968): 465–93. http://www.jstor.org/stable/20090230.

Weeks, Daniel J. *Gateways to Empire: Quebec and New Amsterdam to 1664*. Bethlehem, PA: Lehigh University Press, 2019.

Weeks, Daniel J. *Not for Filthy Lucre's Sake: Richard Saltar and the Antiproprietary Movement in East New Jersey, 1665–1707.* Cranbury, NJ: Associated University Press, 2001.

Weiss, Harry Bischoff, and Grace M. Weiss. *Trades and Tradesmen of Colonial New Jersey.* Trenton, NJ: Past Times Press, 1965.

Wellenreuther, Hermann, ed. *Jacob Leisler's Atlantic World in the Later Seventeenth Century: Essays on Religion, Militia, Trade, and Networks by Jaap Jacobs, Claudia Schurmann, David W. Voorhees, and Herman Wellenreuther.* Münster, Germany: LIT Verlag, 2009.

Wellenreuther, Hermann, and Carola Wessel, eds. *The Moravian Mission Diaries of David Zeisberger, 1772–1781.* University Park: Pennsylvania State University Press, 2005.

Werner, Edgar A., ed. *Civil List and Constitutional History of the Colony and State of New York.* Albany: Weed, Parsons, 1889.

White, Richard. *The Middle Ground: Indians, Empires, and Republics in the Great Lakes Region, 1650–1815.* 1991. Reprint, New York: Cambridge University Press, 2011.

White, Shane. *Somewhat More Independent: The End of Slavery in New York City, 1770–1810.* Athens: University of Georgia Press, 1991.

Whiting, Gloria. "Power, Patriarchy, and Provision: African Families Negotiate Gender and Slavery." *Journal of American History* 103, no. 3 (2016): 583–605. https://doi.org/10.1093/jahist/jaw325.

Whittlesey, Charles Wilcoxson. *Crossing and Re-crossing the Connecticut River: A Description of the River from its Mouth to its Source, with a History of its Ferries and Bridges.* New Haven, CT: The Tuttle, Morehouse and Taylor, 1938.

Wilder, Craig Steven. *In the Company of Black Men: The African Influence on African American Culture in New York City.* New York: New York University Press, 2001.

Wilder, Craig Steven. *A Covenant with Color: Race and Social Power in Brooklyn 1636–1990.* New York: Columbia University Press, 2000.

Wilder, Craig Steven. *Ebony and Ivy: Race, Slavery, and the Troubled History of America's Universities.* New York: Bloomsbury Press, 2013.

Williams, Oscar. "Slavery in Albany, New York, 1624–1827." *Afro-Americans in New York Life and History* 34, no. 2 (July 2010): 154–68. https://www.proquest.com/scholarly-journals/slavery-albany-new-york-1624-1827/docview/749645035/se-2.

Williams, William H. *Slavery and Freedom in Delaware, 1639–1865.* Wilmington, DE: Scholarly Resources, 1996.

Williams-Myers, A. J. *Long Hammering: Essays on the Forging of an African American Presence in the Hudson River Valley to the Early Twentieth Century.* Trenton, NJ: Africa World Press, 1994.

Wilson, James Grant. *Colonel John Bayard (1738–1807) and the Bayard Family of America.* New York: Trow's Printing and Bookbinding Co., 1885.

Wilson, Stephen. *Means of Naming: A Social History.* London: Routledge, 1998.

Winfield, Charles H. *History of the Land Titles in Hudson Country, NJ., 1609–1871.* New York: Wynkoop and Hallenbeck, Printers, 1872.

Winsor, Justin, ed. *The Memorial History of Boston Including Suffolk County Massachusetts, 1630–1880.* Boston: James R. Osgood, 1881.

Wojtowicz, Richard, and Billy G. Smith. "Fugitives: Newspaper Advertisements for Runaway Slaves, Indentured Servants, and Apprentices." In *Life in Early Philadelphia: Documents from the Revolutionary and Early National Periods*, edited by Billy G. Smith, 87–130. University Park: Pennsylvania State University Press, 1995.

Woordenboek der Nederlandsche Taal (WNT). Instituut voor de Nederlandse Taal. Last updated June 9, 2021. https://ivdnt.org/woordenboeken/woordenboek-der-nederlandsche-taal/.

Young, Alfred F. *The Democratic Republicans of New-York: The Origins, 1763–1797*. Chapel Hill: University of North Carolina Press, 1967.

Zabin, Serena R. *The Boston Massacre: A Family History*. Boston: Houghton Mifflin Harcourt, 2020.

Zabin, Serena R. *Dangerous Economies: Status and Commerce in Imperial New York*. Philadelphia: University of Pennsylvania Press, 2009.

Zabin, Serena R., ed. *The New York Conspiracy Trials of 1741: Daniel Horsmanden's Journal of the Proceedings with Related Documents*. Boston, MA: Bedford/St. Martin's, 2004.

Index

Figures, notes, and tables are indicated by f, n, and t following the page number.

Abrahamse, Mattheus, 70
Adam (enslaved person), 85–86, 130, 145
Adams, Julia, 184n5
Adventure (ship), 246n4
Adventure Galley (ship), 230n9
Albany: borderlands conflicts in, 111; elite networks in, 81–82, 83, 159, 162; enslaved persons in, 56–58, 63–64, 101, 173t, 226n105; female networks in, 9, 64–65, 67; Livingston family in, 56–67, 70, 74, 100–101, 149; runaways in, 143–45; trade networks in, 78, 80; Van Rensselaer family in, 70; Vetch family in, 98. *See also* Rensselaerswijck
Alida (enslaved person), 115, 116, 118, 120–21
Allen, John, 231n19
Allyn, Ann, 75
Allyn, John, 46, 73, 79, 81, 226n112, 227n118
Allyn, Matthew, 75
Amandare (ship), 210–11n48
Amsterdam, 21, 35, 43
Ancram (ship), 128, 243n14
Andries (enslaved person), 18–19, 20–22, 62, 193n13
Andros, Governor, 72
Anglo-Dutch elite networks, 39–55
Angola, 26
Ann (enslaved person), 139
Anne and Judith (ship), 246n4
Antigua, 125, 137
antislavery movement, 53–54, 161, 216n103
Aruba, 17, 21, 26
Asiento de Negros, 52

Backer, Jacobus, 40, 49
Backer, Margrietje Stuyvesant, 40
Bailyn, Bernard, 186n17
Balthazar (enslaved person), 24

baptisms, 4, 20, 29–31, 47–48, 71, 102, 195n22, 208n35, 212nn55–57, 252n74
Barbados: Beck in, 48; family networks in, 41f; networks of enslaved persons in, 78; slave trade in, 4, 6, 72, 74–75, 78, 125; sugar industry in, 27, 204n102; trade networks in, 6, 75, 125; Van Cortlandt family in, 61
Bayard, Alida Vetch, 119
Bayard, Anna Stuyvesant, 26, 39–41, 40f
Bayard, Balthazar, 79, 89, 90, 229n149
Bayard, James, 125, 159, 161
Bayard, John, 159, 160f, 161, 162
Bayard, Judith Varlet, 53
Bayard, Lazare, 47, 48
Bayard, Margaretta van Cortlandt, 88
Bayard, Nicholas, 157, 232n48
Bayard, Nicolaes, 51, 52–53, 58, 79–80, 81, 90, 91, 103, 127
Bayard, Peter, 53–54, 216n103
Bayard, Samuel, 26, 40f, 53, 54, 88, 89–90, 125, 150–52, 159–61, 253n3
Bayard, Stephen, 119–20, 125–26, 150
Bayard, Susannah, 125
Bayard, William, 139
Bayard family, 5–6, 5f, 89–90, 91, 125
Beaumont, Adriaen, 208n35
Beck, Matthias, 47–49, 51–52, 74, 211n51, 211n54
Beebe, Samuel, 86
Beeckman, Maria, 93, 95
Beeckman, Willem, 44, 51, 68, 69, 90
Beekman, G. G., 155
Beekman, Gerard, 155
Beekman, William, 155
Behn, Aphra, 204n102
Behrendt, Stephen, 183n4

285

INDEX

Ben (enslaved person), 98–99, 99f, 101–2, 106, 108–9, 250n54
Benjamin (enslaved person), 135
Berlin, Ira, 4, 30, 207n26
Beverwijck, 19–20, 22, 58, 111
Beyerlandt, Gijsbert Cornelissen, 35
Biemer, Linda, 240n80
Blackham, William, 230n9
Blake, Edward, 79
Block, Adriaen, 3
Bly, Antonio, 254n14
Bogardus, Anneken, 31
Bogardus, Everardus, 31
Bogardus, Pieter, 218n14
Bohemia Manor, 53–54, 159–60
Bonaire, 17, 21, 26, 46
Bonomi, Patricia, 219n26
Bonte Koe (ship), 199n59
Boot, Anna Varlet Hack, 41–42, 43, 45, 53, 206n10
Boot, Nicolaes, 42–43
Borland, John, 86, 106
Boston: Bayard family in, 161; elite networks in, 40; enslaved persons in, 230n17; Livingston family in, 58, 76; measles epidemic in, 108, 238n49; revolt following Glorious Revolution, 72; slaveholding culture in, 84–85; trade networks in, 46; Vetch family in, 87, 98, 102–3, 106–8, 112–14
bouwerijs in Manhattan, 23–31, 24f, 36–37, 50–51, 92–95
Bowdoin, Mary, 161
Bradford, William, 46, 127, 211n48
Bradish, James, 113–14
Braveboy (enslaved person), 130
Brazil, 3, 19, 25, 40, 48, 203n101
Breen, T. H., 207n26
Breese, Florah, 144
Breese, John, 143–44, 145
Brewer, Holly, 246n3
Brown, Kathleen, 189n26, 240n88
Brown, Vincent, 8
Browne, John, 46
Bruynvisch (ship), 3, 28, 184–85n9
Burger, Peter, 139
Burnett, William, 119
Bush, Jonathan, 208n33
Byam (ship), 125
Byrd, William, II, 240n88

Caesar (enslaved person), 98, 99f, 102, 114, 122, 131, 132–33

Calico Jack (enslaved person), 247n17
Callender (enslaved person), 115
Campbell, Duncan, 82–83, 85
Campbell, John, 85
Canada: as destination for runaways, 73, 104–5, 247n13; Indigenous peoples in, 72–73, 83; Palatines and, 103; trade networks in, 87
Cane (enslaved person), 68
Cardle, Thomas, 119, 120
Caribbean: family networks in, 41f, 47, 51–52; networks of enslaved persons in, 78; trade networks in, 25–26. *See also specific countries*
Carter, Landon, 240n88
Casparsz, Jacob, 57
Catherine (ship), 147
Catherine and Mary (ship), 251n69
Chaloner, Walter, 137
Chancellor, William, 250n49
Channing, John, 137
Channing family, 134
Charity (ship), 243n9
Charles (ship), 69
Chesapeake: Dutch settlements in, 2; elite networks in, 5, 7; enslaved persons in, 68; family networks in, 11, 40–42, 41f, 44–45, 53, 55, 162–63, 207n26; ironworks in, 128; slaveholding culture in, 27–28, 47, 49; trade networks in, 85, 188n22
children as enslaved persons, 45, 47, 79–80, 82, 84, 86, 91
Christiaensen, Hendrick, 3
Claes, Elisabeth, 218n12
Claes Croes (enslaved person), 60
Clark, George, 130
Clark-Pujara, Christy, 4
Claverack, 67, 94–95
Code Noir (Black Laws), 71, 78
Coleman, Benjamin, 102, 107
Collier, John, 68
Colve, Anthony, 58
Congoij, Emanuel, 29
Coninck Salomon (ship), 49
Connecticut, 136
Coote, Richard, 84
Cortlandt Manor, 100
Crailo (van Rensselaer family manor), 20
criminalization of race, 59–68
Cruger, Henry, 144
Cruger, John, 130
Cuffee (enslaved person), 130

culture: Dutch, 4, 46; of enslavement, 2, 8–10, 14, 37, 108, 163; of family networks, 17, 114; of violence, 108
Curaçao: in Dutch colonial empire, 17; English takeover of New Netherland and, 51; enslaved persons in, 25–26; family networks in, 40–41, 41f, 44, 47–48, 52, 55; as hub for slave trade, 34, 75, 78, 126, 199n59; Livingston family in, 83, 126, 243n9; networks of enslaved persons in, 78; Stuyvesant family in, 25, 33–34; trade networks in, 21, 40, 126

Damen, Marietje, 60–61
Danckaerts, Jasper, 53
d'Angola, Maijken, 94
Daniel (enslaved person), 122, 132
Danish West India and Guinea Company, 53
Dartmouth, Lord, 91
Davids, William, 211n48
Davis, Natalie Zemon, 188n22, 191n32
Dawson, Kevin, 224n80
De Angola, Paulo, 30
Deboras (ship), 243n9
De Bryne, Johannes, 248n19
Decker, Johan de, 43
Dego (enslaved person), 103, 115, 118–19, 120, 121, 241n97
dehumanization, 116, 122
De Laet, Johannes, 184–85n9
Delaware River, 3, 36, 44, 54–55, 147, 249n36
De Meyer, Nicholas, 87
Demos, John, 191n32
Desire (ship), 6, 74, 228n128
De Vries, Jan, 30
De Vries, Symon Janzen, 197n43
De Witt, Petrus, 135–36
Dewulf, Jeroen, 4, 29, 72
Diamond (ship), 136–37
Diana (enslaved person), 98–99, 99f, 102, 106, 107, 108–9, 120, 131
Di Bonaventura, Allegra, 4, 228n126, 228n128, 228n130, 240n80
Dijkeman, Jannetje, 110–11
Dijkeman, Johannes, 108, 110–11, 118, 122
Dijkeman, Johannes, Jr., 111
Dittelbach, Petrus, 217n108
Dongan, Thomas, 71
Dragon (ship), 251n69
Dreeper, Hans, 57
Drisius, Samuel, 45, 209n38

Droilheit, Paul, 232n39
Du Bois, W. E. B., 7
Dudley, Joseph, 87
Dudley, Paul, 87
Dunscomb, Samuel, 151
Dutch East India Company, 20
Dutch Reformed Church, 20, 39, 47–48, 212n55

Eendracht (ship), 203n101
elite networks, 5–6, 5f; Anglo-Dutch networks, 39–55; clandestine trade by enslaved persons and, 65; crossing colonial lines, 45–49; English takeover of New Netherland and, 49–54; expansion of, 41–45; runaways and, 74–79. *See also specific families*
Elizabeth (ship), 137
Ellis, Ellias, 152
Ellis, George William, 209n45
Emanuel (enslaved person), 90
Emanuelse, Barent, 57, 59–60
enslaved children, 45, 47, 79–80, 82, 84, 86, 91
enslaved networks, 10, 141, 147–48
Equiano, Olaudah, 154
Escott, Gabriel, 131
Esopus, 3, 37
Eva (enslaved person), 98, 102, 107, 114
Everson, Nicholas, 145–48
Eyckenboom (ship), 48

family networks: culture of, 17, 114; of enslaved persons, 98–100, 99f; expansion of, 2, 5–6, 5f, 20; in Manhattan bouwerijs, 23–31; map of, 41f; women and, 3, 58–59, 64–67, 88, 141. *See also* elite networks; *specific families*
Finley, Samuel, 161
Fletcher, Benjamin, 81
Flodder, Jacob Jansz, 192n1
Flora (enslaved person), 115, 120, 152
Folkerts, Jan, 194n19
Foote, Thelma Wills, 4
Fort Altena, 44, 51, 93
Fort Amsterdam, 25, 35, 52
Fort Chambly, 142, 247n13
Fort Kromantine, 112
Fort Orange, 204n107
Foy, Charles, 219n25
Francis (ship), 125
Francisco, Jan, 201n77
Franklin, Benjamin, 161

288 INDEX

free Blacks: in Connecticut, 76; elite networks and, 89, 243–44n21; English takeover of New Netherland and, 49–50; legal constructs for, 150–51; in Manhattan bouwerijs, 23, 28, 29–30, 31, 94, 123–24; in New Netherland, 3; property dispossession and, 123–24, 130
Frelinghuysen, Theodorus, 154–55
Frontenac, Louis de Buade, Comte de, 65
Fuentes, Marisa, 4, 57, 191n33
Furman, Abigail Howard, 251n63
Furman, Gabriel, 155, 157, 158, 165, 251n63
Furman, Jane, 153, 158
Furman, Nowell, 155
fur trade, 22, 46, 58, 63, 65, 129

Gabriel (enslaved person), 155
Gallardo, Juan, 197n47, 212n61
Galloway (enslaved person), 143–45, 164
Gardiner, Jacob Jansen, 61
Gardiner, John, 82
geographies of slavery, 148, 191n35, 221n45
Gerrits, Aefje, 66, 68
Gideon (ship), 3, 46, 51, 93
Glorious Revolution, 71–72
Goodfriend, Joyce, 212n55
Graham, James, 61, 62, 220n31
Grange, Arnoldus de la, 53
Green, Bartholomew, 231n19
Green, Gretchen Lynn, 222n53
Gritta (enslaved person), 98, 102, 107, 114
Groth, Michael, 4, 235n8

Hack, Anna Varlet. *See* Boot, Anna Varlet Hack
Hack, George, 44
Hack, Joris, 41, 44
Haes, Gabriel de, 34
Hall, Kim, 189n26
Hall, Prince, 248n28
Hall, William, 248n28
Hallett family, 101–2, 154, 235n15
Hannibal (enslaved person), 117, 120
Hardenbergh, Gerrit, 218n14
Hardesty, Jared Ross, 4, 79, 246n3
Harris, Leslie, 4
Hartgers, Pieter, 22
Hartman, Saidiya, 4, 100, 191n33
Harvard College, 87

Hatfield, April Lee, 188n22, 206n10
Haudenosaunee Confederacy, 3, 12, 65, 70, 144, 222n52, 248n25
Hazard, Samuel, 208n34
Henrick (enslaved person), 103
Henrique, Mathias, 199n59
Herman, Augustine, 41, 44, 49
Herrman, Ephraim, 199n60
Hexham, Henry, 36
Hodges, Graham Russell, 4, 29, 76, 227n121, 247n6
Hollander, Martha, 199n61
Holmes, William, 75
Holyoke, Elizur, 84
Hondius, Dienke, 200n61
Honnich, Maarten, 203n101
Howard, John Randall, 253n3
Hudson River Valley, 21
Hunter, William, 103, 106

Indigenous peoples: attacks on colonial settlements, 36, 68, 111; enslavement of, 6, 37, 49, 115, 144; King William's War (1690) and, 73, 76, 91, 94, 128–29; land grants and, 70; Livingston family and, 103–4, 112, 115; Pequot War (1636–38) and, 6; runaways and, 227n121. *See also specific groups*
Innes, Stephen, 207n26
ironworks, 128–29, 131, 133–35, 245n58
Isabel (enslaved person), 98–102, 99f, 106, 108, 112–13, 122, 131

Jack (enslaved person), 56–57, 62–63, 65
Jackson, Joan, 107–8
Jackson, John, 86
Jacobs, Jaap, 188n25, 194n14, 195n22, 202n83, 205n6
Jamaica, 41f, 86, 126, 128, 136–38, 155, 162
Jamaica Packet (ship), 126, 243n9
James II (king of England), 71, 72
Jan (enslaved person), 57
Jans, Fockke, 214n74
Jans, Marijken, 94
Jansz Douw, Volckert, 22, 195n23
Joe (enslaved person), 115–16, 120
Johnson, Anthony, 28
Johnson, Samuel, 138
Johnston, George, 216n103
Joseph (enslaved person), 48
Jupiter (enslaved person), 115

INDEX

Kane, Maeve, 248n25
Katerickseet, 115
Katherine (ship), 126
Kerrison, Catherine, 191n32
Keteltas, Abraham, 232n39
Keteltas, William, 251n63
Key, Elizabeth, 44, 208n33
Kidd, Thomas, 253n4
Kidd, William, 82–86, 119, 230n9
Kieft, Willem, 29, 46, 49
Kieft's War (1642), 33
Kierner, Cynthia, 219n28
Kierstede, Blandina, 217n110
King Phillip's War (1675–78), 6
Kingsland, Isaac, 149–50
King William's War (1690), 73, 76, 91, 94, 128–29
Kipp, Johannes, 90
Klaverack, 93, 94, 95
Klinckert, Dirck Jansz, 52
Klooster, Wim, 194n17, 203n101, 211n54
Knight, Elizabeth, 107, 237n44
Konijn, Leendert, 116
Koot, Christian, 186n16, 230n14
Kramer, Erin, 67

Labadists, 53–54, 125, 160, 216n103
Labatie, Jan, 18
legal constructs and frameworks: Dutch vs. English, 185n12; in New York, 89, 90; *partus sequitor ventrem*, 44, 208n33; for slaveholding, 9, 68–73, 88, 157, 163; for trade, 59–68; women and, 64, 67–68
Leisler, Jacob, 54, 72, 74, 76, 79
Leisler's Rebellion (1689–91), 8, 72, 76
Lenape, 3
Leonard, Samuel, 146
Leonora (ship), 52
Lepore, Jill, 4, 248n21, 253n4
Leverett, John, 87
Ligon, Richard, 204n102; *A True and Exact History of the Island of Barbados*, 27
Lipman, Andrew, 36
Livingston, Alida Schuyler, 57–61, 63–67, 70, 74–78, 103, 108–10, 113–22, 142
Livingston, Andrew, 87
Livingston, Gilbert, 115, 118, 128, 138
Livingston, Henry, 134, 136–38
Livingston, James, 86–87, 130
Livingston, Joanna, 101, 102, 107–8, 113, 241n97
Livingston, Johannes, 66

Livingston, John, 79, 85–86, 102, 107, 128, 135, 138, 237n44
Livingston, Margaret. *See* Vetch, Margaret Livingston
Livingston, Mary Winthrop, 85
Livingston, Muscor, 138
Livingston, Philip, 83, 99, 104–7, 122, 124–35, 139
Livingston, Philip, Jr., 134, 148–49
Livingston, Robert: Dijkeman family and, 111; elite networks and, 94, 95–96; enslaved people networks and, 77–78; family networks and, 9, 56–66, 81–83, 101, 110–22, 144; Kidd and, 82–85, 86, 230n9; landholdings of, 70; Leisler's Rebellion and, 72, 73; Palatines and, 103; runaways and, 73–79
Livingston, Robert, Jr., 126–27, 128, 130, 132, 133, 135–39, 243n9
Livingston, Robert James, 149–50
Livingstone, John, 58, 77
Livingston family, 5–6, 5f, 10, 57–58, 89, 91
Long Island, 101–2, 105, 113, 119, 127, 162
Loockermans, Govert, 79, 229n149
Loockermans, Maria, 79
Lopez family, 134
Lourisen, Meyndert, 42
Lucaszen, Pieter, 94
Lucia (enslaved person), 48
Lucretia (enslaved person), 24
Lupoldt, Ulrich, 35
Luyck, Ægidius, 31, 202n90
Lydon, James, 183n4

Madeira, 132–33
Mahican, 3, 65, 70, 78, 105
Manhattan, 3, 22–23, 28–29, 32–33, 45, 93, 102, 125
Manor Livingston, 10, 79, 98, 100–104, 109f, 111–22, 115f, 131
Mantet, Daillebout de, 73
Manuel (enslaved person), 22
manumission, 139, 153, 213n69
Margriet (ship), 77
Maria (enslaved person), 144, 145
Maricour ("Stow Stow"), 83–84
Martense, Catherina, 63
Martense, Paulus, 62, 63, 223n67
Martinique, 52
Mary (enslaved person), 57, 67, 116–17, 120, 135
Mary (ship), 85–86

INDEX

Maryland: Bayard family in, 53–55, 125, 159–60; enslaved persons in, 173t; family networks in, 40–41, 53–55; Labadists in, 53–54, 125, 160, 216n103; Leisler's Rebellion and, 72; runaways in, 68; trade networks in, 125
Massachusetts, 84, 136. *See also* Boston
mastery, notions of, 2–3, 5, 70, 73
Mather, Cotton, 84–85, 86, 87, 231n19
Mather, Elizabeth, 238n50
Maurits van Nassau-Siegen, Johan, 29, 200n71
McDonald, Kevin, 247n17
McManus, Edgar 229n147
measles epidemic, 107–8, 238nn49–50
Megapolensis, Johannes, 30, 201n77
Megapolensis, Samuel, 209n38
merchant culture. *See* trade
Merrett, Willem, 90
Merwick, Donna, 188n25
Meuwese, Mark, 186n16
Meyer, Nicolaes de, 34, 215n90
Midtrød, Tom Arne, 235n21
Mijnerts, Pieter, 203n101
Minck (enslaved person), 115
Mingoe (enslaved person), 68
Moesman, Jacob, 42
Mohawk, 103, 104, 235n21
Moll, John, 53
Montagne, Jean de la, 31, 37
Montagne, Johannes de la, 46, 125, 209n43
Montagne, Joseph de la, 125
Montagne, Nicholas de la, 125
Monteiro, Carolina, 29
Montreal, 104–5
Mookinga (enslaved person), 22
Moore, Abraham and Mary, 151
Moore, Philip and Ruth, 76
Moore, Simon, 150–52, 169–71
Moravians, 146, 148
Morgan, Jennifer, 189n26
Morgan, Philip D., 207n26
Morris, John Emery, 209n45
Morris, Lewis, 144
Mosterman, Andrea, 4, 20, 63, 136, 218n15
Murray, Joseph, 145

Native Americans. *See* Indigenous peoples
Neau, Elias, 145
Ned (enslaved person), 154–55
Neger, Jan de, 29–30
Nell (enslaved person), 149–50
networks of enslaved persons, 10, 141, 147–48
Nevis. *See* St. Kitts & Nevis
New Amsterdam: English takeover of, 49–54; enslaved persons in, 24, 28, 29; legal constructs in, 34; settlement of, 198n51; Stuyvesant family in, 24–25, 24f, 36–41; van Rensselaer family in, 18–19, 21–23, 37–38; Varlet family in, 41
Newell, Margaret, 237n38
New England: family networks in, 9, 41f, 55; trade networks in, 46–47. *See also* Boston
New Jersey: Bayard family in, 51, 89, 160–62; enslaved persons in, 142; family networks in, 5; legal constructs in, 64, 91, 157; runaways from, 146–47; Schuyler family in, 128, 133; Stuyvesant family in, 23, 51, 89, 95; Van Horne family in, 155, 158
New London, 74, 76, 107
Newman, Simon, 192n36
New Netherland: English takeover of, 49–54, 70; family networks in, 4–8, 5f, 39–50, 41f; settlement of, 2–3; slaveholding culture in, 3–4, 9–10, 18, 46–47, 49, 66; Stuyvesant family in, 17–22, 24–37; trade networks in, 20–21, 43–44; Varlet family in, 40, 42–43
New Sweden, 3, 36, 41f
Newton, Brian, 25
New York City: Bayard family in, 53, 150, 160–62; bouwerijs in Manhattan, 23–31, 24f, 36–37, 50–51, 92–95; enslaved persons in, 3, 46, 111–12, 118–20, 125, 134–38, 143–46, 148–50, 173–74t, 231n17; family networks in, 5, 5f, 9–10, 114; legal construct for slavery in, 61, 68–71, 89, 90, 91, 104; Leisler's Rebellion and, 8, 72, 76; Livingston family in, 58–59, 61–63, 65, 69–72, 75–80, 83–84, 118–20, 125, 130, 136; Slave Revolt of 1712, 10, 100, 105, 106–7, 122, 163; Stuyvesant family in, 13–14; trade networks in, 54, 83; Van Horne family in, 153–54, 156–58; Vetch family in, 98. *See also* New Amsterdam
Nicholson, Francis, 72
Nicolls, Richard, 1–2, 50, 227n121
Nieuw Haarlem (Manhattan), 45
nonelites, 10, 70, 122
Noorlander, Danny, 71, 212n57

INDEX

North Carolina, 150–52
Nottingham Institute, 161

Odegard, Erik, 29
Olmsted, John, 76
Onckell Philips (ship), 120, 128
Onondaga, 83–84, 104
Oswego (ship), 124–25, 129, 132

Palatines, 103, 105, 118
Panama, 86–87
Paplay, George, 137
Parmenter, Jon, 222n52
Parmyter, Paroculus, 95
partus sequitor ventrem, 44, 208n33
Pastorius, Francis Daniel, 71
patroons, 19, 28, 194n14
Paxton, William, 150
Payton, William, 150
Peddie, William, 211n48
Penn, William, 54
Pequot War (1636–38), 6
Phaeton (enslaved person), 250n54
Philadelphia, 54, 147, 161–62, 249n37
Philip, Philip, 137
Philip, Sarah Johnson, 137
Philipsburg Manor, 69, 100, 143
Philipse, Adolph, 91
Philipse, Frederick, 24, 44, 68, 69, 144, 215n90, 219n25, 247n17
Pieters, Manuel, 94
Pitkin, William, 79
Piwonka, Ruth, 243n21
Plough, Jacob, 239n72
Pompey (enslaved person), 150, 250n54
Ponte, Mark, 21
popery, 79–80
Price, Richard, 191n33
Primus (enslaved person), 13, 13f
Prinses Amelia (ship), 26, 44, 69
Prince van Denemarcken (ship), 203n101
Pritchard, Anna Stuyvesant, 95, 141, 233n64, 247n5
Providence Plantations, 54
Provoost, David, 88
Pygan, Alexander, 76, 228n126
Pynchon, John, 58, 65, 75, 81, 84

Quack (enslaved person), 130, 144, 145
Queen Anne's War (1702–13), 10, 103, 104, 129, 163

Raeff, Sebastiaen, 197n47
Ramezay, Claude de, 105
Rawley, James, 183n4
Rebecca (ship), 75
Rensselaerswijck, 18–20, 21, 23, 29–30, 35, 59, 70, 100, 204n107
Rensselaerswijck (ship), 43
Revenge (ship), 155
Rhea, John, 161
Rhode Island, 46, 125, 128, 133, 142
Rhode Island (ship), 134, 135, 136
Richards, Paul, 143–44, 145, 248n19
Rigaud de Vaudreuil, Pierre de, 87
Ripse, Maria, 218n12
Robin (enslaved person), 152, 164
Rodenborch, Elizabeth, 199n60
Rodenborch, Lucas, 18, 25, 26–27, 46, 199n60
Rodenborch, Lucretia, 199n60
Rodenborch, Trijntjen (Catherina), 18, 20, 26–27, 193n5, 193n7
Roelofs, Sara, 54
Romney, Susanah Shaw, 8, 29, 50, 186n16, 199n61, 206n8, 213n69
Roper, L. H., 188n25
Rose (enslaved person), 115
Rousby, Christopher, 92
Royal Africa Company, 53, 71
Rucker, Walter, 112, 237n38
rum industry, 56, 63, 65–66, 118, 126, 131
runaways, 27, 44, 69–70, 73–81, 87, 104, 118, 138, 142, 159–60, 160f
Rupert, Linda, 27, 186n16, 199n59, 200n61

Saffin, John, 85–86
St. Eustatius, 52
St. Kitts & Nevis, 41f, 52, 53, 83
St. Thomas, 52, 216n96
Sainte Helene, Sieur Le Moyne de, 73
San Antonio (ship), 82
São Tomé, 184n9, 203n101
Sarah (enslaved person), 139
Saxon, Andrew, 127
Schaets, Gideon, 57, 60
Schama, Simon, 199n61
Schenectady, 8, 61, 72–74, 76, 111
Schiebinger, Londa, 189n26
Schmidt, Ariadne, 205n4
Schuyler, Arent, 142
Schuyler, Arnot, 147
Schuyler, Brandt, 65, 88, 90, 223n60

INDEX

Schuyler, Cornelia, 142
Schuyler, Gerrit, 70
Schuyler, Johannes, 83–84
Schuyler, Philip Pietersz, 57, 58, 60, 67, 218n14
Schuyler, Pieter, 57, 81
Schuyler family, 67, 91
Scipio (enslaved person), 13, 13*f*
Seary, Robert, 68
Second Anglo-Dutch War (1665–67), 58
Selijns, Henricus, 24, 31, 45, 47, 195n22, 202n90, 209n38
Senegambia, 26
Sessions, Cato, 76
Sewall, Samuel, 81, 84–86, 219n24, 231nn19–20
Sharpe, John, 220n31
Sierra Leone, 26, 155
Singer, Roberta, 240n80
Slave Revolt of 1712 (New York), 10, 100, 105, 106–7, 122, 163
slave trade: in Barbados, 4, 6, 72, 74–75, 78, 125; in Curaçao, 34, 75, 78, 126, 199n59; elite and family networks invested in, 21–22, 29, 51, 69–70, 125–26, 131, 155; growth of, 26; of Indigenous peoples, 6, 37, 49, 115–16, 144
Sluyter, Hendrick, 54
Sluyter, Henry, 125
Sluyter, Peter, 53
smuggling, 66, 126
Soderlund, Jean, 36, 249n37
South Carolina, 11, 129, 131, 133, 137, 160, 162, 173t, 231n17
Spera Mundi (ship), 45
Springsteen, Jacobus, 155
Staets, Abraham, 22, 67
Staets, Jacob, 57, 62
Staets, Trijntie Wessels, 67
Stavast, Aefje, 63
Stavast, Claes Janse, 62, 63, 223n67
Steedman, Carolyn, 9
Steenwijck, Cornelis, 52, 70, 72, 215n90
Stoffels (enslaved person), 140–43
Storke (ship), 134, 135, 137, 243n9
"Stow Stow" (Maricour), 83–84
Stuyvesant, Anna, 39, 49
Stuyvesant, Balthazar Lazarus, 25, 31, 47, 49, 51–53, 55, 93, 137, 211n51
Stuyvesant, Elisabeth van Slichtenhorst, 92–96
Stuyvesant, Gerardus, 95, 123–24, 130, 233n64

Stuyvesant, Judith Bayard, 25–27, 30–31, 47–48, 156, 212n56
Stuyvesant, Margaret Livingston, 138
Stuyvesant, Maria Beeckman, 69
Stuyvesant, Nicolaes Willem, 25, 31, 92, 93, 95
Stuyvesant, Nicholas Willam (son of Gerardus), 138–39, 247n5
Stuyvesant, Petrus: Allyn and, 75; in Curaçao, 25–27, 48; elite networks and, 89, 93–94; English takeover of New Netherland and, 50–54; family networks and, 1–2, 44, 46, 49; Hallett family and, 102; in Manhattan bouwerijs, 25, 29–31; marriage of, 25–26; slaveholding culture and, 18, 22, 24, 32–33, 37, 200n62; Willet and, 46–47; Winthrop and, 74
Stuyvesant, Petrus (son of Gerardus), 13, 13*f*, 138, 247n5
Stuyvesant, Samuel, 39
Stuyvesant family, 5–6, 5*f*, 23, 89, 125
sugar industry, 27, 34, 48–49, 51, 53, 61, 127, 137, 163, 204n102
Suriname (ship), 58
Surlock, Eve, 139
Susanna (enslaved person), 24
Sweet, John Wood, 247n11
Sydenham, Elisabeth Stuyvesant, 92
Sydenham, George, 92, 93, 95
Symon (enslaved person), 57, 62, 63
Syphax (enslaved person), 13, 13*f*

Tam (enslaved person), 101, 118
Tamandare (ship), 29, 211n48
Taylor, Maureen, 247n11
Teller, Andries, 61
Teller, Willem, 57
Ten Broeck, Dierck, 158, 241n93
Ten Broeck, Tobias, 118, 241n93
Tessemaaker, Peter, 76
Thomas (enslaved person), 103
Thomasz, Jan, 22
Thornton, John, 221n38
tobacco industry, 40, 42–44, 53, 56, 63, 206n10
Toby (enslaved person), 159, 160*f*, 161–62, 164
Tom (enslaved person), 56–59, 62–66, 77, 108, 110, 112–13, 130, 135, 145–48
trade: elite networks and, 1–3, 11; fur trade, 22, 46, 58, 63, 65, 129; legal constructs for, 59–68; merchant culture, 186n17; networks, 6, 20–22, 25–26, 40, 43–47,

54, 63, 75, 78, 80, 83, 85, 87, 125–26, 164, 188n22; rum, 56, 63, 65–66, 118, 126, 131; sugar, 27, 34, 48–49, 51, 53, 61, 127, 137, 163, 204n102; tobacco, 40, 42–44, 53, 56, 63, 206n10
Trebie (enslaved person), 115

Ukawsaw Gronniosaw (enslaved person), 153–54

Van Angola, Jan, 29–30
Van Angola, Marie, 29
Van Angola, Mayken, 24, 139
Van Angola, Sebastiaen, 29–30
Van Bijlaer, Hillegond, 193n11
Van Brugh, Peter, 136–37
Van Campen, Jan, 197n47
Van Cleeck, Catharina, 66, 68
Van Cortlandt, Jacobus, 61, 77, 88, 127
Van Cortlandt, Maria, 22
Van Cortlandt, Oloff Stevenz, 18, 210n46, 215n90
Van Cortlandt, Stephanus, 80, 83, 219n24
Van Cortlandt family, 89
Van Curler, Arent, 67
Van de Langestraet, Jan Jansen, 214n74
Van der Woude, Joanne, 205n6
Van Dijck, Hendrick, 30, 33–34, 36
Van Dijck, Lydia, 30
Vanduersen, John, 139
Vane, George, 107
Van Horne, Abraham, 251n69
Van Horne, Cornelius, 119, 144, 153–54
Van Horne, David, 155
Van Horne, Elizabeth French, 154
Van Horne, Garret, 251n69
Van Horne, James, 153, 156–57
Van Horne, John, 158, 165, 251n69
Van Horne, Samuel, 155
Van Horne family, 5–6
Van Isendoorn, Judith, 202n90
Van Kampen, Pieter, 94
Van Laer, Arnold J. F., 195n28
Van Rensselaer, Jan Baptist, 17, 18–22, 52
Van Rensselaer, Jeremias, 10, 15–19, 16f, 20–23, 31–32, 37–38, 46, 84–85, 87, 121, 209n43
Van Rensselaer, Johannes, 19–20, 193n11
Van Rensselaer, Kiliaen, 19–20, 80, 193n11, 194n19
Van Rensselaer, Maria, 67

Van Rensselaer, Nicolaes, 58, 60, 67, 72, 220n32
Van Ruyvan, Laurens, 49
Van Ruyven, Cornelis, 37
Van Slichtenhorst, Brant, 35, 94
Van Slichtenhorst, Gerrit, 93, 218n12
Van Slichtenhorst, Margaretha, 58
Van Tienhoven, Cornelis, 31, 210n46
Van Twiller, Wouter, 28
Van Veghten, Dirk, Jr., 126
Varlet, Anna. *See* Boot, Anna Varlet Hack
Varlet, Caspar, 40, 43, 207n24
Varlet, Daniel, 43
Varlet, Nicolaes, 40, 41, 43, 49, 89, 90
Varlet family, 39, 45
Venema, Janny, 22
Vergulde Posthoorn (ship), 52
Verlet, Maria, 57
Vetch, Margaret Livingston, 66, 85, 98–99, 101, 106, 107–8, 113, 122
Vetch, Samuel, 85, 87–88, 98–99, 101, 105–6, 113, 234n3, 235n17
Viele, Cornelis Cornelissen, 111
Vincent, Judith, 140, 141–43, 246n4
Vincent, Samuel, 142, 246n4
Virginia, 24, 28, 43–45, 68, 70, 160
Visscher, Femmetje Jans, 57
Visscher, Tjerk Harmense, 57
Vredendael (tobacco plantation), 31
Vrooman, Pieter Meesz, 61

Wadsworth, Benjamin, 81–82; *The Well-Ordered Family*, 98–99
Walter, John, 147
Wapen van Amsterdam (ship), 43–44
Wapen van Leeuwarden (ship), 43
Warren, Wendy, 4, 191n32, 221–22n45
Watts, John, 147
Wax, Darold D., 249n36
Wendell, Evert, 78, 228n141
Wendell, Johannes, 218n14
Wenham, Thomas, 102, 235n17
Wesselsz, Dirck, 241n93
West India Company, 3, 18–19, 24, 27–28, 30, 33–34, 38, 44, 46, 49
Whitefield, George, 154–55, 160–61, 253n4
Wilder, Craig Steven, 4, 131, 158, 250n49
Wilkins, Richard, 84, 85, 231n19
Willet, Mary Browne, 210n45
Willet, Thomas, 46, 55, 209–10n45, 209n42, 210–11n48
William of Orange (king of England), 71

Williams, William H., 208n34
Williams-Myers, A. J., 4, 235n8
Wilree, Jacob Dircksz, 52
Winthrop, Anne, 102
Winthrop, Fitz-John, 74, 76–77, 79, 228n128
Winthrop, John, 74, 77
Wiser, Margaret, 153, 157, 165
Wittepaert (ship), 42
Wolf (ship), 148, 250n49
Wolf, Pedro de, 126, 129
Wolters, Kier, 214n74

women: as baptismal witnesses, 212n55; in Dutch colonial settlements, 40, 96; family networks and, 3, 58–59, 64–67, 88, 141; legal system and, 64, 67–68
Woodbridge, Timothy, 76
Wynant (enslaved person), 115, 116

Yeomans & Escott (trading firm), 129

Zenger, Peter, 127
Zyperius, Anna, 44
Zyperius, Michiel, 44–45, 208n35